HANDBOOKS

# SANTA FE, TAOS & ALBUQUERQUE

ZORA O'NEILL

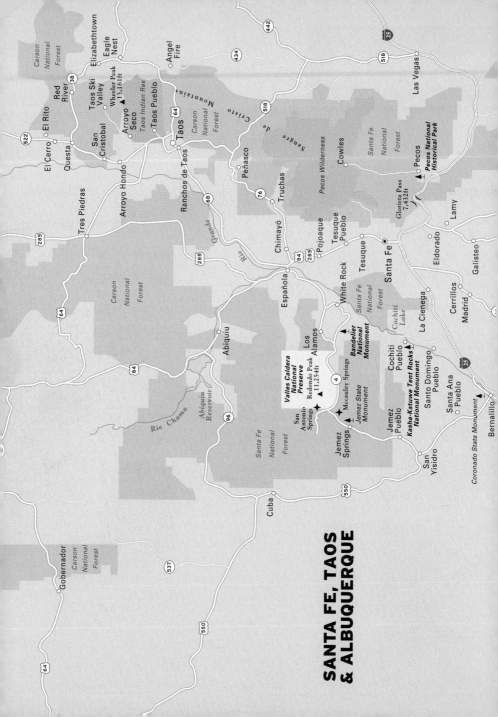

# SANTA FE, TAOS & ALBUQUERQUE

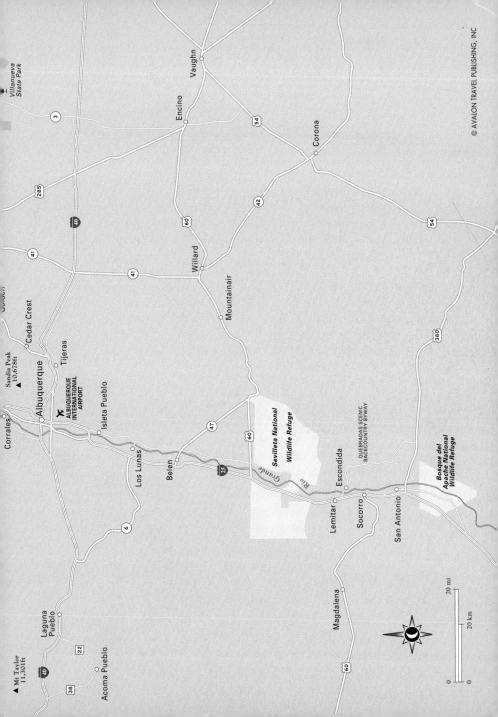

Villanueva State Park

Vaughn

Encino

3

54

285

Corona

42

60

Willard

54

41

41

Mountainair

60

Gordon

Cedar Crest

Sandia Peak
10,678ft

Tijeras

380

Albuquerque

ALBUQUERQUE INTERNATIONAL AIRPORT

Isleta Pueblo

Corrales

47

60

Sevilleta National Wildlife Refuge

Rio Grande

Los Lunas

Belen

25

6

Lemitar

Escondida

QUEBRADAS SCENIC BACKCOUNTRY BYWAY

Socorro

Bosque del Apache National Wildlife Refuge

San Antonio

Laguna Pueblo

Mt Taylor
11,301ft

22

40

38

Acoma Pueblo

Magdalena

60

20 mi

20 km

0

0

© AVALON TRAVEL PUBLISHING, INC

# DISCOVER SANTA FE, TAOS & ALBUQUERQUE

If you explored Santa Fe, Taos, or Albuquerque with your nose alone, you'd find a place that smells like no other: lilac blooms in spring, the ozone of summer thunderstorms, fall's harvest of spicy green chile roasting, and fragrant piñon burning in woodstoves during winter snowfall. Your other senses will get a treat too: If you listen, you'll hear the rough warble of western tanagers, the yelps of coyotes, and the deep throb of drums accompanying bell-clad dancers at American Indian pueblo ceremonies. And that green chile makes everything taste distinct – it sneaks its way onto hamburgers and pizzas and even into ice cream and beer.

But none of that matches the sheer majesty of the view, whether it's across austere, scrub-covered mesas, down narrow sandstone slot canyons, or along densely forested mountain ranges. To visit this region is to feel small – the landscape is simply overwhelming. Even

The hike to Chimney Rock offers great views.

Albuquerque, the state's largest metropolis, where tract houses and steel-and-glass towers cover more than a hundred square miles, shrinks to a mere puddle of population when considered against the mountains that jut 4,500 feet up on its east side and the highways that strike straight off into barren canyon lands to the west. Driving among the towering, red-striped cliffs around the village of Abiquiu, your car is only a fly buzzing at the feet of giants. Look up, and you're nearly flattened by the broad, deep sky, a cloudless dome the precise hue of the turquoise once mined in the Cerrillos hills south of Santa Fe.

The high altitude only enhances the sensory overload – visitors can ease into the area at the airport in Albuquerque, just 5,352 feet above sea level, but Santa Fe is another 1,637 feet up and Taos higher still, in the shadow of Wheeler Peak, New Mexico's highest, at

**Pueblo Indian pottery**

a dizzying 13,161 feet. These communities all provide a bit of comfort amid the massive scale of the surrounding landscape. Albuquerque has just enough big-city glitz to distract you from nature entirely, while the soft curves and golden glow of Santa Fe's all-adobe-finish historic center can make you feel like your normal size again, as you sometimes duck under heavy wooden lintels to enter boutiques, bars, and galleries in snug, whitewashed rooms lit by the glow from corner "kiva" fireplaces. To the north, Taos Pueblo produces the same effect, in more ancient form – this agglomeration of mud bricks, which has been built and rebuilt over nine centuries and counting, is essentially a portion of the earth reshaped to give its residents a cozy, human-scale home at the base of sacred Taos Mountain.

Whether you want to plunge into the empty landscape (New Mexico is one of the least populous states in the union, with an average of 15 people per square mile) or soak up the urban action, you'll find plenty to do. Outdoor adventurers can hike for an hour or a week, through the basalt cleft of the Rio Grande Gorge or along mountainsides thick with yellow-leafed aspens, and skiers can plunge

Cacti abound in New Mexico's drier lower elevations.

through armpit-deep powder at Taos Ski Valley, one of the country's most thrilling downhill runs. Afterward, soothe yourself in a natural hot spring perched on the edge of a rushing river. Elk, eagles, and bighorn sheep occupy the highlands, while the lower desert and river valleys are alive with roadrunners, lizards, and the occasional rattlesnake. With the Rio Grande as a major migration artery, bird life is wonderfully diverse, and you can spot everything from cold-loving rosy finches to elegant sandhill cranes.

Culture mavens will love Santa Fe, with its world-class contemporary art scene and eclectic calendar of international film and live music, not to mention excellent shopping for every imaginable antique treasure, from Navajo jewelry to Afghani rugs. Several world-class museums display work by the Southwest's greatest artists, from anonymous wood-carvers of the 18th century to Georgia O'Keeffe. Taos, which first became known as an arts colony in the early 20th century, shows a more intimate side of the rich creative history of New Mexico; come here to discover raw new work, or to create some of your own.

**Inn at Loretto, Santa Fe**

History buffs will find the past has barely faded here on the frontier of the United States. American Indian pueblos dot the banks of the Rio Grande just as they have for almost a thousand years; in high mountain villages like Truchas, some residents speak much the same language their Castilian ancestors did when they settled here three centuries ago; and vintage neon signs glow along the stretch of historic Route 66 that runs through Albuquerque. You can visit ancient cave dwellings carved out of soft cliff faces, skeletons of mud-brick complexes poking out of valley floors, and crumbling Franciscan mission churches edging hilltops. At the end of the day, pull yourself back into the present with excellent margaritas and cuisine with a chile kick – the final elements of a trip of epic proportions.

**Santa Fe skyline**

# Contents

# MAP CONTENTS

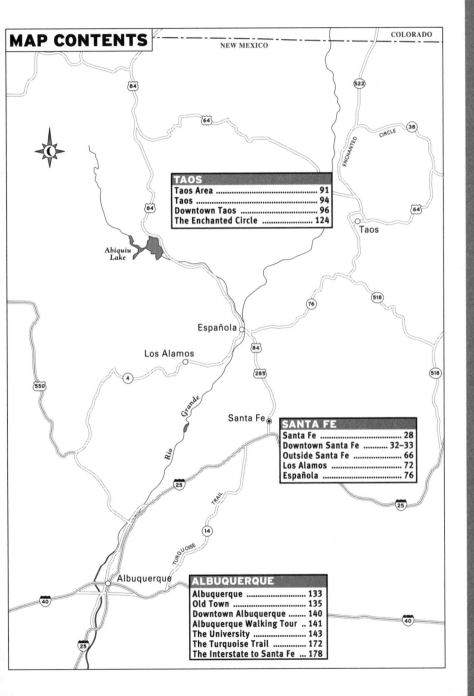

COLORADO

NEW MEXICO

Abiquiu Lake

Española

Los Alamos

Santa Fe

Rio Grande

Albuquerque

ENCHANTED CIRCLE

Taos

TURQUOISE TRAIL

# The Lay of the Land

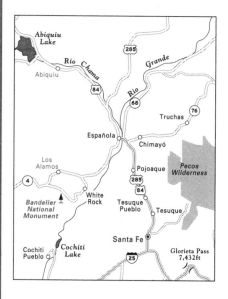

## SANTA FE

A network of little streets winding among thick-walled adobe homes, New Mexico's capital is like no other city in the United States. Santa Fe was the Spaniards' administrative capital for the territory of Nuevo México, so for a taste of that history, you can visit the **Palace of the Governors,** now the state history museum, or the neo-Romanesque **St. Francis Cathedral.** The city's finest galleries line Canyon Road—contemporary art is a significant contributor to the city's economy.

Santa Feans are relentlessly outdoorsy, thanks to great hiking, biking, and ski trails just a few minutes' drive from town. Or head farther, to **Bandelier National Monument,** a canyon lined with the ruins of the Pueblo Indians' ancestors, or to **Abiquiu,** where the scenery inspired famous resident painter Georgia O'Keeffe. Nearby is the town of **Los Alamos,** where the atomic bomb was built.

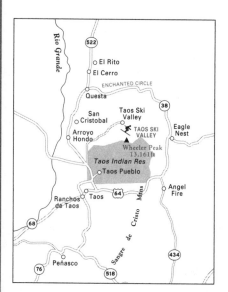

## TAOS

A small town of 4,800 people adjacent to an ancient pueblo, Taos is a remarkable cauldron of artists, trust-fund hippies, spiritual seekers, and ski bums—not to mention the Spanish and American Indian families who've called the place home for centuries. The town itself offers little sightseeing—though **Taos Art Museum at Fechin House** and the **Millicent Rogers Museum** have very strong collections; instead, its atmosphere, cultivated in mellow coffee shops and hidden hot springs, is the real draw. Skiers all praise **Taos Ski Valley,** one of the last purists' resorts that ban snowboards on its near-vertical trails.

A popular day drive from Taos is the **Enchanted Circle,** a loop of two-lane roads running through small towns and high valleys where elk graze. At the loop's center is **Wheeler Peak,** the highest in New Mexico.

# ALBUQUERQUE

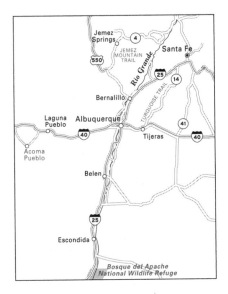

New Mexico's biggest city is not as packed with attractions as its more-visited neighbors to the north, but its beautiful setting, between dormant volcanoes and the Sandia Mountains, is ideal for outdoor recreation.

The city is also well placed for day trips: **Acoma Pueblo,** atop a monolithic mesa on the western plains, rivals Taos Pueblo for the distinction of the oldest city in the United States, while the wetlands of the **Bosque del Apache National Wildlife Refuge** attract thousands of migrating birds. Routes north to Santa Fe include the historic **Turquoise Trail,** passing through ghost towns and rolling hills, and the **Jemez Mountain Trail,** which winds past stunning red-rock outcroppings and natural hot springs.

If you time your trip with the 10-day **Albuquerque International Balloon Fiesta,** you'll catch the city's signature spectacle: pre-dawn mass ascensions of glowing, gem-colored hot-air balloons lifting silently into the sky.

## REGIONAL IDENTITY

New Mexicans have particular ways of identifying themselves and the elements of the state's unique cultural mix. The people who have lived in the highlands and along the Rio Grande for millennia most commonly refer to themselves as Indians, or American Indians in formal situations; or they will call themselves by their pueblo's specific name – Jemez or Santa Clara, for instance. The term "Native American" appears occasionally, but most New Mexican Indians see it as just another inaccurate label.

Those who trace their roots back to the conquistadors call themselves Spanish or Hispano. (The latter is not to be confused with Hispanic, which refers to Spanish-speakers regardless of background.) Hispanos are also distinct from Mexicans and other Latinos, although they do share some similar cultural elements.

The third category is the catch-all term Anglo, which really just means "none of the above" – whether you're white, Asian, or even African American, you could be considered Anglo, a relative latecomer to the state of New Mexico.

# Planning Your Trip

To thoroughly appreciate everything Albuquerque, Taos, and Santa Fe have to offer, you'd need between two and three weeks. More typically, visitors tend to use one place as a base for a week or so, with a day or overnight trip to one of the others. You can also easily dip in for a long weekend in Santa Fe or Taos—either holing up in a romantic old hotel or spending the few days trekking in the wilderness.

North-central New Mexico offers hiking, camping, bicycling, and skiing accessible within just a few miles of city limits. But if you prefer city life, you can get that too—particularly in Santa Fe, where the cultural offerings can keep you busy for weeks. To reach it all, though, you'll have to rent a car or bring your own—bus service won't get you to the out-of-the-way, old Spanish villages like Truchas, or to the trailheads of the more splendid hikes.

Whatever you're planning to do, make your first couple of days easy ones. Most people underestimate the debilitating effect of the high altitude, and your body may react with anything from extreme drowsiness to nausea and headaches. Dehydration is also a chronic problem that few account for in arid New Mexico; even if you're not doing anything more strenuous than strolling around the center of Santa Fe, make sure you drink plenty of water throughout the day.

## WHEN TO GO

Because New Mexico enjoys an average of 300 days of sunshine annually, there's not really a bad time to visit, and your trip will probably coincide with some fiesta, craft market, or ceremonial dance in any season. The one exception is mid-spring, when Taos Pueblo is closed to visitors for about 10 weeks; the precise dates change every year, so call to inquire if you're considering a visit to the pueblo between February and April.

The high tourist season is summer, with hotels charging their peak rates from mid-May through mid-September (they're higher only in the week between Christmas and New Year). If you visit during these months, you can experience some of the region's most notable events, particularly in Santa Fe, where the massive show of Native American art and craftwork called the Santa Fe Indian Market takes place and the Santa Fe Opera season runs on its dramatic open-air stage. Gallery owners also launch some of their strongest shows in the summer. The weather is hot, certainly, but starting in July, the day's heat is often squelched with a strong, brief rainstorm in the afternoon, and nights are still cool. Rafting on the Rio Grande—at its best in early summer, when the mountain snowmelt creates the strongest current—is also a way to cool off. If you want to do any multiday hiking trips at higher elevations, summer is really the only possible season to visit, as many trails are still covered in snow as late as May, and the weather on the peaks gets cruel and windy by September. Winter sees a surge of visitors as well, though they usually head straight to the trails at Taos Ski Valley and Santa Fe Ski Area, so the towns themselves don't feel particularly crowded; many sights are closed or have limited hours, however.

The shoulder seasons have their own appeal, and hotel prices can be quite low, particularly in April, when ski season has finally wound down, and in November, when it hasn't gotten into full swing. In the fall, the crowds disperse, and the residents settle into their routines amid crisp temperatures and generally clear skies through late October. In September, the Feast of San Geronimo is celebrated in Taos Pueblo as well as the town, and the figure of Zozobra ("Old Man Gloom") gets torched in a raucous pagan celebration in Santa Fe. The Albuquerque International Balloon Fiesta takes place over two weeks in October, while in the mountains, the aspen leaves turn a brilliant yellow, accessible by the many beautiful hiking trails. And if winter has been the least bit

wet, springtime produces a burst of wildflowers, turning whole hillsides pink and yellow,
though a last-gasp snowstorm in April or May
is not unheard-of.

If you're planning a visit between Christmas and New Year's day, during any of Santa
Fe's summer art markets, or for the balloon
fest in Albuquerque, book a hotel as far ahead
as you possibly can—Santa Fe's lodging will
book up to a year in advance for the most
tourist-heavy times.

## WHAT TO TAKE

The contents of your suitcase will be deter-
mined largely by what season you'll be visiting
in, but be prepared for a wide range of temperatures whenever you visit. Many people wrongly
assume that New Mexico's desert setting means
heat all day, all year round. In fact, the altitude
yields both extremely hot and cold weather.
Winter temperatures can dip well below freezing even in central Albuquerque, where the elevation is lower than in Taos or Santa Fe (though
Albuquerque sees relatively little snow). If you
think you might attend any ceremonial dances
at a pueblo during the winter months, pack as
many layers as you can imagine. Mittens, dou-
ble-thick wool socks, and a hat with earflaps
will serve you well in these situations.

Summers are quite hot by day (July's average temperature is 92°F), but as soon as the
sun dips below the horizon, the temperature
can drop 20°F or more, especially outside
of asphalt-coated city centers; always keep a
sweater on hand, and a hat can't hurt either.
The summer afternoon "monsoons" can catch
those expecting the bone-dry desert unawares,
so pack an umbrella or rain slicker if you'll be
visiting between July and September. Likewise,
the mud produced by summer rains (and, for
that matter, by spring snowmelt) can be all-
pervasive—if you hike or head out to any rural
areas during this time, expect your boots to get
completely encrusted, and save a nicer pair of
shoes for strolling around town. In the sun,
you'll be more comfortable in long-sleeve,
light-colored shirts and pants in silk or cotton,
rather than skimpy tank tops and shorts—covering up will help deflect the glare, rather than
letting it bake you.

Any time of year, in fact, the sun is a constant, and the thin atmosphere at this altitude
means you'll burn more quickly than you're
used to. You should never be without sun-
glasses, heavy-duty sunscreen, and a brimmed
hat. Wear comfortable shoes that can handle
varied terrains. And don't forget your bathing
suit. Due to the shortage of water in the area,
many hotels don't have swimming pools, but
there are plenty of hot springs, hot tubs, and
spas you might want to take a dip in.

As for clothing, anything goes, and eccentric fashion is welcomed, but a few situations
call for specific items. New Mexicans are very
sensible and casual in their dress—famously,
people attend the Santa Fe Opera in *clean* jeans
and cowboy boots, with a flashy bolo tie to pull
the look together. So if you'll be hobnobbing
in Santa Fe's upper echelons, at the opera or at
some of the city's best restaurants, bring a well-
tailored outfit or two. When visiting churches
and American Indian pueblos, it's respectful to
not show excessive skin—women should avoid
obvious cleavage and super-short skirts. Overall, layering is the key to managing the changes
in temperatures.

# Explore Santa Fe, Taos, and Albuquerque

## 14-DAY GRAND TOUR

While you could conceivably explore Santa Fe, Taos, and Albuquerque for a month or so, seeking out ever more obscure hiking trails and sweeping vistas, two weeks gives ample time to appreciate the distinct character of each community and enjoy the surrounding rural areas and bumpy back roads. A full tour like this one will give you a strong impression of both contemporary and ancient American Indian culture, with visits to pueblos (ideally, time your trip to coincide with a ceremonial dance) as well as to centuries-old Spanish colonial-era villages. You'll also have a chance to appreciate the stark, empty beauty of the high desert and the craggy mountains. This itinerary involves a lot of driving to cover all of the area's most scenic routes, but you'll still have plenty of opportunities for leisurely lunches and other out-of-car activities.

### DAY 1

Arrive at Albuquerque's Sunport airport; transfer to a hotel in the city: El Vado, say, if you want a taste of old Route 66, or one of the excellent, rural-feeling bed-and-breakfasts in the North Valley. Have drinks and dinner in the Nob Hill district.

### DAY 2

Visit the **Indian Pueblo Cultural Center,** then head to the **National Hispanic Cultural Center** to balance it out. Have lunch at funky favorite Barelas Coffee House just blocks away. Spend the afternoon in Old Town.

### DAY 3

Drive to **Acoma Pueblo,** west of Albuquerque. Return by afternoon and take a sunset ride up the **Sandia Peak Tramway.** Enjoy dinner and drinks downtown.

### DAY 4

Drive to Santa Fe via the **Jemez Mountain Trail,** stopping for a dip in some of the many hot springs along the way – how much hiking

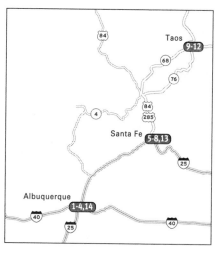

you'd like to do dictates which ones. Pack a picnic lunch, or stop in at Los Ojos Restaurant & Saloon in Jemez Springs for your first green-chile cheeseburger.

### DAY 5

Tour Santa Fe's plaza area, including the

Palace of the Governors, the St. Francis Cathedral, and the Loretto Chapel. Around happy hour, wander down to the Dragon Room Bar on Old Santa Fe Trail, then have a casual pizza dinner at Upper Crust Pizza across the street, while you watch the sun glow on San Miguel Chapel.

## DAY 6

Take in Santa Fe's more contemporary culture, with shopping, gallery-hopping, or a visit to the Museum of International Folk Art. End up on Canyon Road, with drinks and tapas, and maybe even dancing at El Farol.

## DAY 7

Take a day hike up to the peak of Atalaya Mountain or ride a bike to Lamy and the broad Galisteo Basin via a trail along the train tracks. (Or just take the train itself, on the Santa Fe Southern Railway tourist service.) Soothe muscles with an evening visit to the hot tubs at Ten Thousand Waves.

## DAY 8

Drive to Bandelier National Monument to see the ancestral Puebloan ruins. Have a late lunch on "the hill" – in the no-longer-secret town of Los Alamos. If you're up to more driving, head for Abiquiu, where the cliffs glow red in the sunset. Have a hearty New Mexican dinner in Española and return to Santa Fe to sleep.

## DAY 9

Drive to Taos via the high road, stopping at the pilgrimage site of Chimayó and in the villages of Truchas and Las Trampas. Settle into your hotel in Taos after a de rigueur margarita at The Adobe Bar.

## DAY 10

Start with an early visit to San Francisco de Asis Church, followed by breakfast at one of Taos's many great bakeries (the excellent Sweetgrass Café, nearby, stocks goods from several bakers). Then head to the Taos Art Museum at Fechin House for background on the town's art scene. Spend the afternoon visiting more museums, or galleries and shops.

## DAY 11

Visit Taos Pueblo. Then check out some other indigenous architecture: Tour an Earthship on the Solar Survival Tour at Greater World Earthship Development, pausing to peer down into the Rio Grande Gorge on the way. Have dinner at Lambert's, Taos's favorite white-tablecloth spot.

## DAY 12

Pack a picnic lunch and take a leisurely drive around the Enchanted Circle, stopping for a hike along the back side of Wheeler Peak. Depending on your timing, you can get your green chile fix in Questa, or back in Taos at Orlando's.

## DAY 13

Return to Santa Fe via the low road, stopping for lunch in Embudo, and perhaps for a little wine-tasting at the vineyards in this area. Your afternoon is free: Relax in Santa Fe and spend the night here, in a classic old hotel like La Fonda, if you haven't been there already.

## DAY 14

Take the Turquoise Trail south to Albuquerque to catch your late-afternoon flight out.

# THE BEST OF SANTA FE

Get to know the rhythm of New Mexico's capital by following this eight-day itinerary covering the must-see spots in town and allowing for an overnight trip to Taos. The benefit of this schedule is that, with a little modification, it can be done entirely by bus, if you choose, though having a car will of course give you more flexibility and opportunity to explore out-of-the-way hiking trails.

## DAY 1

Arrive at Albuquerque Sunport. Drive or take a shuttle service directly to Santa Fe. If you're not renting a car, choose a hotel or inn close to the center, for easier exploring – the historic Hotel St. Francis, the Madeleine Inn, or an apartment managed by The Chapelle Street Casitas would be a good option. If it's summertime, head to the Bell Tower Bar at La Fonda for an evening margarita and a view of the city. In winter, the lobby bar here is a cozy mix of visitors and oddball residents.

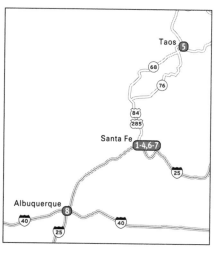

## DAY 2

Tour the plaza area, visiting **St. Francis Cathedral,** the **Loretto Chapel,** and any museums that interest you: the **Palace of the Governors** for a little state history, or the **Museum of Fine Arts.** Check out the American Indian vendors under the portal on the plaza, then walk up to the Cross of the Martyrs for a bird's-eye perspective. Have a casual dinner of shrimp tacos at Bumble Bee's Baja Grill.

## DAY 3

Start the day with a uniquely Santa Fean breakfast at local institution Café Pasqual's, then choose two of the four museums on **Museum Hill** to visit: The Museum of International Folk Art is a must, then you can choose between Spanish and Indian art and culture. If you're adjusted to the altitude by now, in the afternoon drive to **Bandelier National Monument** for an easy hike through Frijoles Canyon to see the cliff dwellings.

## DAY 4

Take a day hike: You can catch a bus to the trailhead for **Atalaya Mountain,** or you can drive to **Rio en Medio,** near Tesuque. If it's fall, you must head to **Aspen Vista;** in the wintertime, stick to lower elevations on the **Dale Ball Trails.** Back in town, have dinner at a casual New Mexican place like the Blue Corn Café – you'll be hungry for a big plate of enchiladas.

## DAY 5

Drive to Taos via the high road. Check in to a room in a classic adobe, such as the Mabel Dodge Luhan House or La Posada de Taos. Spend the afternoon strolling around the plaza area and visiting the **Millicent Rogers Museum.** (Opt for the **Taos Art Museum at Fechin House** and the **Governor Bent House and Museum** if you're not traveling by car.) Have sunset drinks at the Adobe Bar, the town's social nerve center in the lobby of the historic Taos Inn.

## DAY 6

Visit **Taos Pueblo,** then return to Santa Fe via the low road – but be sure to fortify yourself with breakfast burritos from Mante's Chow Cart, and stop at the **San Francisco de Asis Church** on your way out of town. Depending on how long the drive back takes, have dinner in Española at New Mexican classic El Paragua or forge on to Santa Fe for a relaxing splurge at Ristra. Stay overnight in Santa Fe.

## DAY 7

Do a little souvenir shopping and cruise the galleries on **Canyon Road.** In the late afternoon, head for Ten Thousand Waves for a stint in the hot tubs and a relaxing massage.

## DAY 8

Return to Albuquerque via the **Turquoise Trail,** stopping for lunch in Madrid at Mama Lisa's Ghost Town Kitchen if you have time for this scenic drive, or just make a beeline to the airport on I-25. If you're traveling back to the airport by bus or shuttle, use your free morning in Santa Fe for a luxe brunch at the Inn of the Anasazi, or a traditional breakfast burrito at Tia Sophia's.

# WEEKEND GETAWAYS

Even if you have only a few days, getting away to northern New Mexico can be exceptionally refreshing, an easy way to disconnect from your regular routine by immersing yourself in the state's otherworldly architecture and rich history. Just an hour from the Albuquerque airport, Santa Fe lends itself perfectly to a romantic escape. Settle in at one of the many remarkable hotels, and make reservations at a couple of the city's best restaurants (those mentioned here are just a few of the possibilities). With planning, you could also spend an evening at the Santa Fe Opera in the summer. Isolated, countercultural Taos is worth the extra 90-minute drive if you're really looking to get off the map and off the grid, while Albuquerque offers a fun and funky city break, along with great outdoor activities. If you manage to wrangle a four-day weekend, spend it in Santa Fe or Taos—the extra day will be a big help as you adapt to the elevation and the slow pace.

## SANTA FE
### Day 1

Fly into Albuquerque; head to Santa Fe via the scenic Turquoise Trail and check in to your hotel: The Inn of the Five Graces is an exotic, utterly luxurious hideaway. If you're looking for real romantic seclusion, book the weekend at The Galisteo Inn, not far off the Turquoise Trail and about 30 minutes' drive from Santa Fe. If it's summertime, head to **Canyon Road** for the gallery crawl, which gets started around 5 P.M. If it's wintertime,

curl up for a bit by the fire at Staab House, at La Posada de Santa Fe, then walk over to dinner at Café Pasqual's.

### Day 2

Pick up breakfast at the French Pastry Shop, then spend the morning sightseeing **(Museum of Fine Arts, Museum of International Folk Art)** and the afternoon in a private hot tub at Ten Thousand Waves, finishing with a massage and spa treatment. Around happy hour, head to La Casa

Sena – have a drink in the flower-filled patio, then move inside for a candlelit dinner. If you're up for more, go to hip lounge Swig for a cocktail.

## Day 3

Take an early morning hike on the **Dale Ball Trails** or, less strenuously, around the **Santa Fe Canyon Preserve.** Treat yourself to brunch at Inn of the Anasazi, or head out to Harry's Roadhouse, a little north of town, for high-end diner-style goodies (and pie), then drive back down I-25 to catch your flight out.

# TAOS
## Day 1

Fly into Albuquerque; head to Taos via I-25 and the low road. Choose lodging that reflects the area's eco-friendly ideals: the solar Dobson House bed-and-breakfast, perched on the edge of the Rio Grande Gorge, or, more deluxe, El Monte Sagrado Spa & Resort, a lavish resort that happens to recycle all its wastewater. After you check in, stroll the plaza and the galleries along Ledoux Street. Have a haute Mexican dinner at Antonio's, which is conveniently close to the funky Sagebrush Inn, a stop on the small town's limited nightlife circuit.

## Day 2

Visit **Taos Pueblo** in the morning. If you prefer museums, visit **Taos Art Museum at Fechin House** and the **Millicent Rogers Museum;** if you'd rather hike, head for the West Rim Trail along the **Rio Grande Gorge** – it's fairly level, so you shouldn't have too much trouble, despite the elevation. Have green chile for dinner at Orlando's.

## Day 3

Get up early for a dip in **Blackrock hot springs.** Drop by **San Francisco de Asis Church** later in the morning, then fortify yourself for the drive back south with

breakfast at El Taoseño or, more lavishly, with brunch at Joseph's Table. Head out along the high road to Santa Fe, then I-25 to the airport, which takes about four hours, without much stopping; a straight shot back down the low road will shave about 40 minutes off the trip.

# ALBUQUERQUE
## Day 1

Arrive at Albuquerque airport; transfer to your hotel: Try Los Poblanos Inn or another rural-feeling inn in the North Valley, or The Hotel Blue downtown if you want to be in the middle of the action. Stroll around **Old Town** in the afternoon, then dine in Nob Hill (hip finger food at Graze, for instance) or near the university, at New Mexican favorite El Patio. Or just find the nearest Blake's Lotaburger and pick up a green-chile cheeseburger and a cherry Coke.

## Day 2

If you're feeling ambitious, get an early start to drive straight west to **Acoma Pueblo,** which takes about an hour and a half. On your way back toward Albuquerque, stop off on the West Mesa to clamber up the dormant volcanoes, then drive around the base to see **Petroglyph National Monument.** In the late afternoon, drive north through Rio Rancho to the Hyatt Regency Tamaya, where you can have a drink while looking over the lush river valley. In the fading light, drive south through Corrales and have dinner at Casa Vieja.

## Day 3

Get up early again to head for **Sandia Peak:** Either take the tramway up from the foothills or drive around the back side of the mountain and up the winding scenic highway. Allow about three hours for the outing, then stop off at The Frontier for late lunch before catching your flight.

# MESAS AND MOUNTAINTOPS

Not only is New Mexico's mountain scenery stunning, but the population is sparse, so it's very easy to get out of town and enjoy the natural splendor all on your own. This route, which takes nine days, caters to hikers who want to spend as much time as possible outside of the cities. When you arrive in New Mexico and see the scenery, it's tempting to put on your boots and head straight out, but unless you're coming from a comparable elevation, stick to clambering in foothills and scenic drives for the first couple of days. Drink plenty of liquids, and head to bed early.

If you'd prefer not to do the overnight backpacking trip suggested below, take a day hike in Bandelier National Monument instead, then stay the night in nearby Los Alamos or camp at the monument. In the morning, you can squeeze in another quick day hike at Bandelier or drive on toward Jemez and hike to San Antonio Springs. As for timing, don't try this itinerary any earlier than mid-May; even then you will still encounter snowpack at higher elevations. If you're especially interested in rafting, the early part of the summer is the best time to do it, when the river is fullest. Visiting in the fall may be colder, but the glowing yellow aspen groves that stud the mountains are a major attraction.

## DAY 1

Arrive at Albuquerque's Sunport; pick up your rental car and head north to your hotel in Santa Fe. If you arrive on an early flight, take a detour to **Kasha-Katuwe Tent Rocks National Monument** for an easy, hour-long hike – but don't push yourself too hard.

## DAY 2

Rent a bike and get oriented downtown, then head down the rail trail to **Lamy** or cruise around the **Dale Ball Trails** in the Sangre de Cristo foothills. Return to Santa Fe for a leisurely and hearty barbecue dinner at The Cowgirl.

## DAY 3

Take your pick of several hikes in the Santa Fe area: The **Rio en Medio** trail north of Tesuque is a good one, or make the trek along **Raven's Ridge** if you can handle the elevation. At night, relax in the hot tubs at Ten Thousand Waves, then have a late dinner at Kasasoba.

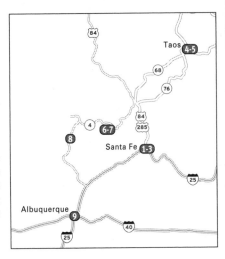

## DAY 4

Drive to Taos via the high road, spending the afternoon around town or on a short hike in **Hondo Canyon** near Taos Ski Valley (grab a burrito at Abe's Cantina y Cocina in Arroyo Seco when you head up this way). At night, meet other outdoorsy types at Eske's Brew

Pub. Bunk at Mountain Light B&B, set on a ridge in **Arroyo Hondo,** with a beautiful view of the mesas.

## DAY 5

Hike or mountain-bike along the **South Boundary Trail,** or go rafting through the white water in the **Taos Box.** Around sunset, head out to the **Blackrock Springs.** Spend the night in Taos.

## DAY 6

Drive back south via the low road and take an afternoon hike in **Valles Caldera National Preserve;** stay the night in Los Alamos or at the campground at **Bandelier National Monument.**

## DAY 7

Head into **Bandelier National Monument** for an overnight backpacking trip to ancestral Puebloan ruins at the Shrine of the Stone Lions.

## DAY 8

Hike out to your car and drive south along the **Jemez Mountain Trail.** Stay overnight in **Jemez Springs,** soothing your muscles with a rest in the hot springs here.

## DAY 9

Return to Albuquerque via the Jemez Mountain Trail; grab a last bite of green-chile stew at The Frontier if you have time before your flight.

# AMERICAN INDIAN HERITAGE TOUR

On this week-long itinerary, you'll concentrate on the culture that developed before the arrival of the Spanish in the 16th century, with visits to both ruined and inhabited pueblos, and to excellent museums that hold some of the region's finest treasures. If you're serious about purchasing art and jewelry, you may want to time your visit with the Santa Fe Indian Market, which takes place every August and showcases more than 1,200 Native American artisans. Otherwise, be sure to visit the gift shops at the Institute of American Indian Arts Museum in Santa Fe or the Indian Pueblo Cultural Center in Albuquerque to get an idea of prices and quality; you can also buy directly from craftspeople at the pueblos.

## DAY 1

Arrive at Albuquerque's Sunport airport and transfer to your hotel. The beautiful Hyatt Regency Tamaya resort is owned by Santa Ana Pueblo; Casita Chamisa in Albuquerque's North Valley even has a small ruin on its grounds, excavated by the owners. If you have time before dark, take a quick visit to **Petroglyph National Monument** on the west side, to see ancient rock carvings and get a great view across the city.

## DAY 2

Visit the **Indian Pueblo Cultural Center** for an overview of the American Indian set-

tlements along the Rio Grande. Have lunch here, at the Pueblo Harvest Café. If you didn't see it yesterday, pop in to Petroglyph National Monument, then continue west to **Acoma Pueblo,** stopping at **Laguna Pueblo** to see its mission church. Return to Albuquerque for dinner.

## DAY 3

Drive to Santa Fe via I-25, stopping off at **Kasha-Katuwe Tent Rocks National Monument** for a short hike through the odd rock formations. On your way back to the highway, drive through **Cochiti Pueblo**

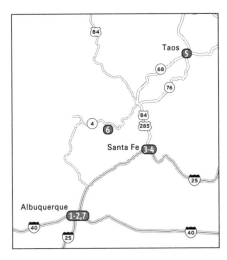

Institute of American Indian Arts Museum, perhaps picking up some craftwork at the gift shop.

## DAY 5

Drive to Taos via the high road. Head straight to **Taos Pueblo;** if you have time, finish the day with a tour of the Native American weaving and pottery collections at the **Millicent Rogers Museum.** Stay overnight in Taos (the owner of Little Tree B&B can give you a history lesson on the area, along with a comfortable bed).

## DAY 6

Get an early start for the drive back south via the low road, then turn off to **Bandelier National Monument,** where you'll make an easy hike through the ancestral Puebloan ruins that fill Frijoles Canyon. Spend the night in Santa Fe.

## DAY 7

Drive down to Albuquerque to catch a flight home. If you book a later flight, you can go via the scenic **Jemez Mountain Trail,** stopping for Indian frybread from the vendors set up in front of the Walatowa Visitors Center; otherwise, take I-25.

to see the old center, built around two huge kivas. Stay in Santa Fe (Hotel Santa Fe, co-owned by Picurís Pueblo, showcases tribal art) and stroll the plaza in the evening.

## DAY 4

Head first to the **Wheelwright Museum of the American Indian** and the **Museum of Indian Arts & Culture.** Then visit the excellent contemporary art collection at the

# SEVEN-DAY ART TOUR

Both Santa Fe and Taos have long histories of fostering creative output, and an amazing amount of art is bought and sold in both places. On this itinerary, you'll see some of the great works created here, then visit the landscapes that inspired them. The Georgia O'Keeffe House is open to tours only in the summer, but it's not an absolutely essential part of the trip—the surrounding views merit a visit on their own. An advantage to this travel schedule is that if you prefer, you need to rely on a rental car only for a few days.

## DAY 1

Fly into Albuquerque; head directly to Santa Fe and choose your accommodations – perhaps a Gallery suite at La Posada de Santa Fe, decorated with work from the most influential local art dealers, or a room at La Fonda, where the lobby is hung with Old West portraits and the hallways are covered in murals.

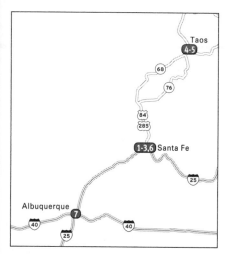

## DAY 2

Get your bearings in Santa Fe, visiting the plaza, the **Museum of Fine Arts,** and the **Georgia O'Keeffe Museum.** Have a leisurely lunch at the O'Keeffe Café, then spend the afternoon visiting galleries, especially along **Canyon Road.**

## DAY 3

Drive to Abiquiu, visiting the **Georgia O'Keeffe House** if possible. Go to Ghost Ranch, where the artist also owned a small studio, and hike up to **Chimney Rock** if you're inclined – keep an eye out for Pedernal Peak, which appears in so many of O'Keeffe's paintings. On your way back, if you have time, visit Rancho de San Juan near Española, where you can hike up to **Windows in the Earth,** a beautiful cavern chapel carved into the cliffs by a contemporary artist. Return to Santa Fe for the night.

## DAY 4

Drive to Taos via the high road, stopping in galleries in Cordova and Truchas. Learn the history of the local art scene at the **Taos**

**Art Museum at Fechin House** and the **Harwood Museum of Art,** both of which have a good collection of work by the Taos Society of Artists, which paved the way for the town to grow as an art colony. Have a drink and dinner at El Monte Sagrado Spa & Resort – keep an eye out for a couple of Basquiats, a Picasso, and a giant Rosenquist canvas. Stay overnight in Taos at the Mabel Dodge Luhan House, where the arts doyenne held her salons.

## DAY 5

Get up by sunrise to see the early-morning light shine on **San Francisco de Asis Church,** likely depicted by every artist who has passed through town. After breakfast, tour the former home of arts patroness Mabel Dodge Luhan (if you're not staying there already), then look for her grave in the nearby cemetery. Enjoy a relaxed lunch at the Dragonfly Café, then spend the afternoon at **Taos Pueblo.**

## DAY 6

Return to Santa Fe via the low road, stopping off in the village of Alcalde to see **Historic Los Luceros Museum,** the former home of Mary Cabot Wheelwright, who established a museum for Native American art. Drive through **Tesuque** to see the Shidoni foundry and Tesuque Glassworks. If you have time, pop in to see the contemporary side of the city's art scene at **SITE Santa Fe.** Dine at chummy Aqua Santa, popular with designers and other members of Santa Fe's creative set. Spend the night in Santa Fe.

## DAY 7

Drive to Albuquerque via the **Turquoise Trail** if your flight time allows, stopping in the galleries in **Madrid** and at **Sandia Park's Tinkertown Museum,** a fantastic collection of homegrown folk art, all made by one very industrious whittler.

# SANTA FE

One of Santa Fe's several nicknames is "Fanta Se," a play on the name that suggests the city's disconnection from reality. This small cluster of mud-colored buildings in the mountains of northern New Mexico does indeed seem to subsist on dreams alone, as more than 20 percent of the 62,000 people who live here are engaged in some sort of creative endeavor—a larger proportion of writers, artists, and performers than in any other city in the United States—and almost 50 percent of the city is employed in the larger arts industry. (Cynics would lump the state legislature, which convenes in the capitol here, into this category as well.)

The city fabric itself is a byproduct of this creativity—many of the "adobe" buildings that make up the distinctive downtown area are in fact plaster and stucco, built in the early 20th century to satisfy a collective vision of what the city ought to look like to appeal to tourists. And the mix of old-guard Spanish, Pueblo Indians, groovy Anglos, and international jet-setters of all stripes has even developed a soft but noticeable accent—a vaguely Continental intonation, with a vocabulary drawn from the 1960s counterculture and alternative healing.

What keeps Santa Fe grounded, to use the local lingo, is its location, tucked in the foothills of the Sangre de Cristos. The outside is never far, even if you're just admiring the mountain view from your massage table at a Japanese-style spa or dining on succulent locally raised lamb at an elegant restaurant. You can be out of town at a trailhead in 15 minutes, skiing down a precipitous slope in 30, or

# HIGHLIGHTS

**◖ Santa Fe Plaza:** On Santa Fe's lively main square, teenage hippies play hacky-sack on one side, while local Pueblo vendors sell their wares under the eaves at the Palace of the Governors (page 29).

**◖ La Fonda:** The Santa Fe Trail came to an end on the doorstep of this hotel, which has witnessed the city's fluctuating fortunes—and harbored its assorted characters—for centuries (page 35).

**◖ Canyon Road:** More than 200 galleries line this winding street that's the heart of Santa Fe's art scene—and its social life, when it's packed with potential collectors and party-hoppers on summer Friday nights (page 36).

**◖ Museum of International Folk Art:** In the main exhibition hall, all the world's crafts, from Appalachian quilts to Zulu masks, are jumbled together in an inspiring, if slightly overwhelming, display of human creativity (page 39).

**◖ Los Alamos:** Driving up to "the City on the Hill," you can't help but imagine what the Manhattan Project scientists must have thought when they arrived in this remote outpost where they would develop the atomic bomb (page 70).

**◖ Bandelier National Monument:** The hidden valley of Frijoles Canyon was once home to the ancestors of today's Puebloans, in an elaborate city complex and cliff-side cave apartments (page 73).

**◖ Ghost Ranch:** The spread where Georgia O'Keeffe kept a house occupies a patch of dramatic red-rock cliffs and wind-blown pinnacles. Hike up to Chimney Rock for the best view across Abiquiu (page 79).

**◖ Chimayó:** The faith is palpable in this village, where an adobe chapel has become known as "the Lourdes of America," thanks to the healing powers attributed to the holy dirt found within its adobe walls (page 80).

**◖ Las Trampas:** In this remote mountain village on the high road to Taos, the San José de Gracia Church is a flawless example of colonial Spanish adobe design. Visit in the summer for a better chance of seeing the beautiful carvings inside (page 83).

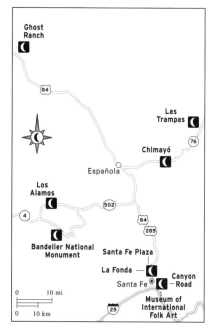

LOOK FOR ◖ TO FIND RECOMMENDED SIGHTS, ACTIVITIES, DINING, AND LODGING.

wandering among the red cliffs you've seen in Georgia O'Keeffe's paintings of **Abiquiu** in 60. To the east of the city is the border of **Pecos Wilderness Area,** a couple hundred thousand acres of dense forest studded with alpine summits like Santa Fe Baldy and Truchas Peak.

Santa Fe's history, too, gives the community strong roots—officially established around 1609, it's the second oldest city in the United States (St. Augustine, Florida, beats it by 44 years). The city is surrounded by American Indian **pueblos** that have been inhabited since well before the Spanish arrived, alongside the remnants of much older cities, such as Tyuonyi in **Bandelier National Monument.** As the former capital of the Spanish territory of Nuevo México, Santa Fe was the gateway to the wilder, emptier lands to the north—and it still is, with two scenic routes running north to Taos: the **high road** winds along mountain ridges through old Hispano villages, while the **low road** follows the Rio Grande through apple orchards and canyons.

If you need a break from Santa Fe and all its history, head for the town of **Española,** a modern and unlikely mix of lowrider-proud cruisers and convert Sikhs, and a great place for New Mexican food. Or seek out isolated **Los Alamos,** home of the atomic bomb—the biggest reality check of all.

## PLANNING YOUR TIME

If you're looking at a short trip, a three-day weekend in the city is a perfectly good getaway; add a few days more to take a hike outside of town or make the drive to Taos, Los Alamos, or Abiquiu. Mobs arrive in July and August, especially for Spanish Market and Indian Market (the latter coincides with closing night at the Santa Fe Opera), so you'll find the city a bit calmer—and the heat less overpowering—in spring and fall. Choose spring if you'll be primarily in the city—lilacs bloom in May, tumbling over adobe walls and filling the air with scent—but opt for the fall if you plan to do a lot of hiking, because October is when the dense groves of aspen trees on the Sangre de Cristo Mountains turn bright yellow, a gorgeous sight enhanced by the crisp, spicy air at that time of year. If you do come in the summer, however, you'll find the gallery scene in full swing—plan to be in the city on a Friday night, when Canyon Road galleries have their convivial openings.

## HISTORY

Founded in 1609, La Villa Real de la Santa Fé (The Royal City of the Holy Faith) was built to be the capital of Spain's northernmost territory in the New World. The Camino Real, the route that connected the outpost with Mexico, dead-ended in the newly built plaza. The 1680 Pueblo Revolt set back the Spanish settlers' plans, but not for long: Don Diego de Vargas returned with troops in 1693, bent on reconquering the city. After a pitched battle, the Spanish moved back in (ousting the Indians from the state house, which they'd turned into storerooms and apartments) and established a shaky truce with the local population, after which more Spaniards began to settle in small villages north of Santa Fe.

Mexico's independence from Spain in 1821 marked a major shift in the city's fortunes, as the new government opened up its northernmost territory to outside trade—something the Spanish had refused to do. Soon enough, the Santa Fe Trail, a route from Missouri to New Mexico first blazed in 1792, was booming with trade, and the city was a cosmopolitan commercial hub where Mexicans and Americans swapped goods and hard currency. But not without a little turmoil: In 1836, the Mexican government appointed Albino Pérez to the governorship—unlike previous leaders, he wasn't a native New Mexican, which angered the populace. A group of protesters fought Pérez's disorganized militia on Black Mesa (the same place a crew of Puebloan holdouts prolonged De Vargas's *reconquista* in 1694), northwest of Santa Fe. Pérez was then hunted down and killed in the Palace of the Governors. This incident helped the Americans earn an easy victory in New Mexico during the Mexican-American War, when General Stephen Kearny peaceably brought the territory under U.S. control in 1846.

# SANTA FE

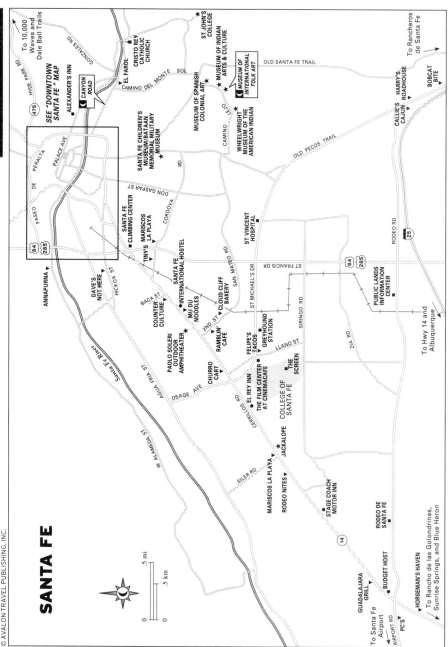

To 10,000 Waves and Dale Ball Trails

HYDE PARK RD

GONZALES RD

475

ST JOHN'S COLLEGE

CRISTO REY CATHOLIC CHURCH

EL FAROL

MUSEUM OF INDIAN ARTS & CULTURE

To Rancheros de Santa Fe

OLD SANTA FE TRAIL

CAMINO DEL MONTE SOL

BOBCAT BITE

HARRY'S ROADHOUSE

CALLIE'S CAJUN

MUSEUM OF INTERNATIONAL FOLK ART

SEE "DOWNTOWN SANTA FE" MAP

ALEXANDER'S INN

CANYON ROAD

MUSEUM OF SPANISH COLONIAL ART

PALACE AVE

PERALTA

PASEO DE

WHEELWRIGHT MUSEUM OF THE AMERICAN INDIAN

CAMINO LEJO

OLD PECOS TRAIL

SANTA FE CHILDREN'S MUSEUM/BATAAN MEMORIAL MILITARY MUSEUM

RD

CORDOVA

DON GASPAR ST

SANTA FE CLIMBING CENTER

MARISCOS LA PLAYA

ST VINCENT HOSPITAL

RODEO RD

25

SAN MATEO RD

ST FRANCIS DR

84 285

TINY'S

SANTA FE INTERNATIONAL HOSTEL

ANNAPURNA

DAVE'S NOT HERE

HICKOX ST

BACA ST

COUNTER CULTURE

MU DU NOODLES

CLOUD CLIFF BAKERY

ST MICHAEL'S DR

PUBLIC LANDS INFORMATION CENTER

Santa Fe River

AGUA FRIA ST

PAOLO SOLERI OUTDOOR AMPHITHEATER

2ND ST

RAMBLIN' CAFE

FELIPE'S TACOS

GREYHOUND STATION

SIRINGO RD

ZIA RD

To Hwy 14 and Albuquerque

CHURRO CART

EL REY INN

THE FILM CENTER AT CINEMACAFE

THE SCREEN

LLANO ST

OSAGE AVE

CERRILLOS RD

COLLEGE OF SANTA FE

W ALAMEDA ST

JACKALOPE

SILER RD

MARISCOS LA PLAYA

RODEO NITES

STAGE COACH MOTOR INN

RODEO DE SANTA FE

14

GUADALAJARA GRILL

BUDGET HOST

HORSEMAN'S HAVEN

To Rancho de las Golondrinas, Sunrise Springs, and Blue Heron

To Santa Fe Airport

AIRPORT RD

PC'S

.5 mi

.5 km

0

0

But Santa Feans still had to contend with the more domineering figure of Bishop Jean Baptiste Lamy, appointed in 1850. For more than three decades, the Frenchman struggled with the local culture (both Spanish Catholic and Indian), and his attempts to "elevate" the city to European standards can be seen in the grandiose stone St. Francis Cathedral.

The Americans had a little more luck taming the frontier capital when the railroad came through, in 1880. Although it effectively killed the Santa Fe Trail (and the trade economy with it), it opened up the city to what's still its lifeblood today: tourism. As locals moved south to do business in the now-booming city of New Albuquerque, where the train tracks went right by their front doors, loads of curious Easterners, who weren't deterred by the 18-mile rail spur up from Lamy, took their places. Along with them came freight cars full of odd materials such as bricks and timber, to build new houses that were the most visible evidence that New Mexico was no longer a Spanish colony.

Some of these early visitors were artists who helped popularize Santa Fe as a retreat well before the territory was granted official statehood in 1912. In that same year, a council of city planners decided to promote Santa Fe as a tourist destination and preserve its distinctive architecture. By 1917, the Museum of Fine Arts had opened, and the first Indian Market was held in 1922, in response to the trend of Anglos collecting the local craftwork. Los Cinco Pintores—a crew of intrepid painters who built their own houses on Canyon Road—were just a handful of the artists who now called the city home.

A new element was added to Santa Fe's mix in 1943, when the building at 109 East Palace Avenue became the "front office" and only known address for Los Alamos, where the country's greatest scientists were developing the atomic bomb under a cloud of confidentiality. But the rational scientists left little mark on Santa Fe—right-brain thinking has continued to flourish, and the city is now a modern, creative version of its old self, a meeting-place where international art dealers swap goods and ideas.

# Sights

## ORIENTATION

For all the things to see in do in Santa Fe, it's easy to forget you're in a small town. Not only are nearly all the major sights within walking distance around the central plaza, but visitors will have little reason to see large swaths of town. Generally, you'll find yourself within the oval formed by Paseo de Peralta, a main road that almost completely circles the central district. On its southwest side it connects with Cerrillos Road, a main avenue lined with motel courts, shopping plazas, and chain restaurants. Compared to the central historic district, it's unsightly, of course, but there are some great local places to eat along this way, as well as the few inexpensive hotels in town.

## ◖ SANTA FE PLAZA

When Santa Fe was established in 1610, its layout was based on strict Spanish laws governing town planning in the colonies—hence the central plaza fronted by the Casas Reales (Palace of the Governors) on its north side. The plaza is still the city's social hub, and the blocks surrounding it are rich with history. In the center of the plaza is the **Soldiers' Monument,** dedicated in 1867 to those who had died in "battles with… Indians in the territory of New Mexico"—the word "savage" has been neatly excised, a policy applied to historic markers throughout the state.

### Palace of the Governors

The former seat of Santa Fe's government is now

# IT'S NOT *ALL* ADOBE

Santa Fe maintains its distinctive historic core through the stringent Historic Styles Ordinance, which dictates even the shade of brown stucco finish required for buildings around the plaza. But look closely, and you'll see several different styles. **Colonial** is the term applied to adobe (or adobe-look) buildings, usually one story, with their typical rounded edges and flat roofs supported by vigas – long cross beams, made of single tree trunks. The style was developed by the Spanish colonists in the 16th, 17th, and 18th centuries, based on their previous experience with adobe architecture and forms they saw in the pueblos. In the 19th century, when New Mexico became a territory of the United States, American influence came in the form of timber-frame houses, often two stories with balconies, and ornamented with brick cornices and Greek revival details, such as carved wood fluted columns.

This **territorial** style, as it's called, can still be seen on the plaza at the two-story Catron Building on the northeast side, but a lot of the best examples were lost during the **pueblo revival** period in the early part of the 20th century. Architects such as John Gaw Meem and Isaac Rapp (the latter designed the Museum of Fine Arts on the northwest corner of the plaza) took their inspiration from both the Spanish colonial-era mission churches and the traditional pueblo buildings, where they saw a clean-lined minimalism that was in keeping with the developing modernist sensibilities. Because they used contemporary frame construction, pueblo revival buildings could be much bigger: Meem's additions to La Fonda make it five stories tall. The architectural trend coincided with the city's aggressive move to court tourism and the idea of developing a comprehensive "look" for the city, so many of the wood-frame territorial houses were simply covered over in a thick layer of plaster. The result is not precisely "historic," but the city planners achieved their goal: Santa Fe looks like no other city in the United States.

the state history museum (120 Washington Ave., 505/476-5090, www.palaceofthegovernors.org, 10 A.M.–5 P.M. Tues.–Sun., $7, free 5–8 P.M. Fri.). Built 1610–1612, it's one of oldest government buildings in the United States, giving it plenty of time to change character (from Spanish colonial adobe to Greek revival wood trim in the territorial era to a brief Victorian phase and back to spiffier adobe in 1909) and accumulate stories: De Vargas fought the Indian rebels here room by room when he retook the city in 1693, ill-fated Mexican governor Albino Pérez was beheaded in his office in 1837, and Governor Lew Wallace penned *Ben Hur* here in the late 1870s.

Currently 80 percent of the museum's collection is in storage, so an approved expansion, slated to finish by 2008, will add a little breathing room. What you can see now: trinkets and photos from the 19th century, including the oldest daguerreotype in the state—which happens to be a portrait of Padre Antonio Martinez, a folk hero of Taos. You'll also see the beautiful 18th-century Segesser hide paintings, two wall-size panels of buffalo skin depicting, on one, a meeting between two Indian tribes, and on the other, a battle between the French and a Spanish expedition in Nebraska. These works, along with the room they're in (trimmed with 1909 murals of the Puyé cliffs) are worth the price of admission. In a couple of the restored furnished rooms, you can compare the living conditions of the Mexican leadership circa 1845 to the relative comfort the U.S. governor enjoyed in 1893.

**Walking tours** depart from the Lincoln Avenue side of the museum daily at 10:15 A.M. ($10), covering all the plaza-area highlights in about two hours. You can also purchase a **museum pass** here for $15 that grants you admission to this and four other exhibition spaces—the Museum of Fine Arts, the Museum of Indian Arts & Culture, the Museum of International Folk Art, and the Museum of Spanish Colonial Art; the pass is good for four days.

## St. Francis Cathedral

Santa Fe's showpiece cathedral (131 Cathedral Pl., 505/982-5619, 7 A.M.–6 P.M. daily, free), visible from the plaza at the end of East San Francisco Street, was built over some 15 years in the late 19th century. It represents a bit of a folly for Jean Baptiste Lamy, who initiated the project. The French priest had been assigned by the church to a newly created post that would formally separate New Mexico's Catholics from those in Mexico, but when he arrived in 1851 full of fire and zeal to uplift the barbarous population, he promptly alienated much of his would-be flock.

Lamy was not only shocked by the locals' ways of worship (the cult of the Virgin of Guadalupe was already well established, and the Penitente brotherhood was performing public self-flagellation), but he was also horrified by their aesthetics. How could a person possibly reach heaven while praying on a dirt floor inside a building made of mud? Lamy took one look at the one-room adobe church dedicated to St. Francis of Assisi and decided he could do better. Construction on the Romanesque revival St. Francis Cathedral began in 1869, under the direction of architects and craftsmen from Europe—they used the old church as a frame for the new stone structure, then demolished all of the adobe save for a small side chapel.

Lamy seems to have financed his very expensive project through a loan from one of the city's wealthiest men: Abraham Staab, one of Santa Fe's leading Jewish merchants. This is the alleged reason for the Hebrew inscription "Yahweh" over the cathedral's main doors and the two six-pointed stars in the place: one visible from the pulpit, another in the vestuary. Even so, Lamy ran short of cash—hence the stumpy aspect of the cathedral's corners, which should be topped with spires.

Inside is all Gothic-inspired light and space and glowing stained-glass windows, but that

St. Francis Cathedral

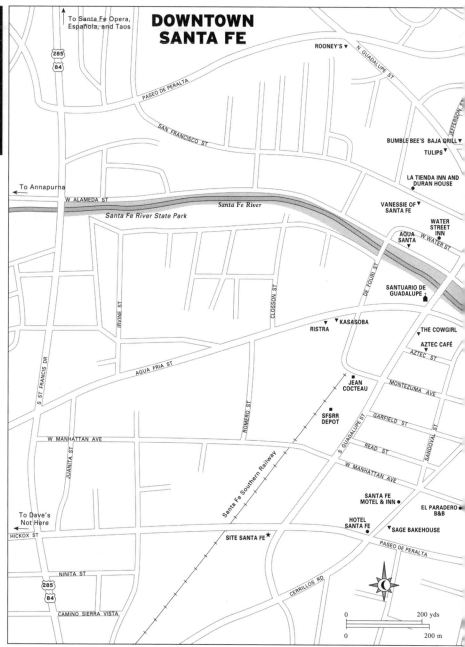

# DOWNTOWN SANTA FE

To Santa Fe Opera, Española, and Taos

285
84

ROONEY'S ▼

N GUADALUPE ST

PASEO DE PERALTA

SAN FRANCISCO ST

JEFFERSON ST

BUMBLE BEE'S BAJA GRILL ▼

TULIPS ▼

LA TIENDA INN AND DURAN HOUSE

To Annapurna

W ALAMEDA ST

Santa Fe River

VANESSIE OF ▼ SANTA FE

Santa Fe River State Park

WATER STREET INN

AQUA W WATER ST
SANTA ▼

DE FOURI ST

SANTUARIO DE GUADALUPE ✝

CLOSSON ST

▼ ▼ KASASOBA
RISTRA

THE COWGIRL

IRVINE ST

AZTEC CAFÉ

AZTEC ST

S ST FRANCIS DR

AGUA FRIA ST

JEAN COCTEAU

MONTEZUMA AVE

ROMERO ST

SFSRR DEPOT

S GUADALUPE ST

GARFIELD ST

SANDOVAL ST

W MANHATTAN AVE

READ ST

JUANITA ST

Santa Fe Southern Railway

W MANHATTAN AVE

SANTA FE MOTEL & INN ●

EL PARADERO ●
B&B

To Dave's Not Here

HOTEL SANTA FE ●

▼ SAGE BAKEHOUSE

HICKOX ST

SITE SANTA FE ★

PASEO DE PERALTA

NINITA ST

CERRILLOS RD

285
84

CAMINO SIERRA VISTA

0          200 yds

0          200 m

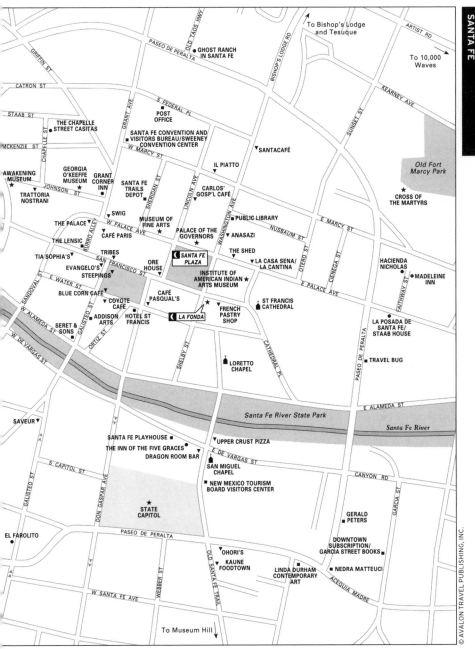

To Bishop's Lodge and Tesuque

ARTIST RD

To 10,000 Waves

GRIFFIN ST

CATRON ST

PASEO DE PERALTA

GHOST RANCH IN SANTA FE

BISHOP'S LODGE RD

KEARNEY AVE

STAAB ST

THE CHAPELLE STREET CASITAS

S FEDERAL PL

POST OFFICE

SUNSET ST

MCKENZIE ST

SANTA FE CONVENTION AND VISITORS BUREAU/SWEENEY CONVENTION CENTER

GRANT AVE

W MARCY ST

SANTACAFÉ

Old Fort Marcy Park

AWAKENING MUSEUM ★

GEORGIA O'KEEFFE MUSEUM

GRANT CORNER INN ★

SANTA FE TRAILS DEPOT

IL PIATTO

CARLOS' GOSP'L CAFÉ ▼

SHERIDAN ST

LINCOLN AVE

WASHINGTON AVE

E MARCY ST

CROSS OF THE MARTYRS ★

TRATTORIA NOSTRANI

JOHNSON ST

THE PALACE ▼

SWIG ▼

MUSEUM OF FINE ARTS

PUBLIC LIBRARY ▼

NUSBAUM ST

CHAPELLE ST

W PALACE AVE

CAFÉ PARIS

PALACE OF THE GOVERNORS ★

ANASAZI ▼

OTERO ST

CIENEGA ST

HACIENDA NICHOLAS

THE LENSIC

BURRO ALLEY

THE SHED ▼

TRIBES ▼

TIA SOPHIA'S ▼

SAN FRANCISCO ST

ORE HOUSE ▼

SANTA FE PLAZA

LA CASA SENA/ LA CANTINA ▼

E PALACE AVE

FAITHWAY ST

MADELEINE INN ●

EVANGELO'S ▼ STEEPINGS ▼

SANDOVAL ST

E WATER ST

INSTITUTE OF AMERICAN INDIAN ARTS MUSEUM ★

BLUE CORN CAFÉ

CAFÉ PASQUAL'S ▼

ST FRANCIS CATHEDRAL ✝

COYOTE CAFÉ ▼

GALISTEO ST

ADDISON ARTS ■

HOTEL ST FRANCIS

LA FONDA

FRENCH PASTRY SHOP ▼

LA POSADA DE SANTA FE/ STAAB HOUSE ●

SERET & SONS ■

ORTIZ ST

W ALAMEDA ST

W DE VARGAS ST

SHELBY ST

CATHEDRAL PL

PASEO DE PERALTA

TRAVEL BUG ■

LORETTO CHAPEL ✝

E ALAMEDA ST

Santa Fe River State Park

Santa Fe River

SAVEUR ▼

SANTA FE PLAYHOUSE ■

THE INN OF THE FIVE GRACES ■ DRAGON ROOM BAR

UPPER CRUST PIZZA ▼

E DE VARGAS ST

SAN MIGUEL CHAPEL ■

CANYON RD

S CAPITOL ST

GALISTEO ST

DON GASPAR AVE

NEW MEXICO TOURISM BOARD VISITORS CENTER ■

GARCIA ST

★ STATE CAPITOL

GERALD PETERS ■

EL FAROLITO ●

PASEO DE PERALTA

DOWNTOWN SUBSCRIPTION/ GARCIA STREET BOOKS ■

OHORI'S ▼

OLD SANTA FE TRAIL

KAUNE FOODTOWN ■

LINDA DURHAM CONTEMPORARY ART ■

NEDRA MATTEUCI ■

ACEQUIA MADRE

WEBBER ST

W SANTA FE AVE

To Museum Hill

OLD TAOS HWY

S FEDERAL PL

could never truly replace the local traditions. The salvaged adobe chapel remains, off to the left of the altar. It is dedicated to the figure of La Conquistadora, a statue brought to Santa Fe from Mexico in 1625, carried away by the retreating Spanish during the Pueblo Revolt, then proudly reinstated in 1693 and honored ever since for inspiring the Spanish to stick with their colonizing project. She glows in her purple robes, under a heavy viga ceiling—all of which probably makes Lamy shudder in his crypt in front of the main altar (he died in 1888).

## Loretto Chapel

Step inside this small chapel (211 Old Santa Fe Tr., 505/982-0092, 9 A.M.–5 P.M. Mon.–Sat., 10:30 A.M.–5 P.M. Sun., $2.50), and you leave the Southwest behind. Initiated by Bishop Lamy in 1873, the building was the first Gothic structure built west of the Mississippi. Lamy was occupied with building the St. Francis Cathedral, so this was a side project, perhaps a way to keep his French architects employed. The decorative elements reflect his fondness for all things European: the stations of the cross rendered by Italian masons, the harmonium and stained-glass windows imported from France, even the stone from which it was built, which was hauled at great expense from quarries up to 200 miles south.

Despite these frills, what really draws the eye is the marvelously simple and elegant—and allegedly miraculous—spiral staircase leading to the choir loft. Made entirely of wood, it makes two complete turns without a central support pole. It was built in 1878 by a mysterious carpenter who appeared seemingly at the spiritual behest of the resident Sisters of Loretto. These nuns—who had in 1853 trooped to New Mexico from Missouri to found a school at Lamy's request—had resorted to prayer because the funding from Lamy hadn't been quite enough. The carpenter toiled in silence for six months, the story goes, then disappeared, without taking any payment. He was never heard from again—though some historians claim to have tracked him down to Las Cruces, where he met

his end in a bar fight. The Sisters of Loretto finally went broke in 1968; the property was desanctified when it sold in 1971, but it's still a very popular wedding spot.

## Museum of Fine Arts

Famed as much for its building as for the art it contains, the Museum of Fine Arts (107 W. Palace Ave., 505/476-5072, www.mfasantafe.org, 10 A.M.–5 P.M. Tues.–Sun., $7, free 5–8 P.M. Fri.) is dedicated to work by New Mexican artists. Built in 1917, it is a beautiful example of pueblo revival architecture, originally designed as the New Mexico pavilion for a world expo in San Diego two years prior. The curvaceous stucco-clad building is an amalgam of iconic pueblo mission churches—the bell towers, for instance, mimic those found at San Felipe. Inside, the collection ranges from Gerald Cassidy's *Cui Bono?,* a perpetually relevant oil painting that questions the benefits of pueblo tourism (it has been on display since the museum opened in 1917), to contemporary video installations. Look out for an excellent collec-

**Museum of Fine Arts**

COURTESY SANTA FE CONVENTION & VISITORS BUREAU/JACK PARSONS

tion of Awa Tsireh's meticulous watercolors of ceremonial dances at San Ildefonso pueblo, alongside other local American Indian artists.

On your way out, don't miss the adjacent St. Francis Auditorium, where three artists adorned the walls with art nouveau murals depicting the life of Santa Fe's patron saint. It's rare to see a secular style usually reserved for languorous ladies in flowing togas used to render such scenes as the apotheosis of Saint Francis and Santa Clara's renunciation, but the effect is beautiful.

### Georgia O'Keeffe Museum
Opened in 1997, this museum (217 Johnson St., 505/946-1000, 10 A.M.–5 P.M. Thurs.–Tues., open daily May–Aug., $8, free 5–8 P.M. Fri.) honors the artist whose name is inextricably bound with New Mexico. The contrary member of the New York avant-garde ("Nothing is less real than realism," she famously said) first visited the state in the 1920s, then moved to Abiquiu permanently in 1949, after her lover, photographer Alfred Stieglitz, died.

Until 2005, the museum was a bit of a hollow monument: All of O'Keeffe's finest works—her signature sensuous, near-abstract flower blossoms, for instance—have already been ensconced in other famous museums the world over, leaving only the rarities here (who knew she did illustrations for a Dole Fruit Co. ad campaign?) to hang alongside loosely related special exhibitions on her contemporaries, or those whose work she influenced or admired. But in mid-2005, the museum received the collection of the Georgia O'Keeffe Foundation, the trust that had been managing the artist's assets since her death in 1986. The transaction will likely bring some exciting new treasures to the space's walls.

### Institute of American Indian Arts Museum
Set in the city's former post office building, this museum (108 Cathedral Pl., 505/988-6211, www.iaiancad.org, 10 A.M.–5 P.M. Mon.–Sat. and noon–5 P.M. Sun., $4) is the showcase for students, professors, and alumni of the pres-tigious IAIA. Come here if you're burned out on old pots in glass cases—instead you'll see the contemporary American Indian experience rendered in oil, charcoal, glass, bronze, and conceptual installations. The collection of works by confident colorist and the institute's most famous prof, Fritz Scholder, is particularly strong. And while the work on the walls is often very experimental, the gift shop stocks a good blend of modern and traditional styles, and is quite well priced.

### The Awakening Museum
Actually a single art installation, the Awakening Museum (125 N. Guadalupe St., 505/954-4025, www.theawakeningmuseum.org, 10 A.M.–6 P.M. daily June–Oct., 10 A.M.–5 P.M. Nov.–May, $3) is the work of French artist Jean-Claude Gaugy. Gaugy, an intense spiritualist who moved to the United States in 1966, was moved to create this room-size work following an epiphany about the nature of humankind's relationship with God. Originally created in an abandoned school gymnasium, the massive allegorical work—which depicts the Last Supper, the Resurrection, and scenes from Revelations—was transferred in 2000 to this room in Santa Fe (formerly a Packard dealership), where Gaugy continued to paint the side panels.

The result is a slightly disorienting immersive experience. Plush carpeting covers the floor, and every surface, including the gracefully curved ceiling crowded with expressionist angels, dances with sinuous figures and vibrant colors. Ethereal music plays, and, in case you're inspired, paper and colored pencils are provided. Although the themes are Christian, Gaugy claims his work is meant to express all human religious experience (the Qur'an, the Popul Vuh, and the Tibetan Book of the Dead are also on hand for your perusal)—and clearly hopes to inspire a similar awakening in its viewers.

### ◖ La Fonda
"The Inn at the End of the Trail," on the corner of San Francisco Street and Old Santa Fe

Trail (see *Accommodations* for more detailed contact information), has been offering respite to travelers in some form or another since 1607. It boomed in the early years of the Santa Fe Trail and the gold-digging era, with a casino and saloon; it hosted the victory ball following General Kearny's takeover of New Mexico in the Mexican-American War; and during the Civil War it housed Confederate general H. H. Sibley during his short-lived attempt to claim New Mexico for the South. Lynchings, shootings, and all the other signatures of Wild West life took place in the lobby. In the 1920s, it got a bit safer for the average tourist, as it became part of the chain of Harvey Houses along the country's railways. From the 1960s on, it's been a family-owned hotel.

The stacked pueblo revival place you see today dates from 1920, and its interior still hums with history—something about the tile floors, painted glass, and heavy furniture conveys the pleasant clamor of conversation and hotel busyness the way more modern lobbies do not. Guests still pick up their keys at an old wood reception desk, drop their letters in an Indian-drum-turned-mailbox, and chat with the concierge below the poster for Harvey's Indian Detours car tour service. Also look around at the great art collection, including wall-size portraits of Kit Carson and Native American dancers, as well as a mural of a Santa Fe Trail wagon train. La Plazuela restaurant, in the sunny center courtyard, is a beautiful place to rest, and the bar is timeless.

# NEW MEXICO STATE CAPITOL

A round building (491 Old Santa Fe Trail, 505/986-4589) with an entrance at each of the cardinal points, the 1966 state capitol mimics the zia sun symbol used on the state flag. Inside it's a maze of concentric halls, many of which are lined with an excellent collection of art by the state's best-known creative types—all accessible for free. On the ground level, check out the halls on the senate side; upstairs galleries combine folk art and rugs with more contemporary work, such as Holly Hughes's giant buffalo-head sculpture. Head to the fourth-floor Governor's Gallery, established in 1973, for more traditional work, and don't miss the stained-glass skylight over the rotunda, which has an Indian basketweave pattern. The floor of the rotunda is a mosaic rendition of the state seal: the Mexican brown eagle, grasping a snake and shielded by the American bald eagle. When the legislature is in session—late January through February in even-numbered years, late January through March in odd—you're welcome to sit in the galleries and watch the proceedings.

# ◖ CANYON ROAD

Ground zero for Santa Fe's art market is the intersection of Paseo de Peralta and Canyon Road, the beginning of a half-mile strip that contains more than 80 galleries. In the summer, Canyon Road is a sea of strolling art lovers, aficionados and amateurs alike. It's especially thronged on Friday evenings, when most galleries have an open house or an exhibition opening. There's a city parking lot at the north end of the road, and public restrooms (9:30 A.M.–5:30 P.M. daily) are near the south end, in the complex at 225 Canyon Road, behind Expressions gallery.

Hard to believe, but this street wasn't always chockablock with thousand-dollar canvases. It used to be farmland (irrigated by the "Mother Ditch," Acequia Madre, which still runs parallel one block to the south), and only a few decades ago, it was still unpaved, a muddy gully when it rained. In addition to the galleries, you'll also pass the mid-19th-century house **El Zaguán,** which contains the offices of the **Historic Santa Fe Foundation** (505/983-2567, www.historicsantafe.com, 9 A.M.–noon and 1:30–5 P.M. Mon.–Fri., free). Named for its long internal hallway *(zaguán),* the building was the home of a local merchant, James L. Johnson, from 1854, then occupied by several other city bigwigs after he lost his fortune in 1881. Its garden, laid out in the late 19th century, is a lovely place to rest in the summer. At 630 Canyon Road, the **Quaker meeting house** (630 Canyon Rd.) is the former home of Olive Rush, who painted the Old Santa Fe Trail mural at La Fonda and willed her house

COURTESY NEW MEXICO DEPARTMENT OF TOURISM/DAN MONAGHAN

© ZORA O'NEILL

Canyon Road's galleries range from ritzy... ...to folky and funky.

to the Quakers after her death. In the 1920s, Los Cinco Pintores, the band of young realist painters who also called themselves the "five little nuts in five mud huts," lived in houses they built around the intersection with Camino del Monte Sol. (Will Shuster is the best known of the five today, in part because he started the Zozobra tradition; Walter Mruk, Fremont Ellis, Joseph Bakos, and Willard Nash were the other four.)

Head beyond the shops and through a residential stretch to the far north end of the road to see John Gaw Meem's enormous **Cristo Rey Catholic Church** (1120 Canyon Rd.), built of 180,000 adobe bricks around a steel frame. It opened in 1940 but looks timeless; inside is a dramatic mid-18th-century baroque stone altarpiece, salvaged from La Castrense, the military chapel that used to occupy the south side of the plaza.

## GUADALUPE AND THE RAILYARD DISTRICT

Guadalupe Street runs south and north from just west of the plaza; its southern stretch de-

veloped around the depot for the 18-mile rail spur up from the main line at Lamy, but today it is lined with a clutch of cafés and shops that feel quite different from the plaza, as Guadalupe is just outside of the historic center, beyond the reach of the most stringent adobe-look codes. The area along the tracks has been slated for substantial redevelopment, with new parks and residential buildings to be added by 2008, as well as an eventual commuter rail service to Albuquerque. In the meantime, a couple of sights merit visitors' attention.

## Santuario de Guadalupe

Built 1776–1796, this is the oldest shrine to the Virgin of Guadalupe in the United States (100 S. Guadalupe St., 505/988-2027, 9 A.M.–4 P.M. Mon.–Sat., free). A century later, it got an odd makeover, with a New England–look wood steeple, tall neo-Gothic arched windows, even a white picket fence, but a renovation in 1975 restored a lot of its original details and shored up its three-foot-thick adobe walls. The interior is spare, just folding chairs set up on the wood floor, in front of a Mexican baroque oil-on-canvas altar painting from 1783. Mass is still said regularly, and musical groups, particularly the Santa Fe Desert Chorale, take advantage of the space's excellent acoustics. A museum in the small anteroom displays relics of the old building, such as Greek-style columns carved in wood, and shows exposed pieces of the adobe walls. The chapel is closed on Saturdays during the winter.

## SITE Santa Fe

In sharp contrast to the Guadalupe chapel, this boxy, modern exhibition space (1606 Paseo de Peralta, 505/989-1199, www.sitesantafe.org, 10 A.M.–5 P.M. Wed.–Sat., 10 A.M.–7 P.M. Fri., noon–5 P.M. Sun., $6, free on Fri.), formerly a Coors beer warehouse, is dedicated to all things new in the art world. It doesn't have a permanent collection, and instead puts on high-concept one-off shows that make use of its very flexible space. SITE hosts the Santa Fe Biennial in even-numbered years, curated by hip critics like Dave Hickey.

## OLD SANTA FE TRAIL

From its end at La Fonda, the historic trade route runs off to the east; just past Paseo de Peralta and the small Santa Fe River, it passes through Barrio de Analco, one of Santa Fe's oldest residential neighborhoods, established by the Tlaxcala Indians who came from Mexico as servants of the first Spanish settlers. The road then runs past the state capitol and to a junction with Old Pecos Trail, the main route to I-25 (and historically the cattle-drivers' route to Mexico).

### San Miguel Chapel

This sturdy adobe building (401 Old Santa Fe Tr., 505/983-3974, 9 A.M.–5 P.M. Mon.–Sat., 10 A.M.–4 P.M. Sun., $1) is the oldest church structure in the United States, built around 1610 by the Tlaxcala Indians as part of Barrio de Analco, then partially rebuilt a century later, after it was set aflame in the Pueblo Revolt; its stone buttresses are the product of a desperate attempt to shore up the sagging walls in the late 19th century. The interior

is snug and whitewashed, with painted buffalo hides on the walls and a splendid altar screen that was restored in 1955 after having been covered over in housepaint for decades. The late-18th-century work is attributed to the anonymous Laguna Santero, a Mexican artist who earned his name from the intricately carved and painted screen at the Laguna Pueblo church, near Albuquerque. The screen functions like an enormous picture frame, with both oil paintings and *bultos* (painted wood statues of saints) inserted in the openings. Below the altar, you can look down into cutouts made into the floor to see the original foundations of the building. On your way out, take a look at the old church bell, now on display in the side room. Allegedly cast in Spain in 1356, it was brought to the New World and installed at San Miguel in the early 19th century.

### Bataan Memorial Military Museum and Library

The **Bataan Death March,** just one of World War II's many atrocities, was a particular tragedy in New Mexico, because most of its national guard, which was drafted as the 200th Coast Artillery, was among the more than 70,000 U.S. and Filipino soldiers subject to torture, malnourishment, random execution, malaria, accidental "friendly fire," and three years' imprisonment. Of the 1,800 who started in the regiment, fewer than 900 came home, and a full third of those men died in the first year back. The catastrophe is recalled with newspaper clippings, maps, and testimonials at this home-grown museum (1050 Old Pecos Tr., 505/474-1670, 9 A.M.–4 P.M. Tues., Wed., and Fri., 9 A.M.–1 P.M. Sat., free), which also contains Civil War memorabilia and exhibits on Native American contributions in U.S. wars, such as the Choctaw and Navajo codetalkers. The museum opens one hour later and closes one hour earlier in winter.

### Santa Fe Children's Museum

Across the parking lot from the Bataan Memorial, kids can have tons of hands-on fun at the Santa Fe Children's Museum (1050 Old Pecos Tr., 505/989-8359, 10 A.M.–5 P.M. Wed.–Sat., noon–5 P.M. Sun., $4). Fitting for New Mexico, pint-size looms give a chance for kids to learn to weave. And then there are the globally appealing bits: a giant soap-bubble pool, face-painting, and fun-house mirrors.

## MUSEUM HILL

The life-size bronze sculpture *Journey's End,* commemorating the Santa Fe Trail and the hardy mule teams that traversed it, marks the entrance to Camino Lejo, a strip of major exhibition spaces on Santa Fe's southeast side. With the Museum of Indian Arts & Culture just next door to the Museum of Spanish Colonial Art, it's an interesting opportunity to compare the two depictions of New Mexican culture and history. One of the city's best tourist deals, a $15 **museum pass,** good for four days, grants access to three of the four institutions on the hill (all but the Wheelwright, which is free), as well as the Palace of the Governors and the Museum of Fine Arts on the plaza. You can purchase it at any of the five participating museums.

### Museum of Spanish Colonial Art

The newest attraction on the hill, the Museum of Spanish Colonial Art (750 Camino Lejo, 505/982-2226, www.spanishcolonial.org, 10 A.M.–5 P.M. Tues.–Sun., $6) opened in 2002 with a strong collection of folk art and historical objects dating from the earliest Spanish contact. The collection had been growing since the Spanish Colonial Arts Society was established in Santa Fe in 1925, and it now has some 3,000 pieces. They're one-of-a-kind treasures—such as the only signed *retablo* by the 19th-century *santero* Rafael Aragón—as well as more utilitarian items salvaged from the colonial past, such as fine tortoiseshell combs, silk mantas, wool rugs, and decorative tin. New work by contemporary artisans is also on display—don't miss Luis Tapia's hilarious *"bulto," The Folk-Art Collectors.*

## Museum of Indian Arts & Culture

This excellent museum (710 Camino Lejo, 505/827-6463, www.miaclab.com, 10 A.M.–5 P.M. Tues.–Sun., $7) is devoted to Native American culture from across the country, though the cornerstone is the permanent exhibit Here, Now & Always, which traces the New Mexican Indians from their ancestors on the mesas and plains up to their present-day efforts at preserving their culture—all through inventive spaces (looking into a HUD-house kitchen on the rez, or sitting at desks in a public schoolroom), sound clips, and stories. Another wing is devoted to contemporary art, while the halls of craftwork display gorgeous beaded moccasins, elaborate headdresses, and more. The gift shop is particularly extensive, stocked with beautiful jewelry and other tidbits from local artisans.

## ◖ Museum of International Folk Art

This marvelous hodgepodge of a museum (708 Camino Lejo, 505/476-1200, www.moifa.org, 10 A.M.–5 P.M. Tues.–Sun., $7) is one of Santa Fe's biggest treats—but the easily overwhelmed should steer clear of the main exhibition space, the collection of modernist designer Alexander Girard. About 10 percent of his collection—10,000 pieces from more than 100 countries—is on permanent display in one hall, hung on walls, set in cases, even dangling from the ceiling. Pieces are juxtaposed to show off similar themes, colors, and materials, an approach that initially seems jumbled but in fact underscores the universality of certain concepts and preoccupations around the world.

Elsewhere in the museum, a wing is dedicated to northern New Mexican Hispano crafts—a good complement to the Museum of Spanish Colonial Art—and a lab area where you can see how pieces are preserved. Temporary exhibits take up the rest of the space, usually with colorful, interactive shows on Carnival celebrations around the world, for instance. Don't skip the gift shop, which stocks some smaller versions of the items in the galleries, along with a great selection of world-music CDs.

## Wheelwright Museum of the American Indian

Mary Cabot Wheelwright, an adventurous East Coast heiress, made her way in the early 1920s to New Mexico, where she met a Navajo medicine man named Hastiin Klah. Together they devised a plan for this museum (704 Camino Lejo, 505/982-4636, www.wheelwright.org, 10 A.M.–5 P.M. Mon.–Sat. and 1–5 P.M. Sun., $3 donation), which opened in 1937 as the House of Navajo Religion. The mission has since been broadened to incorporate all Native American cultures, with exhibits of new work by individual artists rotating every few months. The building—modeled after the typical Navajo hogan, with huge viga timbers supporting the eight-sided structure—has two levels: the ground-floor exhibition space and the basement gift shop, really a re-creation of a 19th-century Navajo trading post. The shop would feel like a tourist trap if it weren't for the authentically creaky wood floors and the beautiful antique jewelry on display in the overcrowded cases.

## SANTA FE METRO AREA
## Cross of the Martyrs

This white cross at the top of a hill overlooking downtown Santa Fe is a memorial to the Spanish settlers who were killed in the Pueblo Revolt. It's actually a newer version of a first cross, raised in 1920 a little bit to the west, off Paseo de la Loma. This new cross is at the end of a zigzagging paved path uphill, each switchback marked with a plaque explaining various points in the city's history. It's not a strenuous walk, and the bird's-eye view from the hilltop is excellent. Behind the cross is **Old Fort Marcy Park,** site of the remnants of the first American fort in the Southwest, built in 1847 by General Stephen Kearny, then abandoned in

a working mill at historic Rancho de las Golondrinas

1894. The path up to the cross begins on Paseo de Peralta just east of Otero Street.

## Rancho de las Golondrinas

The "Ranch of the Swallows" (334 Los Pinos Rd., 505/471-2261, www.golondrinas.org, 10 A.M.–4 P.M. Wed.–Sun. June–Sept., $6), about 15 minutes' drive southeast of Santa Fe, is a 200-acre museum in the form of a restored Spanish colonial *paraje,* a way station on the Camino Real. Museum staff in period costume demonstrate crafts and other aspects of early New Mexican history in the blacksmith shop, the schoolhouse, and the mills. The ranch sometimes hosts big to-dos: a Civil War reenactment in late April, a sheep-shearing fair in early June, a frontier-theme horse show in August, and an October harvest festival, among other theme weekends.

# Entertainment

## BARS

With balmy summer evenings and a populace that seems always able to knock off work a little early, Santa Fe is a great place to savor happy hour. The patio at **The Cowgirl** (319 S. Guadalupe St., 505/988-4227, 8 A.M.–8 P.M. daily) is packed 5–7 P.M. with neighbors swilling margaritas, but sunset is also a great time to hit **The Ore House** (50 Lincoln Ave., 505/983-8687, 2:30–11 P.M. daily), on the plaza, where the upstairs balcony bar serves more than 40 kinds of margaritas (happy hour is only 4–6 P.M., though). Over at La Fonda hotel, the outdoor **Bell Tower Bar** (100 E. San Francisco St., 505/982-5511, Apr.–Oct.) provides a fine view from its fifth-floor rooftop haunt; in wintertime, the regulars decamp to the lobby watering hole, **La Fiesta,** decorated with portraits of rodeo queens; live local country acts grace the small corner stage.

The best happy-hour value is certainly the chichi cocktails-and-Asian-snacks lounge **Swig** (135 W. Palace St., 505/955-0400, 5 P.M.–2 A.M. Tues.–Sat.), where martinis are only $5, and there's a sunset view from the balcony—underappreciated, because everyone's busy looking at each other. The rest of the time, drinks are $11 or more, the price to party with the city's beautiful people and the occasional visitor from Hollywood. Four color-theme rooms allow for dancing, chilling out, or smoking; Thursdays are campy karaoke; Fridays, sultry old-school jazz.

For any time of the night, **El Farol** (808 Canyon Rd., 505/983-9912, 11:30 A.M.–3 P.M. and 5 P.M.–2 A.M. daily) is a perennial favorite. A bar since 1835, it's the gallery-owners' clubhouse after quitting time, a very respectable Spanish restaurant (lots of tasty tapas) around dinner, and occasionally the place for exuberant dancing on the tiny dance floor.

The vintage glam **Staab House** (330 E. Palace Ave., 505/983-0000, 11 A.M.–midnight Mon.–Thurs., 11 A.M.–1 A.M. Fri. and Sat.), at La Posada de Santa Fe, has history of another

kind. The 1882 Victorian home of the prominent Jewish merchant Abraham Staab, it still bears mezuzahs on the doorframes, along with the original ornate woodwork and gas chandelier fixtures. The elegant setting is perfect for a postprandial cognac or a romantic cocktail.

Several funkier venues round out the downtown bar scene: **Evangelo's** (200 W. San Francisco St., 505/982-9014), one block off the plaza, usually has its big windows open, letting the band's blues jam or country tunes spill out into the street. When there's no music, the pool tables and a couple hundred kinds of beer provide distraction. The **Dragon Room Bar** (406 Old Santa Fe Tr., 505/983-7712, 11:30 A.M.–2 A.M. Mon.–Fri., 5 P.M.–2 A.M. Sat., 5 P.M.–midnight Sun.) is so dim you might not notice at first the huge tree growing up from the left side of the bar. Green-chile stew is available at all times, and guys in cowboy hats chat with mountain bikers and dressed-up cocktail drinkers. There's live music Tuesday, Thursday, and Saturday. And even Santa Fe has an Irish pub, of sorts: **Rooney's** (402 N. Guadalupe St., 505/984-9112, 11:30 A.M.–10 P.M. daily), where you can wash down your corned beef with a Guinness—but there's also vegetarian nut loaf on the menu.

## CLUBS AND LIVE MUSIC

Since Santa Fe's one hip dance club shut in mid-2005, many former customers lounge around the small dance floor at Swig and talk about what else might develop. In the meantime, you can head out to **Rodeo Nites** (2911 Cerrillos Rd., 505/473-4138, Wed.–Sun.) for entirely the opposite scene. It's a grand-scale modern juke joint where boot-scooting is the name of the game—although on the weeknights, you'll be doing it as much to Mexican *norteño* music as to Texas two-step. Cover is usually $5 or more.

**Vanessie of Santa Fe** (434 W. San Francisco St., 505/982-9966, 4:30 P.M.–12:30 A.M. Mon.–Sat., 4:30 P.M.–midnight Sun.)

is perhaps the best-lit cabaret in America, creating the incongruity of someone crooning "Crazy" in an airy room done up in light pine furniture. A bit cheesier but chummier is **La Cantina** (125 E. Palace Ave., 505/988-9232, www.lacasasena.com), next to La Casa Sena, where the boa-clad waitstaff belts out show tunes while they serve you drinks and light snacks. You do have to plan ahead and reserve at one of the seatings.

**Paolo Soleri Outdoor Amphitheater** (1501 Cerrillos Rd., 505/989-6318), on the grounds of the Santa Fe Indian School, is a beautiful setting for a summer concert. With some 2,500 seats, the venue attracts big touring bands and festivals.

## PERFORMING ARTS

The 2,128-seat **Santa Fe Opera** (U.S. 84/285, 800/280-4654, www.santafeopera.org) is the city's premier arts venue. The elegant open-air amphitheater seven miles north of Santa Fe acts as "summer camp" for the country's best singers to perform a mix of repertory and modern works during July and August. Even if you think opera is all about tuxes, plush seats, and too-long arias, you shouldn't miss the SFO, where half the fun is arriving early to "tailgate" in the parking lot—a chummy, artsy picnic that involves gourmet goodies, lots of champagne, and time to mill around and check out other attendees' bolo ties. In addition to your picnic dinner (if you like, preorder one from Angel Food Catering, 505/983-2433, www.angelfood.catering.com), also pack blankets to ward off the chill after the sun sets. If you have kids to entertain, look into visiting on a designated "youth night," special dress rehearsals with extra info to introduce young ones to the art form.

Set in a fantastical 1931 Moorishly curlicued palace, **The Lensic Performing Arts Center** (211 W. San Francisco St., 505/988-1234, www.lensic.com) is Santa Fe's best stage after the opera house, with everyone from Ladysmith Black Mambazo to the Santa Fe Chamber Orchestra playing to the 821-seat house. The two-month-long **Santa Fe Chamber Music**

© ZORA O'NEILL

The Lensic Performing Arts Center, Santa Fe's most diverse stage

**Festival** (www.santafechambermusic.org) also schedules events here, as well as at the St. Francis Cathedral, with performances nearly every day in July and August. For the rest of the year, the chamber orchestra of **Santa Fe Pro Musica** performs in Loretto Chapel and other intimate venues (505/988-4640, www.santafepromusica.com). The eclectic organization also sponsors performances by the likes of Loudon Wainwright.

If it's live theater you want, visit the historic **Santa Fe Playhouse** (142 E. De Vargas St., 505/988-4262, www.santafeplayhouse.org), which occupies a small adobe in Santa Fe's oldest neighborhood. It stages a selection of melodrama, folk plays, and work by Latino and gay playwrights. Sundays are "pay what you wish."

## CINEMA

Santa Fe has a number of excellent film outlets, in addition to the megaplexes. Closest to the center of town, **Jean Cocteau** (418 Montezuma St., 505/988-2711, www.transluxmovies

# GOOD-BYE, OLD MAN GLOOM!

Every fall, on the weekend after Labor Day, a raucous chant fills the air in Santa Fe's Fort Marcy Park: "Burn him! Burn him! Burn him!" It's not a witch hunt, but the ritual torching of Zozobra, a 50-foot-tall marionette with long, grasping arms, glowering eyes, and a growly voice. Zozobra, whose name comes from the Spanish word for gloom or anxiety, is said to represent the accumulated worries, sorrows, and chronic problems of the populace; burning him to ashes purges these troubles and allows for a fresh start.

This type of burning ritual has ancient roots, but the tradition in Santa Fe dates only from the 1920s, when artist Will Shuster (a.k.a. "Shus") and a few friends wanted to liven up the annual Fiesta de Santa Fe. Shuster, who had moved to Santa Fe in 1920 to treat the tuberculosis he'd developed in World War I, was inspired by the Mummers Parade, a fixture in his native Philadelphia. He also drew on the traditions of the Yaqui Indians in Tucson, Arizona, who perform a ritual burning of an effigy of Judas during Semana Santa, the week preceding Easter.

The first Zozobra, built in 1924, was just 18 feet high, with a disproportionately small head. By 1926, Shuster had perfected the scale and developed the spectacle. A *Santa Fe New Mexican* article from that year relates:

> Zozobra... stood in ghastly silence illuminated by weird green fires. While the band played a funeral march, a group of Kiwanians in black robes and hoods

stole around the figure. ... [Then] red fires blazed at the foot of the figure ... and leaped into a column of many colored flames. As it burned, ... there was a staccato of exploding fireworks from the figure and round about, and throwing off their black robes the spectators emerged in gala costume, joining an invading army of bright-hued harlequins with torches in a dance around the fires as the band struck up "La Cucaracha."

Shus oversaw the building of Zozobra nearly every year until 1964, when he ceded responsibility to the Kiwanis Club. In the late 1930s, Errol Flynn, in town with Olivia de Havilland and Ronald Reagan to film *The Santa Fe Trail*, set Zozobra aflame. A few years later, during World War II, the puppet's face had the features of the era's baddies – and was called Hirohitlomus. In 1950, Zozobra appeared on the New Mexico state float in the Rose Bowl parade and won the national trophy.

Shus, who died in 1969, is now a local legend – he's also credited with inventing piñon-juniper incense and starting the tradition of citywide bonfires on Christmas Eve. And thanks in part to another of the artist's innovations – collecting and stuffing the figure with outdated police reports, pictures of ex-girlfriends, papers from paid-off mortgages, and other anxiety-inducing scraps of paper – the 30,000 people who gather to watch the conflagration are happy to see Zozobra go up in smoke.

.com) is a charming vintage single-screen theater, with the modern bonus of a small soundproofed VIP room, whether for romantics or for parents with cranky babies. Worth heading farther for is **The Screen** (1600 St. Michael's Dr., 505/473-6494), on the campus of the College of Santa Fe. The enthusiastic curator brings in excellent first-run art films, along with repertory gems. Additionally, the **CCA Cinematheque** (1050 Old Pecos Tr., 505/982-1338, www.ccasantafe.org) has a film program with an emphasis on international titles, and **The Film Center at Cinemacafe** (1616 St. Michael's Dr., 505/988-7414, www.santafefilmfestival .com) couples coffee-house casual with obscure celluloid—it's run by the **Santa Fe Film Festival** (four days in early December), so the selection, from vintage animation to gay-theme hits, is inspired.

## FESTIVALS AND EVENTS

The city's biggest annual event is the **Santa Fe Indian Market** (505/983-5220, www .swaia.org), when 1,200 carefully selected Native American artisans present their jewelry, pottery, weaving, and other wares, ranging from the most traditional forms to wildly inventive ones. Tented booths fill the plaza and surrounding streets, and the city swells with some 100,000 visitors. It's a bit of a frenzy while the selling proper lasts for one weekend near the end of August, but the atmosphere is festive, as the booths are augmented by free music and dance performances, as well as the Native Roots and Rhythms festival at the Paolo Soleri amphitheater.

Along similar lines is the **Spanish Market** (505/982-2226, www.spanishmarket.org), which has been staged every year since 1951. Emphasis is primarily on traditional crafts, with New Mexico's most respected *santeros* and *santeras* selling their work alongside weavers, tinworkers, and furniture-makers. The event usually takes place the last weekend in July; the Spanish Colonial Arts Society also sponsors a smaller Winter Market in early December.

The most recent addition to the calendar is the **International Folk Art Market** (505/476-1166, www.folkartmarket.org), first staged in early July 2004 to showcase traditional crafts from all over the globe: Expect Bhutanese textiles, hand-crafted French knives, and South African beadwork, all contributing to the largest international market in the United States. Unlike the other two markets, this one takes place off the plaza, on Museum Hill, so the city is a bit less disrupted.

After all the frenzy of summer tourism, locals celebrate the arrival of the calmer fall season with the **Burning of Zozobra** (505/660-1965, www.zozobra.org), a neo-pagan bonfire on the Thursday after Labor Day that's as much a part of Santa Fe's social calendar as the opera season. The ritual kicks off the week-long **Fiesta de Santa Fe** (505/988-7575, www.santafefiesta.org), which commemorates De Vargas's reoccupation of the city in 1693, following the Pueblo Revolt. The event, which

has been celebrated in some form since 1712, is marked with a reenactment of De Vargas's *entrada* into the city, then a whole slew of balls and parades, including the Historical/Hysterical Parade and a children's pet parade—eccentric Santa Fe at its finest.

Rodeo Road on the south side of town isn't a nod to Beverly Hills—there really is an annual **Rodeo de Santa Fe** (3237 Rodeo Rd., 505/471-4300, www.rodeosantafe.com), which takes place near the end of June. Expect to see all the competitive events such as barrel racing and bull riding, as well as goofy clowns, trickropers, and a kids' "mutton-busting" show. The event opens with a big parade of everyone in their best cowboy regalia.

Foodies flock to the city in late September for the **Santa Fe Wine and Chile Festival** (505/438-8060, www.santafewineandchile .org), five days of tastings and special dinners at various venues around town. Those who want to just drink, not eat, can attend the **Santa Fe Wine Festival,** which takes place on the Fourth of July weekend at Rancho de las Golondrinas and showcases New Mexican wine producers.

The Burning of Zozobra begins.

# Shopping

Even people who cling hard to their purse strings may be a little undone by the sheer glut of treasures for sale in Santa Fe. Whether you want a 19th-century clay water jar from Taos Pueblo, a ballroom-size Afghan carpet, or a little Wyeth to hang over your mantel, you can pick it up here. Consider these fantastical shops something like going to a museum for free—and an education, so you won't be seduced by the myriad shameless shops in a perpetual state of "liquidation." And of course there are a *few* other outlets that offer less expensive trinkets. In general, you'll find assorted souvenirs and a few very influential galleries downtown around the plaza; galleries of all stripes on and near Canyon Road; and more funky and fun modern stuff on South Guadalupe Street.

## MARKETS

One of the most familiar sights of Santa Fe is the north side of the plaza, where Native American vendors from all over New Mexico spread out their wares under the portal at the **Palace of the Governors,** as they've been doing for more than 80 years. Some 1,000 vendors are licensed to sell here after going through a strict application process that evaluates their technical skills; every morning the 63 spots, each 12 bricks wide, are doled out by lottery, so the selection can change wildly from day to day. Expect anything from silver bracelets to pottery to heishi (shell bead) necklaces to freshly harvested piñon nuts. It's a great opportunity to buy direct from a skilled artisan and learn about the work that went into a piece.

In the railyard park at the corner of Cerrillos Road and Guadalupe Street, the popular **Santa Fe Farmer's Market** (505/983-4098, www.santafefarmersmarket.com, 7 A.M.–noon Tues. and Sat.) is a great place to pick up fresh treats as well as souvenir chile *ristras*. In the wintertime, the market moves into El Museo Cultural (1615-B Paseo de Peralta), for Saturdays only, 9 A.M.–1 P.M.

Once a lovely bit of Saharan-bazaar-style chaos, the **flea market** in Tesuque Pueblo (505/670-2599, www.tesuquepuebloflea-market.com, 8 A.M.–4 P.M. Fri.–Sun.) has unfortunately become quite dull and institutionalized and isn't worth the drive up.

## GALLERIES

With every other storefront downtown occupied by a gallery, aimless wandering is a straight ticket to art burnout. Whether you're just browsing or actually looking to buy, decide first what you're most interested in—American Indian crafts, Taos Society of Artists' work, new abstract painting—and stick with that, at least to start with. Santa Fe's contemporary galleries are increasingly where the buzz is. Summer is the galleries' high season, with openings for new single-artist shows somewhere along Canyon Road every Friday evening, starting around 5 P.M. and lasting until 7 or 8 P.M. In the winter, spaces usually mount survey shows that change every couple of months.

### Contemporary

**Linda Durham Contemporary Art** (1101 Paseo de Peralta, 505/466-6600, 10 A.M.–5 P.M. Tues.–Sat.) helped pull Santa Fe out of the mire of Western Americana with her first gallery in Galisteo, opened in the early 1980s. She has now relocated to a prime spot just around the curve from Canyon Road and deals in big names like Joel-Peter Witkin as well as up-and-comers—her taste runs to punchy, pop, and conceptual.

Similarly influential **LewAllen Contemporary** (129 W. Palace Ave., 505/988-8997, 9:30 A.M.–5:30 P.M. Mon.–Sat., 11 A.M.–5 P.M. Sun.) represents Judy Chicago in Santa Fe, as well as a range of other artists in every medium, though most are figurative to some degree. Around the corner, **Riva Yares** (123 Grant Ave., 505/984-0330, 10 A.M.–5 P.M. Tues.–Sat.) deals in *big*—massive canvases, bold images, and famous names like Frank Stella, Milton Avery, and Esteban Vicente. The mission at **Charlotte Jackson Fine Art** (200 W. Marcy St., 505/989-8688, 10 A.M.–5 P.M. Tues.–Fri., 11 A.M.–4 P.M. Sat.), one block up from LewAllen, is simple: monochrome. But even within this limited mandate, the variety can be surprising and compelling. The owner of the intimate and accessible **Addison Arts** (209 Galisteo St., 505/992-0704, 11 A.M.– 5 P.M. Tues.–Sat.) has wide-ranging taste— you'll see bowling pins rendered in glass, compelling narrative canvases, and near-abstract photography.

On Canyon Road, real cutting-edge work is rare, but do check out **EVO Gallery** (725 Canyon Rd., 505/982-4610, 10 A.M.–5 P.M. Mon.–Thurs., 10 A.M.–7 P.M. Fri. and Sat., 11 A.M.–4 P.M. Sun.), which puts a heavy emphasis on conceptual work and abstraction. Richard Serra and Agnes Martin are on the roster next to upstarts like Ligia Bouton. **Nüart Gallery** (670 Canyon Rd., 505/988-3888, 10 A.M.–5 P.M. daily) showcases lots of Latin American magical realism by painters like Juan Kelly and Jorge Leyva alongside more abstract work. A nice transition from some of the fustier Western galleries to the edgier contemporary scene, **Meyer-Munson Gallery** (225 Canyon Rd., 505/983-1657, 9 A.M.–5 P.M. Mon.–Sat., 11 A.M.–4 P.M. Sun.), established in 1860 in New Haven, opened this branch in Santa Fe in the 1980s. Landscapes are popular here, though this can range from hyperrealism to the spare geometry of Jesse Wood.

## Native American and Southwestern

**Price Dewey** (53 Old Santa Fe Tr., 505/982-8632, 10 A.M.–5 P.M. Mon.–Sat.), upstairs off the plaza, feels very homey—if your home happens to be filled with priceless works of art and clever, conceptual home furnishings. Its stock in trade is Native American jewelry and art, but the place doesn't look like a trinket-filled trading post. The presentation is eclectic— traditional turquoise-and-silver jewelry is displayed next to sharp-edged Knoll leather sofas, with vibrant abstract paintings by Fritz Scholder hanging on the wall. There's a whole room full of flawless Navajo rugs as well.

If you're a "pot head," go straight to **Andrea Fisher Fine Pottery** (100 W. San Francisco St., 505/986-1234, 10 A.M.–6 P.M. Mon.–Sat., noon–6 P.M. Sun.), where only the finest Native American plates, bowls, and figurines are on display—some are antique, such as works by San Ildefonso innovator María Martinez, and others are new and edgy in style. Pieces can run well into the thousands of dollars, but it's a treat to see these works up close, and not behind glass.

Near Canyon Road, **Gerald Peters** (1011 Paseo de Peralta, 505/954-5700, 10 A.M.–5 P.M. Mon.–Sat.) has a bit of everything: 19th- and 20th-century American painters, Taos Society of Artists members, obligatory bronze sculptures of cowboys, and even a very solid stable of contemporary artists, which all tend toward the figurative. The space is so big that several shows are going on at any given time—you're sure to find a room that suits you.

Along with Gerald Peters, **Nedra Matteuci** (1075 Paseo de Peralta, 505/982-4631, 8:30 A.M.–5 P.M. Mon.–Sat.) is the other gigantic art dealer in town. The selection here runs more toward art of the American West, with Taos painters Ernest Blumenschein and Victor Higgins on the roster. Even if that's not your scene, the one-acre sculpture garden out back is a treat.

## Sculpture and More

Definitely in the museum-quality category is **Peyton Wright** (237 E. Palace Ave., 505/989-9888, 10 A.M.–5:30 P.M. Mon.–Sat.), a large house where one-off shows deal in modern American masters (need a Marsden Hartley for your foyer?) as well as Old World treasures that look like they've been culled from a czar's forgotten vault. For quite the opposite feel, lighten up at **Chuck Jones Studio Gallery** (128 W. Water St., 505/983-5999), where you can see original cels and sketches from early Disney films as well as more recent animated hits like *Spongebob Squarepants* and

*The Simpsons.* Or you can just chill out and watch the good stuff on TV.

North of Santa Fe in the village of Tesuque, the bronze foundry **Shidoni** (Bishop's Lodge Rd., 505/988-8001, 9 A.M.–5 P.M. Mon.–Sat.) has been active since 1972. The main attraction is two large gardens full of metalwork sculpture. The gardens are open from sunrise to sunset every day, but if you want to see the foundry in action, show up at noon on a weekday or anytime between 9 A.M. and 5 P.M. on Saturday. Immediately adjacent, **Tesuque Glassworks** (Bishop's Lodge Rd., 505/988-2165, 9 A.M.–5 P.M. daily) has been operating almost as long, since 1975. It functions as a co-op, with a whole range of glass artists using the furnace and materials and displaying their work in the small gallery. To get to Tesuque, head north out of Santa Fe on Washington Avenue, which becomes Bishop's Lodge Road; Shidoni will be on the left side of the street.

## CLOTHING AND JEWELRY

Get the Santa Fe look at **Maya** (108 Galisteo St., 505/989-7590, 10 A.M.–9 P.M. Mon.–Sat., 11 A.M.–9 P.M. Sun.) and **Lucille's** (223 Galisteo St., 505/983-6331, 10 A.M.–6 P.M. Mon.–Sat., 11 A.M.–4 P.M. Sun.), two stores that deal in flowing cotton skirts, bohemian tunics, and chunky jewelry. Lucille's always has good stuff on the sale rack.

At the north end of Canyon Road, **Sybele's** (830 Canyon Rd., 505/988-7045) tends toward trendier looks, with repurposed vintage clothing and a great Marilyn Monroe–style halter dress available in a range of funky fabrics; hours vary daily, but the shop is typically closed Wednesday and Thursday. Artist Richard Campiglio of **Cruz Jewelry Studio** (618 Canyon Rd., 505/986-0644, 10 A.M.–5 P.M. daily) makes heavy, distinctive jewelry in silver and semiprecious stones—Goth cross pendants as well as drop earrings that look like sea urchins. The studio also has a small gallery space and a café in the back.

Back near the plaza, don't miss **Glorianna's** (55 W. Marcy St., 505/982-0353, 10 A.M.–4:30 P.M. Mon., Tues., and Thurs.–Sat.), a

treasure trove of beads, packed to bursting with veritable eggs of raw turquoise, trays of glittering Czech glass, and ropes of African trade beads, as well as boxes full of smaller treasure, like delicate iridescent seed beads and antique sequins. (It's often closed for lunch 1–2 P.M., though.) And you can pick up a pair of boots fit for the Opry at **Back at the Ranch** (209 E. Marcy St., 505/989-8110, 10 A.M.–5:30 P.M. Mon.–Sat., noon–5 P.M. Sun.), stocked floor-to-ceiling with ostrich-skin ropers and loads of belt buckles.

## GIFTS AND HOME DECOR

If it's an odd knickknack, it's at **Doodlet's** (120 Don Gaspar St., 505/983-3771, 9:30 A.M.–5 P.M. Mon.–Sat.), a long-established corner shop filled to the brim with goodies high and low: toy accordions, oven mitts emblazoned with Day of the Dead–esque Mexican skeletons, and every sort of novelty lights you can imagine. Endless browsing potential—and kids can practice the xylophone while you shop.

Traditional New Mexican folk art is the stock in trade at **Móntez** (125 E. Palace Ave., 505/982-1828, 10 A.M.–5 P.M. Mon.–Wed., 10 A.M.–6 P.M. Thurs.–Sat., 1:30–5 P.M. Sun.), where you can find not only elaborate painted-glass-and-tin saints' portraits, but also inexpensive colorful votive holders. (In wintertime, the shop opens an hour later.)

The owner of **Seret & Sons** (224 Galisteo St., 505/988-9151, 9 A.M.–5:30 P.M. Mon.–Wed., 9 A.M.–7 P.M. Thurs.–Sat., 9:30 A.M.–5 P.M. Sun.) is a Santa Fe icon who's reputed to have invented Jimi Hendrix's signature global-boho look when he brought groovy fabrics back from his travels through Turkey, Afghanistan, and Iran. Today he concentrates on dealing finely woven rugs, antique doors, and life-size wooden elephants from his cavernous warehouse just south of the plaza. Each room of the warren is dedicated to a particular item—chances are, you haven't seen so many rugs in one place outside of Istanbul. For funky folk art that won't break the bank, head for the equally gigantic **Jackalope** (2820 Cerrillos Rd., 505/471-8539, 9 A.M.–6 P.M. Sun.–Thurs.,

9 A.M.–7 P.M. Fri. and Sat.), where seemingly acres are given over to mosaic-topped tables, wooden chickens, Mexican pottery vases, and inexpensive souvenirs. Sharing the space is a community of prairie dogs—good distraction for children while adults cruise the breakables.

Stock up on paprika and earthenware crocks at **The Spanish Table** (109 N. Guadalupe St., 505/986-0243, 10 A.M.–6 P.M. Mon.–Sat., 11 A.M.–5 P.M. Sun.), a shop specializing in ingredients and housewares from the Iberian Peninsula. Likewise, **Cookworks** (322 S. Guadalupe St., 505/988-7676, 10 A.M.–5 P.M. Mon.–Sat., 11 A.M.–4 P.M. Sun.) stocks a huge range of kitchen implements and a good array of cookbooks (with many Southwestern titles) in two side-by-side stores.

More goods for foodies: **Todos Santos** (125 E. Palace, 505/982-3855, 10 A.M.–6 P.M. Mon.–Sat., 11 A.M.–4 P.M. Sun.) adds the sweet smell of chocolate to the flower-filled air in Sena Plaza. The closet-size shop blends high and low in the world of confection: Mexican-wrestler Pez dispensers are on the shelves next to Leone pastilles imported from Italy; the glass case is stocked with decadent hand-dipped artisanal truffles, but you can also get a tin full of milk chocolate "sardines." The perfect (if short-lived) Santa Fe souvenir: *milagros,* the traditional Mexican Catholic prayer charms shaped like body parts, here rendered in Valrhona chocolate and covered in a delicate layer of gold or silver leaf. If your preference is for nuts and chews, head to longtime candy vendor **Señor Murphy's** (100 E. San Francisco St., 505/982-0461, 10 A.M.–5:30 P.M. daily) for some "caramales" (chewy balls of caramel and piñon nuts wrapped up in little corn husks) and other New Mexico–inspired sweet treats.

### Collectors' Books and Maps

**Nicholas Potter, Bookseller** (211 E. Palace Ave., 505/983-5434, 10 A.M.–6 P.M. Mon.–Sat., 11 A.M.–4 P.M. Sun.) is a rambling bungalow packed to the rafters with books—a few dog-eared paperbacks, but mostly rare hardbacks. It's eminently browsable, with an owner who knows his stuff. Western history buffs will love **Dumont Maps and Books of the West** (314 McKenzie St., 505/986-6114, 10 A.M.–5 P.M. Mon.–Sat., also noon–5 P.M. Sun. July and Aug.), where first-edition true tales of cowboy life are stacked up against New Mexico travel brochures from the 1920s. **Garcia Street Books** (376 Garcia St., 505/986-0151, 9:30 A.M.–6:30 P.M.) caters to broader interests, and many of the finds in its antiquarian editions (particularly strong on art) are just as juicy. Everyone, from Jane Fonda to local professors, stops by on book tours.

# Sports and Recreation

It's no accident *Outside* magazine has its offices here. On weekends, Santa Feans leave the town to the tourists and scatter into the surrounding mountains on foot or bike. You'll find something to do all four seasons, though serious altitude-gain hikes shouldn't be attempted till mid-May at least. If you're in town in the fall, don't miss the leaves turning on the aspens, usually in mid-October (for a great view, ride the lift at the ski basin if you're not up to for anything more strenuous). The main access point for most activities is via Highway 475—it starts out from the north side of Santa Fe as Artists Road, then the name changes to Hyde Park Road, and farther north locals call it Ski Basin Road.

The **Public Lands Information Center** (1474 Rodeo Rd., 505/438-7840, www.publiclands.org, 8 A.M.–5 P.M. Mon.–Fri.) is the best starting point for any outdoor activity, though you can also pick up some trail maps at the information booth in Sweeney Center, on West Marcy Street at Grant Avenue (8 A.M.–5 P.M. Mon.–Fri.). If you'd like to head out with a guide and perhaps a larger group, contact **Outspire!** (505/660-0394, www.outspire.com), which organizes full- and half-day outings—hiking in summer, snowshoeing in winter.

## SKIING AND SNOWSHOEING

Sixteen miles northeast out of town in the Santa Fe National Forest, **Ski Santa Fe** (Hwy. 475, 505/982-4429, www.skisantafe.com) is a well-used day area (no rental cabins) with 44 fairly challenging trails. A major selling point: Seven lifts, with 2005 plans for an eighth, mean virtually no lift lines, despite the area's popularity.

The only regularly groomed trails for cross-country skiers are the **Norski Trails,** maintained by an enthusiastic local club. About a quarter of a mile before the Ski Santa Fe parking lot, the trails start off the west side of the road. The standard route is about 2.5 miles, winding through the trees and along a ridgeline, and you can shorten or lengthen the tour by taking various loops and shortcuts, as long as you follow the directional arrows—important here because the network sees a lot of use. If you want to blaze your own trail, **Aspen Vista,** on Hwy. 475 just after mile marker 13, is a wide 10-mile-long road with a gradual climb and good views—great for either skiing or snowshoeing. It's closed to motorized vehicles, so relatively peaceful too.

Just seven miles out of town along the road to the ski area, **Hyde Memorial State Park** has a couple of nicely maintained **sledding** runs, as well as some shorter cross-country ski routes. **Cottam's Ski Shop** (Hwy. 475, 505/982-0495, www.cottamsskishops.com) is the biggest rental operation in the area—it's handily located on the way up to Aspen Vista.

## HIKING

Some hikes start very near the center of town, while others call for a half-hour drive at the most. The most popular are the trails in the Sangre de Cristo foothills: the Atalaya, Dale Ball, and Winsor trails. They'll eventually be linked, as the city has purchased the private land that used to break up the area. Mean-while, each segment is separate, but there's still plenty of room to roam on each one.

## Atalaya Mountain

One of the most accessible trails in the Santa Fe area (you can even take the "M" city bus to the trailhead on the campus of St. John's College) is also one of the more challenging. The hike heads up to a 9,121-foot peak, starting out as a gentle stroll along the city's edge, then becoming increasingly steep, for a round-trip of approximately seven miles.

## Santa Fe Canyon Preserve

For an easy saunter close to town, head for this 190-acre patch of the foothills managed by the Nature Conservancy (505/988-3867). The area is open only to people on foot—no distracting mountain bikes, and no pets allowed either. The preserve covers the canyon formed by the now-diverted Santa Fe River, which farmers once attempted to tame by building a two-mile-long rammed-earth dam (a herd of goats did the ramming). An easy interpretive loop trail leads around the area for 1.5 miles, passing the remnants of the dam and winding through dense stands of cottonwoods and willows. The trailhead is on Cerro Gordo Road just north of its intersection with Upper Canyon Road. You can also start out at the adjacent **Randall Davey Audubon Center** (1800 Upper Canyon Rd., 505/983-4609), which runs a free guided bird walk every Saturday at 8:30 A.M.

## Aspen Vista

Heading farther up the mountain, Aspen Vista is the most popular trail in the Sangre de Cristos, but don't be put off by the thought of crowds, as the promised views of golden aspen groves are indeed spectacular—in the densest spots, when the sun is shining through the leaves, the air itself feels yellow. Though at a high elevation, it's an easy hike, on a wide path with a very gradual slope across the 10 miles.

## Raven's Ridge

This is another local favorite, though not too heavily traveled, with great views of Santa Fe

## FALL IN NORTHERN NEW MEXICO

With all its evergreens and scrub trees, New Mexico doesn't seem a likely spot for a vivid display of fall colors. But the deciduous trees that flourish here – aspen, maple, cottonwood – are particularly vibrant and dramatic, wild pockets of color against the rocky landscape, often bright gold against red rocks.

You don't have to drive far to see the colors, which are usually at their peak in mid-October. In Albuquerque, head to the east face of the Sandia Mountains and up the road to the peak, stopping off at Cienega picnic area and Las Huertas picnic area, about midway up the mountain. From the parking area at the top of the mountain, you can hike north along the Crest Trail, past the radio antennas, to North

Sandia Peak, where the mountain face below is solid with aspens – the hike takes about two hours. The drive along the Jemez Mountain Trail, between Bernalillo and Los Alamos, is especially nice, with the cottonwoods contrasting with the red canyon walls as well as plenty of other deciduous trees around Valles Caldera National Preserve (the latter is easily reached from Santa Fe as well). Closer to Santa Fe, just drive up Highway 475 (the road to the ski basin), where pullouts are positioned for the best vistas of the many colorful aspen stands. Abiquiu's dramatic rock formations are also a great backdrop for cottonwoods. From Taos, the entire Enchanted Circle drive passes through various patches of color.

Baldy (elev. 12,622 feet)—while you're busy slogging up and over several peaks yourself. The trail starts at the Winsor trailhead (no. 254) in the Santa Fe ski basin parking lot, but when you reach the wilderness boundary fence, the Raven's Ridge Trail heads to the right, along the outside of the fence. The trail shows up on only one local map (Drake Mountain Maps' *Map of the Mountains of Santa Fe*), but it's easy to follow once you're up there. When in doubt, just head uphill: You'll bag Deception, Lake, and Tesuque peaks in a total of seven miles and a top elevation of 12,409 feet, returning to the ski area parking lot by walking down along the Tesuque chairlift. But this final stretch isn't particularly scenic, so you may want to take in only one or two of the peaks (Lake Peak, the second you reach, is the highest), then retrace your steps.

### Rio en Medio

You can lose the crowds just by heading a little farther from town: Rio en Medio Trail (no. 163) begins north of Tesuque and leads along a clear stream to a series of waterfalls, then up some rather strenuous switchbacks to a large meadow that's filled with wildflowers in springtime. From the trailhead to the first

cascade is 1.7 miles; the meadow is at the 3.5-mile mark, then the trail converges half a mile later with Nambe Trail (no. 160), where you'll probably want to turn around, for a hike that will take a total of four or five hours.

To reach the trailhead, drive north out of Santa Fe on Washington Avenue, which becomes Bishop's Lodge Road (Highway 590). Drive straight through the village of Tesuque, then turn right in less than a mile onto Highway 592, following signs for the village of Rio en Medio. In the village, which you reach after 6.5 miles, the road turns into County Road 78-D, a very unpromising-looking dirt track that winds through front yards for 0.8 mile before ending in a small parking area. A forest road carries on from there for a short stretch, then the trail proper heads off to the right and down along a stream.

### BIKING

Mountain bikers have fantastic outlets very close to Santa Fe, while those who prefer the open road will love the challenges in the winding highways through the mountains north of the city. **Rob & Charlie's** (1632 St. Michael's Dr., 505/471-9119, 9:30 A.M.–6 P.M. Mon.–Sat.) is a reliable shop for road bikers, and **Sun Mountain Bike Company** (102 E. Water St., 505/982-8986, 9:30 A.M.–5 P.M. Mon.–Sat., 10 A.M.–4 P.M. Sun.) is a good friendly shop downtown that rents both mountain bikes and all-around-town cruisers, and also runs shuttles and tours. The shop is closed Sundays in the winter and open later during the summer—best to call ahead.

## Mountain Biking

Named for the local conservationist and avid hiker who pushed to get them established, the **Dale Ball Trails** through the foothills are a 30-mile network of single-track routes used by both hikers and mountain bikers, providing excellent variety and scenery as they wind through stands of piñon and juniper and dip into numerous gullies. There are three sections of trail, accessible from two trailheads: From the northern trailhead, on Highway 475 at Sierra del Norte, the North Section trails vary a bit in elevation, but the Central Section (south from the parking area) is more fun because it's a longer chunk of trails. The southern trailhead, on Cerro Gordo just north of its intersection with Canyon Road, gives access to the Central Section and a newer South Section, which is very difficult, for advanced riders only. Note that the trail that starts at the southern trailhead lot, part of the Santa Fe Canyon Preserve, is for foot traffic only—ride your bike one-tenth of a mile down Cerro Gordo to the start of the Dale Ball system.

A very popular run is **Winsor Trail,** which provides a great range of scenery and terrain. It has become best known as an awesome downhill joy ride, with a local shuttle service providing drop-offs at the top. But local riders would like to strongly discourage you from this tactic—the Forest Service is considering closing the trail entirely to bikes, due to accidents between hot-dogging two-wheelers and hikers as well as damage done by sloppy skidding. Instead, it's recommended you earn the great descent by pedaling up first—there are few deadly steep ascents, so it's tiring but not impossible, and you'll rarely have to hike-a-bike.

The main trail begins near Tesuque: Take Washington Avenue north out of the center of Santa Fe, continuing as it becomes Bishop's Lodge Road (Hwy. 590). After four miles, turn right onto County Road 72-A, following signs for Big Tesuque Canyon; park on the right after a quarter mile. From here, you must go about half a mile through some private land before you reach the trailhead proper (Winsor Trail is no. 254).

It's not cheating too badly to shorten the uphill leg by starting at Chamisa Trail, 6 miles up Highway 475 (Hyde Park Road), which connects with Winsor after 2.5 miles—but you'll need to arrange a pickup at the bottom.

If you just want an easy out-and-back cruise, the **Santa Fe Rail Trail** is perfect. The wide gravel path begins at Rabbit Road (take St. Francis Drive south and under I-25) and runs along the railroad tracks through town and on to Lamy, a trip of about 11 miles that's almost completely level. If you're feeling especially leisurely, you can bike down, then take a train back with the Santa Fe Southern Railway tours (see *Tours*).

## Road Biking

Make sure you're acclimated to the altitude before you set out on any lengthy trip—the best tour, along the **high road to Taos,** will take you through some of the area's highest elevations. The full driving route is described later in the chapter. It's difficult to depart directly from Santa Fe because there's no frontage road all the way along the U.S. 84/285, but starting in Chimayó shaves some not-so-scenic miles off the ride and gives you a reasonable 45-mile jaunt all the way to Taos. The annual **Santa Fe Century** (www.santafecentury.com) ride takes place every May, running a 104-mile loop south down the Turquoise Trail and back north via the old farm towns in the Galisteo Basin, southeast of Santa Fe.

## ROCK CLIMBING

**Diablo Canyon** is the closest climbing area to Santa Fe, a set of two facing cliffs with more than 70 bolted routes and a number of traditional routes, ranging in difficulty from 5.8

to 5.13, with most rated 5.10. The longest one stretches 300 feet. Sun exposure on the cliffs is such that you should be able to find a comfortable spot to climb at any time of day, from early spring through the fall. Farther back is the Grotto, a slot canyon that's shaded most of the day—great during the hottest part of the summer. Be careful, though, as the basalt is loose in spots, particularly on the south-facing cliffs—you must wear a helmet because rock fall is very common.

The canyon is due west of Santa Fe. Drive north on St. Francis Drive, then at the highway junction, double back south on Highway 599 about four miles to the exit for Camino la Tierra. Head west on Camino la Tierra for 12.2 miles until you reach a parking area; the paving gives way to dirt around 4 miles in. Don't be tempted to drive farther than the designated parking area—flash floods from the canyon and falling rocks can do serious damage, even if your car doesn't get stuck in the sand.

If you want to polish up your skills before you tackle the crags, head to **Santa Fe Climbing Center** (825 Early St., 505/986-8944, 5–10 P.M. Mon., Wed., and Fri., 4–10 P.M. Tues. and Thurs., 1–8 P.M. Sat., 1–6 P.M. Sun.), where you can take classes (starting at $25), play around alone on the walls ($12 for a day pass), or sign up for a guided group trip to a nearby climbing site (starting at $60 for half a day).

## HORSEBACK RIDING

The gravel-paved **Santa Fe Rail Trail** to Lamy, primarily a biking trail, is open to horses as well, and there are plenty of pleasant trails to ride in the Sangre de Cristo foothills. The stables at **Bishop's Lodge** (505/819-4013, www.bishopslodge.com), north of Santa Fe, are open to nonguests, running trail rides starting at $45 per person per hour for group trips.

## GOLFING

The city's public course, **Marty Sanchez Links de Santa Fe** (205 Caja del Rio Rd., 505/955-4400, www.linksdesantafe.com), offers great views of the mountains as you tour the 18 holes designed by Baxter Spann; there's also "The Great 28," an additional par-3 9-holer that's exceptionally challenging. With five sets of tees, the course is good for both beginners and experts. True to the ethics of Santa Fe, this is a "water-aware" course that uses indigenous grasses and other plants to minimize water use, and state residents get a hefty discount off the standard greens fees ($49 Mon.–Fri., $51 Sat. and Sun.).

## RAFTING

Most big trips start or end in Pilar, to the north, but you can also float down the more placid Rio Chama. **Kokopelli Rafting** (800/879-9035, www.santafeadventure.com) runs half-day, full-day, and overnight trips, starting at $45 per person; a trip through White Rock Canyon works in a hike through Bandelier National Monument.

## FISHING

Trout teem in the Rio Chama, northwest of Santa Fe. Visit the fly shop **The Reel Life** (500 Montezuma St., 505/995-8114, 10 A.M.–6 P.M. Mon.–Sat., noon–5 P.M. Sun.), where you can also arrange a day trips to nearby waters ($300 for two).

## SPAS

**Ten Thousand Waves** (3451 Hyde Park Rd., 505/992-5025, www.tenthousandwaves.com, 9:15 A.M.–10:30 P.M. Wed.–Sun., 4–10:30 P.M. Tues.) is such a Santa Fe institution that it could just as well be listed under the city's major attractions. This traditional Japanese-style bathhouse just outside of town capitalizes on natural hot springs, with two big communal pools and seven smaller private ones tucked among the trees so as to optimize the views of the mountains all around; many have adjoining cold plunges and saunas as well. The place also offers full day-spa services, with an elaborate menu of intense massages and luxe facials and body scrubs. In the wintertime (Nov.–June), hours are shorter Monday–Wednesday.

In town, **Nirvana Spa** (106 Faithway St., 505/983-7942, www.absolutenirvana.com,

11 A.M.–6 P.M. daily) offers Balinese treatments and massages. Afterward, you can relax in the gardens with a cup of tea and some organic sweets from the adjacent tearoom.

Of all the hotel spas, **Avanyu Spa** (330 E. Palace Ave., 505/954-9630, 8 A.M.–10 P.M.), at La Posada de Santa Fe, is the nicest, with spacious treatment rooms and a really lavish array of beautifying options.

## SPORTS FACILITIES

**Genoveva Chavez Community Center** (3221 Rodeo Rd., 505/955-4001, www .chavezcenter.org, 6 A.M.–10 P.M. Mon.–Fri., 8 A.M.–8 P.M. Sat., 10 A.M.–6 P.M. Sun., $4) is the city's biggest recreational facility, with a large swimming pool with a slide and a separate lap pool (both are indoors); basketball and racquetball courts; a fully equipped gym; and a year-round ice rink. In the winter, there's also a small **ice rink** at **Hyde Memorial State Park** (505/983-7175), seven miles northeast of town on the way to the ski area.

## TOURS

Stefanie Beninato (505/988-8022, www .swguides.com) leads **walking tours** around central Santa Fe and Canyon Road, both for general history and more specialized interests, such as the Jewish-legacy tour or the garden tours; most day trips are $18 per person. If you want to head out of town, call up **Destination 505** (505/424-9500, www.destination505.com), which can organize custom day-long or multiday trips, including studio tours and excellent archaeological outings; one of the owners is a Santa Clara Pueblo member, so she has access and perspectives that a lot of other operators don't.

**HeliNM** (Tesuque, 866/995-1058, www .helinm.com) runs helicopter tours of the area—a great way to appreciate the dramatic geology. Rates start at $71 for a 15-minute flight down the Turquoise Trail; the 30-minute cruise around White Rock and Bandelier ($142) is really impressive, though.

The nifty **Santa Fe Southern Railway** (410 S. Guadalupe St., 505/989-8600, www.sfsr.com) runs vintage train cars from the old depot on South Guadalupe to Lamy. A day train runs year-round, and during the summer, the High-Desert Highball does a 2.5-hour trip starting at sunset, with free snacks and a cash bar. Trips start at $28 per person.

# Accommodations

Santa Fe offers some great places to stay— historic hotels that conjure the old trading days as well as cozy, fantastically decorated bed-and-breakfasts—but none of them are very cheap. Prices quoted here for the bigger hotels are the standard rack rates—chances are, you'll be able to find substantially lower rates just by calling or by booking online, at least at the higher-end properties. Prices spike in July and August; if you're coming for Indian Market (or Christmas), try to book at least eight months in advance.

## UNDER $50

**Budget Host** (4044 Cerrillos Rd., 505/438-8950, www.budgethost.com, $49 d) is miles from the plaza, but it's the only non-dingy motel in this price range in town. You even get access to a small swimming pool.

As hostels go, **Santa Fe International Hostel** (1412 Cerrillos Rd., 505/988-1153, santafehostel@qwest.net) is not the worst, but neither is it one of the more inspiring. Occupying two meandering old motel courts, there is plenty of room, including somewhat dim dorms ($15), private rooms with shared ($35 d) or private bath ($43 d), and a gigantic kitchen (stocked with pantry staples for guests' use). Note that old-school hostel policy still reigns here: Daily chores are required of guests.

If you're **camping,** the closest tent sites to the center are at **Hyde Memorial State**

Park (Hwy. 475, 505/983-7175, $8), about four miles northwest of the city. Or head to the commercial **Rancheros de Santa Fe** (736 Old Las Vegas Hwy., 505/466-3482, www.rancheros.com, Mar.–Nov., $20), which is east of town about seven miles (a 20-minute drive from the plaza) and pleasantly rural. Tent sites are private and shady and well away from the RVs, and there's a pool to swim in. Be sure to reserve ahead in the summertime.

## $50-100

In many ways, budget travelers are better off at **Ghost Ranch in Santa Fe** (401 Old Taos Hwy., 505/982-8539, www.ghostranch.org), an extension of the Presbyterian retreat center in Abiquiu. If the place isn't fully booked with a group, you're welcome to stay in one of the small but perfectly comfortable rooms—a couple have full baths ($90 s, $100 d), but most have only toilets and share tubs and showers down the hall ($75 s, $85 d). A full breakfast is included. Physically, the place has all the charm of a 1970s public elementary school, but the staff is exceptionally nice and welcoming (no religious strings attached), and you're only a few blocks from the plaza.

Leaving aside practicalities like location, **El Rey Inn** (1862 Cerrillos Rd., 505/982-1931, www.elreyinnsantafe.com, $89 d), about two miles from the plaza, counts as one of the best hotels in Santa Fe based on charm alone. Built in 1935, it has been meticulously kept up and adjusted for modern standards of comfort, with beautiful gardens, a hot tub, a big swimming pool, and a fireside open-air Jacuzzi. The 86 rooms, spread over 4.5 acres, vary considerably in style (and in price), from the oldest section with snug adobe walls and heavy viga ceilings to airier rooms with balconies, so ask to see a few before you choose. Rooms at the back of the property are preferable, due to noise from busy Cerrillos Road.

In a similar vein, **Stage Coach Motor Inn** (3360 Cerrillos Rd., 505/471-0707, $79 d) dates from the 1940s, and its 14 rooms around a gravel drive are furnished with lots of pine paneling and vintage oddities like petrified-

wood coffee tables. It's a bit cheaper and more intimate-feeling than El Rey.

A fabulous deal for anyone willing to consider an unhosted place, **The Chapelle Street Casitas** (209 Chapelle St., 505/988-2883, www.casitas.net) offers by-the-night rentals just blocks from the plaza. Every house is a little different, ranging from cozy studios ($84) to big spreads with two bedrooms ($218) and private patios; catch the charming (and very well-priced) "Elvira's Casita" before its sloped wood floors and old-fashioned kitchen get renovated away. Considering that Santa Fe hotels can't change sheets more often than every three days due to water restrictions, you're not missing too much by going it alone at a rental property—and you gain the feeling of being a Santa Fe native, waving at passersby from your front porch and mixing up margaritas in your fully furnished kitchen.

## $100-150

**Santa Fe Motel & Inn** (510 Cerrillos Rd., 505/982-1039, www.santafemotel.com, $119 d) is your best budget bet close to the center, with rooms done up in simple, bright decor that avoids motel sameness despite the generic motor-court layout. A few kitchenettes are available, along with some more private casitas with fireplaces. Lots of nice touches—such as bread from the Sage Bakehouse across the street along with the full breakfast—give the place a homey feel without the tight quarters of a typical bed-and-breakfast.

Just west of Guadalupe Street, a couple of blocks out of the central plaza area, **La Tienda Inn and Duran House** (511 W. San Francisco St., 505/989-8259, $115 d) is on a quiet, narrow residential street. The bed-and-breakfast is two neighboring properties: La Tienda (The Store—the lobby is in what was the neighborhood grocery 60 years back) has seven rooms, most with air-conditioning as well as fireplaces, with typical touches of Southwestern decor, such as stepped-diamond headboards and Navajo rugs. Duran House's four rooms are done in a different (and preferable) style, with Spanish and American antiques set against whitewashed wood; the upstairs Aurora room has a great view of the mountains, and two of the downstairs rooms have fireplaces.

With 12 rooms in an old adobe, plus an adjacent Victorian with two suites, **El Paradero B&B** (220 W. Manhattan St., 505/988-1177, www.elparadero.com, $120 d) has a variety of room configurations that can suit families, solo travelers, and friends traveling together. Upstairs rooms have balconies, and a few others have fireplaces. Two rooms with private baths across the hall dip below the $100 level.

East of the plaza, a trio of excellent bed-and-breakfasts, all run by the same woman, offer any ambience you could want: The rooms at **Hacienda Nicholas** (320 E. Marcy St., 505/992-8385, www.haciendanicholas.com, $145 d) have a tasteful Southwest flavor, decorated with a few cowboy trappings and Gustave Baumann prints; two of the rooms have fireplaces. Across the street, **Madeleine Inn** (106 Faithway St., 505/982-3465, www.madeleineinn.com, $145 d) is set in a towering wood Victorian, the former home of a railroad tycoon, but the guest rooms aren't lacy—they're done in rich Balinese fabrics and antiques. There's also a good day spa and organic tea room on the premises. If you're planning a longer stay, or just want somewhere with a kitchen, look into **Alexander's Inn** (529 E. Palace Ave., 505/986-1431, www.alexanders-inn.com, $200 d), a bit further east. One cottage apartment has a full kitchen and a beautiful loft sleeping area; there's another casita adjacent with the same amenities, as well as two more full apartments a few blocks away. Wherever you stay, you get plush perks like robes and slippers; breakfast is a continental spread, but that doesn't mean you'll go away hungry—the banana bread is fantastic.

Only 20 minutes from Santa Fe, ◖ **Rancho Jacona** (277 County Rd. 84, 505/455-7948, www.ranchojacona.com, $135 d) feels entirely rural. The working farm is dotted with 11 separate casitas, each with a kitchen, laundry, fireplace, and private patio. With trundle beds, sleeper sofas, and the like, each place sleeps at least three people, and some sleep up to eight—ideal for families. Kids will also love the lush

grounds crawling with animals: a huge rabbit warren, rare breeds of chickens (you'll likely get some of their fresh eggs to use for breakfast), even peacocks. There's a three-day minimum, but chances are, you'll want to stay longer.

## $150-250

Well worth the half-hour drive from Santa Fe, ◖ **The Galisteo Inn** (9 La Vega Rd., Galisteo, 866/404-8200, www.galisteoinn.com, $165 d) is a stylish hideaway in a quiet village where the stars crowd the sky and the crickets buzz at night. The hip guest rooms are done up in vibrant turquoise and orange with a few well-chosen paintings and Western-theme antiques—the sort of style that would cost you double anywhere inside the city limits. Another bonus: Three small rooms are available for solo travelers (or very loving couples) for $105 or less. Admittedly, there's not much to do in Galisteo after you've had your continental breakfast—just lounge around the pool or take a horseback ride from the inn's stables. But if you're looking for a few days of beautiful solitude, this is the place to enjoy them.

Another restful spot is **Houses of the Moon** (3451 Hyde Park Rd., 505/992-5025, www.tenthousandwaves.com, $190 d), the guest cottages at Ten Thousand Waves spa—some have more of a local feel, with viga ceilings and kiva fireplaces, while others are straight from Japan (both samurai era and contemporary anime). The Zen-spare aesthetic doesn't apply to amenities—rooms all have coffeemakers, microwaves, CD players, and private patios with hibachis. Rates include access to the communal hot tubs.

The gracious **Hotel St. Francis** (210 Don Gaspar Ave., 505/983-5700, www.hotelstfrancis.com, $179 d), a California mission–style building that dates from 1923, has a pleasingly authentic historic feel. The 82 rooms vary considerably, from a cozy, lace-filled nook good for solo travelers to bigger suites with big windows, dark-wood furniture, and quilts on the brass beds. The capacious art deco–inflected lobby bar and front veranda are excellent places to rest after a day of sightseeing.

Majority-owned by Picurís Pueblo, ((( **Hotel Santa Fe** (1501 Paseo de Peralta, 800/825-9876, www.hotelsantafe.com, $219 d) is both a successful business experiment and a very nice hotel, with one of the few large outdoor pools in town, set against the neo-pueblo hotel walls. The standard rooms are a bit small—it's worth upgrading to the junior suite if possible. If you book online, rates for the ultra-luxe Hacienda wing, where the huge rooms all have fireplaces and butler service, and where niches in the hallways are filled with Native American treasures, are a steal compared to other high-end places in town.

A very nice bed-and-breakfast in this category is **El Farolito** (514 Galisteo St., 505/988-1631, www.farolito.com, $180 d), where the eight rooms have private entrances, small patios, and fireplaces. Decor ranges from Southwestern to international folk art (in Casita Peralta, which has two double beds), and the breakfast is very good.

Also try **Water Street Inn** (427 W. Water St., 505/984-1193, $175 d), which will serve your morning meal in your room, if you don't feel up to the full chummy bed-and-breakfast experience—though the sunny kitchen and deck do make a nice venue for savoring the rich pastries and fresh fruit. Rooms are a restrained mix of country-comfy and Southwest detail, and many have fireplaces, balconies, or private patios.

For more frills and a prime location, head to the **Grant Corner Inn** (122 Grant Ave., 505/983-6678, www.grantcornerinn.com, $165 d), a pretty wood Victorian that somehow survived the adobification of downtown. The kitchen serves a varied, full breakfast with excellent baked goods and entrées that go beyond the familiar frittatas, and guest rooms are elegant and well appointed.

A 20-minute drive southwest from Santa Fe, **Sunrise Springs** (242 Los Pinos Rd., 505/471-6500, www.sunrisesprings.com, $105 s, $175 d) is a lovely spa resort, with an emphasis on alternative healing and spiritual wellness—sweat lodges, reiki, and yoga are all on offer. The guest quarters have a relaxing spareness to them; the spa rooms, each with one double bed, are perfect for people seeking a solo retreat.

## OVER $250

From the outside, ((( **The Inn of the Five Graces** (150 E. De Vargas St., 505/992-0957, www.fivegraces.com, $360 per suite) looks like a typical historic Southwestern lodge, a collection of interconnected adobe casitas. But inside, there's a certain air of opium dream—the sumptuous suites are done entirely in stock from Mideast exotica purveyor Seret & Sons, from the antique Turkish kilims on the walls to the pottery that was broken to make the elaborate mosaic details around the deep tubs. The result is certainly not typical "Santa Fe style," but it perfectly captures the Santa Fe aesthetic: decadent international bohemian. A member of the exclusive Garrett Hotel Group, Five Graces offers all the sorts of luxuries that make these properties so nice to visit: a minibar stocked with complimentary freshly made margaritas, daily walking tours and wine, and a no-tipping policy.

((( **La Posada de Santa Fe** (330 E. Palace Ave., 888/367-7625, www.rockresorts.com, $289 d) is the only hotel in the center of town with grounds, giving it a resort feel within walking distance of the plaza. The informal rooms are individually furnished with fine New Mexican antiques; some of the nicest are no. 197 (two queen beds, a sitting room, and a fireplace) and no. 215 (which has a private patio and lofty ceilings). Deluxe suites above the palatial Avanyu Spa have a more contemporary style, while a few rooms in the old Staab House are redone in perfect Victoriana, and "gallery suites" showcase the best local artwork. But there's room on the lower end too: Two cozy "artist studio" rooms (usually about $209) are great for singles.

While other hotels have put a hip gloss on their history, **La Fonda** (100 E. San Francisco St., 505/982-5511, www.lafondasantafe.com, $259 d), just off the plaza, remains pleasantly unchanged and still family-owned, its lobby of waxed saltillo tile floors and heavy Span-

La Fonda, "The Inn at the End of the Trail"

ish-style wood decorated as it has been for decades, its bar populated by a mix of cowboys, layabouts, and lunchtime schmoozers. Despite the high price tag, this is not really a luxury hotel—you're paying for the feel of Santa Fe before it was a trendy spa-and-shopping destination. The cozy rooms are done up with the occasional New Mexican antique, and some have their original kiva fireplaces and *latilla* ceilings; open-plan deluxe rooms are actually a bit more comfortable than the subdivided suites. If you do want some modern trappings, spring for the Terraza-level penthouse suites done in chic earth tones.

Outside of Santa Fe to the north, **Bishop's Lodge** (1297 Bishop's Lodge Rd., 505/983-6377, www.bishopslodge.com, $279 d) occupies 450 acres centered on the former country estate of Bishop Lamy (his personal chapel is now used regularly for weddings). Just a 10-minute drive from the plaza, the resort is still far enough into the foothills that you can go horseback riding or hiking in solitude; the vast grounds give kids lots of room to run around. Fifteen separate lodges offer a variety of styles: South Lodge rooms are the oldest, with creaky porches and thick adobe walls, while Chamisa Lodge is all new, with huge bathrooms and gas fireplaces. The Ridge Lodge capitalizes on the view across the valley.

# Food

Dining is one of Santa Fe's great pleasures—considering the tiny population, it's remarkable what a range of flavors and what high quality you can choose from. While you can always get a cheese-smothered, crazy-hot plate of green-chile chicken enchiladas, most restaurants skew toward a more cosmopolitan "Santa Fean" cuisine that cheerfully incorporates Asian, Southwestern, and Mediterranean flavors, with an emphasis on organic and holistic. Prices included reflect the average entrée price.

## SANTA FE PLAZA

Food is a bit ho-hum on the plaza itself (except for the fajita cart, when it's set up), but the blocks surrounding it, within the ring formed by Alameda Street and Paseo de Peralta, contain some classic Santa Fe spots that everyone makes a trek to at some point, along with a few hidden treats.

### Coffee and More

Although Starbucks is near the plaza, disguised by an adobe facade, you might want to get your latte at a local joint: **Tribes** (139 W. San Francisco St., 505/982-7948, 8 A.M.–6:30 P.M. daily, $4) is a good bet, serving excellent café mochas as well as truly monster-scale sandwiches—a half portion is ample.

Hidden back on the top floor of a shopping complex just west of the plaza, **Steepings** (112 W. San Francisco St., 505/986-0403,

8 A.M.–11 P.M. Mon.–Sat., 8 A.M.–7 P.M. Sun., $3) offers more than 40 varieties of tea leaves and herbal tisanes, as well as a mellow oasis in the midst of the downtown frenzy. If you're not relaxed after a simple chamomile infusion, then maybe a hemp kava latte will do the trick.

If you like dark-roast coffee, head straight for **Ohori's Coffee, Tea & Chocolate** (507 Old Santa Fe Tr., 505/988-7026, 8 A.M.–6 P.M. daily, $3), Santa Fe's small-batch coffee epicures. You can drink a cup of the black-as-night brew there and buy a pound or two to take home.

## Breakfast and Lunch

Pretty bed-and-breakfast **Grant Corner Inn** (122 Grant Ave., 505/983-6678, 8:30–10 A.M. Mon.–Fri., $12) serves breakfast, brunch, and afternoon tea to the public as well as to its guests. Come here when you're burnt out on chile and adobe—the big white Victorian looks like it should be in Savannah, Georgia, rather than Santa Fe, and the menu includes challah French toast with candied pecans, hearty home fries, and lox and bagels; you can also reserve for afternoon tea on the wraparound porch, served Friday and Saturday at 5 P.M., and reasonably priced at $12 per person.

The **French Pastry Shop** (100 E. San Francisco St., 505/983-6697, 6 A.M.–5 P.M. daily, $7) and the **Café Paris** (31 Burro Alley, 505/986-9162, 8 A.M.–9:30 P.M. daily, $7) give you two chances at sweet crepes, buttery pastries, *croque monsieurs,* and chewy baguette sandwiches. The latter place is also open for dinner, serving bistro favorites like *salade niçoise* and duck confit. Early mornings at the French Pastry Shop attract a fascinating crew of Santa Fe regulars.

Set off a patio inside a shopping plaza, **C** **Carlos' Gosp'l Café** (125 Lincoln Ave., 505/983-1841, 8 A.M.–3 P.M. Mon.–Fri., 11 A.M.–3 P.M. Sat., $6) is packed at lunch, as locals make a run on the fat deli sandwiches, like the Miles Standish (turkey with cranberry, cream cheese, and mayo), or hearty Hangover

Santa Fe's plaza is a main hub of the city.

© ZORA O'NEILL

Stew, a veggie green-chile chowder. Breakfast is mellow—you can hear the proffered gospel soundtrack and read the paper in peace.

**Tia Sophia's** (210 W. San Francisco St., 505/983-9880, 7 A.M.–2 P.M. Mon.–Sat., $6) is one of the last greasy-spoon places in the plaza area, serving old-time New Mexican plates without a touch of fusion—so authentic, in fact, the kitchen claims to have invented the breakfast burrito.

The glowing stone-walled dining room of **Anasazi** (113 Washington Ave., 505/988-3236, 7–10:30 A.M., 11:30 A.M.–2:30 P.M., and 5:30–10 P.M. daily, $8), at the Inn of the Anasazi, is very good for a luxe breakfast, with choices like blackberry flapjacks or huevos rancheros with chorizo and black beans. (Skip dinner—it's a little overwrought.)

## New Mexican

**The Shed** (113½ E. Palace Ave., 505/982-9030, 11 A.M.–2:30 P.M. and 5:30–11 P.M. Mon.–Sat., $11) has been serving up platters of enchiladas since 1953—bizarrely, with a side of garlic bread. But that's just part of the tradition at this colorful, comfortable, marginally fancy place that's as popular with tourists as it is with die-hard residents. There are perfectly decent distractions like lemon-garlic shrimp and fish tacos on the menu, but it's the red chile you really should focus on.

Standard New Mexican dishes get the modern-diner treatment at the **Blue Corn Café** (133 W. Water St., 505/984-1800, 11 A.M.–10 P.M. daily, $10): fresh ingredients and clean flavors, all in a family-friendly, casual, slightly chain-restaurant setting. The chiles rellenos benefit especially well from the modernizing, and of course the tacos and enchiladas get at least a visual boost from the blue corn tortillas. Burgers and ribs are also on the menu.

In 2005, the old politico power center **The Palace** (142 W. Palace Ave., 505/982-9891, 11:30 A.M.–3 P.M. and 5:30–9 P.M. Mon.–Sat., $18) was remade as a family-friendly but still slightly hip restaurant. (The building was formerly a house of ill repute presided over by the self-made madam and expert monte dealer Doña Tules—the only remaining evidence is the painting of a scantily clad Indian maid.) On the menu are fish tacos as well as spaghetti with meatballs. Old-timers will miss the gritty saloon feel of the dark-wood bar, which is now a bit more cleaned up, but there's also a pleasant patio.

## Mexican

At **(( Bumble Bee's Baja Grill** (301 Jefferson St., 505/820-2862, 7:30 A.M.–9 P.M. Mon.–Fri., 11 A.M.–9 P.M. Sat. and Sun., $5) fat bumblebee piñatas dangling from the ceiling set a cheerful tone. The specialty at this upscale taco joint is Baja shrimp tacos—but made healthy by grilling rather than frying. They're garnished with shredded cabbage and a creamy sauce, plus a spritz of lime and your choice of house-made salsas. Lamb tacos are also delicious, as are that Tijuana classic, Caesar salad, and the fried-fresh tortilla chips. In the morning, equally fresh and tasty breakfast burritos are served.

## Santa Fe Eclectic

Open since the mid-1970s, **(( Café Pasqual's** (121 Don Gaspar St., 505/983-9340, 7 A.M.–3 P.M. and 5:30–9:30 P.M. Mon.–Sat., 8 A.M.–2 P.M. and 5:30–9:30 P.M. Sun., $26) has defined its own culinary category. Its breakfasts are legendary, but the food is delicious any time of day—just brace yourself for the inevitable line, as the brightly painted dining room seats only 50 people, and loyal fans number in the thousands. Expect nearly anything on the menu: smoked-trout hash or Yucatán-style *huevos motuleños* are what's for breakfast; at dinner, sure, the mole enchiladas are good, but don't miss the Vietnamese squid salad.

In a cozy tin-roof house on Guadalupe, **Tulips** (222 N. Guadalupe St., 505/989-7340, 6–10 P.M. Tues.–Sat., $28) is a tranquil setting for fresh, inventive food based on local and seasonal ingredients. The weekly menu, which always includes a couple of vegetarian options, melds Southwestern, Mediterranean, and Asian preparations into unlikely sounding but delicious dishes such as the signature green-chile lobster spring rolls or coffee-rubbed quail.

## Italian

Of all of the opportunities in Santa Fe to blow your rent money on a decadent dinner, **(( Trattoria Nostrani** (304 Johnson St., 505/983-3800, 5:30–10 P.M. Mon.–Sat., $29) is one of the most worthy—even though it incorporates absolutely none of its Southwestern surroundings. The cuisine in this four-room house with glossy wood floors and white tablecloths is pure northern Italian, executed flawlessly: delicate fritto misto to start, rich ravioli filled with salt cod and potato and topped with lump crab, or simple, insanely creamy *burrata,* a super-fresh mozzarella flown straight from the motherland. An ethereal *panna cotta* or biscotti served with sweet *vin santo* makes the perfect finishing touch.

Locals head to amber-lit **Il Piatto** (95 W. Marcy St., 505/984-1091, 11:30 A.M.–2 P.M. and 5:30–9:30 P.M. Sun.–Thurs., 11:30–2 P.M. and 5:30–10 P.M. Fri. and Sat., $16) for casual, unfussy Italian and a neighborly welcome from the staff, who seem to be on a first-name basis with everyone in the place. Hearty pastas like *pappardelle* with duck are served in generous portions—a half order will more than satisfy lighter eaters. This is a great place to take a breather from enchiladas and burritos without breaking the bank.

With the options of whole-wheat crust and green chile as a topping, the pies at **Upper Crust Pizza** (329 Old Santa Fe Tr., 505/982-0000, 11 A.M.–10 P.M. Mon.–Thurs., 11 A.M.–11 P.M. Fri.–Sat.), next to Mission San Miguel, are actually more Santa Fean than Italian. Hot deli sandwiches and big, super-fresh salads round out the menu. Delivery is free, but then you'd be missing the live music on the little front deck.

## Fine Dining

Just because it's right next door to the Georgia O'Keeffe Museum doesn't mean the **C O'Keeffe Café** (217 Johnson St., 505/946-1065, www.okeeffecafe.com, 11 A.M.–3 P.M. and 5:30–10 P.M. daily, $21) is your standard museum-cafeteria-style canteen. In fact, it's a refined sit-down place done up in black and white—a serene setting that allows the vibrant combinations of local produce to shine, in new-American dishes like seared duck breast with a beet-and-butternut-squash puree. Alongside, pick from the judicious wine list (with a section of bottles "No Higher Than Twenty-Six")—or let the staff do the work for you and opt for the four-course wine-paired set menu. Or you can just pop in at lunch for a lamb-terrine sandwich and a single glass of wine. Either way, the place is a great value, easily as satisfying as places that charge $10 more for entrées.

**Coyote Café** (132 W. Water St., 505/983-1615, 6–9 P.M. Sun., Mon., and Thurs., 5:30–10 P.M. Fri. and Sat., $26) started the contemporary Southwestern trend, bringing chipotle chiles to the masses in 1987. The restaurant got a big renovation in 2005, along with renewed attention from its star chef, Mark Miller. In the elegant earth-tone dining room, you're served dishes that blend Mexican, Spanish, and Southwestern ingredients: pork loin brined in Mexican cinnamon with a mission-fig mole sauce, for instance, or squash empanadas with a sherry glaze. Or just head to the Rooftop Cantina for a Smokin' Margarita, topped with a splash of smoky-flavored mescal (Apr.–Oct. only).

At elegant **La Casa Sena** (125 E. Palace Ave., 505/988-9232, 11:30 A.M.–3 P.M. and 5:30–10 P.M. Mon.–Sat., 5:30–10 P.M. Sun., $29), the emphasis is on hearty meats: chorizo-stuffed pork tenderloin, for instance, or the "jackalope" mixed grill, a combo of fire-cooked rabbit and antelope loins. Even the fish dishes need to be attacked with gusto: The trout baked in adobe gets cracked open at the table, releasing a perfectly moist and tender fish. In summer, Sunday brunch is also served (10 A.M.–3 P.M.), with dishes like lobster ceviche and eggs Benedict with jalapeño hollandaise. The patio is a dreamy place to dine in the warm months, but do go inside to admire the fantastic art collection (bigwig gallery proprietor Gerald Peters owns the building).

Set in an 1857 adobe, **Santacafé** (231 Washington Ave., 505/984-1788, 11:30 A.M.–2 P.M. and 6–10 P.M. Mon.–Sat., 6–10 P.M. Sun., $24) is an institution—which doesn't necessarily mean the food is great. But the scene, especially when the legislature is in session, is lively, with politicos seated next to ladies serious about their lunches. Stick to standards and items with a distinct Southwestern flair—the more inventive international dishes often miss the mark. Sunday brunch, served only in summer, is a safe bet, too.

## Groceries

**Kaune Foodtown** (511 Old Santa Fe Tr., 505/982-2629, 8:30 A.M.–7 P.M. Mon.–Sat.) is the closest proper grocery store to the plaza, for those who are self-catering. It's small but very well stocked with gourmet treats and quality meats and produce, as well as some prepared take-out food. (Sound like a native: The name's pronounced CON-ee, as it has been since it opened in 1896.)

# GUADALUPE AND THE RAILYARD DISTRICT

An easy walk from the plaza, these few square blocks hold some of the better, quirkier dining options in town.

## Cafés

In a funky wood house off Guadalupe Street, **Aztec Café** (317 Aztec St., 505/820-0025, $5) pours java for Santa Fe's tattooed and guitar-strumming youth. An impromptu acoustic serenade on the side porch shouldn't distract from the food, which is inexpensive and veggie-friendly—bagels heaped with tomatoes and sprouts, for instance. Even coffee addicts should consider the Mexican hot chocolate.

Tiny **Saveur** (204 Montezuma St., 505/989-4200, 7:45 A.M.–4:45 P.M. Mon.–Fri., $7) is a cafeteria line where you're just as likely to find duck confit with a port demiglace as a big slab of meatloaf—a good place to stock up for a picnic (though it's closed on the weekends).

Make room in your morning for an almond croissant from ◖ **Sage Bakehouse** (535 Cerrillos Rd., 505/820-7243, 7 A.M.–5 P.M. Mon.–Sat., $4). Washed down with a mug of coffee, these butter-soaked pastries will have you set for hours. Before you leave, pick up some sandwiches for later—classic combos like smoked turkey and cheddar on the bakery's excellent crust. And maybe a pecan-raisin wreath. And a cookie too.

## American

All things Texan are the specialty at **The Cowgirl** (319 S. Guadalupe St., 505/988-4227, 8 A.M.–8 P.M. daily, $13), a kitsch-filled spot that's as friendly to kids as it is to margarita-guzzling, rib-gnawing adults. Mesquite-smoked brisket is popular, as is the chicken-fried steak. Non-meat-eaters won't feel left out: An ooey-gooey butternut squash casserole comes with a salad on the side. Both carnivores and veggies should save room for pineapple upside-down cake and the ice-cream "baked potato."

## Japanese

Hip and delicious **Kasasoba** (544 Agua Fria St., 505/984-1969, 11:30 A.M.–2 P.M. and 5:30–9 P.M. Mon.–Fri., 5:30 A.M.–9:30 P.M. Sat. and Sun., $14), where the walls are hung with anime panels and monster-movie posters, whisks its fish in straight from the Tsukiji market in Tokyo, so a piece of black bass is sitting in front of you, steamed in sake with enoki mushrooms, barely 24 hours after it's caught. Sushi is of course available, as is a delicious selection of noodles.

## Fine Dining

Where Santa Fe foodies eat on a casual night, ◖ **Aqua Santa** (451 W. Alameda St., 505/982-6297, noon–2 P.M. and 5:30–9 P.M. Wed.–Fri., 5:30–9 P.M. Tues. and Sat., $18) feels like dining at a friend's house—the open kitchen occupies more than a third of the small building, leaving space for just a handful of tables in the whitewashed room with a fireplace. Dinner, served on old-fashioned flower-print plates, capitalizes on punchy combinations, such as a salad of fennel, parsley, and olives with a blood-orange dressing, and entrées are limited to five or so very strong choices, like linguine with clams and lamb sausage. Wash it down with a glass of Lillet, and you're set for the night.

Elegant but not flashy, regulars' favorite **Ristra** (548 Agua Fria St., 505/982-8608, 5:30–9:30 P.M. daily, $23) applies a French treatment to Southwestern cuisine: Squash blossoms are fried up like ethereal beignets, foie gras gets a deconstructed *al pastor* treatment, drizzled with a surprisingly delicate pineapple-red chile sauce. It's in a white-walled bungalow with tables in the front yard in warm weather; service is gracious.

# CANYON ROAD

Gallery-hopping can make you hungry—but there are only a handful of places to eat on Canyon Road, and not many of them are all that satisfying. For a caffeine hit, stop into the café at **Cruz Jewelry Studio** (618 Canyon Rd., 505/986-0644, 10 A.M.–5 P.M. daily), or jog off the strip to **Downtown Subscription** (376 Garcia St., 505/983-3085, 7:30 A.M.–7 P.M.), an airy coffee shop that stocks perhaps a million magazines and attracts potential readers for even the most obscure titles. Wednesday nights occasionally see poetry readings after normal hours.

At the north end of Canyon Road, stalwart **( El Farol** (808 Canyon Rd., 505/983-9912, 11:30 A.M.–3 P.M. and 5 P.M.–2 A.M. daily, $8) is a very popular bar, but its selection of Spanish tapas is also worth noting—grilled octopus with olive pesto, for instance—and you can also take in a bigger meal in a small side room that's quieter than the main bar; the *zarzuela* (fish soup) is recommended. Just next door, **Sol Café** (802 Canyon Rd., 505/989-1949, 8 A.M.– 8 P.M. daily, $9) dresses up the burger-and-fries experience, with tablecloths, frosty beers, and good service. It also has a nice patio for people-watching. Of the two splurgy restaurants on Canyon Road, **The Compound** (653 Canyon Rd., 505/983-4353, noon–2:30 P.M. and 5– 9 P.M. Mon.–Fri., 5–9 P.M. Sat. and Sun., $29) is the better. Signature dishes like sweetbreads and foie gras emphasize decadence, while the lamb loin with favas, morels, and peas is a showcase for local agricultural products. **Geronimo** (724 Canyon Rd., 505/982-1500, 11:30 A.M.–2 P.M. and 6–10 P.M. Tues.–Sun., 6–10 P.M. Mon., $30), which also gets a lot of press, is a bit more of a show, what with an ostentatious clientele and somewhat gaudy food (though the peppered elk tenderloin is simple and delicious); the snug bar with a fireplace is a good place to rest your feet after a Canyon Road cruise—it's open between lunch and dinner, though very quiet.

## CERRILLOS ROAD

Cerrillos isn't Santa Fe's most scenic zone, but you'll find some great culinary gems out this way.

### Cafés

**Ramblin' Café** (1420 2nd St., 505/989-1272, 7 A.M.–4 P.M. Mon.–Fri., 7 A.M.–2 P.M. Sat., $6) is very light on charm—it's in a near-abandoned strip mall, and the interior is largely kitchen space—but its food more than makes up for it. Try the spinach-and-green-chile quesadilla, or a big BLT, also laced with green chile;

in the morning, a smothered breakfast burrito gets you moving.

The decor—all light pine, metal, and chalkboard menus—at **Counter Culture** (930 Baca St., 505/995-1105, 8 A.M.–3 P.M. Mon.–Sat., 8 A.M.–2 P.M. Sun., $7) is spartan, but the colorful crowd of, well, countercultural types fills the void. The eclectic menu runs from fat burgers to cold sesame noodles; in general, Asian flavors are good, as are the soups. Breakfast, served till 11 A.M., is great—then you can indulge in the gigantic muffins and coffee cakes as a main meal, rather than dessert; on Sunday, breakfast is served all day.

## New Mexican

The white-stucco dining room is too bright, and the beer-sign-filled lounge is too dim, but that's part of the charm at **Tiny's** (1015 Pen Rd., 505/983-1100, 11:30 A.M.–2 P.M. and 6– 10 P.M. Mon.–Fri., 11:30 A.M.–1 P.M. Sun., $8), a haven of undiluted New Mexico style, right down to its name. All the old favorites are on the menu—the only concession to "modern" trends is that you might get butter with your sopaipillas.

Chile still not hot enough for you? Head to **Horseman's Haven** (4354 Cerrillos Rd., 8 A.M.–8 P.M. Mon.–Sat., 8:30 A.M.–2 P.M. Sun., 505/471-5420, $6), which claims to serve the hottest green chile in Santa Fe. The atmosphere is pure greasy spoon (the place is off to the side of a gas station parking lot, after all), even featuring a portrait of John Wayne, but the loyal clientele of cops and construction workers doesn't seem to mind.

**PC's** (4220 Airport Rd., 505/473-7164, 11 A.M.–2:30 P.M. and 5:30–9 P.M. Tues.– Fri., 9 A.M.–2:30 P.M. and 5:30–9 P.M. Sat., 9 A.M.–2:30 P.M. Sun., $7) is old-school New Mexican, served in a cavernous room filled with Spanish-speaking families, all chowing down on big burritos and stuffed sopaipillas. Diner-style breakfast, with chile ladled on top, is served Saturday and Sunday. At the very end of Cerrillos Road, it's a hike, but worth a cruise just for a reality check on central Santa Fe.

## Mexican

You can tell **[C] Mariscos La Playa** (537 Cordova Rd., 505/982-2790, 11 A.M.–9 P.M. Wed.–Mon., $10) is authentic Mexican because it serves up ceviche and shrimp *cocktel* the standard beachfront way, with little packets of saltine crackers. If you can't decide what sort of seafood you'd like, opt for the "come back to life" soup *(caldo vuelve a la vida)*, studded with shrimp, fish, calamari, clams, and more. Go at off-peak times, or be prepared for a line—even with a second location (2875 Cerrillos Rd., 505/473-4594), La Playa can't manage the adoring crowds.

**Guadalajara Grill** (3877 Cerrillos Rd., 505/424-3544, 10:30 A.M.–9 P.M. Mon.–Fri., 10:30 A.M.–10 P.M. Sat., 10 A.M.–9 P.M. Sun., $12) is another popular spot for south-of-the-border seafood dishes—the grilled shrimp, bathed in butter and garlic and served with guacamole, are particularly good. Alas, a beer-and-wine license means no margaritas and the ambience is nonexistent.

For a more *norteño* experience, stop off at **La Diligencia,** a little wood cart trimmed in red-painted horseshoes, in the parking lot of cowboy-supply store Casa Macias (301 Airport Rd.). A loyal, all-Mexican clientele orders big burritos, soft tacos, and imported pure-cane-sugar Coca-Cola—all so tasty, you might be inspired to pop into the shop and buy a pair of ostrich-skin boots and a lasso when you're done. The cart is usually open for lunch only.

Another parking-lot treat: the **churro cart** in the parking lot of **Pepe's Tacos** (1925 Cerrillos Rd.). Hours are highly erratic, though weekend nights seem to be a good bet to pick up cinnamon-dusted fritters straight from the deep fryer. Ask for a double helping of sticky-sweet *cajeta* (goat's-milk caramel) on top—it's to churros what ketchup is to fries.

Even more fleeting is **Lucky Barbeque/ Barbacoa con Suerte,** which sets up its smoker on Baca Street across from Counter Culture. If it's there, it's serving an array of tender meats, dished up on paper plates.

## Asian

A little oasis of Asian-inflected organic food in a chain-restaurant part of town, **Mu Du Noodles** (1494 Cerrillos Rd., 505/983-1411, 5:30–9:30 P.M. Tues.–Sat., $18) cuts the strip-mall glare with warm-hued walls and bamboo screens. The menu ranges from Central Asia to Japan, offering lamb pot stickers, coconut-spicy Malaysian *laksa,* and Indian yellow curry along the way. Reviving citrus-ade with ginger is delicious hot or cold, or you can order beer or wine.

## SANTA FE METRO AREA

Head farther afield for hefty burgers or enlightened spa food in a lush setting.

## Café

A big airy barn west of the Guadalupe district, **Cloud Cliff Bakery** (1805 2nd St., 505/983-6254, 7:30 A.M.–5 P.M. Mon.–Fri., 8 A.M.–3:30 P.M. Sat. and Sun., $9) is a gathering place for Santa Fe's dreadlocked activists as much as it is a café—though certainly the hearty granola pancakes and the spinach-and-tofu stir-fry are not bad ways to start the day. For lunch, expect garden burgers and bigger plates like lamb with quinoa. In the evening, the bakery is often a venue for readings, debates, and the like.

## New Mexican

Reputedly named for the former owner's cop-dodging practices, or else a Cheech and Chong routine that seemed funny back in the day, **[C] Dave's Not Here** (1115 Hickox St., 505/983-7060, 10 A.M.–9 P.M. Mon.–Sat., $7) is a homey one-room joint best known for its giant hamburgers, from meat ground fresh daily, and its cheesy and hot chiles rellenos.

## Mexican

In a strip mall off St. Michael's Drive, **Felipe's Tacos** (1711-A Llano St., 505/473-9397, 9 A.M.–4:30 P.M. Mon.–Fri., 9 A.M.–3:30 P.M. Sat., $4.50) makes soft tacos just like you get down south: steaming corn tortillas wrapped around grilled chicken or steak, or the chile-soaked pork *al pastor,* then topped with radish slices, salsa, and lime. Bigger appetites will want a hefty burrito—The Original is your choice of meat, plus cheese, beans, and generous lashings of avocado. Wash it down with the fresh limeade. Breakfast burritos (9– 11 A.M. only) are great, too.

## Burgers and More

Perhaps the world's only burger joint owned by a vegetarian, **Bobcat Bite** (420 Old Las Vegas Hwy., 505/983-5319, 11 A.M.–7:50 P.M. Wed.–Sat., $7) doesn't seem to suffer from the proprietor's preferences. Burgers, from freshly ground meat, are plenty thick, piled high with chopped green chile and oozy cheese. Pork chops and rib-eye steaks are on the menu too, for heartier eaters. It's well worth the drive out this way (Old Las Vegas Highway is the frontage road on the north side of I-25), and the wait in line—try to go near the end of typical lunch hours to avoid the crowds.

For dessert, you'll want to head back toward town and **Harry's Roadhouse** (96-B Old Las Vegas Hwy., 505/989-4629, 7 A.M.–10 P.M. daily, $7), where chocolate mousse pie, lemon meringue pie, and coconut cream pie could be crowding the pastry case at any given time. And if you're looking for a reason to spend even more time on the shady front patio with a great view across the flatlands, the rest of the menu is solid, too: cold meatloaf sandwiches, catfish po'boys, lamb stew, and shrimp satay, not to mention tasty margaritas and an awe-inspiring breakfast burrito.

Also look for **Callie's Cajun** (Old Las Vegas Hwy., 505/438-7012, $8), a small blue trailer parked on the south side of Old Las Vegas Highway just east of the intersection with Old Pecos Trail. When it's there (usually weekdays between noon and 8 P.M.), it serves insanely rich crawfish pies, meat-filled spicy jambalaya, and scores of other straight-from-the-bayou specials—get the gumbo if you can.

## Indian

Santa Feans have embraced Albuquerque transplant **Annapurna** (905 W. Alameda St., 505/988-9688, 10 A.M.–8 P.M. Mon.–Sat., $5) with open arms—its mellow feel and Ayurvedic menu are just what the city's vegans have been hankering for. But even folks without particular dietary needs won't say no when a giant *masala dosa,* bursting with perfectly spiced veggies, gets plopped down on the table. Wash it down with some richly spiced *chai.*

## Fine Dining

**Blue Heron** (242 Los Pinos Rd., 505/471-6500, 7:30–10 A.M. Mon. and Tues., 7:30 A.M.–2 P.M. and 5:30–9 P.M. Wed.–Sun., $24), at the Sunrise Springs resort southwest of the city, makes an excellent romantic retreat, especially in the summer, when you can sit on the terrace overlooking a series of ponds. The food applies Japanese and other Asian flavors to local organic produce and meats—it's light and spa-friendly without being insubstantial.

Another beautiful dining destination is **La Mancha** (9 La Vega Rd., Galisteo, 505/466-3663, 6–9 P.M. Wed.–Sat., $20), at the old adobe Galisteo Inn, a half-hour drive southeast of Santa Fe. The small dining room, with only eight tables, is warmed by a fireplace in winter and opens onto a cottonwood-shaded courtyard in summer. The menu adds Spanish accents—mushrooms sautéed in sherry, Cabrales blue cheese—to straightforward grilled meats such as locally raised lamb chops. A lavish brunch is served on Sundays, as is lunch on Saturdays, but you must reserve these ahead of time.

# Outside Santa Fe

Within less than an hour's drive from Santa Fe lie all manner of fascinating destinations, whether you're interested in the six-century-old ruins of ancestral Puebloan culture at Bandelier or the 20th-century atomic developments in Los Alamos, home of the Manhattan Project. Abiquiu, best known as Georgia O'Keeffe country, is a landscape of rich red rocks along the tree-lined Rio Chama, while Pecos Wilderness Area, east of the city, is a great spot to hike to alpine meadows. The most popular day or overnight outing from Santa Fe is to Taos, but even that presents two possibilities: the low road along the Rio Grande or the high road that passes through tiny Hispano mountain villages.

## PECOS AND VILLANUEVA

Santa Fe backs up against the vast **Pecos Wilderness Area,** the second-largest nature reserve in the state (after the Gila), 223,000 acres of high country where the mountain streams seethe with trout and elk ramble through emerald-green meadows. The former logging town of Pecos, where mountain men now rub shoulders with alternative healers and monks, is the jumping-off point for any trip into the woods. (While you're there, check out **San Antonio de Padua Church,** another Gothic-style project by Bishop Lamy.) To reach the village, head east along I-25 to Glorieta (exit 299) and Highway 50; or there's an alternate route via Highway 63 (exit 307), which passes the ruins of Pecos Pueblo, the regional power before the Spanish arrived. Villanueva, a small village near a gem of a state park, is 14 miles farther on I-25, then 10 miles south.

On the drive out, near exit 295, you pass the site of the westernmost Civil War battle in the United States. The **Battle of Glorieta Pass** raged March 26–28, 1862, part of a Confederate plan to invade the West with a force of Texans—a plan that was foiled in this decisive rout. Look for annual reenactments of the fight.

## Pecos National Historical Park

The largest pueblo when the Spanish made first contact in 1540, Pecos was home to some 2,000 people, who lived among four- and five-story complexes built of stone sealed with mud. The ruins of this grand community (Hwy. 63, 505/757-6032, www.nps.gov/peco, $3) are accessible to visitors via Highway 63, then a 1.5-mile paved interpretive trail that winds through the remnants of the Pecos Pueblo walls, a couple of restored kivas, and, most striking, the remainder of a Franciscan mission. Free guided tours around various parts of the site run daily at 2 P.M. during the summer.

The Pecos Pueblo setting—on a ridge facing out to the plains to the northeast and to the mountains behind—provides a beautiful view today; around 1100, when the area was being settled with the first villages, it also provided a livelihood. The ridge was part of a natural

ruins of a Franciscan mission inside Pecos National Historical Park

© ZORA O'NEILL

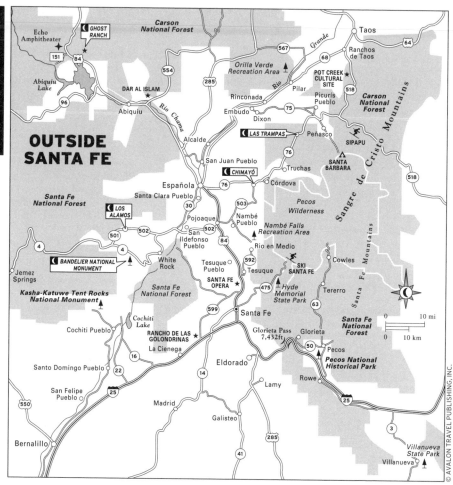

**OUTSIDE SANTA FE**

© AVALON TRAVEL PUBLISHING, INC.

trade path between the Rio Grande farmers and the buffalo hunters of the Great Plains—both groups met in Pecos, itself an agricultural community, to barter. What began as a series of small villages consolidated very quickly in the 14th century into a city, with a layout so orderly it appears to have been centrally planned, and by 1450, the fortress of Pecos was the major economic power in the area.

Perhaps it was the city's trading culture and relative worldliness that made the Pecos Indians welcome Francisco Vásquez de Coronado and his men in 1540 with music and dancing, rather than bows and arrows. Nearly 60 years later, Don Juan de Oñate visited the area and ordered that a mission church be built—a dramatic, imposing structure with six bell towers and buttresses 22 feet thick in some spots. The building was destroyed during the Pueblo Revolt, however, and the Pecos people dug a kiva smack in the middle of the ruined convent area—symbolic architecture, to say the least. But soon

# TRIBAL ECONOMIES IN THE GAMING AGE

North of Santa Fe on U.S. 84/285, Cities of Gold Casino looms up beside the road, a sight that would've dazzled any conquistador in search of El Dorado. This, it seems, is the true fabled jackpot of the New World.

Pojoaque opened Cities of Gold in the 1990s, after much deliberation in the small pueblo. The main argument in favor of gaming – effectively permitted by the federal Indian Gaming Regulatory Act in 1988, then legalized in New Mexico in 1994 – was simply the status quo: Pre-casinos, unemployment and poverty rates in some pueblos were almost inconceivably below national standards. With virtually no industry on pueblo lands, up to 72 percent of residents were jobless, and the average income in many communities was less than $10,000 per year.

Although Pojoaque now boasts zero unemployment, as well as attractive new apartment housing and a beautifully appointed museum funded by casino profits, not all pueblos have followed that community's lead down the gaming path. For instance, Picurís's social conservatism as well as more practical concerns, such as

its remote location, deterred the pueblo from opening its own gambling palace; the elders did eventually agree to co-owning the Hotel Santa Fe, a venture initiated by a few Anglo entrepreneurs who saw an opportunity to capitalize on a unique relationship with a pueblo. Jemez Pueblo remains staunchly reliant on its own agriculture and crafts, and does not even take advantage of its status to sell tax-free cigarettes. The divisions between gaming and non-gaming pueblos are not dramatic, but they are visible – especially as they're enhanced by difference in economic status.

Puebloans and Anglos alike complain about the aesthetics of the gaudy, brightly lit casinos springing up on previously empty land, and others worry about the apparent loss of tradition that goes along with courting lowest-common-denominator tourism. But for many people who had previously been not much more than a scenic backdrop in New Mexico – a mute patch of "local color" – there's no incongruity at all. As George Rivera, the former lieutenant governor of Pojoaque has put it, "You don't have to be poor to have your culture."

enough, the Spanish were back, and they were even welcomed and aided at Pecos. When they built a new church in the early 1700s, it was noticeably smaller, maybe as a form of compromise. But even as a hybrid Pueblo-Spanish culture was developing, the Indian population was gradually falling victim to disease and drought. When the Santa Fe Trail opened up in 1821, Pecos was all but empty, and in 1838, the last city-dwellers marched to live with fellow Towaspeakers at Jemez Pueblo, 80 miles west; their descendants still live there today.

## Pecos Wilderness Area

Stop in at the **ranger station** (Hwy. 63, 505/757-6121, 8 A.M.–4:30 P.M. Mon.–Fri.) on the north end of Pecos town to buy topographical maps and inquire about hiking conditions at Pecos Wilderness Area, as well as the state of various campsites—eight developed areas are usually open, though some have not fared so well from recent bark-beetle invasions and forest fires. At this high elevation, summer temperatures are rarely above 75°F and can dip below freezing at night, so plan accordingly when you pack, especially for multiday trips.

Highway 63 runs north out of town, following the Pecos River past the tiny settlement of Tererro and several fishing access points. At the general store in Tererro, inquire about **horseback-riding** trips (Hwy. 63, 505/757-6193). The road then narrows and rises, to reach the former mining camp of Cowles— now just a wide spot in the road. Immediately north, Forest Road 223 leads 4.5 miles to Iron Gate Campground and **Mora Flats Trail,** a fairly level 3.8-mile hike to a wide-open meadow—look out for wild strawberries among the myriad wildflowers.

At the end of Highway 63 (bear right where the dirt road forks), **Cave Creek Trail,** which runs out of Panchuela Campground, is an easy 3.6-mile out-and-back that follows a small waterway up to some caves that have been carved out of the white limestone by the stream's flow. You can make this hike more ambitious by pressing on past the caves, up a steep hillside, and on to Horsethief Meadow; this adds an extra 3 (very strenuous) miles, and you could make this into an overnight trip, as the meadow is a beautiful place to camp. More ambitious still is the 7.5-mile trek to **Pecos Baldy Lake,** which goes out of Jacks Creek Campground and should be done as an overnight hike. All trails in this area require a $2 trailhead parking fee; additional fees apply for camping or picnicking, depending on the spot.

## Food and Accommodations

At the main crossroads in Pecos, where Highway 50 meets Highway 63, **Frankie's Casanova** (Hwy. 63, 505/757-3322, 7 A.M.–2 P.M. and 5:30–9:30 P.M. Tues.–Sat., 8 A.M.–2 P.M. and 5:30–9:30 P.M. Sun., $9) is the best all-around restaurant in town, serving massive breakfasts (pork chops!), giant lunches (burgers stuffed with green chile and cheese!), and also rather large dinners, which range from plain old enchiladas to pasta alfredo with shrimp. During the winter, the place is open only for breakfast and lunch.

If you want to get an early start hiking, consider staying the night in Pecos. The **Benedictine Monastery** (Hwy. 63, 505/757-6415, www.pecosabbey.org, $50 s) maintains four austere hermitages with beautiful views; the rate is a suggested donation. **Pecos Paradise Inn** (14 Hwy. 63, 505/757-3669, www.pecosparadiseinn.com, $125 d) offers a few more worldly comforts: fluffy beds, a pleasant porch to lounge on, and a big fireplace in the living room. (Note that breakfast is not included.) Several mountain lodges, such as **Los Pinos Ranch** (505/757-6213, www.lospinosranch.com, $125 pp), offer multiday packages with all meals and a variety of outdoor activities.

## Villanueva

If you want a change of scenery from the mountains, drive a bit farther on I-25, to exit 323, then south on Highway 3, to reach the small but beautiful **Villanueva State Park** (505/421-2957, $5 day use), which occupies a bend in the Pecos River against 400-foot-tall sandstone cliffs. Because the parkland is small, it doesn't draw big crowds—even in the summer, it's only busy on the weekends. During the week, you'll probably have the 2.5-mile Canyon Trail to yourself, and the choice of **camping** ($8) either on the cottonwood-shaded river bottom or up on the canyon rim amid juniper and piñon. The river is stocked with trout and is deep enough for canoeing. Spring comes early in the river valley, making for flower-filled paths by late April; fall is a burst of red scrub oak and yellow cottonwood leaves, in sharp contrast against the evergreens.

# THE PUEBLOS

Between Santa Fe and Taos lie seven pueblos, each set on a separate patch of reservation land. Unlike scenic Taos Pueblo, which opens its centuries-old buildings to visitors, most of the others are not worth visiting for their ancient architecture—they're typically a mix of old and new, and some are closed to outsiders all or part of the year. Do visit on feast days or for other ceremonial dances if you can, though.

Directly north of Santa Fe, U.S. 84/285 runs right through the lands of Tesuque and Pojoaque—the overpass bridges are decorated with the original Tewa names of the pueblos. Though this stretch of casinos and tax-free cigarette shops isn't particularly scenic, don't be tempted to race through it—the area is a major speed trap.

## North of Santa Fe

**Tesuque** (Te Tesugeh Owingeh, "village of the cottonwood trees") is marked by **Camel Rock,** a piece of sandstone on the west side of the highway that has eroded to resemble a creature that looks right at home in this rocky desert. The old village, established in 1200, is closed

# CEREMONIAL DANCES

This is only an approximate schedule for ceremonial dances at pueblos in the Santa Fe area – dates can vary from year to year, as can the particular dances. Annual feast days typically involve carnivals and markets in addition to dances. Confirm details and start times – usually afternoon, but sometimes following an evening or midnight Mass – with the Indian Pueblo Cultural Center (505/843-7270, www .ipcc.org) before setting out.

## JANUARY 1
- San Juan: cloud or basket dance

## JANUARY 6
- Nambé: buffalo, deer, and antelope dances
- Picurís: various dances

## JANUARY 22
- San Ildefonso: vespers and firelight procession at 6 P.M.

## JANUARY 23
- San Ildefonso: Feast of San Ildefonso, with buffalo, Comanche, and deer dances

## JANUARY 25
- Picurís: Feast of San Pablo

## FEBRUARY 2
- Picurís: various dances for Candlemas (Día de la Candelaria)

## MARCH/APRIL (EASTER)
- Nambé: bow dance
- San Ildefonso: various dances

## JUNE, FIRST SATURDAY
- Tesuque: corn dance for blessing of the fields

## JUNE 13
- San Juan and Picurís: Feast of San Antonio

## JUNE 24
- San Juan: Feast of San Juan Bautista

## JULY 4
- Nambé: celebration at the waterfall

## AUGUST 9
- Picurís: dances after sunset Mass

## AUGUST 10
- Picurís: Feast of San Lorenzo

## OCTOBER 4
- Nambé: Feast of San Francisco de Asís

## NOVEMBER 12
- Tesuque: Feast of San Diego

## DECEMBER 11
- Pojoaque: night dances

## DECEMBER 12
- Pojoaque: Feast of Our Lady of Guadalupe

## DECEMBER 24
- Picurís: torchlight procession at sundown, followed by Los Matachines dances
- San Felipe, Tesuque, and Nambé: various dances, beginning after midnight Mass

## DECEMBER 25
- San Ildefonso and Picurís: Los Matachines dances
- Tesuque: various dances

## DECEMBER 28
- Picurís: children's dances to celebrate Holy Innocents Day

to the public some days; call ahead (505/983-2667) if you're planning to visit, though the only real sight is the new-old church, which was reconstructed after it was destroyed by arson. The new construction uses an interesting new eco-friendly building material called Rastra—a lightweight mix of concrete mixed with recycled styrofoam that takes particularly well to an adobe finish.

**Pojoaque** manages the **Poeh Museum** (U.S. 84/285, 505/455-3334, 10 A.M.–4 P.M. Mon.–Fri., 11 A.M.–2 P.M. Sat., free), a striking old-style adobe building that incorporates a cutting-edge museum, thanks to casino profits; the permanent display on Pueblo culture, set to open in late 2005, is a multimedia bonanza, with separate "experiences" for English- and Tewa-speakers. The adjacent restaurant, **Ó Eating House** (505/455-5065, 7 A.M.–3 P.M. Mon.–Sat., $6), serves really tasty hot doughnuts.

### Near Española

**San Ildefonso,** best known for the black-on-black pottery of María Martinez and her husband, Julian, is off Highway 502, on the way to Los Alamos. A small **museum** (Hwy. 502, 505/455-3549, 8 A.M.–4:30 P.M. Mon.–Fri., $3) shows the pottery-making process, and there are several crafts shops, but otherwise, there's not much to see. **Santa Clara** (Kha P'o, or "shining water"), on Highway 30 south of Española, contains the beautiful Puyé Cliff Dwellings, but they have been closed since the Cerro Grande fire of 2000, with no stated plans to reopen; the pueblo, too, is generally closed to visitors. If you do hear that Puyé has reopened, go—the place is worth seeing. Immediately north of Española, at the junction of the Rio Chama and the Rio Grande, is **San Juan,** the birthplace of Popé, who led the Pueblo Revolt. You pass through its boundaries on Highway 68, but its center is west along the river—worth seeking out for the **Oké Oweenge Crafts Co-op** (505/852-2372, 9 A.M.–4:30 P.M. Mon.–Sat.) and the odd brick **San Juan Bautista Church,** built in 1919.

## █ LOS ALAMOS

Unlike so many other sights in New Mexico, which are cloaked in centuries of history, Los Alamos is an emblem of the modern age. During World War II, what had been only an elite, rugged boys' school was requisitioned by the army to become the top-secret base for development of the nuclear bomb, home for a time to J. Robert Oppenheimer, Richard Feynman, Neils Bohr, and other science luminaries. The Manhattan Project and its aftermath, the Cold War arms race, led to the establishment of Los Alamos National Labs (LANL) and the growth of the makeshift military base into a town of nearly 20,000 people (more if you count the "suburb" of White Rock, just down the hill on Highway 4).

The highway up the mountainside is wider than it used to be, but the winding ascent to "Lost Almost"—as the first scientists dubbed their isolated, officially nonexistent camp—still carries an air of the clandestine. The town itself has a jarring newness about it, only emphasized by the dramatic, timeless landscape spreading out in all directions from the mesa edge on which it's perched. The scenery is still recovering from the Cerro Grande forest fire that tore through in 2000, when the entire town had to be evacuated, but it's still a beautiful starting point for hikes—after you've gone to the museums and cruised Bikini Atoll Road, Trinity Boulevard, and Oppenheimer Drive.

### Orientation and Information

Los Alamos is spread out over three long mesas that jut like fingers from Pajarito Mountain. Highway 502 arrives in the middle mesa, depositing you on Central Avenue and the main downtown area; the north mesa is mostly residential, while the south mesa is occupied by the labs and two routes running back down the mountain and connecting with Highway 4. (Stray too far off the beaten track, and you start passing ominous "Explosive Area" signs.) Stop at the **tourist info center** (109 Central Park Square, 505/662-8105, http://visit.losalamos.com, 9 A.M.–5 P.M. Mon.–Fri., 9 A.M.–4 P.M. Sat.) for thorough maps to the area and the handy *50 Hikes in the Los Alamos Area* booklet. There's another helpful office in **White Rock** (Hwy. 4, 505/672-3183, 9 A.M.–4 P.M. daily) on Highway 4; both offices are also open 10 A.M.–3 P.M. Sunday in the summer.

## Los Alamos Historical Museum

Even a manufactured town like Los Alamos has a history. See what the area was like pre–Manhattan Project at this fascinating museum (1921 Juniper St., 505/662-6272, 10 A.M.–4 P.M. Mon.–Sat. and 1–4 P.M. Sun. in winter, 9:30 A.M.–4:30 P.M. Mon.–Sat. and 11 A.M.–5 P.M. Sun. in summer, free) set in an old building of the Los Alamos Ranch School, the boys' camp that got the boot when the army moved in. The exhibits cover everything from relics of the early Tewa-speaking people up to juicy details on the social intrigue during the development of "the gadget," as the A-bomb was known.

Ideally, you'd take one of the free **walking tours** of the blocks around the museum (2 P.M. Sun. and 11 A.M. Mon.), led by longtime residents with great stories to tell. Otherwise, pick up a flyer for a self-guided walk around the old school grounds and the lab site, to see how bare-bones dorms meant for toughening up teens in the winter got turned into barely more luxurious apartments for the country's top physicists.

In front of the museum is historic **Fuller Lodge,** originally the Ranch School's dining room and kitchen. It was built by John Gaw Meem, who hand-picked the vertical logs that form the seemingly unsound walls and even designed the cowboy-silhouette light fixtures hanging outside. It houses the **Los Alamos Art Center** (10 A.M.–4 P.M. Mon.–Sat.), which showcases local students and often has very attractive, well-priced items in its gift shop.

The museum is just west of the main street, Central Avenue—you'll see Fuller Lodge on Central, with the museum set back behind it. And you can tell this is a town full of scientists: Summer hours start with daylight saving time.

## Bradbury Science Museum

This LANL-sponsored exhibit (Central Ave. at 15th St., 505/667-4444, 10 A.M.–5 P.M. Tues.–Sat., free) on the miracles of atomic energy has the feel of a very-high-grade science fair, with plenty of buttons to push and gadgets to play with. There's also an air of a convention sales booth—the museum's mission is definitely to sell the public on LANL's work and nuclear technology in general, though a public forum corner gives space to opposing views. More interesting are the relics of the early nuclear age: the Fat Man and Littleboy shell casings, gadgetry from the Nevada Test Site, and the like.

## The Black Hole

An enormous shop dealing in engineering equipment tossed from LANL, The Black Hole (4015 Arkansas Ave., 505/662-5053, 10 A.M.–5 P.M. Mon.–Sat.) is more like a 17,000-square-foot museum of obsoleteness: Geiger counters, stacks of IBM punch cards, vacuum tubes, and –ometers of all kinds. Who knows what you'll find here: FBI agents even raided the place in 2004, taking too literally a gag planted in the front display window, a computer hard drive marked "secret." Owner Ed Grothus also maintains the Omega Peace Institute next door, an anti-nuclear shrine. To get there, head toward the north mesa on Diamond Drive, then turn left on Arkansas Avenue.

## Recreation

The mountains and canyons around Los Alamos are filled with some excellent **hiking** trails, in addition to those at Bandelier National Monument, farther west. One short route is **Mortendad Cave Trail,** an out-and-back (1.6 miles round-trip) that takes you to an Ancestral Puebloan site consisting of an old kiva set among a cluster of cave dwellings; the ceiling of the kiva cave is carved with very well-preserved petroglyphs. You can do the route year-round, and it's easy enough for children. To reach the trailhead, turn from Highway 4 onto East Jemez Road (also known as the truck route, up the back of the hill to the labs), then park on the right (north) after 0.7 mile. The

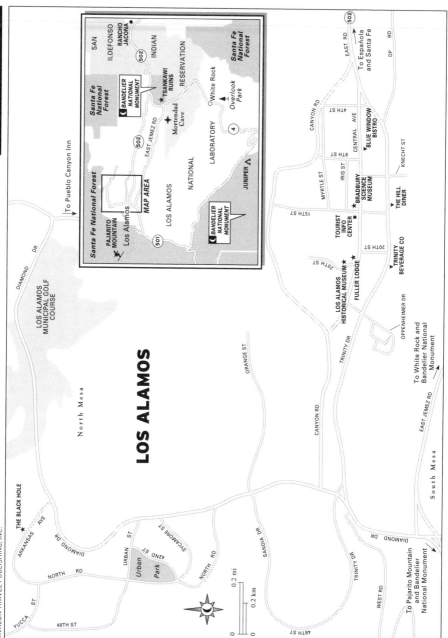

# LOS ALAMOS

LOS ALAMOS MUNICIPAL GOLF COURSE

North Mesa

South Mesa

THE BLACK HOLE

Urban Park

To Pajarito Mountain and Bandelier National Monument

To White Rock and Bandelier National Monument

To Española and Santa Fe

BLUE WINDOW BISTRO

THE HILL DINER

BRADBURY SCIENCE MUSEUM

TOURIST INFO CENTER

TRINITY BEVERAGE CO

LOS ALAMOS HISTORICAL MUSEUM

FULLER LODGE

To Pueblo Canyon Inn

**MAP AREA**

BANDELIER NATIONAL MONUMENT

TSANKAWI RUINS

Mortendad Cave

White Rock

Overlook Park

Santa Fe National Forest

SAN ILDEFONSO INDIAN RESERVATION

RANCHO JACONA

Santa Fe National Forest

PAJARITO MOUNTAIN

Los Alamos

LOS ALAMOS NATIONAL LABORATORY

JUNIPER

502

501

502

4

EAST JEMEZ RD

0 0.2 mi
0 0.2 km

© AVALON TRAVEL PUBLISHING, INC.

trail begins at a gap in the fence on the opposite side of the road.

In White Rock, the **White Rock Rim Trail** runs three miles along the cliff edge—you'll have suburban tract homes to your back and a dizzying canyon out in front of you. The walk starts at Overlook Park; follow signs from Highway 4 at the first stoplight in town. You can also take a strenuous hike into the gorge along the **Red Dot Trail,** which passes a few petroglyphs on its way down to the Rio Grande; ask at the White Rock visitors center for directions to the trailhead, which is at the back end of a subdivision.

Thanks to the canyon walls, White Rock is also popular with **rock climbers,** who most frequently head to **The Overlook,** a 65-foot basalt wall below Overlook Park. The Los Alamos Mountaineers (www.losalamos.org/climb) organization maintains a very good website with detailed route guides and information on smaller area walls; the group also helps organize the annual Meltdown climbing competition in September.

A bit of a locals' secret, **Pajarito Mountain** (505/662-5725, www.skipajarito.com, 9 A.M.–4 P.M. Fri.–Sun. and holidays) offers good **skiing and snowboarding** cheap ($39 for a full day), with five lifts giving access to bunny slopes as well as double-black-diamond trails. The area is just a few miles northeast of Los Alamos, off Highway 501, and luckily escaped all damage from the Cerro Grande fire.

## Accommodations

The few hotels in Los Alamos cater primarily to visiting engineers, which is a shame, considering the city's proximity to Valles Caldera National Preserve—it's a handy place to bunk if you want to get an early start on a hike. One very pleasant place, **Pueblo Canyon Inn** (199 San Ildefonso Rd., 505/662-9200, $85 d), however, does give you ample opportunity to enjoy the town's beautiful setting, as it sits on a big lot of tall junipers and cedars on the north mesa. It's a very spacious, comfortably furnished house, with great views from the back hot tub and upstairs rooms.

## Food

Perhaps the best-loved restaurant on the hill is **Blue Window Bistro** (813 Central Ave., 505/662-6305, 11 A.M.–2:30 P.M. and 5–9 P.M. Mon.–Fri., 8:30 A.M.–2:30 P.M. and 5–9 P.M. Sat., $15), a cheerful place done up in bright Mexican colors. The menu is all over the place—crab cakes alongside chile relleno crepes—but the flavor combos are all spot-on, and the ingredients very fresh. It's great for lunch, too; enormous sandwiches are about $7.

As hip as Los Alamos gets, **Trinity Beverage Co.** (2201-G Trinity Dr., 505/662-3800, 11 A.M.–midnight Mon.–Wed., 11 A.M.–2 A.M. Thurs.–Sat., noon–midnight Sun., $9) is a good spot for a locally brewed beer and a burger, or other typical bar snacks—the patio gets lively after work.

The Los Alamos old guard favors **The Hill Diner** (1315 Trinity Dr., 505/662-9745, 11 A.M.–8 P.M. daily, $8), where the vibe is Early Cold War: wood paneling, checked tablecloths, massive slices of coconut cream pie, and hot dinners like chicken-fried steak served with your choice of two sides. It's open an hour later in the summer. For very special occasions, everyone heads to **Katherine's** (121 Longview Rd., 11:30 A.M.–1:30 P.M. and 5–9 P.M. Tues.–Sat., 5–9 P.M. Sat., $22), an unlikely gourmet outpost in White Rock, where you can get chipotle-rubbed New York strip served in white-tablecloth ambience.

## ◖ BANDELIER NATIONAL MONUMENT

One of New Mexico's most atmospheric ancient Indian sites, Bandelier ($10 per vehicle, $5 per person) comprises 23,000 acres of wilderness, including the remarkable Frijoles Canyon, which is lined on either side with cave "apartments," while the remnants of a massive settlement from the 16th century occupy the valley floor. The near-Edenic canyon and the fun of clambering up ladders and around caves make for a grand day out—but everyone else thinks so too, and the place is packed from late April through the end of the summer. Come early on a weekday, if at all possible, or plan an overnight hike in the backcountry to avoid the crowds. Better still, join a torch-lit, silent **night walk** into Frijoles Canyon, a trip that sparks the imagination. They typically fall on Thursday nights; check online (www.nps.gov/band) for the schedule and for other special events, including those for Bandelier's 90th anniversary through 2006.

Start your day at the **visitors center** (505/672-3861, 8 A.M.–4:30 P.M. daily in winter, 8 A.M.–6 P.M. daily in summer, 9 A.M.–5:30 P.M. daily in spring and fall), built by the Civilian Conservation Corps in the late 1930s, almost 50 years after self-taught anthropologist Adolph Bandelier first set foot in Frijoles Canyon, brought there by Cochiti guides. The info center has a small museum and the usual array of maps and guides; pick up a Falls Trail guide even if you're not hiking that way, as it has good illustrations of the various plants and wildflowers that grow in the area. You can also get a free backcountry permit and thorough topo maps here.

## Main Loop Trail and Ceremonial Cave Trail

A paved walkway leads out the back of the visitors center into Frijoles Canyon, passing the ruins of the major settlements—or at least the ones that have been thoroughly excavated. You first reach **Tyuonyi** (chew-ON-yee), a circle of buildings that was settled for about 200 years, beginning in the 1300s. Built of bricks cut from tuff (the volcanic rock that makes up most of the area) and adobe plaster, some of the 250 rooms at one time stood several stories tall.

The trail then goes up next to the cliffs, dotted with small caves dug out of the soft stone, and to **Long House,** the remnants of a strip of condo-style buildings tucked into the rock wall. Paintings and carvings decorate the cliff face above. If you're here near sunset, keep an eye on the **bat cave** near the end of the strip, home to about 10,000 of the animals.

After Long House, the trail continues another half-mile to the **Ceremonial Cave,** where you can climb up to a restored kiva high up

in the cliffs—well worth the extra mileage, as well as facing any fear of heights (the 140 feet of ladders do require a lot of concentration, however). Rangers run free guided walks around the main loop trail a few times a day, or you can pick up the trail guide for a small fee in the visitors center.

## Other Trails

**Falls Trail,** which leads southeast from the visitors center, is a showcase for the area's geology, rather than archaeology—the 2.5-mile route leads down through a canyon to two separate waterfalls. Allow about two hours for the full trip, as the going can be steep and very hot in the summer.

Well before you reach the main entrance to Bandelier, you pass **Tsankawi** on the east side of Highway 4. Unique pottery excavated in this separate section, disconnected from the main park, suggests that it was inhabited by a different people from those who settled in Frijoles Canyon, and some sort of natural border seems to have formed here, despite a shared cliff-dwelling culture: Today the pueblos immediately north of the Bandelier area speak Tewa, while those to the south speak Keresan. A 1.5-mile loop, with ladders to climb along the way, leads past unexcavated ruins, cave houses, and even a few petroglyphs.

Two popular overnight hikes are to the **Shrine of the Stone Lions,** two weathered sandstone carvings of mountain lions on a mesa top about 10 miles from the visitors center, and **Painted Cave,** which requires a 12-mile hike to see a 50-foot swath of rock covered in layers of ancient artwork.

## Camping

**Juniper Campground** ($12), just inside the park's northern border, is usually open year-round, with 94 sites. There are no hookups or showers—you're directed to the Los Alamos YMCA up the hill instead. No reservations are taken, but it's usually not full. The scenery up on the plateau isn't as striking as down in the canyon, but you will get an early start on the day if you stay overnight here.

# ESPAÑOLA

Although it's just a few miles from San Gabriel, the first town established by Don Juan de Oñate in 1598, Española itself is a relatively modern city of about 10,000 people, founded in the 1880s as a stop on the Chili Line, the railway between Denver and Santa Fe. It's still a crossroads: Take Highway 68 (called Riverside Drive in town) north from here to Taos, or continue on U.S. 84/285 to Abiquiu. Highway 76 leads east to Chimayó, then to Truchas and the other high-road towns on the way to Taos. Highway 30 is the back road to Los Alamos.

Superficially, the place is not enticing—fast-food joints line the main highway, and Wal-Mart seems to be the biggest social scene in town. One token museum, the **Bond House** (706 Bond St., 505/747-8535, noon–5 P.M. daily, free), tries to scrape up some historic pride, but really, Española is all about the food: Come here for authentic northern New Mexican cuisine, never watered down for interlopers' tastes. Española is also the state's unofficial lowrider capital—keep your eyes out for cruisers in, say, the Wal-Mart parking lot, or at the Saints and Sinners package liquor store (its neon sign should also get landmark status) on U.S. 84/285 at the south end of town.

## Chimayó Trading Post

No, you haven't made a wrong turn—you're still in Española. This adobe trading post (110 Sandia Dr., 505/753-9414, 9 A.M.–4 P.M. Mon.–Sat.) on the west side of the main highway relocated here in the 1930s, after several decades at its original location in Chimayó. Now it's a listed landmark, as one of the last remaining historic trading posts, and it has

# YOGIS IN ESPAÑOLA

At first glance, Española's street culture is all lowriders, baggy pants, and blaring hip-hop. But look closer, and you'll notice a high proportion of Anglos clad in white kurtas and tightly wrapped turbans – these are members of the Sikh Dharma community in Sombrillo, just east of Española. The group is an unlikely product of the commune era, one of the oldest and largest ashrams established by Sikh Dharma's leader, Harbhajan Singh Khalsa Yogiji.

The India-born yogi first came to New Mexico in 1969, to teach yoga to the assembled hippie masses. Twinkly eyed, white-bearded Yogi Bhajan, as he became known, had a knack for inspiring his followers not only to make their bodies strong ("healthy, happy, holy" are the tenets of his teaching, a New Age-inflected version of orthodox Sikhism), but to build up their bank accounts as well. In particular, he focused on "turning chicks into eagles" – his term for teaching women to empower themselves financially – and he encouraged all of his students to start businesses. The first Sikh Dharma-owned enterprise was Yogi Tea, followed by Golden Temple Foods, and then – in radical departures from the stereotype of

Sikh culture – Sun and Son Computers and Akal Security. The security firm was founded in Española in 1980 by a would-be police officer, turned down for jobs because of his beard and turban: "Start a company, and the police will work for you," Bhajan counseled his student. Akal has grown to become the fourth-largest security provider in the United States, with nearly every federal courthouse protected by its guards.

Based on these contributions to the state economy, as well as directly to the Democratic and Republican parties, Yogi Bhajan became very influential in New Mexico politics – his birthday party was attended every year by prominent lawmakers and former governors – and at his funeral in 2004, just after his 75th birthday, Governor Bill Richardson paid his respects in the keynote speech.

Although they might look out of place to visitors, the Sikhs are an accepted part of Española and don't merit a second glance from locals. The best evidence of their integration? The all-veggie "Khalsa Special" burrito at El Parasol takeout stand – a savvy business move that Yogi Bhajan himself surely admired.

## ESPAÑOLA

To Rancho de San Juan and Abiquiu

To Taos

FAIRVIEW LN

PASEO DE OÑATE

SPRUCE ST

BOND ST

BOND HOUSE

PASEO DE OÑATE

To Los Alamos

N RIVERSIDE DR

MCCURDY RD

JOANN'S RANCH O CASADO

EL PARASOL/ EL PARAGUA

SANTA CRUZ DE LA CAÑADA CHURCH

BUS STATION

CHIMAYÓ TRADING POST

CORLETT RD

MATILDA'S

S RIVERSIDE DR

To Chimayó and Truchas

Rio Grande

0     0.75 mi
0     0.75 km

To Santa Fe

everything you'd expect from such status: creaky wood floors, dim lighting, and a jumbled stock of treasures that includes not only Chimayó rugs but also ones from Iran; Nepalese silver jewelry; cut-tin candleholders, made locally; long skeins of handmade wool yarn; postcards; and even free coffee. You could easily spend hours in here.

## Santa Cruz de la Cañada Church

Take a right turn midway through town at Highway 76 to reach the village of Santa Cruz, established in 1695. The sizable church (varied hours, free) that's here now (turn left at the traffic light after one mile) dates from 1733, and its altar screen is another colorful work attributed to the Laguna Santero, who also painted the *reredos* at San Miguel Mission in Santa Fe and the church at Laguna Pueblo. It is dated 1795 but was completely painted over—with the same images—in the mid-19th century, presenting a particular challenge to the preservationists who cleaned and restored the piece in 1995. Each panel presents a different combination of the original artist's work and the "fresh coat" applied half a century later.

## Food

Española is the place to go for hearty, inexpensive New Mexican. If you're just driving through on your way north, stop off for a quick bite at **El Parasol** (602 Santa Cruz Rd., 505/753-8852, 7:30 A.M.–9 P.M. daily, $3), a takeout stand with picnic tables under cottonwood trees and a Spanglish menu ("pollo with guacamole taco"); burritos are big but not as tasty as the freshly fried crispy tacos. If you've got more time, head indoors to neighbor **El Paragua** (505/753-3211, 11 A.M.–9 P.M. Mon.–Thurs., 11 A.M.–9:30 P.M. Fri. and Sat., 11 A.M.–8 P.M. Sun., $15) in a big two-story hacienda filled with wagon wheels, wrought-iron bric-a-brac, and vintage newspaper clippings. The place is constantly packed with locals stuffing themselves with big plates of carnitas, chiles rellenos, and the most delectable, perfectly fried sopaipillas in the region—which doesn't mean you shouldn't also get some flan or *capirotada* (bread pudding) for dessert. Turn for both of these places at the sign for Highway 76, which is called Santa Cruz Road in town—the restaurants are immediately on the left.

For a smaller, quieter dining experience, look for **Matilda's** (424 Corlett Rd., 505/753-7200, 10:30 A.M.–8 P.M. Tues.–Thurs., 10:30 A.M.– 9 P.M. Fri., 9 A.M.–9 P.M. Sat. and Sun., $7) to the southeast off the main road (if you're heading north and pass the Chimayo Trading Post, you've gone too far). The place strikes a homey tone from its front steps, which are filled with pots full of geraniums, and Matilda herself, who has owned the place since the 1950s, still presides over the tables. Her family cooks up the very traditional (read: heavy on the chile, light on the cheese) northern New Mexican goods, often using ingredients they've grown themselves.

On the main drag (Highway 68/Riverside Dr.), diner-style **JoAnn's Ranch O Casado** (938 N. Riverside Dr., 505/753-1334, 7–9 A.M. Mon.–Sat., 7 A.M.–4 P.M. Sun., $6) serves breakfast all day, along with very good and inexpensive enchiladas, fajitas, and more. The kitsch factor is high—check out the mini-waterfall.

## Rancho de San Juan

While you're up this way, head north on U.S. 285 about 10 miles to the Relais & Chateaux–managed Rancho de San Juan. On the grounds is **Windows in the Earth,** a warren of vaulted-ceiling caves carved into the sandstone cliffs by artist Ra Paulette; visitors may **hike** to the amazing structure after registering at reception (closed after noon on Sun. and all day Mon.).

The resort itself (505/753-6818, www.ranchodesanjuan.com, $225 d) is quite lovely; it's 38 miles from Santa Fe but worth the drive if you're looking for solitude. Scattered over 225 acres, even the standard rooms have private patios and fireplaces. The **restaurant** (open to nonguests with reservations) is also excellent, devising a new set four-course meal every day, with choices like organic New Mexico lamb shank and rack of venison with Moroccan spices.

## ABIQUIU

Northwest of Española, along U.S. 84, the valley formed by the muddy Rio Chama is one of the most striking landscapes in northern New Mexico. Lush greenery on the river bottom clashes with bright red mud; roaming sheep and cattle graze by the roadside. The striated hills represent dramatic geological shifts, from 200-million-year-old purple stone from the dinosaur era to red clay formed by forests, then gypsum from sand dunes, then a layer of lava, from only 8 million years back.

More recently, Abiquiu has become inextricably linked with the artist Georgia O'Keeffe, who made the valley her home for more than 40 years, entranced all the while by the glowing light and the dramatic skyline. It's also the birthplace of Padre Antonio Martinez, the controversial Taos priest who clashed with Bishop Lamy in the mid-1880s. Years before that, in the mid-1700s, the Hispanicized Indian settlers *(genízaros)* had a reputation for harboring witches, an idea that still hasn't quite worn off—the vast Ghost Ranch is better known as *el rancho de los brujos,* or "witch ranch."

Although Abiquiu often refers to the whole river valley, the unofficial town center is **Bode's** (505/685-4422, 6:30 A.M.–7 P.M. Mon.–Fri., 7 A.M.–8 P.M. Sat. and Sun.), an old-fashioned general store (the name's pronounced BO-deez) where you can get gas, sandwiches, and fishing licenses and tackle. The actual village of Abiquiu, established in 1754 by the *genízaros* through a land grant from the Spanish Crown, is up the hill on the opposite side of the road. O'Keeffe's house forms one side of the old plaza; on the other is the Santo Tomas de Abiquiu Church, built in the 1930s after the community opted for the legal status of village rather than pueblo. Continue uphill past O'Keeffe's house to see the village *morada,* dramatically set on a hilltop. You're not really encouraged to poke around, however—the village maintains a privacy policy similar to those of the pueblos.

## Poshuinge Ruin Trail

About two miles south of Abiquiu proper, on the west side of the road, this half-mile trek leads to an ancestral Tewa site, literally the "village above the muddy river," inhabited only between 1420 and 1500—why it was abandoned is unclear. The village contained about 137 rooms, as well as surrounding field grids, though there's not much to see today (thorough excavations took place in 1919, and it has been left to melt away since then). Nonetheless, it's a good place to get out and stretch your legs and take in the view from the hilltop.

## Georgia O'Keeffe House

The artist's main residence, where she lived 1949–1984, fronts the small plaza in the village center of Abiquiu. The house is open to guided tours mid-March–November (505/685-4539, 9:30 A.M., 11 A.M., 2 P.M., and 3:30 P.M. Tues., Thurs., and Fri., $20). The rambling adobe, parts of which were built in the 18th century, is interesting, but in many ways the landscape reflects O'Keeffe's work more than her home does. Tours depart from the Abiquiu Inn on U.S. 84; you must make reservations in advance.

# ANCIENT EGYPT IN NORTHERN NEW MEXICO

Adobe, the word for the sun-dried mud bricks the Spanish used to build their houses for the first few centuries they lived in New Mexico, is derived from Arabic *(al-tub)* and Coptic, which probably has its roots in the language of the ancient Egyptians. But this shared heritage didn't help Egyptian architect Hassan Fathy communicate when he arrived in Abiquiu to build the mosque and the madrassa that would be the cornerstone of Dar al Islam, a newly established community of American-born Muslims.

Fathy had earned a reputation as a champion of vernacular architecture in the 1940s, when he built the village of New Gourna near Luxor in Egypt. His use of adobe made modernist architects scoff, but it provided cheap, efficient, and even elegant housing for people who could be easily trained to help construct the home and make their own repairs.

By the time the Dar al Islam community hired him in 1980, Fathy was in his 80s, but he nonetheless came to New Mexico to personally help build the mosque. It was his first and only commission in North America, and he was excited to work so near the pueblos, where, he noted, the proportions of the mud bricks were nearly the same as those that make up the Temple of Hatshepsut. He brought with him two Nubian assistants and hired a team of locals to help with the actual construction.

But what could've been a bonding experience over the global utility of mud-brick architecture – the very tenet Fathy had built his career on – became an awkward culture clash. Fathy was built up as an expert to local *adoberos,* who resented the deference, especially when he proved to be wrong. In particular, they were critical that his construction was not adapted to the cold climate, and he used techniques that could not be applied after he left. The minaret proved too expensive, and an additional plan to build individual homes in Dar al Islam had to be scrapped due to building codes that no longer permitted the use of adobe bricks without additional framing.

The innovations he did bring are lovely, though: arched doorways and roofs, and – best of all – the unsupported adobe domes and barrel vaults that were Fathy's signature, derived from ancient Nubian temples. The gentle curves of the complex's roofline and its rounded, whitewashed interior spaces echo the nearby Plaza Blanca hills, so the building seems beautifully integrated into its surroundings – so long as you don't compare it to its Spanish-style adobe neighbors.

## Dar al Islam

In another chapter of New Mexico's long utopian history, a few American converts to Islam established Dar al Islam (505/685-4515, www.daralislam.org), an intentional religious community, in 1979. A village for about 150 families on 8,300 acres just south of the village of Abiquiu proper, it was meant to be a place in which Muslims could practice their religion in every aspect of life, from food (cattle for halal slaughter were to be raised) to education. With funding from the Saudi royal family, the group hired renowned Egyptian architect Hassan Fathy to build the mosque and madrassa (school) that formed the core of the site. The group also established local businesses, such as the Abiquiu Inn.

The village concept never quite took off, though, and Dar al Islam has now been reinvented as a retreat center that's open to visitors—Fathy's adobe mosque, all organic sinuous lines, is beautiful and harmonizes flawlessly with the land surrounding it. The most direct route to the community is via Highway 554, which runs east from U.S. 84 south of Abiquiu (follow signs for El Rito); immediately after crossing the river, turn left on County Road 155, which leads to the main entrance.

If you leave the mosque by the far side, continuing on County Road 155 on its loop back to meet U.S. 84, you pass the towering gypsum formations of **Plaza Blanca** (White Place), an oft-photographed patch of land that looks like a pile of bleached bones. You can park your car anywhere and wander among the pinnacles.

## Abiquiu Lake

An Army Corps of Engineers dam project created this 4,000-acre lake with fingers running into the canyons all around. The view coming in is marred by the power station, but past that the water glimmers at the base of the flat-topped flint mountain Pedernal Peak, the distinctive silhouette that found its way into so many of O'Keeffe's paintings. ("It's my private mountain," she often said. "God told me if I painted it often enough, I could have it.") The overly paved campground at the lake is open year-round, but water and electric hookups are available only in the summer.

## Ghost Ranch

Ghost Ranch (U.S. 84, 505/685-4333, www.ghostranch.org), a 21,000-acre retreat now owned by the Presbyterian Church, is famous for several things: First, Georgia O'Keeffe owned a small parcel of the land and maintained a studio here (a drawing she did of a cow skull is now the ranch's logo). Then, in 1947, paleontologists combing the red hills discovered about a thousand skeletons of the dinosaur *Coelophysis* ("hollow form," for its hollow, birdlike bones), the largest group discovered in the world. More recently, the dramatic red cliffs have formed the backdrop of such essential westerns as *City Slickers* and *Silverado.*

The grounds are open to visitors by day, to see the **Florence Hawley Ellis Museum of Anthropology** and the **Ruth Hall Museum of Paleontology** (9 A.M.–5 P.M. Tues.–Sat., $2), which have small but interesting collections displaying the local finds, including remnants of the prehistoric Gallina culture that lived on the ridge above the valley, santos carved by sixth-generation New Mexican Max Roybal, and an eight-ton chunk of *Coelophysis*-filled siltstone in the process of being excavated.

Both museums are also open 1–5 P.M. on Sundays in the summer. Guided tours of the ranch grounds, with an emphasis on O'Keeffe's legacy, run mid-March–November (Tues., Thurs., and Sat., $20).

You can also hike on your own after registering with reception. The best trek, which takes about 1.5 hours round-trip, is to **Chimney Rock,** a towering landmark with panoramic views of the entire area. Don't be daunted—the steepest part of the trail is at the start—but do slather on the sunscreen, as there's no shade on this route. **Box Canyon** is an easier, shadier, all-level walk that's about four miles round-trip. **Kitchen Mesa Trail,** which starts at the same point, is much more difficult, requiring some climbing to get up the cliffs at the end (though you could hike the easy first two-thirds, then turn around).

## Echo Amphitheater

This bandshell-shape rock formation, a natural wonder of acoustics, is a great place to let kids run around and yell to their hearts' content. It's four miles north of Ghost Ranch; there are pleasant picnic areas tucked among the brush and a couple of campsites ($2 day-use).

## Food and Accommodations

The **Abiquiu Inn** functions as the area's visitors center. Its restaurant (8 A.M.–8 P.M., $7) serves *barbacoa* wraps and other modern Mexican dishes, as well as bigger entrées like grilled trout. Lodging ($89 d) consists of some pretty casitas at the back of the property, with great views of the river, and a cluster of motel rooms closer to the front (opt for rooms 2–6, which face away from the road). Midway between Española and Abiquiu, **Casa del Rio B&B** (505/753-2035, casadelrio@newmexico.com, $100 d) is an earthy ranch house smack up against a towering red cliff. Escape out here for dense stars at night and a meditation room during the day.

You can also stay at **Ghost Ranch** (U.S. 84, 505/685-4333, www.ghostranch.org) when it's not full for retreats—cabins start at

$45, or you can camp for $16. Thirteen miles down a rocky dirt track, **Christ in the Desert Monastery** (Forest Rd. 151, www.christdesert.org, $50 s) delivers on solitude; overnight visitors are welcome in the hermitage section for a suggested donation. Out the same road (at the 11.5-mile mark), **Rio Chama Campground** is remote but beautiful—preferable to Abiquiu Lake if you really want to get away from it all.

## THE HIGH ROAD TO TAOS

Córdova, Truchas, Las Trampas, Peñasco—these are the tiny villages strung, like beads on a necklace, along the winding highway north through the mountains. This is probably the area of New Mexico where Spanish heritage has been least diluted—or at least relatively untouched by Anglo influence, for there has been an exchange between the Spanish towns and the adjacent pueblos. In any case, the local dialect is distinctive, and residents can claim ancestors who settled the towns in the 18th century. The first families learned to survive in the harsh climate with a 90-day growing season, and much of the technology that worked then continues to work now; electricity was still scarce even in the 1970s, and adobe construction is common. These communities, closed off by geography, can seem a little insular to visitors, but pop in at the galleries that have sprung up in a couple of the towns, and you'll get a warm welcome. And during the **High Road Arts Tour** (www.highroadnewmexico.com), over two weekends in September, craftspeople famed particularly for their wood-carving skills open their home studios.

The drive straight through takes only about an hour and a half, but leave time to dawdle at churches and galleries, take a hike, or have lunch along the way. There's also an excellent overnight hike just north of Las Trampas. Start the driving route by leaving Santa Fe via North St. Francis Road, then continuing on U.S. 84/285 to the junction with Highway 503; turn right, following signs for Nambé Pueblo.

### Nambé Pueblo

To the right off Highway 503 just a few miles is **Nambé Falls Recreation Area** (505/455-2304, $5 day-use fee), open to the public for swimming and fishing; it also has beautiful camping spots. The highlight is the falls themselves, a double cascade through a narrow crevice, marking the break between the Sangre de Cristo Mountains and the Española Basin.

Nambé Pueblo was a major religious center from its founding around 1300 until the conquest; as such, it received unfortunately thorough attention from the Catholic church and was nearly destroyed. Today it's home to about 1,700 people, and much of its culture has blended with the surrounding Hispano villages. The Nambé line of high-end housewares has nothing to do with the pueblo—weaving and micaceous pottery are some of the traditional crafts here. The biggest annual event is Fourth of July, celebrated with dances and a crafts market.

### ◖ Chimayó

Continue on Highway 503 to a T junction where you make a hard left to follow the main road and begin the descent into the valley of Chimayó, site of the largest mass pilgrimage in the United States. During Holy Week, some 50,000 people arrive in town on foot, starting days in advance to arrive on Good Friday and often bearing large crosses (or at least police-issued glow-sticks while they're walking the highways at night). Smaller crowds participate in pilgrimages on Mother's Day and in early June.

The inspiration for the group treks, a tradition begun in 1945 as a commemoration of the Bataan Death March, is the **Santuario de Chimayó** (www.holychimayo.us, 9 A.M.–4 P.M. daily Oct.–Apr., 9 A.M.–6 P.M. May–Sept.), a small chapel that has gained a reputation as a healing spot, as it was built in 1814 at the place where a local farmer, Bernardo Abeyta, is said to have dug up a miraculously glowing crucifix.

Unlike many of the older churches in this area, which are now open very seldom, Chimayó is an active place of prayer, always busy

# WALK ON, SANTO NIÑO

According to Spanish Catholic legend, when the Christians were battling the Moors in the medieval period, around 1300, the Muslims imprisoned a number of people after a particularly brutal battle in Atocha, near Madrid, and would not allow the captives' families to visit them. After many desperate prayers on the part of Atocha's Christian women, a mysterious child appeared, carrying food and water, to care for the prisoners, and the populace guessed that it must be the child Jesus. Thus Santo Niño de Atocha became the patron saint of prisoners, and he is still depicted carrying a pail for bread and a gourd for water and wearing a large hat emblazoned with a scallop shell, the symbol of pilgrims.

In northern New Mexico, the figure is a popular one – in Chimayó alone, the Santo Niño de Atocha is installed in the main Santuario de Chimayó, as well as in a separate 1857 chapel just a block away. He is seen now as a broader intercessor, an object of prayer not just for those imprisoned, but also for the chronically ill. New Mexicans have developed a unique folk practice, placing (too-small) baby shoes at the Santo Niño's feet, on the assumption that his own have worn out while he was walking in the night.

with tourists as well as visitors seeking solace. (Mass is said weekdays at 11 A.M. and on Sunday at noon year-round.) As you approach from the parking area, you will see that previous visitors have woven twigs into the chain-link fencing to form crosses, each set of sticks representing a prayer. Outdoor pews made of split tree trunks accommodate overflow crowds, and a wheelchair ramp gives easy access to the church.

But the little adobe chapel seems untouched by modernity. The front wall of the dim main chapel is filled with an elaborately painted altar screen from the first half of the 19th century,

the work of Molleno (nicknamed "the Chile Painter" because forms, especially robes, in his paintings often resemble red and green chiles). The vibrant colors seem to shimmer in the gloom, forming a sort of stage set for Abeyta's crucifix, Nuestro Señor de las Esquípulas, as the centerpiece. Painted on the screen above the crucifix is the symbol of the Franciscans: a cross over which the arms of Christ and Saint Francis meet.

But most visitors make their way directly to the small, low-ceiling antechamber that holds *el posito,* the little hole where the cross was allegedly first dug up. From this pit they scoop up a small portion of the exposed red earth, to later apply to withered limbs and arthritic joints, or to eat in hopes of curing internal ailments. (The parish refreshes the well each year with new dirt, after it has been blessed by the priests.) The adjacent sacristy, formerly filled with hand-written testimonials, prayers, and abandoned crutches, is now a bit tidier and devoted to a shrine for Santo Niño de Atocha, a figurine that is also said to have been dug out of the holy ground here.

Chimayó has also been a weaving center for centuries, commercially known since 1900, when local Hispano weavers started selling locally crafted "Indian" blankets to tourists. **Ortega's** (County Rd. 98, 505/351-2288, 9 A.M.–5 P.M. Mon.–Sat., 10 A.M.–4 P.M. Sun.) is one of the longest-established shops, at the intersection with Highway 76. Right around the corner from Ortega's is the tiny **Chimayó Museum** (505/351-0945, www.chimayomuseum.org, 11 A.M.–3 P.M. Tues.–Sat. Apr.–Sept., free), on the old fortified plaza and housing a neat collection of vintage photographs.

If you want to spend the night in the area, **Casa Escondida** (Hwy. 76, 505/351-4805, www.casaescondida.com, $99 d) is a lovely place, with a big backyard, a hot tub, and a sunny garden.

For lunch head right across the parking lot from the Santuario de Chimayó to **Leona's** (505/351-4569, 11 A.M.–5 P.M. Thurs.–Mon., $2), where you can pick up bulk chile and pistachios as well as delicious tamales and crumbly *bizcochitos*. For a more leisurely sit-down lunch, **Rancho de Chimayó** (County Rd. 98, 505/351-4444, www.ranchodechimayo.com, 11:30 A.M.–9 P.M. Tues.–Sun. Nov.–Apr., 11:30 A.M.–9 P.M. daily May–Oct., $9) offers great red chile on a beautiful terrace—or inside the old adobe home by the fireplace in wintertime. The place is also open for breakfast on weekends, 8:30–10 A.M., and it's a popular special-occasion spot for Santa Feans.

## Córdova

Turning east (right) on Highway 76 (west takes you directly to Española), you begin the climb back up the Sangre de Cristo Mountains. Near the crest of the hill, about three miles up, a small sign points right and down into Quemado Valley to Córdova, a village best known for its unpainted, austere santos and *bultos* done by masters such as George López and José Dolores López. Another family member, **Sabinita López Ortiz** (9 County Rd. 1317, 505/351-4572, variable hours), sells her work and that

of five other generations of wood-carvers. **Castillo Gallery** (County Rd. 1317, 505/351-4067, variable hours) mixes traditional styles with more contemporary work.

## Truchas

Highway 76 continues to wind along the peaks, eventually reaching the little village of Truchas (Trout), founded in 1754 and still not much more than a long row of buildings set into the ridgeline and facing the expansive valley below. On the corner where the highway makes a hard left to Taos is the village *morada,* the meeting place of the local Penitente brotherhood; head straight down the smaller road to reach the old **Nuestra Señora del Rosario de Truchas Church,** tucked into a small plaza off to the right of the main street. It's open to visitors only June–August—if you do have a chance to look inside the dim, thick-walled mission, you'll see precious examples of local wood carving. Though many of the more delicate ones have been moved to the Taylor Museum in Colorado Springs, those remaining display

Truchas Peak

© ZORA O'NEILL

an essential New Mexican style—the sort of "primitive" thing that Bishop Lamy hated; they're preserved today only because Truchas residents hid them in their houses during the late 19th century. Santa Lucia, with her eyeballs in her hand, graces the altar, and a finely wrought crucifix hangs to the right, clad in a skirt because the legs have broken off.

In this part of town, you'll also find the most established gallery, **Hand Artes** (505/689-2443, variable hours)—Jack Silverman's silk-screen prints of American Indian textile patterns are particularly fine. If you keep going down the road out of town, you'll eventually reach the beautifully isolated **Rancho Arriba Bed & Breakfast** (Hwy. 76, 505/689-2374, www.ranchoarriba.com, $70 d), a farmhouse built by hand by its owner. Guests no longer have to use an outhouse, but breakfasts are still cooked on a wood stove.

## ◖ Las Trampas

Back on Highway 76, heading toward Taos, the village of Las Trampas was settled in 1751, and its showpiece, **San José de Gracia Church** (10 A.M.–4 P.M. Sat. and Sun. June–Aug.), was built nine years later. It remains one of the finest examples of New Mexican village church architecture. Its thick adobe walls, which are covered with a fresh coat of mud every year or two, are balanced by vertical bell towers; inside, the clerestory at the front of the church—a very typical design—lets light in to shine down on the altar, which was carved and painted in the late 1700s. Other paradigmatic elements: the *atrio,* or small plaza between the low adobe boundary wall and the church itself, utilized as a cemetery; and the dark narthex, where you enter, confined by the choir loft above, but only serving to emphasize the sense of light and space created in the rest of the church by the clerestory and the small windows near the viga ceiling. Unfortunately, chances are slim that you'll be in town when the church is open—but it's worth trying the door anyhow.

As you leave the town heading north, look to the right—you'll see a centuries-old acequia

that has been channeled through a log flume to cross a small arroyo. Less than a mile north of the village, you pass the turn for El Valle and Forest Road 207, which leads to the **Trampas Lakes** trailhead. This 6.1-mile hike goes through gorgeous alpine scenery—steep rock walls jutting up from dense forest, myriad wildflowers, and the two lakes themselves, which are clear and frigid. A spur trail at the last junction leads to Hidden Lake (2 miles round-trip). This route makes a very pleasant overnight trek, giving you time to fish and relax at the end, but with an early start, you could also do the trail as an intense all-day outing.

## Peñasco

The next community along the road is Peñasco, best known to tourists as the home of the delicious **Sugar Nymphs Bistro** (15046 Hwy. 76, 505/587-0311, 11 A.M.–2:30 P.M. and 5:30–8 P.M. Thurs.–Sat., 11 A.M.–2 P.M. Sun., $10), where you can get all kinds of treats such as grilled lamb, fresh-pressed cider, piñon couscous, and pizzas. Hours can be more limited in the winter, so it's best to call ahead. If you've already eaten lunch, stop in **Peñasco Valley Food Store** (8 A.M.–6 P.M. daily) for an ice-cream cone or root-beer float. This is also the northern gateway to the **Pecos Wilderness Area**—turn on Forest Road 116 to reach Santa Barbara Campground and the Santa Barbara Trail to Truchas Peak, a 23-mile round-trip that requires a good amount of advance planning.

## Picurís Pueblo

For all the signs that point to Picurís, from every possible surrounding highway, you would imagine it's a glittery tourist extravaganza. In fact, as one of the few Rio Grande pueblos that has not established a casino, Picurís Pueblo instead capitalizes on its beautiful natural setting, a lush valley where bison roam and aspen leaves rustle. You can picnic here or dine at the **Hidden Valley Restaurant,** or fish in small but well-stocked Tu-Tah Lake. After the **San Lorenzo de Picurís Church** collapsed due to water damage in 1989, pueblo members rebuilt it by hand, following exactly the form of the original 1776 design—a process that took eight years. A museum tells the history of the pueblo, the smallest in New Mexico, with only a few hundred members, and along with Taos Pueblo, the only Tiwa-speakers. As at Nambé, local traditions have melded with those of the surrounding villages; the Hispano-Indian Matachines dances are well attended on Christmas Eve. Start at the **visitors center** (505/587-1099, 10 A.M.–5 P.M. Mon.–Sat.) to pick up maps and tips. The pueblo is a short detour from the high road proper: Just past Peñasco, turn left (west) from Highway 76 onto a well-marked access road, which leads to the pueblo in a few miles.

## Sipapu

Detouring right (east) along Highway 518, you reach Sipapu (Hwy. 518, 800/587-2240, www.sipapunm.com), an unassuming, inexpensive **ski resort**—really, just a handful of cabins at the base of a 9,255-foot mountain. Cheap lift tickets ($36/day) and utter quiet make this a bargain getaway.

You can also take a nice afternoon hike along **Cañon Tio Maes,** a two-mile trail up to a meadow filled with flowers and aspen trees—plan about 2.5 hours for a leisurely round-trip. A longer hike—more like 6 miles and 4 hours round-trip—goes to **Gallegos Peak** (10,258 feet), where you can look over to the snow-capped Truchas Peaks, another 2,800 feet up. The Cañon Tio Maes trailhead (no. 5) is 3.2 miles east on Highway 518, before you reach Sipapu; it's unmarked coming from this direction—look for a paved road on the left side that doubles back along the highway for a short stretch. For Gallegos Peak, drive to the Flechado Canyon Campground, 5.4 miles east of the junction, immediately past Sipapu; the trailhead is across the road.

Returning to the junction, continue on to Taos via Highway 518, which soon descends into a valley and passes **Pot Creek Cultural Site** (505/587-2255, 9 A.M.–4 P.M. Wed.–Sun. July–Aug.), a mildly interesting diversion for its one-mile loop trail through ancestral Puebloan

ruins from around 1100. You arrive in Taos at its very southern end—really, in Ranchos de Taos, just north of the San Francisco de Asis Church on Highway 68. Turn left to see the church, or turn right to head up to the town plaza and to Taos Pueblo.

## THE LOW ROAD TO TAOS

The lush farmland around the Rio Grande is the highlight of this drive north—this valley filled with apple orchards is as green as New Mexico gets. The road is at first a bit unpromising, as it passes through the modern town of Española, but it soon winds into an ever-narrower canyon and finally arrives on the llano, the dramatic point where the high plains meet the mountains. This route is more direct than the high road and has fewer scenic stopping points, so if you're pressed for time, this is the way to go.

## Alcalde

The chief attraction in this riverside farm town, **Historic Los Luceros Museum** (505/852-1895, 8:30 A.M.–5 P.M. daily Apr.–Oct., by appointment Nov.–Mar.), is eight miles north of Española; turn left across from the Oñate monument onto County Road 0048, which dead-ends after half a mile at the gates to the ranch.

The 140-acre spread is the former home of Boston heiress Mary Cabot Wheelwright, who lived here 1923–1958 and established what's now the Wheelwright Museum of the American Indian in Santa Fe. After much restoration work on the Casa Grande—the main two-story territorial-style house—it was opened to the public in 2004. Visitors can tour the main house and its period furnishings, often with the help of docents who have lived or worked on the property since Wheelwright's time. Outside, donkeys, goats, rabbits, and the occasional peacock stroll the grounds, which are maintained as a working farm and orchard, and the *bosque* is flourishing with cottonwoods and willows.

Next door to the farm, you can visit **Ice's Tea Room** (County Rd. 1097, 505/852-2589, www.icestearoom.com, noon–5 P.M. Tues., Wed., and Thurs. Mar.–Nov., $20) for an afternoon tea made from local organic ingredients; call ahead, though—it's by reservation only.

## Embudo

The village of Embudo is really just a bend in the river, but it offers a couple of good eating options. First up is beautiful **Embudo Station** (Hwy. 68, 505/852-4707, 11:30 A.M.–9 P.M. Tues.–Sun. Apr.–Oct., $14), a little lodge right on the water where you can have a lunch of smoked trout under the shade of a big cottonwood; wash it down with a house-brewed beer. Friday–Sunday, **Sugar's** (Hwy. 68, 505/852-0604, 11 A.M.–7 P.M. Wed.–Mon., $5), just up the road on the right, does a big barbecue dinner with ribs, brisket, sausage, and two sides; the rest of the week you can get a simple pulled-pork sandwich or chicken-fried steak. It's take-out only, but there are a few plastic picnic tables where you can sit down. Just around the bend is the enigmatic **Classical Gas Museum,** a haphazard array of vintage pumps and old gas-guzzlers, with grass growing up around their bases. Rarely is anyone ever around to explain the collection.

If you're into wine, keep an eye out for the various wineries just north of here: **Vivác** is on the main highway (2075 Hwy. 68, 505/579-4441, 10 A.M.–6 P.M. Mon.–Sat., noon–6 P.M. Sun.), and **La Chiripada** (505/579-4437, 10 A.M.–5 P.M. Mon.–Sat., noon–5 P.M. Sun.)

is down Highway 75 a few miles in the pleasant little gallery/farming town of Dixon.

## Pilar

This small cluster of houses is best known as a river access point. Beginning just south of Pilar and stretching several miles north, **Orilla Verde Recreation Area** ($3 parking) is public land along either side of the Rio Grande, used primarily as a put-in or haul-out for **rafting,** but you can **camp** on the riverbanks as well—Petaca and Taos Junction are the best campgrounds ($7 per night). The **Vista Verde Trail** runs about 1.2 miles one-way along the west rim, an easy walk with great views and a few petroglyphs to spot in a small arroyo about a third of the way out; the trailhead is half a mile up the hill from the Taos Junction Bridge, on Highway 567 (turn left off the highway in Pilar, then follow signs into Orilla Verde). Stop first on the main highway at the **Rio Grande Gorge Visitors Center** for maps and other information (Hwy. 68, 505/758-8851, 7:45 A.M.–4:30 P.M. Mon.–Sat. June–Aug.). Across the road, **Pilar Yacht Club** (Hwy. 68, 505/758-9072, 7:30 A.M.–6:30 P.M. daily) is the center of the action, serving food to hungry river rats and functioning as an office for a couple of outfitters; TNM&O buses to and from Taos also stop here. You can also go horseback riding nearby with **Cieneguilla Stables** (505/751-2815, melcieneguillastables@hotmail.com), starting at about $40 per hour.

# Information and Services

## TOURIST INFORMATION

The **Santa Fe Convention and Visitors Bureau** (800/777-2489, www.santafe.org) maintains a small information kiosk with a helpful staff in the Sweeney Convention Center on West Marcy Street, at the corner of Grant Avenue (8 A.M.–5 P.M. Mon.–Fri.). This is smaller but better located than the **visitors center** near San Miguel Chapel (491 Old Santa Fe Tr., 505/827-7336, 8 A.M.–

5 P.M. Mon.–Fri.), which is run by the New Mexico Department of Tourism.

For info on the outdoors, head out to the very comprehensive **Public Lands Information Center** (1474 Rodeo Rd., 505/438-7840, www.publiclands.org, 9 A.M.–4:30 P.M. Mon.–Fri.) on the far south side of town—you can pick up heaps of free flyers, including detailed route descriptions for the most popular area day hikes, as well as buy guidebooks, detailed topo maps for all the wilderness areas, and hunting and fishing licenses.

## Books and Maps

Santa Fe has two particularly good bookshops right in the center of town. **Travel Bug** (839 Paseo de Peralta, 505/992-0418, 7:30 A.M.–5:30 P.M. Mon.–Sat., 10 A.M.–3 P.M. Sun.) specializes in maps, travel guides, gear like luggage and GPS gadgets, and free advice. The stock of New Mexico hiking and other outdoor guides is especially thorough, and you can load up on topo maps here if you're headed out to the woods. For more general stock, **Collected Works** (208-B W. San Francisco St., 505/988-4226, 9 A.M.–9 P.M. Mon.–Sat., 10 A.M.–6 P.M. Sun.), directly across from The Lensic, is the place to go—excellent staff recommendations, and a trove of local-interest titles.

## Local Media

The *Santa Fe New Mexican* is Santa Fe's daily paper, which publishes events listings and gallery news in its *Pasatiempo* insert on Fridays. For left-of-center news and commentary and an exceptionally good food column by Gwyneth Doland, the *Santa Fe Reporter* is the free weekly rag, available in most coffee shops and cafés.

## Radio

Santa Fe supports a number of niche radio stations: KLBU (102.9 FM) brings Ibiza-style chill-out electronica to the mountains, while "Lucky's Belvedere Lounge," a rockabilly fest on Thursday nights, is one of the most popular shows on KBAC (98.1 FM) a.k.a. Radio Free Santa Fe. Tune in Friday afternoons for news on the gallery scene. For NPR news and other public radio programs, tune in to KSFR (90.7 FM).

# SERVICES
## Banks

**First National Bank of Santa Fe** (62 Lincoln Ave., 505/992-2000, 9 A.M.–5 P.M. Mon.–Fri.) is on the west side of the plaza. **First State Bank** (100 N. Guadalupe St., 505/946-4100, 9 A.M.–5 P.M. Mon.–Thurs., 9 A.M.–6 P.M. Sat.) is walking distance from the plaza, but also easily accessible by car.

## Post Office

Santa Fe's **main post office** (120 S. Federal Place, 505/988-2239, 8:30 A.M.–5:30 P.M. Mon.–Fri., 9 A.M.–4 P.M. Sat.) is just north of the plaza, behind Sweeney Convention Center and near the district courthouse.

## Internet

**Travel Bug** (839 Paseo de Peralta, 505/992-0418, 7:30 A.M.–5:30 P.M. Mon.–Sat., 10 A.M.–3 P.M. Sun.) bookstore offers free Internet access and also serves coffee. **Santa Fe Public Library** (145 Washington St., 505/955-6780, www.santafelibrary.org, 10 A.M.–9 P.M. Mon.–Thurs., 10 A.M.–6 P.M. Fri. and Sat., 1–5 P.M. Sun.) has several public Internet terminals with free access; call ahead to reserve a time slot if you can.

## Laundry

Most self-service laundromats are located on or near Cerrillos Road. One of the largest and nicest is **St. Michael's Laundry** (1605 St. Michael's Dr., 505/989-9375, 6 A.M.–11 P.M. daily), across from the College of Santa Fe, a couple of blocks east of Cerrillos Road. For drop-off service that's a bit cheaper than what most hotels offer, try **La Unica Quality Cleaners** (647 Cerrillos Rd., 505/983-1182, 7:30 A.M.–6 P.M. Mon.–Fri., 9 A.M.–3 P.M. Sat.) or **New Method Cleaners** (1911 St. Michael's Dr., 505/982-0271, 7 A.M.–6 P.M. Mon.–Fri., 9 A.M.–1 P.M. Sat.).

# Getting There and Around

## BY AIRPLANE

**Santa Fe Airport** (SAF; 505/955-2900) isn't really a viable option. The small airstrip southeast of the city receives flights only from Denver, on **Great Lakes Aviation** (800/554-5111, www.greatlakesav.com)—so it's better to fly via Albuquerque (ABQ), less than an hour's drive away.

## BY CAR

**Hertz, Budget, Avis,** and **Thrifty** all have branches on Cerrillos Road; only **Enterprise** (100 Sandoval St., 505/989-8859) has an office close to the plaza. **Best Car Rental** (3281 Cerrillos Rd., 505/473-4852, 9 A.M.–6 P.M. Mon.–Fri., 9 A.M.–5 P.M. Sat.) is the only locally owned operation.

## BY BUS AND SHUTTLE

**Santa Fe Shuttle** (888/833-2300, www.sfshuttle.com) runs a shuttle van from the Albuquerque airport to various hotels in Santa Fe eight times daily 6:30 A.M.–10:45 P.M. ($21 one-way). **Sandia Shuttle Express** (888/775-5696, www.sandiashuttle.com) does hourly pickups from the airport 8:45 A.M.–10:45 P.M. and will deliver to any hotel or B&B ($23 one-way).

**TNM&O** (806/763-5389, www.tnmo.com) typically runs from Albuquerque's main bus station three times daily to Santa Fe, arriving in Santa Fe a little more than an hour later.

Coming from Taos, TNM&O's service leaves once a day, in the early evening; the trip takes about an hour and half. Santa Fe's **main bus station** is at 858 St. Michael's Drive (505/471-0008).

Within town, the reasonably useful city bus system, **Santa Fe Trails** (505/955-2001, www.santafenm.gov), can take you to all of the major sights from the handy central depot on Sheridan Street just north of the plaza. The "M" route goes to Museum Hill; Route 2 runs along Cerrillos Road, and Route 6 goes down to Rodeo Road, past the Public Lands Office and the community center. Buses on all routes don't run very frequently—generally, between every 30 and 60 minutes—so check out the schedule first. The Museum Hill and Cerrillos Road buses run on Sundays. Fare is $1.

## BY TRAIN

**Amtrak** (800/872-7245, www.amtrak.com) runs the Southwest Chief through Lamy, 18 miles south of Santa Fe and a dramatic place to step off the train—you'll feel very Wild West, as there's no visible civilization for miles around. Trains arrive daily at 2:24 P.M. from Chicago and at 2 P.M. from Los Angeles. Amtrak provides a shuttle van for passengers coming and going to Santa Fe.

# TAOS

Though adobe houses cluster around a plaza, and art galleries, organic bakeries, and yoga studios proliferate, the town of Taos is much more than a miniature Santa Fe. It's more isolated, reached by curving two-lane roads along either the winding mountain-ridge route or the fertile Rio Grande river valley, with a rougher, muddier feel. The glory of the landscape, from looming Taos Mountain to the staggered blue mesas dissolving into the flat western horizon, can be truly breathtaking; add to that the intense mysticism surrounding Taos Pueblo and the often wild creativity of the artists who have lived here, and the lure is irresistible. People flock here on pilgrimages—to the ranch where D. H. Lawrence lived, to the hip-deep powder on the slopes at Taos Ski Valley, to the San Francisco de Asis Church that Georgia O'Keeffe painted—then simply wind up staying. The waitress pouring your coffee probably has a variation on this same story.

Celebrity residents like Julia Roberts and Donald Rumsfeld have lent the place a certain reputation of wealth and exclusivity, but this is hardly the case: Spanish farmers in Valle Valdez scrape by on their acequia-fed farm plots just as they have for centuries; the same goes for residents of old Taos Pueblo, the living World Heritage Site that still uses no electricity or running water. Add to that a strong subculture of ski bums, artists, off-the-grid eco-homesteaders, and spiritual seekers, and you have a community that, while not typically prosperous, is more loyal and dedicated to preserving its unique way of life than perhaps any other small town in the western United States.

© ZORA O'NEILL

# HIGHLIGHTS

**◖ Taos Art Museum at Fechin House:** In the early 1930s, Russian artist Nicolai Fechin designed his home in a fantastical fusion of Tartar, Spanish, and American Indian styles. Today, his paintings hang next to the wood lintels and furniture he carved (page 96).

**◖ Millicent Rogers Museum:** A 1950s' socialite amassed an astounding trove of American Indian and Spanish artwork in just a few short years in Taos. Her collection is on view in her former house, and it provides a thorough introduction to the region's oldest cultures (page 97).

**◖ Mabel Dodge Luhan House:** See where America's counterculture thrived in the mid-20th century, as encouraged by the arts doyenne who made Taos her home. Countless writers, painters, and actors visited Mabel here in her idiosyncratic home (page 100).

**◖ San Francisco de Asis Church:** With its massive adobe buttresses and rich earthy glow, this 350-year-old Franciscan mission is one of the most recognizable in the world, thanks to its frequent depiction in paintings and photographs (page 101).

**◖ Taos Pueblo:** The stepped adobe buildings at New Mexico's most remarkable pueblo seem to rise organically from the earth. Don't miss the ceremonial dances here, about eight times a year (page 101).

**◖ Rio Grande Gorge:** Think how dismayed the first homesteaders must have been when they reached "New Mexico's Grand Canyon," an 800-foot-deep channel cut through the rock to the west of Taos. Think how overjoyed today's whitewater rafters are in the spring, when mountain run-off surges through the rift (page 103).

**◖ Taos Ski Valley:** This is the purist's mountain: deep powder, no pretension—and no snowboards. Don't ski? Drive up here just to crane your neck up at the top, and consider taking lessons (page 107).

**◖ Vietnam Veterans National Memorial:** Set on a low ridge overlooking the bowl of a high valley, this elegant white chapel, erected in 1969, was built to honor one man's fallen son. Since then, it's grown to become a national monument (page 125).

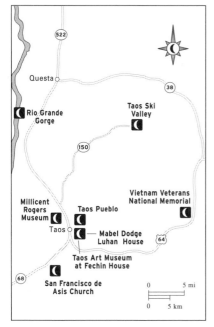

LOOK FOR ◖ TO FIND RECOMMENDED SIGHTS, ACTIVITIES, DINING, AND LODGING.

**TAOS**

North and east from Taos, the grandly named **Enchanted Circle** scenic byway loops around Wheeler Peak, the highest mountain in New Mexico at 13,161 feet. The area was settled primarily by miners and ranchers in the late 19th century, so it has a different atmosphere from centuries-old Spanish-and-Indian Taos. Along the way, you can stop at a mining ghost town, a moving Vietnam veterans' memorial, or a rowdy Old West–style steakhouse. Likewise, the ski resorts of Angel Fire and Red River offer a somewhat less extreme, but no less fun, alternative to Taos Ski Valley.

## PLANNING YOUR TIME

Taos's busiest tourist season is the arid summer, when a day's entertainment can consist simply of gallery-hopping then settling in to watch the afternoon thunderheads gather and churn, or the sun set under lurid red streaks across the broad western mesas. Wintertime is of course busy with skiers between November and April, but as they're all up on the mountain during the day, museums scale back their hours, and residents reclaim the town center, curled up with books at one of the many coffee shops. The Taos Pueblo also closes to visitors for up to 10 weeks in February and March. By May, the peaks are relatively clear of snow, and you can hike to high meadows filled with wildflowers; fall is dominated by the smell of wood smoke and the beat of drums, as the pueblo and the rest of the town turn out for the Feast of San Geronimo at the end of September.

If you're coming straight from Albuquerque, the trip takes about 2.5 hours along the slightly more direct "low road" through the river valley, or 3 hours along the high road; you'll want to stay over at least a couple of nights to make the drive worthwhile. From Santa Fe, it's possible to visit Taos as a day trip—as hundreds do in the summertime—but you'll of course get a better sense of the place if you stay overnight. A three- or four-night visit will give you a chance to explore at a leisurely pace, with an afternoon at Taos Pueblo, a couple of mornings at galleries and museums, time for hiking or

skiing, and a day tour of the Enchanted Circle. But you can also get a nice taste of Taos over a weekend, and a number of distinctive bed-and-breakfasts make it a perfect place for a short romantic getaway.

As for the Enchanted Circle, the 84-mile drive is typically done as a day trip, but you may want to stay overnight in the old gambling town of Eagle Nest or in Red River (a.k.a. "Little Texas"), the better to take in the skiing, hiking, and rock climbing in the area. By no means attempt to visit Taos and do the Enchanted Circle loop in a single day—you'd be terribly rushed, and this is hardly the spirit of Taos.

## HISTORY

The first full-time inhabitants of the area at the base of Taos Mountain were Tiwa-speaking descendants of the Ancestral Puebloans (also called Anasazi) who migrated from the Four Corners area in around A.D. 1000. Taos, from Tiwa for "place of the red willows," was a thriving village when Spanish explorers, part of Francisco de Coronado's crew, arrived in 1540. By 1615, settlers had arrived and established their own small community.

The Spanish initially had difficulty establishing a toehold, however. The Pueblo Revolt of 1680, led by Popé in Taos, succeeded in driving Spanish settlers out of New Mexico for 12 years. Under the heavy hand of Governor Diego de Vargas, most of the area was reclaimed in 1692, but the Taos Pueblo Indians held out for four more violent years before they formally surrendered. The only thing that held the truce was that the Pueblo people and the Spanish both had to defend themselves against Comanche and Jicarilla raiders.

By the middle of the 18th century, Taos had become moderately more secure and was an integral part of a brisk trade network, thanks in part to French fur trappers who had discovered wealth in beaver pelts from the lakes in the surrounding mountains. The little village became a place to gather and swap goods brought from Mexico and in from the surrounding wilderness. At the trade fairs, rug-

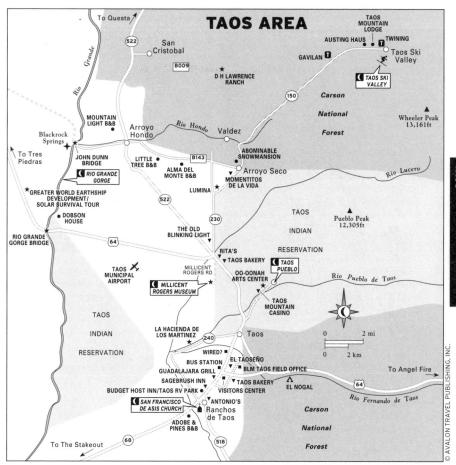

**TAOS AREA**

ged mountain men met and mingled with wealthy Spanish merchants, mule-train runners up from Mexico, and local Indians selling their wares.

Early in Taos's history, the population was so scarce and life so hard that it took only one energetic person to have a significant impact. Padre Antonio José Martínez, son of an established trader, was one of the area's most dynamic leaders in the first half of the 19th century. In 1835, he acquired the first printing press in the American west and began producing books and a newspaper, *El Crepus-culo de Libertad,* which was published off and on well into the 20th century; he also established a co-ed school, a seminary, and a law school. Jean-Baptiste Lamy, the Frenchman appointed bishop of Santa Fe in 1853, earned the enmity of Taoseños by curtailing the popular Padre Martínez's work, even filing an order to excommunicate him. Although the papers don't appear to have been processed, Martínez claimed to have been cast out of the church, and he set up a private chapel at his house, from which he ministered until he died in 1867.

# TAOS IN PRINT

Just as San Francisco de Asis Church has inspired countless painters and photographers, the people of Taos and their struggles have found their way into novels and short stories, covered with only the barest veneer of fiction – but that's because the true stories happen to be just as fascinating as what any writer could dream up.

First brush up on the basic tales floating around town with Bill Hemp's *Taos Landmarks & Legends* (Boulder: University Press of Colorado, 2002), which dedicates chapters to historical figures like Kit Carson as well as more recent Taos happenings, such as the dynamics behind the New Buffalo commune. It's all served up with a generous sprinkling of anecdotes, hearsay, and even recipes.

One of Taos's more revered figures is Padre Antonio Martinez, a popular priest and leader in the mid-1800s. So some Taos residents aren't fond of Willa Cather's *Death Comes for the Archbishop* (New York: Vintage, 1990), even if it is a highly lauded literary classic. The 1927 novel is based on the mission of Jean Baptiste Lamy, who became archbishop of Santa Fe, with sympathy for his efforts to straighten out "rogue" Mexican priests like Martinez. The *padre* gets more balanced coverage in *Lamy of Santa Fe* (Middletown, Conn.: Wesleyan University Press, 2003), a biography by Paul Horgan that won a Pulitzer Prize after it was published in 1975.

Frank Waters, famous Western novelist and a Taos resident for almost 50 years, fictionalized the story of Edith Warner, a woman who ran a small café frequented by the Los Alamos scientists while they were developing the nuclear bomb. *The Woman at Otowi Crossing* (Athens, Ohio: Swallow Press, 1987) is his portrait of a woman who seeks isolation in the New Mexico wilderness but is nonetheless drawn back into the world through the largest event of her time. The novel is very true to Warner's life, but it's rounded out nicely by a full biography, *The House at Otowi Bridge: The Story of Edith Warner & Los Alamos* (Albuquerque: University of New Mexico Press, 1979), written by Peggy Pond Church, who herself lived at Los Alamos for 20 years, in the years before the area was taken over by the military.

Another Taos writer, John Nichols, earned acclaim for his comic novel *The Milagro Beanfield War* (New York: Owl Books, 2000), which was later made into a film by Robert Redford. The war of the title is an escalating squabble in a tiny New Mexican village over the acequia, the traditional irrigation ditch that's still used in Valle Valdez and other agricultural communities in the area. But if you think it takes comic melodrama and a star like Redford to make irrigation interesting, look into the beautiful and fascinating *Mayordomo: Chronicle of an Acequia in Northern New Mexico* (Albuquerque: University of New Mexico Press, 1993), Stanley Crawford's memoir about his term as "ditch boss" in the valley where he runs his garlic farm.

And if that's all too highbrow, you can find pure pulp in Ruth Laughlin's *The Wind Leaves No Shadow* (Caldwell, Id.: Caxton, 1978), a bodice-ripper based on the steamy life of Doña Barcelo Tules, who was born a pauper but grew up to be a powerful madam and gambling queen in 1830s Taos, then decamped to Santa Fe to run a high-end card house. She was the lover of Manuel Armijo, the last Mexican governor of New Mexico, then attended the U.S. Victory Ball in 1846 on the arm of American general Stephen Kearny. Allegedly.

When Mexico declared its independence from Spain in 1821, little changed for Taos, but the transition to U.S. rule in 1846, following the Mexican-American war, caused much more upheaval. Wealthy Spanish landowners and Catholic priests (including Padre Martinez) both foresaw their loss of influence under the Americans and secretly plotted a rebellion. Twice delayed, it finally started January 19, 1847, as the leaders incited a mob, many of them Indian, to kill New Mexico's first American governor, the veteran merchant Charles Bent; elsewhere in town and the larger region, scores of other Anglo landowners were massacred before U.S. cavalry came from Santa Fe to squelch the uprising.

The last half of the 1800s saw the establishment of a mining industry in Twining (now Taos Ski Valley) and a gold rush in nearby Elizabethtown, but the 1879 arrival of the railroad in Raton to the north bumped Taos from its role as trading hub, and it slipped into backwater status. Nonetheless, the era brought colorful characters to town, some of whom would soon work their way into local legends. The six-foot-tall outlaw "Long" John Dunn, for instance, made a business in toll bridges across the Rio Grande (only one of the three survived the ravages of floodwaters), monopolizing road travel to the west; he also set up a gamblers' hotel and was the first car owner in Taos. He finally died in 1955.

Equally legendary: Bert Geer Phillips and Ernest Blumenschein, two painters on a jaunt from Denver in the summer of 1898 who "discovered" Taos when their wagon wheel snapped near town. After being happily waylaid in this inspirational place, Phillips stayed, marrying the town doctor's sister, Rose Martin; Blumenschein eventually returned with others, such as Oscar E. Berninghaus, Eadgar Irving Couse, Joseph Sharp, and W. Herbert "Buck" Dunton. Together, the six established the Taos Society of Artists (TSA) in 1915. In the 12 years of the TSA's existence, not only did these and other artists make names for themselves as painters of the American West, but they also put Taos on the map. A deal with the Santa Fe Railway even promoted travel in exotic New Mexico with works by TSA painters in its brochures and posters. In another forward-thinking move, in 1923, Bert Phillips and Victor Higgins encouraged a wealthy local widow to donate some of her property for a permanent home for the TSA's legacy from the previous eight years; the Harwood Museum is still open on Ledoux Street. The TSA name also helped creative locals survive in the lean years—during the Depression, the Works Progress Administration funded several projects in the area, including the work of master wood-carver Patrocinio Barela, whose santos were later exhibited at the Museum of Modern Art in New York City.

More important, the TSA piqued the curiosity of influential East Coasters. One was Mabel Dodge Luhan, a well-off, free-thinking woman who had fostered art salons in New York City and Florence, then decamped to Taos in 1916, much to the fascination of cultural critics of the day. Her name is now inextricably linked with Taos's 20th-century history because she had an eye for budding artists and writers and encouraged them to come live with and meet one another at one of her several homes around town; by the 1920s, D. H. Lawrence, who spent some time in Taos at her behest, had taken to calling the place "Mabeltown," and figures as grand and varied as Greta Garbo, Willa Cather, Ansel Adams, Georgia O'Keeffe, Robinson Jeffers, and Carl Jung were making the long trek to this dusty mountain town. Mabel's steamy memoirs, published in the 1930s after Lawrence's death, reveal the feuds and affairs that fueled the massive creative output of this period.

The next generation, in the 1960s, was even more dedicated to living together and sharing ideas: This was when dedicated hippies, attracted by New Mexico's isolation, established several communes in the area. The New Buffalo commune in Arroyo Hondo inspired Dennis Hopper when he filmed *Easy Rider,* which in turn led to another wave of countercultural immigrants. Longtime locals, living by very traditional mores, were horrified at the naked, hallucinogen-ingesting, free-loving, long-haired aliens who had appeared in their midst; more than a decade of antagonism followed. Eventually, however, the most extreme communes disbanded and everyone mellowed a bit with age; even members of old Spanish families now talk about maximizing the solar gain of their adobe houses.

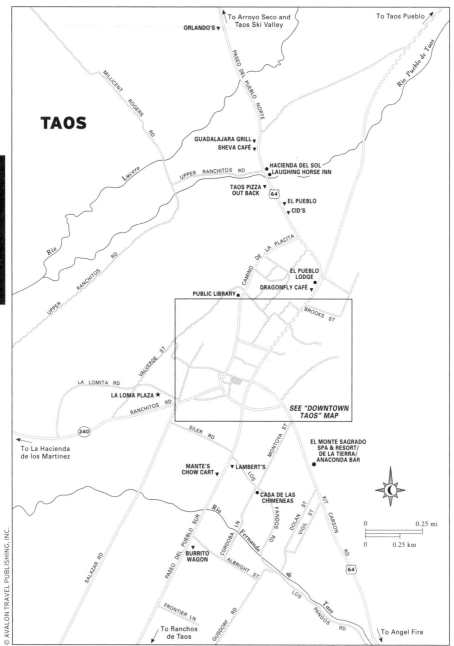

**TAOS**

To Arroyo Seco and
Taos Ski Valley

To Taos Pueblo

ORLANDO'S ▼

PASEO DEL PUEBLO NORTE

MILLICENT ROGERS RD

Rio Pueblo de Taos

GUADALAJARA GRILL ▼
SHEVA CAFÉ ▼

Lucero

UPPER RANCHITOS RD

HACIENDA DEL SOL
LAUGHING HORSE INN

TAOS PIZZA
OUT BACK ▼

64

● EL PUEBLO

▼ CID'S

Rio

UPPER     RANCHITOS     RD

CAMINO DE LA PLACITA

● EL PUEBLO
LODGE

DRAGONFLY CAFÉ ▼

PUBLIC LIBRARY ▪

BROOKS ST

VALVERDE ST

LA LOMITA RD

LA LOMA PLAZA ★

RANCHITOS RD

SEE "DOWNTOWN
TAOS" MAP

240

SILER RD

MONTOYA ST

EL MONTE SAGRADO
SPA & RESORT/
DE LA TIERRA/
ANACONDA BAR
●

To La Hacienda
de los Martinez

MANTE'S
CHOW CART ▼

▼ LAMBERT'S

LOS

● CASA DE LAS
CHIMENEAS

DOLAN LN

VIGIL ST

KIT CARSON RD

0          0.25 mi

0          0.25 km

Rio

PANDOS RD

CORDOBA LN

Fernando

SALAZAR RD

PASEO DEL PUEBLO SUR

▼ BURRITO
WAGON

ALBRIGHT ST

de

64

LOS PANDOS RD

Taos

FRONTIER LN

GUSDORF RD

To Ranchos
de Taos

To Angel Fire

# Sights

## ORIENTATION

The area usually referred to as Taos encompasses not only the historic old town, which fans out from a main plaza, but a number of smaller surrounding communities. If you come via the low road, on Highway 68, you pass first through Ranchos de Taos; once a distinct village, it's now connected to Taos Plaza by the least scenic part of town, a stretch of chain stores and cheap motels. Paseo del Pueblo Sur, as Highway 68 is called from Ranchos on, continues north to the central crossroads, the intersection with Kit Carson Road (a.k.a. U.S. 64).

After the light, the street name changes to Paseo del Pueblo Norte; where it curves west, at the northern end of the central business district, a smaller road continues north about two miles to Taos Pueblo. Paseo del Pueblo Norte carries on through the village of El Prado (now also overtaken by greater Taos) to a four-way intersection that will likely forever be called "the old blinking light," even though the flashing red signal was replaced with a newfangled three-color job in the 1990s. Here U.S. 64 regains its true name, shooting west to the Rio Grande, and Highway 522 leads northwest to the outlying village of Arroyo Hondo, then to Questa and the Enchanted Circle. Highway 150, commonly called Taos Ski Valley Road, goes north to Arroyo Seco, another peripheral town that usually gets lumped in with Taos, and eventually to the base of the ski area.

## TAOS PLAZA

Even more confusing than the patchwork of interlinked towns and highways is the fact that you can drive straight through Taos and completely miss its historic center if you're not careful. The plaza, enclosed by adobe buildings with deep portals, is just west of the main intersection of Kit Carson Road and Paseo del Pueblo Sur. Once an informal area at the center of a cluster of settlers' homes, the plaza was established around 1615 but then destroyed in the Pueblo Revolt of 1680. New homes were

built starting in 1710, but fires over the centuries repeatedly gutted the block-style homes and the large gate that was used to seal off the community and protect it against Indian raids. The buildings that currently edge the plaza all date from around 1930. In the center of the plaza is a monument to New Mexicans killed in the Bataan Death March of World War II; the U.S. flag flies day and night, a tradition carried on from a point during the Civil War when Kit Carson and a crew of his men hoisted the flag and guarded it to keep Confederate sympathizers from taking it down. On the plaza's north side, the old **Taos County courthouse** contains a series of WPA-sponsored murals painted in 1934 and 1935 by Emil Bisttram and a team of other Taos artists. The door isn't always unlocked, but definitely try to get in: Enter on the ground floor through the North Plaza Art Center and go upstairs, toward the back of the building.

### A Walking Tour

Many of the main historical and cultural sights are described in more detail below, but a short stroll to get oriented would take you around the plaza, then out the southwest corner to **Ledoux Street** and the museums and galleries there. Make a short jog down Lower Ranchitos Road to **La Loma Plaza,** a farm settlement in the 1780s and now a quiet courtyard. From there head back north along Ranchitos, which merges into Camino de la Placita. After a couple of blocks, turn east on Bent Street, passing the home of the first American governor, Charles Bent. End at the **Taos Inn,** distinguished by its large glowing thunderbird sign, the oldest neon sign in town. The inn was as central to previous generations of Taoseños' lives as it is now. Granted, today it's the hotel bar that everyone goes to, but starting in the 1890s, it was the home of Dr. T. P. Martin, Taos's first and only county doctor, who had a good reputation for accepting chickens or venison from his poorer patients in lieu of cash.

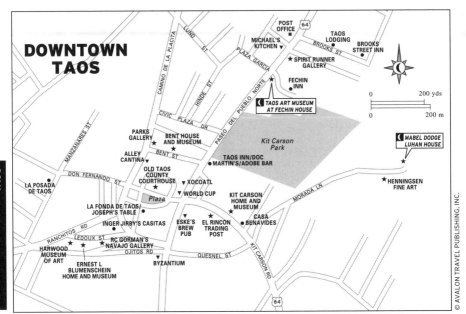

© AVALON TRAVEL PUBLISHING, INC.

His home looked out on a small plaza and a well—what has since been covered over and made into the hotel lobby.

## MUSEUMS

The Museum Association of Taos (www .taosmuseums.org) manages five museums in town—all of those listed below except for the Governor Bent House and the Kit Carson Home and Museum. At any of the museums, you can purchase a $20 pass, valid for a year, that grants you a single admission to all six. With individual admissions costing $6 or more, it's worth it if you visit four places, and it's transferable, so you can pass it along to a friend if you don't use it up.

### ◖ Taos Art Museum at Fechin House

This sunny space (227 Paseo del Pueblo Norte, 505/758-2690, 10 A.M.–5 P.M. Tues.–Sat., noon–5 P.M. Sun. May–Oct., 10 A.M.–4 P.M. Wed.–Sun. Nov–Apr., $6), former home of artist and wood-carver Nicolai Fechin, is a

showcase not only for a great collection of paintings, but also for Fechin's lovely woodwork. When the Russia native moved to Taos in 1927, hoping to cure his tuberculosis, he purchased seven acres of land, including the small two-story house, and, with the tools that are hidden in a small cabinet in the dining room, proceeded to hand-carve the lintels, staircases, bedsteads, and more, in a combination of Russian Tartar and local styles. He also designed all of the metal trim, as well as the fireplaces. His blending of traditions is flawless and natural—a small altar, also in the dining room, is set with Orthodox icons but could just as easily hold local santos. Although Fechin was devoted to traditional styles, he had no qualms about adapting the house to modern life. The stove in the kitchen is electric, installed in 1928 when power first arrived in town, and he engineered a central heating system.

The collection of paintings shown here is eclectic: Victor Higgins's 1936 *Indian Nude* recalls Gauguin, while Dorothy Brett's *Rainbow and Indians* from 1942 is more enamored of the powerful landscape. One room is dedicated to Fechin's own portrait work, characterized by broad, dynamic brushstrokes and a canny eye for distinctive facial features. One work is an etching of the same set of haggard, mustachioed twins rendered in oil by Ernest Hennings on a canvas hanging at the Harwood Museum. After all the work he did on the house, Fechin stayed in Taos only six years, when his wife divorced him. He moved on to Los Angeles with his daughter, Eya (her sunny study, on the ground floor, contains the child-scale furniture that her father made for her). After her father died in 1955, Eya, by then practicing psychodrama and dance therapy, returned to live in the studio (the back building that also houses the gift shop) and helped establish the main house as a museum. While you're on the grounds, head farther back from the road to see the lobby of the Fechin Inn, a small hotel and convention center opened in 1996—the astonishing woodwork that fills the space, all of it following Fechin's designs and planned under Eya's guidance, took 52 artisans working three years to finish.

## ◖ Millicent Rogers Museum

While today's style-makers jet to Reykjavík, Dakar, and Bhutan for inspiration, Millicent Rogers, a dashing, thrice-married New York City socialite and designer, moved to Taos in 1947 on a tip from a friend, Hollywood actress Janet Gaynor. Rogers brought her eye for style with her, adopting Navajo-style velvet broomstick skirts and *concho* belts and donning pounds of turquoise-and-silver jewelry for photo spreads in *Vogue* and *Harper's Bazaar.* Though she died just six years after she moved, in 1953 at the age of 51, she managed to accumulate a fantastic amount of stuff. Her namesake museum (1504 Millicent Rogers Rd., 505/758-2462, 10 A.M.–5 P.M. daily Apr.–Oct., 10 A.M.–5 P.M. Tues.–Sun. Nov.–Mar., $6), was established by her son, Paul Peralta-Ramos, and is set in the warren of adobe rooms that make up her former home. It reflects her discerning taste, with flawless pieces of pottery, rugs, and jewelry—both local works and her own designs. Peralta-Ramos has also recently started contributing his own growing collection, including beautiful pieces of Hispano devotional art that were put on display in 2005.

The hand-built Fechin House is as beautiful as the art collection it contains.

© ZORA O'NEILL

TAOS

Aside from the individual beauty of the works, they also make up an excellent broad introduction to the artisanal work of the area, from ancient times to modern. Look for the beautiful black-on-black pottery of María Martinez, santos by Patrocinio Barela, and fine examples of the distinctive *colcha* embroidered rug style. But it's not all rooted in local culture: Rogers's quirky, goofy illustrations of a fairy tale for her children fill the last room. The gift shop here is particularly thorough and includes beautiful (though pricey) vintage jewelry and very old rugs.

## Harwood Museum of Art

This museum (238 Ledoux St., 10 A.M.–5 P.M. Tues.–Sat., noon–5 P.M. Sun., $7) set in the sprawling pueblo revival–style home of the Harwood patrons, tells the story of Taos's rise as an art colony, beginning with Ernest Blumenschein's fateful wagon accident, which left him and his colleague, Bert Phillips, stranded in the tiny town in 1898. Modern Taos painters are represented as well in the temporary exhibit spaces upstairs, and it's interesting to see the same material—the mountain, the pueblo, the river, local residents—depicted in different styles over the decades, from the Taos Society of Artists' early realist works with a certain genre bent to later cubist and abstract efforts. Also upstairs: a small but very good assortment of Hispano crafts, including a couple of santos by Patrocinio Barela, the Taos wood-carver who modernized the art in the 1930s, and some beautiful 19th-century tinwork. A separate back wing is dedicated to the ethereal abstractions of painter Agnes Martin, who relocated to Taos 50 years before she passed away in 2004; in addition to bringing renewed attention to Taos through her well-received work, she was discovered to have been a generous anonymous donor to many local cultural establishments.

## Ernest L. Blumenschein Home and Museum

Ernest Blumenschein, one of the founding fathers of the Taos Society of Artists, moved into this house (222 Ledoux St., 505/758-0505, 9 A.M.–5 P.M. daily May–Oct., 10 A.M.–4 P.M. daily Nov.–Apr., $6) in 1919 with his wife, Mary Shepard Greene Blumenschein, who was herself an accomplished artist, having earned medals at the Paris Salon for her painting. The house's decoration largely reflects her taste, from the sturdy wood furnishings in the dining room to the light-filled studio and the cozy wood-paneled library. Throughout, the walls are hung with sketches and paintings by their contemporaries; some of the finest are in the back "Green Room," including a beautiful monotype of Taos Mountain by Oscar E. Berninghaus. The main bedroom, entered through a steep arch, is decorated with Mary's lush illustrations for *The Arabian Nights.* Throughout, you can admire the variety of ceiling styles, from rough-hewn split cedar *(rajas)* to tidy golden aspen boughs *(latillas).*

## La Hacienda de los Martinez

The word *hacienda* conjures a sprawling complex and rich surrounding lands, but the reality in 19th-century Taos was quite different, as this carefully restored adobe home (708 Hacienda Rd., off Ranchitos Rd., 505/758-1000, 9 A.M.–5 P.M. daily May–Oct., 10 A.M.–4 P.M. daily Nov.–Apr., $6) from 1804 shows. Its builder and owner, Severino Martinez, was a prominent merchant who often hosted the Taos trade fairs at the hacienda and eventually became the mayor of Taos in the 1820s. His oldest son was Padre Antonio Martinez, the valley leader who clashed with the French bishop Jean-Baptiste Lamy. Despite the family's high social standing, life was fairly rugged, cramped, and cold: 21 simple rooms arranged around two courtyards made room for sleeping, cooking, and, in the single room with a wood floor, dancing. Some of the spaces have been furnished to reflect their original use; others are dedicated to exhibits, such as a very interesting display on slavery in the area, and an especially creepy wood carving of Doña Sebastiana, lady death, with her glittering mica eyes, in the collection of Penitente paraphernalia. During the summer months, local craftspeople are on hand

© ZORA O'NEILL

Get a glimpse of colonial life at La Hacienda de los Martinez.

to demonstrate weaving, blacksmithing, and the like in the house's workshops; in the fall, the trade fair is reenacted.

## Kit Carson Home and Museum

Reopened after renovation in May 2005, the Kit Carson Home and Museum (113 Kit Carson Rd., 505/758-4741, 10 A.M.–6 P.M. daily, $5) is set in the former house of this legendary scout. With old photographs, memorabilia, and assorted trinkets from the frontier era, it conjures the spirit of the definitive mountain man and the other solitary scouts, trackers, and trappers who explored the American West on foot and horseback. Carson was an intrepid adventurer who, after a childhood on the barely settled edge of Missouri, joined a wagon train headed down the Santa Fe Trail as a teenager; he arrived in Taos in 1826. His talent for tracking, hunting, and translating from Spanish and various Indian languages soon put him in high demand. But whether he was scouting for explorer John C. Frémont as Frémont mapped the trails west to Los An-

geles or serving as an officer in the Civil War (or, less heroically, forcing the Navajos on their "Long Walk" to Fort Sumner), he used Taos as his base camp and eventually called the place home. He purchased this house in 1843 with his third wife, Josefa Jaramillo; he and Josefa died there in 1868.

## Governor Bent House and Museum

Although it's not a member of the Museum Association of Taos, this dusty little backroom exhibit space (117 Bent St., 505/758-2376, 9 A.M.–5 P.M. daily June–Aug., 10 A.M.–4 P.M. daily Sept.–May, $2) is definitely worth a visit. It's the former residence of Charles Bent, who, following the Mexican-American War, was appointed the first governor of the territory of New Mexico in 1846, based on his extensive experience as a western trader (he and his brother had built Bent's Fort, an important trading center in Colorado). But Bent died a grisly death in 1847, at the hands of an angry mob dissatisfied by the new American government. Amid the slightly creepy clutter (a malevolent-looking ceremonial buffalo head, Eskimo knives, photos of Penitente rituals from an old *Harper's* magazine) is the very hole in the very wall that Bent's family quickly dug to escape, while Bent tried to reason with murderous crowd. The back room only gets stranger, with surreal taxidermy, sinister doctor's instruments from 1905, and lots of old guns. The whole place may feel like an antiques store where nothing's for sale, but it still gives a surprisingly good overview of the period.

## ◀ MABEL DODGE LUHAN HOUSE

Now used as a conference center and B&B, arts patroness Mabel Dodge Luhan's home (240 Morada Ln., 505/751-9686, 9 A.M.–5 P.M. daily, free) is open to curious visitors as well as overnight guests. Knock at the main building first; the caretaker will give you information for a self-guided tour. Bordering the Taos Reservation, the house was built to her specifications starting in 1918, a year after she had moved to New Mexico to be with her third husband (she was Mabel Dodge Sterne at that point), then divorced him. This intrepid woman, who shaped Taos's arts culture for decades to come, also exercised a firm hand when designing her own place. Alongside a small original structure—a low row of adobe rooms that were already a century old at that point—she added a three-story main building, topped with a huge sunroom open on three sides. This, and the similarly glass-enclosed bathroom on the second floor, seemed a bit scandalous to her neighbors, the pueblo residents. One of them, however, didn't seem to mind—Tony Luhan, the foreman of the construction project, became her next husband. But Mabel's custom love-nest brought out some latent prurience even in D. H. Lawrence, who objected to the curtainless bathroom windows; to soothe his sensibilities, if not Mabel's, he painted colorful swirls directly on the glass; you can still see them today.

Other parts of the house did not fare so well; after Mabel's death in 1962, subsequent residents did some serious damage. Dennis Hopper, for instance, reputedly was in the habit of riding his motorcycle across the roof of the string of guest rooms. Fittingly, the only remaining original furniture, in the second-floor bedroom, is Mabel's sturdy pine bed—perhaps simply because its Taos-style spiral posts made it too big and heavy to move. Downstairs is a cozy reading wing as well as a vast dining room, over which portraits of Mabel and Tony preside.

## KIT CARSON CEMETERY

After seeing where Mabel Dodge Luhan lived, you can also visit her grave, in Taos's oldest cemetery. A shady sprawl of gravestones in a corner of Kit Carson Park, on Paseo del Pueblo Norte north of the Taos Inn, it was established in 1847 to bury the dead from the Taos Rebellion (the same melée in which Governor Charles Bent was murdered). First known simply as El Cementerio Militar, it earned its current name when the bodies of Mr. Carson and his wife were moved here in 1869, according to his will. Many of Taos's oldest families, particularly the merchants of the late 1800s, are buried here. Mabel had been a very close friend of the trader Ralph Meyers, and they often joked about being buried together. When Mabel died in 1962, a few years after Ralph, writer Frank Waters (who had based a character in *The Man Who Killed the Deer* on Meyers) recalled their wishes, and suggested that Meyers's grave be scooted over to make room for Mabel; she was the last person to be buried in the cemetery, in 1962, and her grave is squeezed into the far southwest corner. Other local luminaries at rest here include Padre Antonio Martinez, who stood up to Catholic bishop Lamy, and Englishman Arthur Manby, whose grave actually stands outside of the cemetery proper, thanks to his lifetime of shady business deals, land grabs, and outright swindles perpetrated in town. Manby was found beheaded in his mansion in 1929, and the unsympathetic populace was happy to call it natural causes. (Another Waters book, *To Possess the Land*, tells Manby's story.)

# ◖ SAN FRANCISCO DE ASIS CHURCH

Just as photographs of the Great Pyramid of Cheops seldom show the sprawl of modern Cairo crowding up to its base, San Francisco de Asis Church (east side of U.S. 68 in Ranchos de Taos, 505/758-2754, 9 A.M.–4 P.M. daily, Mass 7 A.M., 9:30 A.M., and 11:30 A.M. Sun., donation) as depicted in, say, Emil Bisttram's or Georgia O'Keeffe's paintings, or in Ansel Adams's photographs, is always a shadow-draped fortress isolated on a hilltop. So it's often a surprise to visitors to see the cluster of buildings that ring the small plaza in front of the church, which was built in the first half of the 18th century as a Franciscan mission for the farming community of Ranchos de Taos.

Today the adobe houses around the church hold more T-shirt shops than homes, but you can nonetheless see what has fascinated so many artists. The clean lines, the shadows created by the hulking buttresses, the rich glow of the adobe in the sun—these are all appealing aesthetic details, but at bottom, the church is a sort of living architecture, as much a part of the earth as something raised above it. As with every traditional adobe structure, it must be refinished every year with a mix of clay, sand, and straw; it is then coated with a fine layer of water and sand, and buffed with sheepskin. Each year, the structure changes ever so slightly and grows marginally thicker. Artists' renderings of the church become more like portraits than simple representations of a building.

## The Shadow of the Cross

Inside, the whitewash walls are covered with santos and *retablos;* in an adjoining room is another, more modern attraction, an 1896 painting by a French-Canadian artist named Henri Ault ($3 donation). The eight-foot-high canvas depicts Jesus in front of the Sea of Galilee; when the lights in the small room are extinguished, it begins to luminesce, and the life-size figure of Christ soon appears ready to step off the rocks and into the room. Some people also see the shape of a cross over Christ's shoulder, or a glowing halo. This "miracle" paint-

ing caused quite a sensation when Ault first made it—he claimed to be baffled by the odd phenomenon—and it was even shown at the World's Fair in St. Louis in 1904. After years of exhibition in Europe, a wealthy Texan woman bought the painting, known as *The Shadow of the Cross,* and donated it to the church.

## ◖ TAOS PUEBLO

Even if you've been in New Mexico awhile and think you're inured to adobe, Taos Pueblo (505/758-1028, www.taospueblo.com, 8 A.M.–4:30 P.M. daily, closed for 10 weeks around Feb.–Mar., $10) is an amazing sight. Two clusters of mud-brick buildings, one up to four stories high and the other up to five, make up the core of this village, which claims, along with Acoma Pueblo, to be the oldest continually inhabited community in the United States. The current buildings, though annually repaired and recoated with mud, essentially date from the 1200s and house about 150 people year-round (the total population of the Taos reservation is about 2,000). The dedication of

early apartment-living at Taos Pueblo

COURTESY NEW MEXICO DEPARTMENT OF TOURISM/MARK NOHL

TAOS

# PUEBLO DANCES: WHAT TO EXPECT

Visiting a pueblo for a ceremonial dance or feast-day celebration is one of the most remarkable things you can do on your trip to northern New Mexico. The animal dances are particularly transporting – dressed in pelts and mimicking the movements of a deer, for instance, the dancers transform the plaza into a forest glade. Whereas the state's American Indian culture can occasionally seem exploited for its tourism value, a pueblo dance is not at all for the benefit of tourists: It is a ceremony and a religious ritual, not a performance; you are a guest, not an audience.

Keep this in mind to guide your own behavior – applause is not appropriate, nor is conversation during the dance. Queries about the meaning of the dances are generally not appreciated. Never walk in the dance area, and try not to block the view of pueblo locals. The kivas, as holy spaces, are always off-limits to outsiders. During feast days, though, some pueblo residents may open their doors to visitors, perhaps for a snack or drink – though be considerate of others who may also want to visit, and don't stay too long. Photography is strictly forbidden at dances, sometimes with the exception of Los Matachines, which is not a religious ritual. Don't even think about trying to sneak a shot with your camera phone, as tribal police will be more than happy to confiscate it.

On a practical level, be prepared for a lot of waiting around. Start times are always approximate, and everything depends on when the dancers are done with their kiva rituals. There will usually be a main, seasonal dance – such as the corn dance – followed by several others. If you go in the winter, dress very warmly, but in layers – a Christmas Eve Mass may start inside the close-packed, overheated church, then dances may continue outside in the near-freezing cold.

pueblo residents along with the town's designation as a UNESCO World Heritage Site have kept the place remarkably as it was in the pre-Columbian era—though the use of adobe bricks as the main structural material, as opposed to rock and puddled mud, was introduced by the Spanish. The apartment-like homes, stacked up in stages and connected by wood ladders, have no electricity or running water. The windows and doorways are the byproduct of better security in recent centuries; originally, the only entrance to the separate rooms was through the roof. The sole concessions to modernity are the occasional use of a wood stove, as opposed to the traditional fireplaces, and the odd pickup truck.

As you explore, be careful not to intrude on spaces that are not clearly marked as stores, and stay clear of the ceremonial kiva areas on the east side of each complex. These kivas form the ritual heart of the pueblo, a secret space within a generally private culture. Kivas are where drummers prepare before dances, for instance, and where the tribal governor and war chief are elected by consensus (among the men only) every year.

## San Geronimo Church

The path past the admission gate leads directly to the central plaza, a broad expanse between the **Red Willow Creek** (source of the community's drinking water, flowing from sacred Blue Lake higher up in the mountains) and San Geronimo Church. The latter, built in 1850, is perhaps the newest structure in the village, a replacement for the first mission church the Spanish built in 1619, using forced Indian labor. Visitors are allowed inside, as long as they are respectful and quiet. The Virgin Mary presides over the room roofed with heavy wood vigas; her clothes change with every season, a nod to her dual role as the Earth Mother. Directly in front of the churchyard is where ceremonial dances take place periodically. (Taking photos is strictly forbidden inside the church at all times and, as at all pueblos, at dances as well.)

The older church, to the north behind the main house, is now a cemetery, fitting given the tragic form of its destruction. It was first torn down during the 1680 Pueblo Revolt; the Spanish rebuilt it about 20 years later. In 1847 it was again attacked, this time by American troops sent in to quell the rebellion against the new government—retaliation for the murder of Governor Charles Bent. The counterattack brutally outweighed what had sparked it: More than 100 pueblo residents, including women and children, had taken refuge inside the church when the Americans bombarded and set fire to it, killing everyone inside and gutting the building. Since then, the bell tower has been restored, but the graves have simply intermingled with the ruined walls and piles of dissolved adobe mud. All of the crosses—old carved wood to new finished stone—face sacred Taos Mountain.

## Pueblo Crafts

You are welcome to wander around a bit and enter any of the handful of craft shops and galleries that are open—a good opportunity to see inside the mud structures, as well as to purchase some of the distinctive Taos pottery, which is only very lightly decorated but glimmers with mica from the clay that is particular to this area. On your way out of the pueblo, you may want to stop in at the **Oo-oonah Arts Center** (505/770-2110, 10 A.M.–4 P.M. daily Apr.–Oct.), where the gallery displays the work of pueblo children and adults enrolled in its craftwork classes—you can often find very talented work here that's quite well priced. Twenty-five percent of the sales benefit the work of the nonprofit center, and the remainder goes to the artists. Another attraction on the road out: **Tewa Kitchen** (505/751-1020, 11 A.M.–5 P.M. Wed.–Mon., $8), which serves simple traditional food, such as grilled buffalo and heirloom green chile.

## ◨ RIO GRANDE GORGE

Heading west on U.S. 64 from the "old blinking light," you pass the Taos airstrip on the left, then, after a few more miles, the ground sim-ply drops away. This is the Rio Grande Gorge, plunging 800 feet deep in malevolent-looking black basalt at its most alarming point. The river winds below, but it's not just millions of years of rushing water that have carved out the canyon—seismic activity has also caused a rift in the earth's surface. The crack extends north to just beyond the Colorado state line and south almost to Española. The elegant, unnervingly delicate-looking bridge that spans it was built in 1965, to supplement entrepreneur John Dunn's rickety old toll crossing eight miles north. Critics mocked it as "the bridge to nowhere" because the highway on the western bank had yet to be built, but the American Institute of Steel Construction granted it the Most Beautiful Span award in 1966; at 650 feet above the river, it was, and still is, the second-highest suspension bridge in the United States. On either side of the bridge is the stretch of canyon called the Taos Box, two words that will inspire wild tales in any seasoned river-runner. The Class III and IV rapids, which start around the John Dunn Bridge to the north, are held to be the best place for white-water rafting in New Mexico.

## Arroyo Hondo and Blackrock Springs

A less adrenaline-fueled way to enjoy the water here is at one of several hot springs that seep up next to the river, a byproduct of the seismic upsets. The easiest ones to reach are those at the old John Dunn Bridge. To reach them, backtrack to the old blinking light, then head north on Highway 522. After about six miles, the road dips down to the Rio Hondo; immediately after the bridge, turn left on County Road B-005, which runs along the north edge of the arroyo. Drive slowly through this village, as the dirt roads are bumpy and there are often children playing. It's hard to imagine now, but this is where the New Buffalo commune was in the late 1960s—all traces of hippie influence seem to have evaporated. The road crosses the small Hondo River, then climbs a hill and descends again, winding toward the Rio Grande, where you cross the John Dunn Bridge to reach

# NEW MEXICO'S COMMUNES

Something about New Mexico's vast empty spaces inspires utopian thinking, as if the landscape were a blank slate, a way to start over from scratch and do things right. Spanish settlers felt it in the 16th century. Would-be gold miners banked on it in the 1800s. And in the 1960s, hippies, free-thinkers, free-lovers, and back-to-the-landers fled crowded cities and boring suburbs to start life fresh in communities such as the Hog Farm and the New Buffalo Commune, both near Taos. For a while, New Mexico was the place to be: Dennis Hopper immortalized New Buffalo in his film *Easy Rider*, Janis Joplin chilled out in Truchas, and Ken Kesey drove his bus, "Further," through the state.

Today these experimental communities and their ideals seem to have been just a brief moment of zaniness – their only legacy appears to be Hog Farm leader Wavy Gravy's consecration on a Ben & Jerry's label. But some of the ideals set down by naked organic gardeners and tripping visionaries have taken root and sprouted in unexpected ways. For instance, Yogi Bhajan, an Indian Sikh who taught mass kundalini yoga sessions in New Mexico in 1969, eventually became a major contributor to the state economy through all the businesses he established. Buddhist stupas dot the Rio Grande Valley, the product of Anglo spiritual seekers working with Tibetan refugees who were brought to New Mexico by Project Tibet, a nonprofit organization cofounded by John Allen, who also ran the commune Synergia Ranch.

Synergia, which still exists as a retreat center, just off Highway 14 on the plateau south of Santa Fe, began as an avant-garde theater group but evolved into a hard-working cult with properties around the globe, its members dedicated to, among other things, building sustainable mini-ecosystems, or biospheres. Luckily, one of the ranch's more devoted adherents was Edward Bass, renegade son of a Texas oil family. He invested some $100 million in Biosphere 2, a glass dome in the Arizona desert filled with 3,800 living species; in 1991, it was sealed up with eight people inside, to test its environmental sustainability as a possible model for a Mars colony. After two two-year runs, Bio2 wasn't as inspirational as Allen and Bass had hoped, but it wasn't a complete failure. Bass arranged for Columbia University to take over operations and use the place as a lab, to measure carbon-dioxide damage in coral reefs and other problems facing the changing Earth. But in 2004, Columbia abandoned the project, and it's now open solely as a tourist attraction, a relic of perhaps the most utopian vision yet to have sprouted in New Mexico.

the west side; turn left, then park at the first switchback. From there, it's a quarter-mile hike down the rocks and downstream to the springs. Don't crowd in if several people are already in the spring, and never leave trash behind.

## Greater World Earthship Development

If you brave the slender suspension bridge and continue on the west side of the gorge on U.S. 64, you soon see some odd apparitions along the right side of the road. These whimsically curved and creatively stuccoed houses are Earthships: modular, low-priced homes that function entirely separate from the public utility grid by using collected rainwater and wind and solar power. Architect Michael Reynolds has been honing his Earthship design for more than three decades here in New Mexico. Whether it's due to the latent hippie culture or the awe-inspiring landscape, the homes have proved very popular, and you'll see them dotted around the area, as well as clustered together here at Greater World, the largest of three all-Earthship subdivisions in the area.

Although they look like fanciful Hobbit homes or Mars colony pods on the outside, Earthships are made of rather common stuff: The walls, usually built into hillsides, are stacks of used tires packed solid with rammed earth,

© ZORA O'NEILL

TAOS

View the inner workings of an ecosensible home on the self-guided Solar Survival Tour.

while bottles stacked with cement and crushed aluminum cans form front walls and colorful peepholes. Windows along the front wall are angled to maximize heat from the sun during the winter, while planters filter gray water and black water, creating a humid greenhouse atmosphere inside that's very welcome in arid New Mexico.

The Greater World subdivision maintains a visitors center, 1.8 miles past the bridge, that's the most unconventional model home and sales office you'll ever visit. You can take the self-guided **Solar Survival Tour** (505/751-0462, www.earthship.com, 10 A.M.–4 P.M. daily, $5) of a basic Earthship and watch a video about the building process and the thinking behind the design. If you're hooked, you can of course get details on buying a lot in the development, or purchasing the plans to build your own place. Or try before you buy: Two Earthships here are for rent on a nightly or weekly basis, starting at $150 (less for longer stays); the one-bedroom classic design is warm and romantic, tucked in an almost suburban-feeling

cul-de-sac with a clutch of other homes, while the other house is a big two-bedroom place, furnished with a slick kitchen and a giant flat-screen TV, to make clear that living off the grid doesn't have to mean going without.

## Tres Piedras

Usually only rock climbers go the additional 26 miles to Tres Piedras, a handful of houses scattered around the intersection of U.S. 64 and U.S. 285. Its name (Three Stones) comes from the rock formations that spike up from the utterly flat plain, looking as though they should be in Australia or Greece. Otherwise, you can stop to browse at **The Old Pink Schoolhouse Gallery** (U.S. 64 at U.S. 285, 505/758-7826, erratic hours, so call ahead), an absorbing accretion of Mexican and New Mexican artwork and trinkets, all crammed in the village's former school-turned-mill. Then refresh yourself at **The Diner** (junction of U.S. 64 and U.S. 285, 505/758-3441, 8 A.M.–4 P.M. Mon.–Sat., 9 A.M.–4 P.M. Sun., $5), a tiny old Valentine box that has been overseeing the town's

## GREENBACKS MEET GREEN LIVING

While devoted ecoarchitect Michael Reynolds builds Earthships in isolation on Taos's western frontier, catering to a particular sort of earnest back-to-the-lander, Tom Worrell, a media magnate turned environmental evangelist, has gone about the same task in precisely the opposite way. Worrell, who hails from North Carolina but became enamored of Taos on skiing visits, built a $20 million luxury resort. His reasoning: The term "sustainability" has a whiff of deprivation about it, which people, especially rich and influential people, want no part of.

To counter this negative association, he created an intimate 36-room resort, called El Monte Sagrado (The Sacred Mountain), as a showcase for inventions produced by his engineering company, Dharma Living Systems: Curoxin, a nontoxic alternative to highly poisonous chlorine, solar-panel "trees," and a seven-phase wastewater-processing system. The trick is that there's no hint you're in an "ecoresort" – no gratuitous hemp products here, just priceless antiques and paintings decorating the magnificent suites, a lavish spa, a vast wine cellar, and of course, very, very high-thread-count sheets. Unless you're told, you would never guess that the lily-covered fish ponds and babbling brooks running through the central courtyard are what

Worrell calls Living Machines: a chemical-free means of treating sewage waste to produce water that is then used for the lush gardens and greenhouse plants.

Whether Worrell's ecological paradise will bring out the latent green in the world's wealthiest people remains to be seen – the resort opened only in late 2003. Meanwhile, Worrell has not wooed the people of Taos so well, it seems. He has antagonized some long-time locals, who see him as swooping in and throwing around a shocking amount of cash in this not-so-well-off town. But he has forged a working relationship with Michael Reynolds, and the two are planning projects together that will merge Dharma Living Systems' technology with the Earthships' more comprehensive energy-use strategies.

Despite the lone survivalist mentality that "off the grid" implies, both Reynolds and Worrell advocate the use of their technologies in areas with denser populations. Reynolds envisions an Earthship city of pyramid-shaped stacks of the modules, with shared cisterns and water processing. Worrell says he intentionally chose the site of El Monte Sagrado in town, half a mile from the plaza, rather than outside of Taos, to show that sustainable architecture isn't something that's "out there," in the wilderness, but something we can live with every day.

---

blinking-light intersection since 1953. Frito pie (especially tasty) and meaty green-chile stew are among the typical dishes.

## ARROYO SECO

Bemoaning the gallerification of downtown Taos? The sheer touristy mayhem? From the old blinking light, head north on Highway 150 to the village of Arroyo Seco, a cluster of buildings at a bend in the road to the ski area, and you'll slip back a couple of decades. Sure, there's some art up here too, but this smaller community, though only a half-hour drive from the plaza, maintains an even more laid-back and funky attitude than Taos—if such a

thing is possible. It has been a retreat for decades: Frank Waters, celebrated author of *The Man Who Killed the Deer* and *The Woman at Otowi Crossing,* lived here off and on from 1947 until his death in 1995.

"Downtown" Arroyo Seco has grown up around **La Santísima Trinidad Church,** set back from Highway 150 on the left. Built in 1834, its adobe walls are alarmingly eroded in patches, but it sports a cheery red metal roof; the spare traditional interior is decorated with santos and *retablos,* but the doors are often locked. Better to pop in at one of the secular gathering places on the road. **Arroyo Seco Mercantile** (Hwy. 150, 505/776-8806,

10 A.M.–5:30 Mon.–Sat., 11 A.M.–5 P.M. Sun.) is the town's former general store, now a highly evolved junk shop that has maintained the beautiful old wood-and-glass display cases. Its stock ranges from the practical (books on passive-solar engineering and raising llamas) to the frivolous and beautiful, like antique wool blankets. Across the street, **Abe's Cantina y Cocina** is a very old-style bar propped up by locals for countless decades; visit the adjacent lunch counter and peek in the side, if you don't fancy making a dramatic front-door entrance to a crowd of taciturn old Spanish men in cowboy hats. Taos Cow, the coffee shop next door, known as **"The Cow,"** is the hangout for everyone who doesn't fit in at Abe's—many of them guests at The Abominable Snowmansion hostel down the block.

Taos Ski Valley has near-vertical ski slopes.

### The Rim Road and Valle Valdez

Continuing on, the main road toward the ski valley eventually makes a hard right, and the so-called "rim road" heads to the left. It runs the length of a canyon edge, overlooking Valle Valdez below, where tidy farm plots are set along Rio Hondo and the traditional acequia irrigation model that has been used here for more than four centuries. In typical modern real estate distribution, the not-so-well-off native Taoseños value their fertile soil, while wealthy arrivistes (Julia Roberts, most famously) have claimed the swoon-inducing views on the rim road, which was only developed in the later part of the 20th century. The one exception is on the north side of the valley, where the ritzy Turley Mill development (formerly the site of a still that produced the powerful bootleg hooch known as "Taos lightning" from the 1700s to 1847) is home to Donald Rumsfeld and other occupants of million-dollar casitas.

### TAOS SKI VALLEY

A relentlessly winding road weaves through the Hondo Canyon, the steep mountain slopes crowded with tall, dense pines. In the wintertime, the mountaintops are often obscured by a wreath of clouds. The road dead-ends at Taos Ski Valley, a resort area that is technically an incorporated village, but of course only the mountain, along with the snow on top of it, matters to most people. When you finally get out of the car at the base of the ski runs and take in the vertiginous view toward Kachina Peak (elevation 12,481 feet, and often white-capped even in July), you'll see why it inspires legions of reverential skiers every winter, when an average of 305 inches of snow fall on the mountain—almost 10 times the amount they get down in town. And note that's *only* skiers who come here, as Taos Ski Valley is one of just three remaining resorts in the country that don't allow snowboarding. Many claim it's too dangerous on the seriously precipitous slopes here (more than half the trails are rated expert level, and many of them are left ungroomed), but with such a fanatical customer base, it's also true that TSV doesn't need to cater to another market.

In the summertime, Hondo Canyon's many trails make for very good hiking or picnicking. The road is dotted on either side with picnic areas and campgrounds—Cuchilla del Medio is a particularly nice area for a picnic. **Rio Grande Stables** (505/776-5913, www.lajitasstables.com) does **horseback-riding trips** in the mountains around the ski valley, starting at $40 for one hour.

# Entertainment

Taos is a small town—that means no glitzy dance clubs, no bars where you're expected to dress up. Nighttime fun is concentrated in a handful of bars that, if you visit frequently enough, you'll get to know quickly. And the various town-wide celebrations draw a full cross-section of the population.

## TAOS PUB CRAWL

Starting around 5 P.M., **The Adobe Bar** (125 Paseo del Pueblo Norte, 505/758-2233), in the lobby of the Taos Inn, is where you'll run into everyone you've seen over the course of the day, sipping a Cowboy Buddha ($9.50) or some other specialty margarita—the best in town. Mellow jazz or acoustic guitar sets the mood Wednesday–Sunday. To give the poor hotel residents a break, the bar closes at 10 P.M., which forces all the regulars to move on down the road to the next phase of the evening: the dance floor at the **Sagebrush Inn** (1508 Paseo del Pueblo Sur, 505/758-2254). It gets packed

with cowboy-booted couples stepping lively to decent country cover bands whose members always seem to resemble Kenny Rogers. The scene encompasses all of Taos, from artists to pueblo residents to mountain men with grizzled beards. Booze is a bargain, and the fireplace is big. After the band wraps up around midnight, dedicated boozers move on to **The Alley Cantina** (121 Teresina Ln., 505/758-2121) for another hour or so. This warren of interconnected rooms (one of which claims to be the oldest in Taos…but don't they all say that?) can be potentially baffling after a few drinks. There's shuffleboard for entertainment if you're not into the ensemble onstage—its name usually ends in "Blues Band"; a $3 or $4 cover applies on weekends. The kitchen is open till 11 P.M., and it's not a bad place for a lunchtime burger ($6.50) either.

## OTHER BARS

In addition to the Big Three, a few other watering holes draw a crowd, usually for live music of some kind. Wood-paneled **Eske's Brew Pub** (106 Des Georges Ln., 505/758-1517) is across from the plaza, tucked back from the southeast corner of the intersection of Paseo del Pueblo Sur and Kit Carson Road. With live music on Fridays and Saturdays, it serves its house-made beer to a chummy après-ski crowd. You're in New Mexico—you should at least try the green-chile ale.

Named for its location near the landmark traffic signal, **The Old Blinking Light** (1 Hwy. 150, 505/776-8787) is a casual, sprawling restaurant and bar where locals head for live bands; longtime local singer-songwriter Michael Hearne often graces the stage. The food is only so-so (except for the deadly Mud Pie), but the atmosphere is very mellow and friendly, especially on weekend afternoons, when people bring their kids to run around the back garden. If you're on the lookout for Julia Roberts (probably sans twins), this is a good bet; so far, Donald Rumsfeld hasn't been spotted.

© ZORA O'NEILL

In the lobby of the Taos Inn, The Adobe Bar is an essential part of Taos nightlife.

Taos's swankiest boîte—really, the only place in town that could be called a boîte—is the moodily lit **Anaconda Bar** in El Monte Sagrado resort (317 Kit Carson Rd., 505/758-3502), where deep semicircle leather booths curve around tables built of African drums. Skilled bartenders whip up pomegranate margaritas, and the list of wines by the glass is varied; the sommelier offers quickie wine classes on Thursday nights. Starting around 9:30 P.M. most nights, there's not-too-intrusive live music. Another plus: the reasonably priced, wide-ranging bar menu, executed by the excellent De la Tierra restaurant.

**Taos Mountain Casino** (505/737-0777, 8 A.M.–1 A.M. Mon. and Tues., 8 A.M.–2 A.M. Wed.–Sun.) claims to be the "coziest" in New Mexico, and it certainly is an intimate gambling spot, just inside the pueblo entrance. All the basic slots plus blackjack and craps, but perhaps the biggest perk is that it's smoke-free.

## CINEMA AND THEATER

**The Storyteller** (110 Old Talpa Canyon Rd., 505/758-9715, www.transluxmovies.com) shows first-run films with an occasional arty bent. Given the high concentration of artists of all stripes, it's no surprise that Taos's theater scene is very rich for such a small town. Check at the **Taos Center for the Arts** (133 Paseo del Pueblo Norte, 505/758-2052, www.taoscenterforthearts.org) to find out what shows may be on.

## FESTIVALS AND EVENTS

Taos's biggest annual festivity, for which many local businesses close, is the **Feast of San Geronimo,** the patron saint thoughtfully assigned to Taos Pueblo by the Spanish when they built their first mission there in 1619. The holiday starts the evening of September 29 with vespers in the pueblo church and continues the next day with foot races and a pole-climbing contest. La Hacienda de los Martinez usually reenacts a 19th-century Taos trade fair, with mountain men, music, and artisans' demonstrations.

In the realm of modern culture, the long-running Taos Talking Pictures film festival is

### CEREMONIAL DANCES AT TAOS PUEBLO

In addition to the Feast of San Geronimo, visitors are welcome to attend ceremonial dances. This is only an approximate schedule – dates can vary from year to year, as can the particular dances. Contact the pueblo (505/758-1028, www.taospueblo .com) for times, or check the *Tempo* entertainment listings for that week.

**JANUARY 1**
- Turtle dance

**JANUARY 6**
- Deer or buffalo dance

**MAY 3**
- Feast of Santa Cruz: corn dance

**JUNE 13**
- Feast of San Antonio: corn dance

**JUNE 24**
- Feast of San Juan: corn dance

**JULY, SECOND WEEKEND**
- Taos Pueblo Powwow

**JULY 25 AND 26**
- Feast of Santiago and Santa Ana: corn dances and foot races

no more, but the four-day **Taos Picture Show** (505/751-3658, www.taospictureshow.com) in early April looks like a good bet to replace it, with a wide-reaching program of internationally flavored indies. Since 1977, grape fanatics have been living it up at the 10-day **Taos Winter Wine Festival** (www.skitaos.org) at the end of January; seminars and special dinners are held at the ski valley resort center and many restaurants around town. Taos galleries put out their finest at the spring (Apr.–May) and fall (Sept.–Oct.) **Taos Arts Festival** (www.taosfallarts.org), two-week-long exhibitions of the works of more than 150 Taos County artists. Since 1983, the **Taos Wool Festival** (www.taoswoolfestival.org) has drawn textile artists as well as breeders—admire the traditional Churro sheep or an Angora goat, then pick up a scarf made from its wool. And if it's counterculture you're after, every June the **Taos Solar Music Festival** (www.solarmusicfest.com) takes place at an off-the-grid stage near the Earthship development west of the Rio Grande Gorge. The event draws a wild mix of dedicated campers and sun-worshippers, as well as diverse performers, including Steve Earle, Harry Belafonte, and Los Lobos.

The glow of luminarias and torchlight on snow produces a magical effect—perhaps that's why Taos has so many winter events. On the first weekend in December, the **tree-lighting ceremony** on the plaza draws the whole town, and the rest of the season sees numerous celebrations, such as the reenactments of the Virgin's search for shelter, called Las Posadas, which take place at Our Lady of Guadalupe Church west of the plaza on the third weekend in December. At the pueblo, vespers is said at San Geronimo church on Christmas Eve, typically followed by a children's dance. On Christmas Day, the pueblo hosts either a deer dance or the Spanish Los Matachines dance.

Farther afield, the ski town of Red River has a rowdy Memorial Day Motorcycle Rally, as well as a surprisingly large Fourth of July parade, when they really lay on the Texan charm. The biggest stretch of all for this town of 400, though, is the annual Mardi Gras street party. Contact the Red River chamber of commerce for more details (505/754-2366, www.redrivernewmex.com).

## Shopping

As you might imagine, Taos Plaza is ringed with less-than-inspiring T-shirt shops and souvenir stores. Two further clusters of boutiques and art dealers lie just north of the plaza—very pleasant places to browse, though you certainly won't find any bargains. The beginning stretch of Kit Carson Road has a more varied selection of shops with more affordable prices.

### GALLERIES

If you're in the market for something precious, pick up a copy of the *Collector's Guide,* a booklet listing the most discerning galleries, many of which are open only by appointment. If, on the other hand, you're hoping to discover Taos's next big art star, poke around smaller operations on back streets and in Arroyo Seco, or just keep your eyes out when you get your morning coffee—nearly every business doubles as a gallery in this town.

Otherwise, visiting some of the town institutions can round out your experience at the museums. **Spirit Runner** (303 Paseo del Pueblo Norte, 505/758-1132, 10 A.M.–5 P.M. Tues.–Sun.), for instance, is operated by Ouray Meyers, son of Ralph Meyers, the first Anglo man to deal in Indian art in his trading post. His gallery is as much a social hub as an art dealership, and he has some tales to tell. Summertime usually sees an all-nude show, complete with paper covering the windows, and plenty of wine.

**R. C. Gorman's Navajo Gallery** (210 Ledoux St., 505/758-3250, 11 A.M.–5 P.M. daily) represents the best-known American Indian artist, who died in late 2005. Gorman sold art in Taos—and all over the world—since 1968, when he moved here from Chinle, Arizona. Even if you don't recognize his name, you will likely recognize his work: His fluid representations of American Indian women have achieved near-iconic status.

Stop in **Blue Rain Gallery** (117 S. Taos Plaza, 505/751-0066, 10 A.M.–6 P.M. Mon.–Sat.) to see Tammy Garcia's modern takes on traditional Santa Clara pottery forms—she sometimes renders bowls in blown glass or applies the geometric decoration to jewelry. Other skilled artists in the gallery are Navajo and Hopi.

The town's best gallery for contemporary art is **Parks Gallery** (127 Bent St., 505/751-0343, 10 A.M.–5:30 P.M. Mon.–Fri., 11 A.M.–4 P.M. Sat.), where the selection of styles and media is extremely varied, from Melissa Zink's collages to Arthur Lopez's quirky modern *bultos*.

Out near the Mabel Dodge Luhan House, **Henningsen Fine Art** (235 Morada Ln., 505/758-1434, 10 A.M.–5 P.M. daily) is an eye-catching vanity project, but the beautiful mini-malist gardens merit a visit, even if you're not in the market for a life-size neonified nude por-trait. Somewhat more restrained are Henning-sen's zippy, abstract photo collages and more austere sepia and black-and-white landscapes.

Halfway to Arroyo Seco, turn off High-way 150 to reach **Lumina** gallery and sculp-ture gardens (11 Hwy. 230, 505/758-7282, 10:30 A.M.–5 P.M. daily), which has a very broad stable of artists, from a local from Santa Clara Pueblo who inlays pottery bowls with turquoise and shells to very contempo-rary photomontages. The former owner of the house in which the gallery is set developed the elegant Japanese gardens, now studded with monumental sculptures.

## GIFTS AND JEWELRY

Gussy yourself up in Western trappings from **Horse Feathers** (109-B Kit Carson Rd., 505/758-7457, 10:30 A.M.–5:30 P.M. daily), where you can pick up a full cowpoke get-up, from 10-gallon hat to jingling spurs. The big money is in the room full of vintage cowboy boots, but you can find less expensive, eclec-tic gift items, such as giant belt buckles or campfire cookbooks from 1900, in one of the other big rooms packed with stuff. **El Rincon Trading Post** (114 Kit Carson Rd., 505/758-

9188, 10 A.M.–5 P.M. Tues.–Sun.) is equally crammed with stuff, some of it perhaps dating back to 1909, when Ralph Meyers established the Mission Shop, the first trading post to deal in American Indian art. Today the trove is man-aged by his daughter, who has put aside many of the best pieces in an informal "museum," but there are still plenty of one-of-a-kind *con-cho* belts and other jewelry, as well as beads and baubles from elsewhere in the world.

A little farther down Kit Carson Road, **Twining Weavers** (129-E Kit Carson Rd., 505/758-9000, 10 A.M.–5 P.M. Tues.–Sun.) is an old-fashioned toy and gift shop, with little hand-carved animal figurines, fuzzy woven blankets and elaborate quilts, and jointed toy bears. Across the street is its hip mod-ern equivalent, **FX/18** (140 Kit Carson Rd., 505/758-8590, 10 A.M.–5 P.M. Thurs.–Sun., noon–5 P.M. Wed.). From groovy housewares to lively kids' stuff to nifty stationery, the col-orful shop has a great selection of goodies to give as gifts or to treat yourself. Despite all the placeless kitsch (bottle-cap necklaces, for in-stance), it doesn't forget it's in Taos—the selec-tion of contemporary Southwest-style jewelry is particularly good.

If you're overloaded on New Mexican knick-knacks, head to **Wabi-Sabi** (216-A Paseo del Pueblo Norte, 505/758-7801, 10 A.M.–6 P.M. Mon.–Sat., 11 A.M.–5 P.M. Sun.), which tran-scends the roadrunner paperweight with simple and beautiful Japanese (or Japanese-inspired) items for around the home. From gleaming shell knives to rough stoneware, it's all func-tional yet beautiful, and the store as a whole is a wonderful place to relax.

Less soothing, but a whole lot of fun, **Taos Drum** (3956 Hwy. 68, 505/758-9844, 8 A.M.–5 P.M. Mon.–Fri.) is a giant shop and factory dedicated to making Taos Pueblo–style per-cussion instruments, from thin hand drums to great booming ones made of hollow logs. Try-ing out the wares is encouraged—it's a good place to bring the kids. The shop is located on the west side of the highway 5 miles south of the plaza.

TAOS

# Sports and Recreation

If you don't go hiking, mountain biking, or skiing in Taos, you're missing most of the town's appeal—the wild setting presses in all around, and Taos Mountain looms up behind every town view. Downhill skiing is the main draw in the winter, just a 45-minute drive from central Taos, but you can also try more solitary snowshoeing and Nordic skiing. In summer, peak-baggers will want to strike out for Wheeler Peak, the state's highest, while rafters, rock climbers, and mountain bikers can head the other direction, to the dramatic basalt cliffs of the Rio Grande Gorge, where river-runners defy death in the churning rapids of the legendary Taos Box (late May and early June is the best season for this).

A complete list of tour operators can be found online at Taos Outdoor Recreation (www.taosoutdoorrecreation.com), and the sites maintained by the Bureau of Land Management (www.nm.blm.gov) and the National Forest Service (www.fs.fed.us/r3/carson) can also give you a more detailed overview of the area before you arrive. Sudden thunderstorms are common in the summer months, as are flash floods and even freak blizzards. Well into May, snow can blanket some of the higher passes, so wherever you go, always carry more warm clothing than you think you'll need, and don't skimp on the sunscreen, even when it's below freezing.

## SKIING AND SNOWSHOEING

**Taos Ski Valley** (800/485-1894, www .skitaos.org, $55 full-day lift ticket) is the premier spot for Alpine skiing. The resort is open from late November through the first weekend in April, with 110 trails served by 12 lifts and snow-making capacity on all beginner and intermediate areas in dry spells. The truly dedicated can do the hike up to Kachina Peak, an additional 632 feet past where the lift service ends. Don't be too intimidated by the trails: The highly regarded Ernie Blake Ski School is one of the best places to learn the basics or

polish your skills. Novice "yellowbirds" can take one ($70) or two ($105) days of intensive instruction specially geared to new skiers. For those with some experience, a six-day improvement program costs $195, plus lift tickets, or you can opt for a two-day, 10-hour crash course ($165). Lift tickets are half price in the two weeks following Thanksgiving.

For cross-country skiing and snowshoeing, **Enchanted Forest** near Red River offers miles of groomed trails, and there are also easy access points in the Carson National Forest—at Capulin Campground on U.S. 64, for instance, 5 miles east of Taos; along **Manzanita Trail** in the Hondo Canyon on the road to the ski valley; and, especially good for snowshoeing, the **Bull of the Woods Trail,** which starts at Twining campground, in the ski area parking lot, and leads in about 2.5 miles to a high pasture, then another 5.5 miles up to Wheeler Peak, if you're feeling extremely energetic. Visit the **Carson National Forest Supervisor's Office** (208 Cruz Alta Rd., 505/758-6200, www.fs.fed.us/r3/carson, 8:30 A.M.–4:30 P.M. Mon.–Fri.) for full details and snow status before you set out.

Don't have your own gear? **Cottam's Ski & Outdoor** (207-A Paseo del Pueblo Sur, 505/758-2822, 7 A.M.–7 P.M. Mon.–Fri., 7 A.M.–8 P.M. Sat. and Sun.) has the biggest stock of rental skis, for both downhill and cross-country, even snowboards and snowshoes. The shop also sells everything else you'll need to get out and enjoy the snow; there's another location at the ski valley (505/776-8719) and one at Angel Fire (505/776-8256).

## HIKING AND BACKPACKING

With Taos Mountain in the backyard, hiking around here ranges from rambles along winding rivers to intensive hauls that gain 2,000 feet in less than four miles. Be prepared for a cold snap or storm at any time, and don't plan on doing much before May—it takes that long for the snow to thaw, though you might still hit some of the white stuff in the highest alpine meadows even in high summer. The most accessible and varied trails are along the road to Taos Ski Valley: At Twining campground, in the base of the ski valley, the grueling trail to **Wheeler Peak** begins, a 16-mile roundtrip that only the very fit should attempt in one day. The **Gavilan Trail** is also recommended—it's plenty steep as well but leads to a high mountain meadow. The route is 5 miles roundtrip, but you can also connect with other trails once you're up on the rim. If this sounds too strenuous, you can always take the chairlift up to the top of the mountain ($7, Thurs.–Mon. late June–Sept.), then wander down any of several wide, well-marked trails, all with stunning views. A variety of trails course through **Taos Canyon** east of town, with numerous campgrounds and trailheads off U.S. 64, including the **South Boundary Trail,** 22 miles up and over the pass, with views onto Moreno Valley.

If you'd like to do a backpacking trip over several days, the options are almost endless, although one popular route is to Wheeler Peak up the back of the mountain, beginning near Red River and taking two or three days to do a 19-mile loop. Consult with the BLM and the Carson National Forest offices to make sure you've got the maps you need and details on campsites and water sources. If you don't want to haul all the gear yourself, you can go trekking with **Wild Earth Llama Adventures** (800/758-5262, www.llamaadventures.com), which can arrange multiday expeditions March–November with expert naturalist guides. Or you can just "take a llama to lunch" on a day hike ($79) into the surrounding mountains or down in the Rio Grande Gorge.

## BIKING

A popular trail ride close to town is along the west rim of the Rio Grande Gorge, either from the suspension bridge up to John Dunn Bridge, about 15 miles round-trip, or from the suspension bridge south to the Taos Junction bridge near Pilar, about 18 miles out and back. Either way, you'll have great views

and fairly level but rugged terrain. A more aggressive ride is the 22-mile South Boundary Trail (see *Angel Fire* in *The Enchanted Circle* section). **Native Sons Adventures** (1033-A Paseo del Pueblo Sur, 505/758-9342, www.nativesonsadventures.com) can provide maps and shuttle service to and from trailheads. It also runs half- and full-day tours to these and several other trails, as well as hiker-biker combo trips. Angel Fire and Red River both open their slopes to mountain bikers in the summer, with access to the peaks on the chairlift.

If you prefer road touring, you can make a pleasant loop from Taos through Arroyo Hondo and Arroyo Seco. The 25-mile route has no steep grades and is a good way to get adjusted to the altitude. Head north up Paseo del Pueblo Norte, straight through the intersection with Highway 150, then turn right in Arroyo Hondo onto County Road B-143; this road winds up into Arroyo Seco, eventually dead-ending on Highway 230. Turn right, and you'll merge with Highway 150 in a couple of miles. The standard challenge is the 84-mile Enchanted Circle loop; every September sees the Enchanted Circle Century Bike Tour, sponsored by the Red River chamber of commerce (800/348-6444 for information). A mountain-biking race takes place the day before.

**Gearing Up** (129 Paseo del Pueblo Norte, 505/751-0365, 9:30 A.M.–6 P.M. daily) rents mountain and hybrid bicycles for $35 per day, with discounts for longer terms. The bike-fanatic couple who own the shop are very knowledgeable and can point you to less-traveled roads and trails. If you're bringing your bicycle with you, consider having it shipped here, and they'll reassemble it and have it waiting when you arrive.

## ROCK CLIMBING

From popular sport-climbing spots like the basalt Dead Cholla Wall in the Rio Grande Gorge to the more traditional routes at Tres Piedras, Taos is a climber's dream. One of the most impressive pitches is at Questa Dome, north of Taos on Highway 378, where the flawless granite on the Questa Direct route is graded 5.10 and 5.11. And you're not limited to the summer months, as winter sees some terrific ice climbs at higher elevations. **Taos Mountain Outfitters** (111 South Plaza, 505/758-9292, 10 a.m.–6 p.m. Mon.–Sat., 11 a.m.–5 p.m. Sun.) can provide maps, ropes, and more details. For climbing lessons or guided tours, contact **Mountain Skills** (505/776-2222, www.climbingschoolusa.com) in Arroyo Seco.

## RAFTING AND TUBING

The **Taos Box,** the 16-mile stretch of the Rio Grande south of the John Dunn Bridge down to near Pilar, provides perhaps the best rafting in New Mexico, with Class III rapids ominously named Boat Reamer, Screaming Left-Hand Turn, and the like. The river mellows out a bit south of the Taos Box, then leads into a shorter Class III section called the Racecourse—the most popular run, usually done as a half-day trip. Beyond this, in the Orilla Verde Recreation Area around Pilar, the water is wide and flat, a place for a relaxing float with kids or other water newbies; you can flop in an innertube if you really want to chill out. **Native Sons Adventures** (505/758-9342, www.nativesonsadventures.com) leads trips to all these spots and does a couple of tours that combine rafting with other activities. The best season is late May and early June, when the water is high from mountain runoff but marginally less bone-chilling than in the winter months.

## HUNTING AND FISHING

Taos's mountain streams and lakes teem with fish; the feisty cutthroat trout is indigenous to Valle Vidal, north of Questa, or you can hook plenty of browns in the wild waters of the Rio Grande. Eagle Nest Lake and Cabresto Lake (northeast of Questa) are both stocked every year. If you'd like a guide to show you around, **Van Beacham's Solitary Anglers** (866/502-1700, www.thesolitaryangler.com) can't be beat; clients can have exclusive access to a few private river leases, including on the Cimarron River immediately south of

the Eagle Nest dam. For tackle, see **Los Rios Anglers** (126 West Plaza Dr., 505/758-2798, www.losrios.com, 9 a.m.–5:30 p.m. daily).

Elk are the primary target in hunters' rifle scopes, but you can also bag mule deer, bear, and antelope; **High Mountain Outfitters** (505/751-7000, www.huntingnm.com) is one of the most experienced expedition leaders, and it has access to private land for hunting exotics. Visit the website of the New Mexico Game & Fish Department (www.wildlife.state.nm.us) for details on seasons, permits, and licenses.

## SPAS AND SPORTS FACILITIES

**Taos Spa & Tennis Club** (111 Doña Ana Dr., 505/758-1980, www.taosspa.com) is an affordable place to work out muscles made sore from skiing or biking. The $65 for a one-hour massage entitles you to free use of the hot tubs, steam room, and swimming pool for the rest of the day, or you can purchase a day pass to the fitness center for $12. Facials, body scrubs, and other spa treatments are also available.

The **Don Fernando Swimming Pool** (124 Civic Plaza Dr., 505/737-2622, $3, plus $2 for shower) is an unremarkable indoor pool, but it'll do the trick if this is your preferred form of exercise. Hours for recreational and lap swims change seasonally—call to check. The **Kit Carson Park Ice Rink** (505/758-4160, $3) is open from Thanksgiving through February. Hours vary according to the weather and day of the week; call ahead. With skate rental included in the price, it's perhaps the best bargain winter sport in the Taos area.

## TOURS

**Roberta Meyers,** who hosts a weekly storytelling hour at the Fechin Inn, also leads very dramatic walking tours around town, describing the juiciest historical moments as she goes (505/776-2562). **Rob Hawley,** co-owner of the Taos Herb Co. (710 Paseo del Pueblo Sur, 505/758-7641, www.taosherb.com) since 1979, leads day-long walks in the mountains, pointing out local wild treatments and discussing how to prepare them.

# Accommodations

Because Taos is awash in centuries-old houses with impressive cultural and historic pedigrees, bed-and-breakfasts have thrived, even to the exclusion of proper hotels, which are typically of the generic chain variety. For those skeptical of B&Bs, don't despair: The majority of them have private bathrooms, separate entrances, and not too much country-cute decor. Certainly, just as in Santa Fe, the Southwest decor can be applied with a heavy hand, but wood-burning fireplaces, well-stocked libraries, hot tubs, and big gardens can make up for that. Also consider staying outside of Taos proper. Arroyo Seco and Arroyo Hondo are about a half-hour drive from the plaza, and some inns in these two communities, as well as in Ranchos de Taos to the south, offer excellent value. In the summer, the lodges near the ski valley cut their prices by almost half—a great deal if you want to spend some time hiking in the canyon and don't mind driving into town for food and entertainment. If you're arriving in town without a car, a few good budget choices are served by Taos's Chile Line bus, which caters to skiers in the winter, from down on the southern end of town all the way up to the ski valley.

## UNDER $50

The best lodging bargain in the Taos area is **The Abominable Snowmansion** (Hwy. 150 in Arroyo Seco, 505/776-8298, www.taoswebb.com/hotel/snowmansion, $22 pp, $3 HI discount). Conveniently set midway to the Taos Ski Valley, in bustling "downtown" Arroyo Seco, this is a cheerful HI hostel offering bunks in dorm rooms or, in the summertime, tepees. As the name suggests, winter sports fanatics are the main clientele; if you don't want to be woken at the break of dawn by skiers racing for the Chile Line bus outside, opt for an individual cabin with shared bath, or a private room with en suite bathroom (though the latter runs $52 in high ski season). There's also room to camp in the summer, and breakfast is included in the price.

If you want to be closer to the plaza, **Budget Host Inn** (1798 Paseo del Pueblo Sur, 505/758-1989, www.taosbudgethost.com, $40 d) is the best of the string of cheapies along the highway at the southern end of Taos. The rooms in the cheerily painted two-story motel building are a little worn but kept very clean, and you get cable TV, wireless Internet access, and a free continental breakfast. Rates can vary according to the season and overall occupancy, but they're never higher than $70. The same owners manage the **Taos RV Park** next door, which maintains the same tidy standards. If you're on a strict budget, book well ahead here or at the Snowmansion, because many other hotels in this category can be quite grim indeed.

If the Budget Host is booked, your next best option is **Hacienda Inn Taos** (1321 Paseo del Pueblo Sur, 505/758-8610, www.haciendainntaos.com, $45 d), a basic motel in the same area. Refurbishing hasn't yet reached all of the rooms, so ask to see a few, and stick with the ones with newer carpeting. There's a pool on-site, and you get cable TV.

## $50-100

**El Pueblo Lodge** (412 Paseo del Pueblo Norte, 505/758-8700, www.elpueblolodge.com, $69 d) is a budget operation with slightly spacey management but nice perks like free laundry; rooms vary wildly, from a tiny, very atmospheric nook in the oldest adobe section to new, slick motel rooms complete with gas fireplaces. The rooms in the 1960s motel strip are a good combo of atmosphere and tidiness. The grounds are quite pleasant, with a heated pool, a hot tub, and hammocks slung up between the big cottonwoods in the summertime.

**The Laughing Horse Inn** (729 Paseo del Pueblo Norte, 800/776-0161, www.laughinghorseinn.com, $68 d), one of Taos's most popular budget B&Bs, cultivates an eccentric reputation, with a guest list of starving artists and Europeans on vision quests.

Ten rooms in the main adobe house give new meaning to the word "snug" and share three bathrooms, while the penthouse A-frame room, which conjures some of the bygone hippie charm, has a big deck and room for six to sleep ($150 for two). An honor-system kitchen, a clothing-optional hot tub, and continental breakfasts from organic, locally farmed foodstuffs add to the hippie throwback feel.

Not a hotel at all, but simply a clutch of well-maintained one- and two-bedroom private casitas (formerly used as homes for wayward women, as it happens), **Taos Lodging** (109 Brooks St., 505/751-1771, www.taoslodging.com, $79 studio) is in a quiet, convenient block about 10 minutes' walk north from the plaza. The eight cottages, arranged around a central courtyard, have assorted floor plans and perks (one has a washer and dryer, for instance), but all have porches, full kitchens, and living rooms, as well as access to a shared outdoor hot tub. The smallest, a 350-square-foot studio, sleeps two comfortably; the largest, at 800 square feet, sleeps up to six.

In addition to being a tourist attraction, the ◖**Mabel Dodge Luhan House** (240 Morada Ln., 505/751-9686, www.mabeldodgeluhan.com, $95 d) also functions as a homey bed-and-breakfast. Choose one of the snug little rooms in the oldest adobe section, all furnished with rickety antiques, floors worn down from years of treading, and tiny fireplaces; or one of the rooms in the main house: Mabel's original bedroom ($180) is the grandest (you can even sleep in her bed), but for those who don't mind waking at the crack of dawn, the upstairs solarium is gloriously sunny with gorgeous views of the mountain. Either way, you'll feel a little like you're bunking in a historical museum.

**Casa Benavides** (137 Kit Carson Rd., 505/758-1772, www.taos-casabenavides.com, $89 d) calls itself a B&B, but now it feels a bit more like a small hotel, as it sprawls down Kit Carson Road in a series of interconnected buildings, one of which is a wood Victorian built around 1900. The longtime owners, a local family, have put a lot of care into the decoration of the 38 rooms with Taos-style furniture and Western artifacts. Each one is different, which makes the choices a little overwhelming—the artist's studios are nicely secluded, and the two small (and cheap) upstairs rooms in the Benavides family home have balconies with mountain views. Otherwise, pick the price you're comfortable with (they range up to $300), and go from there.

Tucked away in Arroyo Hondo, ◖**Mountain Light B&B** (off Hwy. 522, 505/776-8474, www.mtnlight.com, $55 s, $85 d) is not only a great bargain, but also a wonderful place to feel like a real resident of the area. The owner, a photographer, is particularly encouraging to fellow artists (who can rent an Airstream trailer for longer retreats). Her beautiful tower-shaped house has two guest rooms, which share a bath; they're cozy and simple, decorated with quilts and tucked in the natural curves of the house. You can eat breakfast out on the deck, with an absolutely stupendous view over Valle Valdez—one that hasn't changed much in decades.

About a mile from the base of the ski area, **Austing Haus** (1282 Hwy. 150, 505/776-2649, www.austinghaus.com, $72 d) oozes alpine charm, with exposed beams, lace curtains, and great views of the mountain scenery. The 24 rooms are done in European antiques—a pleasant escape if you're maxed out on Southwest chic—and the location on the road to the mountain is great for skiers or summer hikers. Several rooms have extra beds in sleeping lofts, so you can squeeze in a couple more people; wood-burning fireplaces are another perk in most rooms. Continental breakfast is included.

## $100-150

The owners of the friendly ◖**Brooks Street Inn** bed-and-breakfast (119 Brooks St., 505/758-1489, www.brooksstreetinn.com, $100 d) have their priorities straight: The morning meal outshines those at much higher-priced establishments. The six very well-kept rooms, while not grand, are certainly comfortable (robes and slippers are supplied). Three rooms with private entrances are set back in the walled garden, with wood-burning kiva fireplaces; the other three rooms, in the main house, have wood floors.

( **La Posada de Taos** (309 Juanita Ln., 505/758-8164, www.laposadadetaos.com, $124 d) hits the sweet spot between luxury comforts and casual charm—all the amenities are here, such as wood fireplaces (in five of the six rooms) and whirlpool tubs (in three), but the overall atmosphere is very homey and informal, and the decor is distinctly Taos without being heavy-handed, with sparing country touches. The price is right too, coming in on the lower end compared to other places with the same perks. El Solecito, in the older adobe section with its own back terrace, is recommended.

**Adobe & Pines B&B,** tucked just off the road into Ranchos de Taos (4107 Hwy. 68, 505/751-0947, www.adobepines.com, $100 d), is a little out of the way, but it's especially pretty in the summer, when the large central garden is in bloom. If you like pastels, though, don't come here—the colors throughout are vibrant and strong, with each of the seven rooms painted a different hue. All but the tiniest (snug Puerta Azul, in the old main house) have staggeringly grand bathrooms: Puerta Rosa, for instance, has its own dry sauna and soaking tub, as well as a fireplace.

Everything at **Hacienda del Sol** (109 Mabel Dodge Ln., 505/758-0287, www.taoshaciendadelsol.com, $115 d) is built in relation to Taos Mountain, which looms up in the backyard with no other buildings cluttering the view. Even the smallest rooms feel expansive in the summer, as doors open onto a vast courtyard and, of course, the view (which you can also enjoy from the hot tub). The 11 rooms, spread over several adobe outbuildings, are cozy without being too oppressively Southwestern in their design, and perks like robes, bathtubs, and mini fridges approximate hotel service, while a collection of Taos-related books waits by the bedside.

The **Fechin Inn** (227 Paseo del Pueblo Norte, 505/751-1000, www.fechin-inn.com, $114 d, $208 suite) is set back from the road behind the Taos Art Museum at Fechin House. Its showpiece is its stunning lobby, all done in the Russian wood-carver's style. The rooms, however, aren't quite as thoroughly decorated and have a somewhat bland sameness to them. If you're looking for the amenities of a full-function hotel (such as wireless Internet and a gym), though, you'll find them here at a very good price. Also, Roberta Meyers, storyteller extraordinaire, spins yarns at 6 P.M. and 8 P.M. every Wednesday.

Of the two landmark hotels in town, **Hotel La Fonda de Taos** (108 South Plaza, 505/758-2211, www.hotellafonda.com, $100 d) is preferable to the Taos Inn (which is less expensive, but not so well kept). After a full renovation in 2002, the rooms are very comfortable, if not oozing historic atmosphere, as the wood fireplaces have been replaced with tidier gas. But the beds are very nice, there's DSL in every room, and you can feel quite grand opening your balcony doors over the plaza—no. 301, an extra-spacious front-facing room, is the best

Hotel La Fonda de Taos houses a collection of D. H. Lawrence's erotic paintings.

deal for this. Don't miss the small collection of D. H. Lawrence's erotic paintings ($3 admission); they're tucked in a small room behind the front desk.

Out near Arroyo Hondo, the house-proud owner of ◖ **Little Tree B&B** (226 Hondo–Seco Rd., 505/776-8467, www.littletreebandb.com, $135 d) is a history buff—his expertise is a perk that comes with a stay at this snug inn with four rooms. The house and its small outbuilding are rare examples of old-school adobe (no stucco finish) *without* the stamp of history; a Taos Pueblo expert built them in 1990 using a range of mud finishes and decorative techniques. The feeling is rustic, authentic, but also very comfortable: One room has a private hot tub; all have wood-burning fireplaces or stoves.

**Dobson House** (475 Tune Dr., 505/776-5738, www.taosnet.com/dobsonhouse, $110 d), off U.S. 64 west of town, is a bed-and-breakfast in a modified Earthship. It's a bit more comfortable than staying at the Greater World Earthship development—you have the guarantee of well water, for one, in addition to a phone line—and you don't have to be a fan of eco-architecture to appreciate the stunning view off the eastern edge of the Rio Grande Gorge; hot springs are a short hike away. The setting is isolated but no farther from the plaza than Arroyo Hondo or Seco.

## $150-250

Although the location of **Casa de las Chimeneas** (405 Cordoba Rd., 505/758-4777, www.visittaos.com, $165) a few blocks south of the plaza is very convenient for sightseeing, the place is also a skier's delight, with snow reports via email in the winter, plus a hot tub and wet and dry saunas to soothe aching muscles. The B&B label doesn't quite conjure the right image; breakfast is served, but the layout and the generously appointed rooms feel more like a small luxury lodge than someone's adapted home. The largest suite has its own private steam sauna as well as a whirlpool tub, and skylights, fireplaces, reading nooks, and gigantic tubs are some of the

perks in the other rooms, furnished in tasteful if slightly bland style.

For a larger group or a family, an excellent option in this price range is **Inger Jirby's Casitas** (207 Ledoux St., 505/758-7333, www.jirby.com, $175 suite). The two full guesthouses, side by side on historic Ledoux Street just off the plaza, are furnished very tastefully by the Swedish artist owner with colorful Indian rugs. Five people can sleep comfortably in the multilevel apartments that let in lots of light through clerestory windows. Both have full kitchens, stereo systems, cable TV and Nintendo, and gas fireplaces upstairs and down.

Set in the flat land between Taos and the ski valley, **Alma del Monte B&B** (372 Hondo–Seco Rd., 505/776-2721, www.almaspirit.com, $165 d) has a sprawling hacienda feel, with plenty of public space, as well as nice details like Bose stereos and iPods loaded with local music in the five rooms. Each room feels very secluded and private, perfect for a romantic weekend in; lavish three-course breakfasts ensure that you won't want to do much more than languish in your in-room Jacuzzi or outdoor hot tub.

Much closer to the slopes, **Taos Mountain Lodge** (1346 Ski Valley Road, 505/776-2229, www.taosmountainlodge.com, $175 suite) rents 10 four- and six-person condos with full kitchens and plenty of space. They're a bargain in the summer, at only $80, and close to a lot of good hiking trails.

## OVER $250

A successful experiment in sustainable development is also Taos's most luxurious lodging option: **El Monte Sagrado Spa & Resort** (317 Kit Carson Rd., 505/758-3502, www.elmontesagrado.com, $345 suite), a soothing retreat that's still walking distance from the plaza. Eclectic luxury is the byword here: In the main entrance, an original Basquiat hangs alongside handcrafted jewelry from the pueblo, and the standard suites are named after American Indian leaders, from Black Elk to Jim Thorpe, or feature colorful Taos artwork.

Larger casitas and two-bedroom suites conjure the world's most exotic spots; needless to say, the Indian Kama Sutra suite is very popular. The spa offers pampering galore—it's open to nonguests as well. One very tangible perk of the resort's eco-friendly stance: The pool is treated not with chlorine, but with a nontoxic, non-smelly substance developed by the resort owner's research company. And if guests tire of this soothing hideaway, they can arrange overnight outings to a luxe base camp in the Latir wilderness 30 minutes north of town.

# Food

For a town of its size, Taos has a surprisingly broad selection of restaurants, including quite a few splurge-worthy options with entrée pricing hovering around $30; alas, few vacationers will have the budget to sample all of them, but it's a treat to have a choice. If you're in town during a holiday or peak ski season, you might want to make reservations, but otherwise they're not necessary, and the whole Taos dining scene is exceptionally casual, with waiters often inquiring about your day skiing along with your preference for red or white wine. For less spendy meals, as with hotels, you'll find many options along Paseo del Pueblo Sur, but you won't be priced out of the center of town either. At one of the New Mexican places, be sure to try some posole—it's more common here than in Albuquerque or Santa Fe, often substituted for rice as a side dish alongside pinto beans. Also, the breakfast burrito—a combo of scrambled eggs, green chile, hash browns, and bacon or sausage wrapped in a flour tortilla—is commonly wrapped up in foil and served to go, perfect if you want an early start hiking or skiing.

## COFFEE AND DESSERT

The location of **World Cup** on the corner of the plaza (102-A Paseo del Pueblo Norte, 505/737-5299, 7 A.M.–6 P.M. daily, $3) makes it a popular pit stop for both tourists and locals—the latter typically of the drumming, dreadlocked variety, lounging on the stoop. If you want a bit more room to maneuver, head to **The Bean** (1033 Paseo del Pueblo Sur, 505/758-5123, 6:30 A.M.–4 P.M. Mon.–Fri., 7 A.M.–4 P.M. Sat. and Sun., $6.50), which

serves a full breakfast menu till 2 P.M., along with pastries and incredibly strong, organic coffee. This is an all-day hangout for some regulars, who start with a crossword puzzle and move on to grander projects, all while most of the rest of town files in and out.

In Arroyo Seco, most people start the day at **Taos Cow** (485 Hwy. 150, 505/776-5640, 7 A.M.–7 P.M. daily), a chilled-out coffee bar par excellence, with writers scribbling in one corner and flute players jamming in another. But it's really the ice cream that has made the Taos Cow name (you'll see it distributed all around town, and in occasional spots elsewhere in New Mexico and Colorado). The most popular flavors are tailored to local tastes: Café Olé contains cinnamon and Mexican chocolate chunks, while Cherry Ristra is vanilla with piñon nuts, dark chocolate, and cherries.

Back on the plaza, the raison d'être of **⟨ Xocoatl** (121 North Plaza, 505/751-7549, 11:30 A.M.–5 P.M. Thurs.–Tues., $3) is chocolate, especially its signature Mayan hot chocolate, which is intense and a tiny bit spicy. Other treats include rich flourless chocolate cake and handmade truffles in flavors like lavender-vanilla and banana-cashew. If you feel decadent eating chocolate on an empty stomach, have a crepe, salad, or some other savory dish from the café menu—*then* go for dessert.

For more pastries and artisanal bread, head for **Taos Bakery** (1223 Gusdorf Rd., 505/751-3734, 7 A.M.–3 P.M. Mon.–Fri., 7 A.M.–2 P.M. Sat., $3), which turns out drool-inducing fig tarts, apricot turnovers, and artisanal bread using all organic flour. A smaller but easier-to-locate branch is at 1229 Paseo del Pueblo Norte on the north side (505/758-0434, same opening times).

Taos Bakery pastries are just one attraction at mellow, pro-organic **Sweetgrass Café** (4153 Hwy. 68, 505/737-5200, 7 A.M.–5 P.M. Mon.–Fri., 8 A.M.–5 P.M. Sat., $3), in Ranchos de Taos, where you can also pick up great granola, a breakfast bagel, or a generous plate of scones with whipped cream and homemade jam.

## BREAKFAST AND LUNCH

**Michael's Kitchen** (304-C Paseo del Pueblo Norte, 505/758-4178, 7 A.M.–8:30 P.M. daily, $7) is famous for New Mexican breakfast items like huevos rancheros and blue corn pancakes with pine nuts, served all day, but everyone will find something they like on the extensive menu at this down-home wood-paneled family restaurant filled with chatter and the clatter of dishes. "Health Food," for instance, is a double order of chile cheese fries. The front room is devoted to gooey doughnuts, cinnamon rolls, and pie.

At the homey **C Dragonfly Café** (402 Paseo del Pueblo Norte, 505/737-5859, 7 A.M.–3 P.M. daily, 6–8 P.M. Fri.–Sun., $7), you can choose your table according to which novelty set of salt-and-pepper shakers you prefer. The breakfast menu, served till 11.30 A.M., is wide-ranging, from homemade granola to smoked-trout-and-potato pancakes. It's all supplemented with a delicious array of European-style baked goods. Lunches are equally eclectic and hearty (a roast duck wrap, for instance, or a veggie-filled bowl of Korean *bibimbop*), and a very well-priced dinner menu is served Friday, Saturday, and Sunday (entrées about $14).

In the Taos Inn, elegant **Doc Martin's** (125 Paseo del Pueblo Norte, 505/658-1977, 7:30 A.M.–2:30 P.M. and 5:30–9 P.M. daily, $7) is open all day, but breakfast is when the kitchen really shines—especially on dishes like the Kit Carson (poached eggs on yam biscuits topped with red chile) or blue corn pancakes with blueberries. The lunch menu is also tasty and doesn't reach the stratospheric prices of dinner. Despite the trendy flavor combos on the menu, the chile and beans are made by a Taos local as they have been for decades.

**Sheva Café** (812-B Paseo del Pueblo Norte, 505/737-9290, 7 A.M.–10 P.M. Mon.–Fri., 5–9 P.M. Sat., 10 A.M.–9 P.M. Sun., $10) conjures the tastes of the Middle East, starting with fluffy house-made pita bread and extending to stuffed grape leaves and assorted dips and salads—all of which happen to be vegetarian. The only meaty tastes are the organic lamb and fish on Fridays; otherwise, you can get a savory, fresh-tasting all-veggie variety plate. Early mornings are dedicated to coffee and chill-out music, to ease the young hippie clientele into the day.

Up in Arroyo Seco, **C Abe's Cantina y Cocina** (489 Hwy. 150, 505/776-8516, 7 A.M.–5:30 P.M. daily, $3.50), a creaky old all-purpose general store–diner–saloon, has earned fans from all over for its satisfying and cheap breakfast burritos; and don't miss the sweet, flaky empanadas (delicately spiced prune, apple, and pumpkin are the usual choices) next to the register. For coffee, though, you'll want to go next door to **Taos Cow.**

Just down the street, **Gypsy 360 Café** (Hwy. 150, 505/776-3166, 8 A.M.–4 P.M. Mon.–Sat., 9 A.M.–3 P.M. Sun., $8) serves up huge Thai beef wraps, Vietnamese meatball subs, and spicy Jamaican fish on candy-colored plates; you can sit outside on the small deck or in the cozy sun-porch. There's espresso, too, if your spirits are flagging on the drive up the valley.

For nourishment in Taos Ski Valley, fortify yourself with a green-chile cheeseburger at **Tim's Chile Connection** (Taos Ski Valley, 505/776-2894, 8 A.M.–9 P.M. daily, $12), which gets busy after 3 P.M., when tired skiers come down from a day on the slopes. It's a good place to start in the morning too, with breakfast burritos and huevos rancheros.

## NEW MEXICAN

A small, gaily painted place on the north side of town, the family-run **Orlando's** (1114 Don Juan Valdez Ln., 505/751-1450, 10:30 A.M.–3 P.M. and 5–9 P.M. daily, $10) is invariably the first restaurant named by anyone, local or visitor, when the question of best chile comes up. That said, there have been occasional whisperings about inconsistency (the sort of talk that borders on heresy!), but it still generally serves very satisfying, freshly made New Mexican standards, such as green-chile chicken enchiladas. The posole is quite good too—perfectly firm, earthy, and flecked with oregano. It's always busy, but a fire pit outdoors makes the wait more pleasant.

If Orlando's strikes you as a bit too fancy, **El Taoseño** (819 Paseo del Pueblo Sur, 505/758-4142, 6 A.M.–9 P.M. Mon.–Thurs., 6:30 A.M.–10 P.M. Fri. and Sat., 6:30 A.M.–2 P.M. Sun., $6.50) is a simple diner with everything from chiles rellenos to steak and eggs, all distinctly ungussied-up; fittingly, it's a favorite with Taos's old, old guard (the neighboring wood-floor lounge hosts a "senior dance" on Sunday afternoons).

**El Pueblo** (625 Paseo del Pueblo Norte, 505/751-9817, 6 A.M.–midnight daily, $6) has the most generous opening hours in Taos, so you're bound to end up squeezed into this snug little room at some point, eavesdropping on your neighbors' late-night yarn-spinning. The menu is New Mexican standards, though you can get basic diner fare, like grilled ham-and-cheese sandwiches, as well.

## MEXICAN

It takes a talented chef to rise above the inevitable Mexican/New Mexican confusion (and perhaps chauvinism, if you ask locals what they prefer), but the man in charge at the small, elegant **⬛ Antonio's** (4167 Hwy. 68, 505/758-9889, 11 A.M.–2 P.M. and 5:30–9:30 P.M. Mon.–Sat., $15) has managed, delivering flawless versions of proper Mexican classics like tortilla soup and *chiles en nogada* (stuffed poblano peppers in walnut sauce); the pit-roasted lamb is also recommended. Antonio will likely visit your table to convince you that south of the border is where it's at, food-wise. But if you're still craving *New* Mexican for some reason, the obligatory red and green enchiladas can be found on the back of the menu.

For a less expensive Mexican alternative, stop in at **Guadalajara Grill** (1384 Paseo del Pueblo Sur, 505/751-0063, 10:30 A.M.–9 P.M. Mon.–Sat., 11 A.M.–9 P.M. Sun., $10). It may be in a strip mall, but the food transports you straight to western Mexico, with enormous portions of gooey *queso fundido* (fondue-like cheese) and shrimp sautéed in garlic. There's a branch on the north side as well (822 Paseo del Pueblo Norte, 505/737-0816).

## FINE DINING

Chef Joseph Wrede, of **Joseph's Table** (108-A South Plaza, 505/751-4512, 5:30–11 P.M., $26) in the La Fonda hotel on the plaza, runs the most lauded—and probably the most beautiful—restaurant in Taos. The moodily lit room glitters with gilt butterflies and pussy-willow chandeliers, the better to appreciate decadent treats like duck-fat French fries, citrus-marinated quail, and duck breast with French lentils. You can also enjoy a smaller menu of more casual items at the bar, or the diverse Sunday brunch. Wrede relies on the freshest ingredients from local farms, and he does a great vegetarian special every night.

Like its host hotel, El Monte Sagrado, **De la Tierra** (317 Kit Carson Rd., 505/758-3502, 5:30–10 P.M. daily, $34) is probably the most expensive place to dine in Taos. The markup may be partially for the privilege of dining under a giant James Rosenquist canvas, on exquisitely comfortable chairs, attended to by polished waitstaff, but certainly the food earns its price. The kitchen uses largely organic and local products—most of the produce is grown on the resort's own farm plot—to create pitch-perfect seasonal dishes, such as the wintry braised duck with Alsatian choucroute, all paired with an adventurous wine list. If anything, go just for dessert: The pastry chef elevates familiar tastes like key lime pie to art. (As a last resort, go for breakfast and order the pastry sampler.)

Open since 1988, **Lambert's** (309 Paseo del Pueblo Sur, 505/758-1009, 5:30–9 P.M. daily, $28) is a Taos favorite, where everyone goes for prom, anniversaries, and other landmark

**TAOS**

events. Its New American menu is a bit staid, but everything is executed perfectly—trend-following foodies can't quibble that the chile-dusted rock shrimp with house-made cocktail sauce don't taste good. Get the caribou if you can; otherwise, the signature pepper-crusted lamb is fantastic. A full liquor license means excellent classic cocktails, which you can also enjoy in the snug, clubby couch-filled lounge.

**C Byzantium** (La Placita and Ledoux St., 505/751-0805, 5–10 P.M. Thurs.–Sun., $30) is set in a groovy room with only a few tables and a mix of Taos fixtures and ultra-cool modern touches—mirror tiles trim a traditional spiral pine pillar, for instance. The food follows the same theme, and there's substance underneath the style: Standards like Caesar salad are presented with incredible flair, baked halibut with golden-raisin couscous towers on the plate, and familiar Toblerone inspires an amazing dessert. Great service directly from the owner and an interesting wine list round out this offbeat dining experience. It's pricey, but portions are more than generous.

Hidden away in Arroyo Seco, **Momentitos de la Vida** (470 Hwy. 150, 505/776-3333, 5:30–11 P.M. Tues.–Sun., $26) also pulls out all the stops on beautiful design: Glowing candles illuminate delicate painting on mud walls, while the skillfully prepared food hits all the luxe high points, with standards like oysters, blackened filet mignon, and lobster risotto. But chef Chris Maher has a creative streak that inspires the frequently changing menu, with items like smoked-trout éclairs and plum-glazed duck. Next door, the **Bar at Vida** is one of the most beautiful rooms in Taos: deep sofas with heavy vigas overhead and beautiful murals on the adobe walls; Friday's jazz duo is a popular draw.

Another worthwhile drive is to the **Stakeout** (nine miles south of Taos on Hwy. 68, 505/758-2042, 5–9:30 P.M. daily, $29) for the view across the valley at sunset—the restaurant is halfway up the mountainside south of town. Unlike at many restaurants where the view is paramount, the food holds its own. Hearty steaks and rich seafood such as oysters Rockefeller are aug-mented with a few token vegetarian options like ravioli with porcini mushrooms (Chef Mauro hails from Italy); there's homemade gelato for dessert. A roaring fireplace adds to the ambience in the winter. Coming from town, turn left at the sign about four miles south of the last houses in Ranchos de Taos.

## QUICK BITES

At some point during your stay, you have to grab a snack at the venerable **C Burrito Wagon,** a temporary-looking van set up in the Super Save parking lot (519 Paseo del Pueblo Sur, $3.50) that has in fact been in operation since 1970. Burritos come with your choice of meats and pinto beans, while lighter eaters can opt for a soft taco. Don't let winter weather deter you; you can huddle next to the space heater set up under the awning, or request a double dose of the green-chile salsa. Hours vary, but it's generally open from about 8 A.M. (for breakfast burritos, of course) through late afternoon.

Hands down, **Taos Pizza Out Back** (712 Paseo del Pueblo Norte, 505/758-3112, 11 A.M.–10 P.M., $12) serves up the best pie in town, using mostly local and organic ingredients. A glance at the menu—with items like Thai chicken, green chile and beans, and the popular portabello-camembert combo—often make first-timers blanch, but after a bite or two they're converts, like everyone else in town. Soups and salads are also available, if you want to round out your meal.

The small roadside shack that is **Rita's** (1638 Paseo del Pueblo Norte, 505/751-4431, 7:30 A.M.–8 P.M. Mon.–Fri., 8 A.M.–6 P.M., Sat. and Sun., $1.50) is the place to stop in for tamales, served either plain in their cornhusks or smothered in chile; burritos (breakfast and otherwise) are also tasty.

A drive-through never offered something so good: **Mante's Chow Cart** (402 Paseo del Pueblo Sur, 505/758-3632, 7 A.M.–9 P.M. Mon.–Sat., $4) specializes in breakfast burritos, as well as genius inventions like the Susie: a whole chile relleno wrapped up in a flour tortilla with salsa and guacamole. Perfect road food.

## GROCERIES AND LIQUOR

Planning a picnic? Stop at **Bravo!** (1353-A Paseo del Pueblo Sur, 505/758-8100, 11 A.M.–9 P.M. Mon.–Sat.) for Taos's best selection of wines, as well as gourmet takeout—plenty of cold salads and the like to choose from. **Cid's** grocery (623 Paseo del Pueblo Norte, 505/758-1148, 7:30 A.M.–7 P.M. Mon.–Sat.) also has great takeout food, as well as freshly baked bread and a whole range of organic and local goodies, from New Mexican wines to freshly hunted elk steaks.

# The Enchanted Circle

The loop formed by U.S. 64, Highway 38, and Highway 522, going past the ski resorts of Angel Fire and Red River as well as a handful of smaller towns, is perhaps too generously named, but the views of the Sangre de Cristo mountains, including Wheeler Peak, the tallest in the state, are breathtaking. The area is also a cultural change of pace from Taos: Many of the towns along the north and east sides of the loop were settled by Anglo ranchers and prospectors in the late 1800s, and the "Wild West" atmosphere persisted well into the 20th century, today reinforced by the large population of transplanted flatlander Texans enamored of the massive peaks. You can easily drive the 84-mile route in a day, with time out for a short hike around Red River or a detour along the Wild Rivers scenic byway.

Most guides and maps run the route clockwise, heading north out of Taos to Questa, but if you're doing the outing as a day trip, it makes more sense to head counterclockwise, going through Angel Fire and arriving in Red River or Questa, where there's better food, around lunchtime (or you could pack a picnic lunch to enjoy at any of the picnic areas along the small river west of Red River). You'll also enjoy fantastic views at the end of the drive, descending into the Taos valley from Questa. If you're staying overnight, either direction will work, with the most lodging available in Red River. Because the ski areas value their customers, the roads are generally cleared quickly in the winter; the only patch that may be icy is Palo Flechado Pass west of Angel Fire.

To start, head east on Kit Carson Road, which eventually turns into U.S. 64, winding through the Taos River valley and numerous campgrounds and hiking trails, as well as the Institute for Buddhist Studies. At the pass, the road descends into the high Moreno Valley, a gorgeous expanse of green in the spring and a vast tundra in the winter.

## ANGEL FIRE

A right turn up Highway 434 leads to this tiny ski village. Although the mountain here looks like a molehill in comparison to Taos Ski Valley, **Angel Fire Resort** (800/633-7463, www.angelfireresort.com, $45 full-day lift ticket), with a summit elevation of 10,677 and a vertical drop of 2,077 feet, has one important thing going for it: A massive chunk of the runs are devoted to snowboarding, including four terrain parks and a half-pipe designed by Chris Gunnarson. For those with no snow skills at all, the three-lane, 1,000-foot-long tubing hill provides an easy adrenaline rush. Otherwise, there are few independent attractions in the cluster of timber condos at the base of the mountain. If you're around in the winter, visit **Roadrunner Tours** (Hwy. 434 in town, 505/377-6416) to book a sleigh ride ($25 for 35 minutes)—especially grand on a moonlit night when the snow gleams across the whole valley. The company can also arrange horseback tours and dinners.

In the summer, in addition to the small, trout-stocked Monte Verde Lake and the 18-hole golf course at **Angel Fire Country Club,** both managed by the ski resort, the main

TAOS

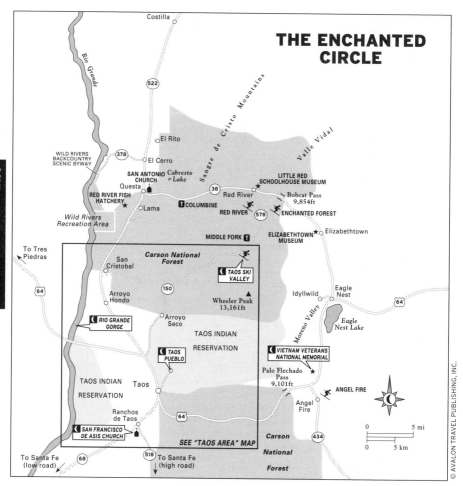

**THE ENCHANTED CIRCLE**

© AVALON TRAVEL PUBLISHING, INC.

diversion here is mountain biking. On the mountain itself, the resort maintains about 30 miles of trails; you can also explore the Elliott Barker Wilderness Area nearby. But the real challenge is the storied **South Boundary Trail,** which runs from a trailhead off Forest Route 76 near Angel Fire to Taos—about 5 vertical-seeming miles up and over the pass, then another 22 or so back to El Nogal trailhead on U.S. 64 about half a mile east of Taos. (Only the truly masochistic would go

the other direction—which doesn't mean it's not done.) Maps are a must; contact **Native Sons Adventures** in Taos (505/758-9342, www.nativesonsadventures.com).

For a lunch of burgers or brisket, stop off at **Zebediah's** (Hwy. 434, 505/377-6358, 11 A.M.–9 P.M. daily), a big wood-paneled room that caters to hungry snowboarders in the winter and folks fishing at Eagle Nest in the summer. The bar, which is open till about 2 A.M., is the main hangout in the area.

## **◖ Vietnam Veterans National Memorial**

Back on U.S. 64, a few miles past the turn for Angel Fire, a swooping white structure rises on the hill to your left. This is the Vietnam Veterans National Memorial (505/377-6900, 9 A.M.–7 P.M. daily June–Aug., 9 A.M.–5 P.M. daily Sept.–May), built by Victor Westphall as a remembrance for his son David, who died in the war. When Westphall commissioned Santa Fe architect Ted Luna to design the graceful white chapel in 1968, it was the first such memorial for the casualties of Vietnam; an adjacent visitors center was built later and has expanded over the years. The complex is a site of pilgrimage for many, and the front grounds and bulletin boards testify to veterans' and families' devotion, as they are covered with additional informal monuments and messages.

## **EAGLE NEST**

Heading north on U.S. 64 from the Vietnam memorial, you soon see Eagle Nest Lake on the left. The lake was created in 1918 with the construction of a dam on the Cimarron River; funded by ranchers and built using Taos Pueblo labor, the 400-foot-wide structure is the largest one in the United States built with private money. In addition to agricultural and mining uses, the lake also supplied an ice-block industry in the winter. Today it's a state park, stocked with trout, and a popular summertime recreation spot (the huge Fourth of July fireworks display is legendary). Vacation homes are clustered down by the water, but the town itself is farther north, at the junction with Highway 38. A small strip of wooden buildings are all that's left of what was a jumping (illegal) gambling town in the 1920s and 1930s, when enterprising businessmen would roll slot machines out on the wooden boardwalks to entice travelers on their way to Raton and the train, and bars like the **Laguna Vista Saloon** hosted roulette and blackjack. The Laguna Vista even claims to host its own phantom, the so-called "Ghost of Guney," a woman whose husband disappeared during their honeymoon stay at the lodge and who was forced into work as

a saloon girl. The restaurant at the Guney is **Texas Reds** (505/377-2755, 5–9:30 P.M. daily, $12), a beloved legend in Red River, which opened a branch here after a fire in 2004. It's recommended for giant steaks or its tasty burgers (dinner only).

## **ELIZABETHTOWN**

Blink and you'll miss it: A small sign on the right side of the road 4.8 miles past Eagle Nest points the way to the former gold-rush site of Elizabethtown, the first incorporated village in New Mexico. Once home to more than 7,000 people, it's now mostly a ghost town overshadowed by the stone ruins of the Mutz Hotel, the former center of social activity. The only signs of life are, ironically, in the **cemetery,** which is still used by residents of Colfax County and contains graves dating as far back as 1880. The **Elizabethtown Museum** (505/377-3420, 9 A.M.–5 P.M. daily June–Aug., $2 donation) details Elizabethtown's brief but lively history, from the discovery of gold in 1866 through assorted gunfights to the town's slow fade after a dredge-mining project failed in 1903.

Continuing on Highway 38, you reach **Bobcat Pass** (505/754-2769, www.bobcat-pass.com), a popular spot for year-round recreation: snowmobiling in the winter and summertime horseback riding and "cowboy evenings" of live music, campfires, and big steaks. Halfway down the pass, the **Enchanted Forest** cross-country ski area (505/754-2374, www.enchantedforestxc.com) has more than 20 miles of well-groomed trails winding through the trees and ascending the mountainside. Nonskiers can rent snowshoes; the nighttime snowshoe tour is especially good.

## **RED RIVER**

Descending into the valley, a somewhat bizarre apparition awaits: tidy rows of wooden buildings, all done up in Old West–look facades, complete with boardwalks and swinging saloon doors. No, it's not Elizabethtown of yore, it's the ski town of Red River (the giveaway: the alpine-theme touches, such as Der Markt grocery store). Although Taos loyalists dismiss the

**Red River Ski & Snowboard Area** (505/754-2223, www.redriverskiarea.com, $49 full-day lift ticket) as an amateur's playground, it's nothing if not convenient: The trails run right into town, so it's walking distance from anywhere to the chairlift. The mountain is fairly evenly divided among beginning, intermediate, and advanced trails.

Like Elizabethtown, though, Red River was once a community of wild prospectors, carving copper, silver, and gold out of the hillsides. When that industry eventually went bust, the town salvaged itself by renting out abandoned houses to vacationers needing a respite from the summer heat at lower elevations (the average summer temperature is just 75°F, dipping to 38°F at night). Luckily, just when air-conditioning started to become widespread, the ski area opened in 1959, saving the town from a major slump. Red River still manages to thrive, with a year-round population of only about 450. For an overview of the community's history, visit the 1914 **Little Red Schoolhouse Museum** (702 E. Main St., 505/754-6564, 10 A.M.–12:30 P.M. Mon., Tues., Fri., and Sat., 6–9 P.M. Thurs., donation), behind the library at the Y junction on the east end of town.

### Hiking

This is the back side of Wheeler Peak, so the ascents are much more gradual, while still yielding dramatic views. Stop in at the **visitors center** (505/754-1708, www.redriver.org, 8 A.M.–5 P.M. daily), in the conference center next to Brandenburg Park, for area maps and trail guides. The least strenuous hiking option is Red River's chair lift, which runs in the summer, weekends only in May and early June, then daily from mid-June through September ($8, plus $15 for a day bicycle pass). It deposits you at the start of numerous hiking and mountain-biking trails back down the slope. If you prefer to stick to the lowlands, the **Red River Nature Trail** starts in town at Brandenburg Park and runs two miles one-way, with signs identifying plants and geological formations. Follow Highway 578, which heads south from town, about six miles to the

turn for Forest Road 487 and **Middle Fork Road,** a pleasant, moderately challenging trail leading seven miles to a small lake. West of town, the road leads past a number of trailheads that make for a good amble. **Columbine Trail,** on the left seven miles out, starts out easy, crossing Deer Creek, but soon moves to a series of long switchbacks that lead through a large aspen grove, then above the tree line to the ridge, a total of about five miles. As an incentive, wild berry bushes flourish alongside the trail in the late summer. The right side of the road, however, is a little less scenic because a molybdenum mine has stripped a good chunk of the mountain. "Molycorp: minerals for tomorrow's technology today" boasts the company, though the future looks awfully bleak right here.

### Food

Red River is a good place to stop for a late lunch if you're craving meat—but if you're hungrier for spicy New Mexican, hold out till Questa. The town's most legendary eatery is **Texas Reds** (505/764-2964) open since 1967 but gutted by a fire in late 2004; the owners were rebuilding next to Brandenburg Park at last check, though how they'll re-create the smoke-stained wallpaper and vintage photos is unknown. In the meantime, **The Red River Dairy Bar** (401 E. Main St., 505/754-2479, 11 A.M.–8 P.M., $5) serves big juicy burgers in an old-fashioned diner atmosphere. If you're around in the evening, **Sundance** (Copper King Trail at High St., 505/754-2971, 5–9 P.M. daily, $10), one block uphill from the main road, serves reasonably good New Mexican food.

## QUESTA

Arriving in Questa, at the junction of Highway 38 and Highway 522, you're back in Spanish New Mexico—the town, which now has a population of about 1,700, was established in 1842 and is still primarily a Hispano farming village, though a few Anglo newcomers have set up art galleries here. The only real sight is the San Antonio Church, a handsome white stucco structure with a red metal roof and the distinctively New Mexican spiral-carved pine columns on either side of the front door; inside, santos and *retablos* by local artisans adorn the altar and the side niches.

## Food

Turning south on Highway 522, you're on the final leg of the Enchanted Circle loop; the **Questa Café** (505/586-9631, 6 A.M.–10 P.M. Mon.–Sat., 6 A.M.–3 P.M. Sun., $6), about half a mile south of the junction, is the best place in town for hearty New Mexican home cooking. Or **Paloma Blanca** (505/586-2261, 7 A.M.– 6 P.M. Mon.–Sat., $3), Questa's only coffee-house, owned by a local blacksmith, offers a pick-me-up for the end of the drive.

## Wild Rivers Recreation Area

Visitors usually breeze straight through Questa on their way to the Wild Rivers Recreation Area, a portion of Carson National Forest that encompasses the confluence of the Rio Grande and Red River, and the dramatic canyons forged by the two flows. Steep hiking trails lead down into the gorge and along the river, so you can make a full loop, and white-water rafting is very popular here in the Class III rapids of the Red River Confluence run. Five developed campgrounds (but no RV hookups) on the rim can be reached by car, or you can hike in to campsites by the river. The area feels very remote and wild, especially once you get down one of the trails—you will probably see red-tailed hawks circling over the gnarled, centuries-old piñon and juniper trees that line the rim of the gorge. The access road is 3 miles north on Highway 522 from the main Questa intersection, then west on Highway 378, which leads through the town of El Cerro and to the area's visitors' center (505/770-1600, 10 A.M.– 5 P.M. Fri.–Sun., $3 day use, $7 camping).

At the southern edge of the recreation area, but reached by going south 3.5 miles on Highway 522 from Questa, the **Red River Fish Hatchery** produces almost 400,000 trout every year to stock lakes all over northern New Mexico. Dedicated anglers, or just people whose kids are getting antsy in the back seat, can stop into the visitors center (9 A.M.–5 P.M. daily), where you can take a free self-guided tour and feed "trout chow" to the growing guppies.

## The D. H. Lawrence Ranch

After Questa, the view opens up as you descend into the valley, with mesas stretching far to the west. Just south of San Cristobal, a turn to the left (Taos County Road B-009) leads five miles on a rutted road to the ranch where English writer and provocateur D. H. Lawrence lived in 1924 and 1925 with his wife, Frieda, and the painter Dorothy Brett. The 160-acre spread, originally called the Kiowa Ranch, was a gift to Lawrence and his wife from Mabel Dodge Luhan, who had invited them. Lawrence soon returned to Europe, but Frieda stayed on; after the writer died of tuberculosis in France in 1930, she eventually decided to exhume his body and have the ashes returned to New Mexico. This plan sparked anger among Lawrence's other friends, including Mabel Dodge, who characterized Frieda's planned site for the ashes as "that outhouse of a shrine." Tales abound about how Lawrence's ashes never quite made the trip, whether by accident or sabotage, but visitors to the ranch remain undeterred. Some of the earliest to pay their respects to the place include Tennessee Williams and Georgia O'Keeffe, whose dramatic painting *The Lawrence Tree* is based on the view from the base of a gnarled pine. The aforementioned shrine is indeed small and now very run-down, as the University of New Mexico, which runs the ranch as a retreat center, has been neglectful; aside from what may or may not be Lawrence's ashes mixed into a concrete slab, the modest building contains a guest book and a small altar of oddments left by previous literary pilgrims. To reach the ranch coming from the north, turn left at the second sign for Taos County Road B-009 (the first is in the town of San Cristobal); coming straight from Taos, look for the historic marker on the right side of the road, immediately before the turn.

# Information and Services

## TOURIST INFORMATION

The **Taos Visitors Center** (505/758-3872, www.taoschamber.com, 9 A.M.–5 P.M. Mon.–Sat.), maintained by the Taos chamber of commerce, is an expansive and helpful place on Paseo del Pueblo Sur (Hwy. 68) a few miles south of the plaza. Stop here for flyers and maps galore, free coffee, and a copy of the very thorough weekly news and events bulletin, which includes all gallery listings, music, and more. The staff can also advise on the Enchanted Circle. Take a peek at the side room maintained by Taos Pueblo, which displays pieces by local artisans; it's all paid for with casino money and is very tastefully done.

If you're planning to go hiking, mountain biking, or cross-country skiing, stop in at the **Carson National Forest Supervisor's Office** (208 Cruz Alta Rd., 505/758-6200, www.fs.fed.us/r3/carson, 8:30 A.M.–4:30 P.M. Mon.–Fri.) for advice, booklets on recommended trails, and maps. Just down the street, the **Bureau of Land Management Taos Field Office** (226 Cruz Alta Rd., 505/758-8851, www.nm.blm.gov, 7:45 A.M.–4:30 P.M. Mon.–Fri.) can help you prepare for a rafting or longer camping trip, with plenty of maps and brochures.

For the Enchanted Circle area, the **Red River Chamber of Commerce** (100 Main St., 505/754-2366, www.redrivernewmex.com, 8 A.M.–5 P.M. Mon.–Fri.), in the town hall in the center of town, opposite Brandenburg Park, can advise on lodging and other activities in and around the town. The **Angel Fire Chamber of Commerce** (Centro Plaza, Hwy. 434, 505/377-6661, www.angelfirechamber.org, 9 A.M.–5 P.M. Mon.–Fri., 9 A.M.–4 P.M. Sat.) maintains a visitors center as well; the lobby is open 24 hours, so you can load up on glossy brochures even when the office is closed.

### Books and Maps

**Moby Dickens** (124-A Bent St., No. 6 Dunn House, 505/758-3050, 10 A.M.–6 P.M. Sun.– Thurs., 10 A.M.–7:30 Fri. and Sat.) is Taos's best bookstore, exceedingly well informed on local history and culture, stocking plenty of maps, as well as rare books, a good CD collection, and assorted gift items.

### Local Media

The *Taos News* comes out every Thursday, and it contains the *Tempo* entertainment section, with music, theater, and film listings. Many hotels offer free copies of *Tempo* to their guests. The *Albuquerque Journal* publishes a special Northern edition daily, focused on local issues, but if you really want to dip in the muck of local politics, pick up a free copy of the gossip-mongering *Horse Fly,* published monthly as the voice of cantankerous Taos; you can even read up on the Web ahead of your visit (www.horseflyonline.com). In the Red River area, the free *Sangre de Cristo Chronicle* is about as hard-hitting as it gets.

On the northeast corner of the plaza, **Fernandez de Taos** (109 N. Taos Plaza, 505/758-4391, 10 A.M.–6 P.M. Sun.–Wed., 10 A.M.–7:30 P.M. Thurs.–Sat.) is a run-of-the-mill bookstore, but it has the town's best newsstand, with the *New York Times,* lots of magazines, and local papers like *La Herencia,* a bilingual journal devoted to northern New Mexico Hispano culture.

### Radio

While you're in town, don't miss tuning in to KTAO (101.9 FM), a local radio station that's all solar-powered. The musical programming is broad, and you're sure to learn an interesting tidbit about the community in the process. You can keep up with the outside world on KRZA (88.7 FM) and KXMT (99.1 FM), which carry National Public Radio news.

## SERVICES
### Banks

**First State Bank** (120 W. Plaza, 505/758-6600, 9 A.M.–5 P.M. Mon.–Fri.), just off the southwest corner of the plaza, is the most convenient bank and ATM while on foot. The drive-through service at **Centinel Bank of Taos** (512 Paseo del Pueblo Sur, 505/758-6700, 9 A.M.–5 P.M. Mon.–Fri.) is easily accessible from the main drag.

## Post Offices
The Taos **post office** (318 Paseo del Pueblo Norte, 505/758-2081, 8:30 A.M.–5 P.M. Mon.–Fri.) is on the west side of Paseo del Pueblo Norte, next to the Dragonfly Café. Another post office farther north (1518 Paseo del Pueblo Norte, 505/758-4810, 8:30 A.M.–4:30 P.M. Mon.–Fri., 8:30–11:30 A.M. Sat.) is open Saturdays as well.

## Internet
**Wired?** (705 Felicidad St., 505/751-9473, 7 A.M.–8 P.M. Mon.–Sat., 9 A.M.–7 P.M. Sun.), off behind Raley's La Posta Rd., is a laid-back Internet café with a big garden, light snacks, and free wireless access for laptops; other-wise, computer use is $7 per hour. The Fechin Inn also has a wireless hot spot in its lobby. The **Taos Public Library** (420 Camino de la Placita, 505/758-3063, 10 A.M.–5 P.M. Mon.–Sat.) has less atmosphere, but it's also cheaper, at $2 per hour for users without a library card.

## Laundry
Taos's only laundromat is the **Spin & Sparkle,** a few blocks south of the plaza (106 Siler Rd., 505/758-5150, 7 A.M.–7:15 P.M. daily); you can also drop off your laundry and have them do it for you.

## Classes
Donner Ranch offers **Fechin Art Workshops,** four-day live-in retreats at a ranch just north of Taos in the mountains above the village of San Cristobal. Seminars have 14–20 students, guaranteeing personal critiques from the various instructors, most of whom specialize in oil painting, especially landscapes.

# Getting There and Around

## BY AIRPLANE
**Westward Airways** (877/937-8927, www .westwardairways.com) runs two flights daily between the Albuquerque Sunport (ABQ) and Taos Municipal Airport (TSM), an airstrip halfway down U.S. 64 on the way to the Rio Grande Gorge. Fares are about $90 one-way.

## BY CAR
**Enterprise** has an office at the Taos airport and one in town (334 Paseo del Pueblo Sur, 505/737-0514), though **Friday Motors** (1040 Paseo del Pueblo Sur, 505/758-2252), a car dealership at the south end of town, is sometimes more willing to cut a deal.

## BY BUS AND SHUTTLE
**TNM&O** (806/763-5389, www.tnmo.com) operates bus service from Albuquerque to Taos, with an early-morning departure. The three-hour ride costs $27 one-way; it also stops in Santa Fe. The bus station in Taos is at 1008 Paseo del Pueblo Sur (505/758-1144). Coming from Taos, TNM&O's service leaves at 5:45 A.M. and 6:30 P.M.

   **Faust's Transportation** (505/758-3410) runs a twice-daily shuttle between Albuquerque Sunport and Taos ($45 one-way), Taos Ski Valley ($50), Angel Fire, and Red River (both $55). It stops in Santa Fe, so you can use it to travel to Taos from the capital ($35). The company also provides taxi service in town.

   Within Taos, the **Chile Line bus** (505/751-4459) runs north–south from the Ranchos de Taos post office to the Taos Pueblo, extending all the way up to Taos Ski Valley in the wintertime. Buses run approximately every 30 minutes 7 A.M.–9 P.M. The fare is 50 cents, or $1 for an all-day pass.

TAOS

# ALBUQUERQUE

As a tourist destination, Albuquerque may labor in the shadow of the jet-set arts colonies to the north, but as a city, it's a thriving haven for those who pride themselves on being down-to-earth and sensible. If Santa Fe is the "City Different" (a moniker any Albuquerquean will razz for its pretentiousness), then New Mexico's largest city, with a population of nearly 800,000, is proudly the "City Indifferent"—unconcerned with fads, cultivated quirkiness, and museum-quality building facades.

Which is not to say the city doesn't have its pockets of historic charm, well away from the traffic-clogged arteries of I-40 and I-25, which intersect in the center in a graceful tangle of looping, turquoise-trimmed bridges. The Duke City was founded three centuries ago, its cumbersome name that of a Spanish nobleman, but its character is the product of later eras: the post-1880 downtown district; the University of New Mexico campus, built in the early 20th century by John Gaw Meem, the architect who defined pueblo revival style; and Route 66, the highway that joined Albuquerque to Chicago and Los Angeles beginning in 1926.

Spread out on either side of the Rio Grande, from volcanic mesas on the west to the foothills of the Sandia Mountains along the east, Albuquerque enjoys a striking natural setting. Easily accessible hiking and biking trails run through diverse environments: In the morning, you can stroll under centuries-old cottonwood trees along the wide, muddy river through the center of the city; in the afternoon, you can hike along the edge of a windswept mountain range

© ZORA O'NEILL

# HIGHLIGHTS

◖ **Rio Grande Nature Center State Park:** Savor a bit of country in the city in this bird-filled sanctuary along the river. Hiking and biking trails head north and south along the cottonwood-shaded irrigation channels (page 138).

◖ **San Felipe de Neri Church:** Built in 1793, this adobe church is the most striking building in Albuquerque's historic Old Town. It's still in regular use by local parishioners (page 139).

◖ **Nob Hill:** Hobnob and boutique-hop in Albuquerque's quirkiest shopping district, developed in sleek modern style in the 1940s. Sidewalk cafés and bars provide a place to rest up afterward (page 145).

◖ **National Hispanic Cultural Center:** This grand new institution, built in a historic barrio south of downtown, contains a great museum displaying art by Spanish-speakers from all over the globe; try to catch a flamenco performance in the beautiful auditorium (page 145).

◖ **Sandia Peak Tramway:** Zip up the world's longest single-cable tram to the crest of the mountain that looms over Albuquerque. At the top, you'll get a vertigo-inducing view across the whole metro area and out to the west (page 145).

◖ **Petroglyph National Monument:** The city's west mesa is covered with fine rock carvings made centuries ago by the ancestors of the local Pueblo people. Don't miss the views across the city from the dormant volcanoes at the top of the ridge (page 146).

◖ **Acoma Pueblo:** This windswept village on a mesa west of Albuquerque is one of the oldest communities in the United States. Visit for the views as well as for the delicate black-on-white pottery made only here (page 168).

◖ **Valles Caldera National Preserve:** In the crater formed by a collapsed volcano, some 89,000 acres of grassy valleys are set aside for very controlled public access. You must make reservations to hike here, but it's worth planning ahead (page 178).

**ALBUQUERQUE**

LOOK FOR ◖ TO FIND RECOMMENDED SIGHTS, ACTIVITIES, DINING, AND LODGING.

with views across the vast empty land beyond the city grid. And at the end of the day, you'll see Albuquerque's most remarkable feature, the dramatic light show that results from the setting sun reflecting bright pink off the Sandia (Watermelon) Mountains.

The city is also an excellent (and reasonably priced) base for exploring the many interesting pueblos and natural attractions nearby, and it's just an hour's drive to Santa Fe, allowing for easy day trips or long scenic drives through the mountains in between. The main outing is the

65 miles west to Acoma Pueblo, a thousand-year-old settlement atop a natural fortress of stone. Naturalists will want to head south to the Bosque del Apache, one of the United States' largest bird sanctuaries, which attracts some 15,000 sandhill cranes in November; drive down before dawn to see the birds at their most active, then wind your way back north via the Quebradas Backcountry Scenic Byway, a meandering dirt route through rainbow-striped hills.

Whether you're en route to Santa Fe or just making a day loop, you have several ways to head north. The most direct is I-25, which cuts through dramatic rolling hills; take a short detour to Kasha-Katuwe Tent Rocks National Monument, where bizarrely pointed white rocks tower above a narrow canyon. Beginning east of Albuquerque, the historic Turquoise Trail winds along the back side of the Sandias, then through the former mining town of Madrid, resettled as an arts colony, with galleries occupying the cabins built against the black, coal-rich hills.

The most meandering route north is along the Jemez Mountain Trail, a scenic byway that heads northwest out of Albuquerque and runs through the brick-red rocks surrounding Jemez Pueblo, then past a number of natural hot springs. The road runs along the border of Valles Caldera National Preserve, a vast, pristine valley where the daily number of visitors is carefully limited, so you can enjoy the vistas in solitude.

## PLANNING YOUR TIME

Because Albuquerque's major historic attractions are few, the city really fares best as the primary focus of a trip, when you have time to enjoy the natural setting and the people. So ideally, you would spend a leisurely week here soaking up a little Route 66 kitsch, enjoying the downtown entertainment, hiking in the Sandias, taking scenic drives, and bicycling along the Rio Grande.

But given the rich history and scenic splendor farther north, it is difficult to recommend spending more than a couple of days in Albuquerque if you're also planning to visit Santa Fe and Taos in a limited time. In this case, you'll probably want to allocate only a couple of days on your way in or out—preferably the latter, because Albuquerque's modern, get-real attitude is best appreciated after you've been in the adobe dreamland of Santa Fe for a bit. Spend a day driving west to Acoma Pueblo, then the next relaxing and knocking around Old Town and the shops in Nob Hill. Or if you prefer a last dose of open sky, take the tramway up to Sandia Peak and hike along the crest trail—at the end of your trip, you'll be able to handle the elevation with no problem.

Any time of year is enjoyable in the city proper—even the winters are quite mild in the low basin around the river, though the Sandias start getting snow in December. As elsewhere, summer heat is usually broken by heavy afternoon rainstorms. And because Albuquerque is *not* top on tourists' lists, there's rarely a time when major attractions are unpleasantly mobbed. Hotel prices are highest in summer, but not a dramatic hike from low-season rates.

## HISTORY

Even before the steady traffic of tourists to points north, Albuquerque was a way station. It was established in 1706 as a small farming outpost on the banks of the Rio Grande, where Pueblo Indians had already been cultivating crops since 1100, and named after a Spanish duke, then a viceroy in Mexico. When the Camino Real, the main trade route north from Mexico, developed decades later, the Villa de Alburquerque (the first "r" was lost over the years) was ideally situated, and the town soon prospered and outgrew its original adobe fortress, the central plaza ringed with one-story haciendas and a grand church.

Life continued relatively quietly through the transition to U.S. rule in 1848, but then, in 1880, the railroad came through town—or near enough. The depot was some two miles from the original plaza, but investors were quick to construct "New Town," which became the downtown business district. Railroad

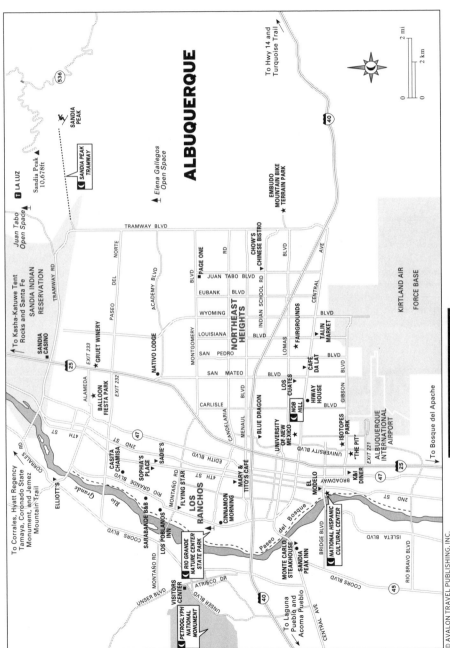

ALBUQUERQUE

Avenue—later named Central Avenue—connected the two communities, though increasingly "Old Town" fell by the wayside, its old adobe buildings occupied primarily by the Mexican and Spanish population maintaining their rural lifestyle, while Anglos dominated commerce and the construction of the new city. Developers rapidly built up the land around the train station, with hotels, banks, shops, and more, while other visionaries looked to "the heights"—the sand hills east of the tracks—as the site for a new university. In the early 20th century, Albuquerque's crisp air began to be lauded for its beneficial affect on tuberculosis patients, and a number of sanatoriums flourished. Then Route 66 was laid east–west down Central Avenue in the 1930s; by the next decade car traffic and business was booming, and by the 1950s, the characteristic neon signage on the numerous motor-court hotels and diners was in place.

Albuquerque's character again changed drastically following World War II, when recruits trained at Kirtland Air Force Base returned to live where they'd learned to be pilots; at the same time, the escalating Cold War fueled Sandia National Labs, established in 1949, and engineers relocated to work on defense technology (thanks to the labs, Albuquerque still has more PhDs per capita than any other major city in the United States). Streets were carved into the northeast heights in anticipation of the tract houses these new workers would inhabit, and over the course of the 1940s, the population exploded from 35,000 to 100,000; by 1959, 207,000 people lived in Albuquerque.

Growth has been steady ever since, and in the 1990s, the city experienced another development boom, helped along by the construction of one of Intel's largest American manufacturing plants. Subdivisions have spread across the West Mesa, and small outlying communities such as Bernalillo and Placitas have been incorporated into the larger metro area. Now they're primarily wealthy suburbs, though portions, such as Corrales and Los Ranchos de Albuquerque, both north of central Albuquerque along the river, retain a village feel that's not too far from the city's roots as a farming community three centuries back.

# Sights

## ORIENTATION

Albuquerque's greater metro area covers more than 100 square miles, but visitors will likely be in only a handful of neighborhoods, all of which are linked by Central Avenue (historic Route 66), the main east–west thoroughfare across town. Visitors typically start in Old Town, where the city's best museums are clustered a few blocks from the Rio Grande, which runs north–south through the city. East from Old Town lies downtown, where most of the city's bars and clubs are located, along with the bus and train depots. Central Avenue then continues under I-25 and past the University of New Mexico campus. Just east of the school, the Nob Hill shopping district occupies about 10 blocks of Central. After this, the rest of Albuquerque blurs into the broad area known as the Northeast Heights, where there are only a few attractions of note—visitors will want to come up this way, to the farthest edge of the heights, to hike in the foothills and ride the Sandia Peak Tramway to the top of the mountain. The other notable parts of town—technically, separate villages—are Los Ranchos de Albuquerque and Corrales. These are two districts in the North Valley—the stretch of the river north of Central—that contain a few of the city's better lodging options; from Old Town, head north on Rio Grande Boulevard to reach Los Ranchos, then jog west over the river and north again to Corrales.

When you're trying to get your bearings, do as the locals do and keep your eyes on the mountains, which run along the east side of the city. Additionally, street addresses are fol-

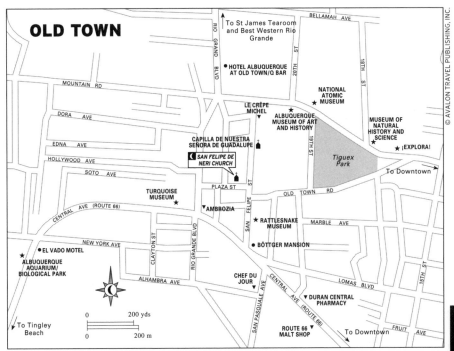

lowed by the city quadrant (NE, NW, SE, SW); Central Avenue forms the dividing line between north and south, while the east–west border is roughly along 1st Street and the train tracks, with numbers increasing as they go away from the dividing lines. The two intersecting highways, I-40 (east–west) and I-25 (north–south), also divide the city into regions, though you won't need to use the freeways for much until you head east to the foothills or west to Petroglyh National Monument and Acoma Pueblo.

## OLD TOWN AND THE RIO GRANDE

Until the railroad arrived 1880, Old Town wasn't old—it was the *only* town, a cluster of one-story haciendas on the riverbank with the formal title of La Villa de San Felipe de Alburquerque. Today this area is primarily a tourist destination, the labyrinthine old adobes repur-

posed as souvenir emporiums and galleries; most of the city's major museums are nearby on Mountain Road. Despite all the chile pepper magnets and cheap cowboy hats, though, the residential areas surrounding the shady plaza retain a strongly rooted Hispano flavor and the historic Old Town buildings have a certain endearing scruffiness—they're lived-in, not polished to museum-quality shine. Because there are few formal sights but plenty of lore in the neighborhood, a free walking tour with the Albuquerque Museum of Art and History is recommended if you have time. A few blocks west of Old Town runs the Rio Grande, which creates a ribbon of green space through the city and a quiet reminder of the city's agricultural history.

### Albuquerque Biological Park

This-kid friendly park (2601 Central Ave. NW, 505/764-6200, 9 A.M.–5 P.M. daily Sept.–May,

# UP, UP, AND AWAY: ALBUQUERQUE'S HOT-AIR BALLOON HISTORY

How did it come to be that one of the most iconic sights in Albuquerque is a 127-foot-tall Mr. Peanut figure floating in front of the Sandias? The city's balloon-friendly air currents were tested for the first time in 1882, when an adventurous bartender piloted a hydrogen-filled craft into the sky as part of the New Town's Fourth of July celebrations, much to the delight of the assembled crowd, which had waited most of the day for *The City of Albuquerque*, as the balloon was dubbed, to fill. "Professor" Park Tassell, the showman pilot, went aloft alone and landed successfully; the only mishap was that a ballast sandbag was emptied on a spectator's head.

But then it took another 90 years before Albuquerque again drew attention as a place to pursue this gentle sport – in 1972, the first balloon fiesta was held, with 13 aircraft participating. The gathering, centered around a single race, was organized by a local balloon club largely as a publicity stunt for a local radio station's 50th anniversary celebrations. The spectacle drew 20,000 spectators, most of whom had never even seen a hot-air balloon before, but within a few short years,

the event was an annual spectacle of international renown.

Albuquerque, it turns out, enjoys the world's most perfect weather for navigating hot-air balloons: A phenomenon called the "Albuquerque Box," created by the steep mountains adjacent to the low river bottom, enables pilots to move at different speeds at different altitudes, and even to backtrack if necessary. Couple that with more than 300 days of sunshine per year, and it's no wonder that now more than 700 balloons – including "special shapes" like Mr. Peanut – convene annually to show off their colors and compete in precision flying contests.

Boosters of the scene include locals Ben Abruzzo, Larry Newman, and Maxie Anderson, who in 1978 made the first Atlantic crossing by balloon in the Double Eagle II helium craft. Abruzzo and Anderson also crossed the Pacific and set a long-distance record (5,678 miles) in the Double Eagle V. These pioneers are honored at **The Anderson-Abruzzo Albuquerque International Balloon Museum** (505/880-0500, www.balloonmuseum.com), which opened in 2005 in Balloon Fiesta Park.

Thousands turn out for the mass ascensions at the Albuquerque International Balloon Fiesta.

9 A.M.–6 P.M. daily June–Sept., $7) on the riverbank just west of Old Town contains two components: On one side is a small but well-done aquarium, with a giant shark tank, and a creepy tunnel full of eels, and displays on underwater life from the Gulf of Mexico and up the Rio Grande. The other half of the park is devoted to botanical gardens, including a desert hothouse and a butterfly habitat. The most New Mexico–specific installation, and the most interesting, is the 10-acre Rio Grande Heritage Farm, a re-creation of a 1930s operation with vineyards, apple orchards, and a cider press. The farm maintains heirloom apple varieties, as well as rare types of livestock, such as Percheron horses and Churro sheep. It's an idyllic setting near the river and fun for kids (especially if you're there for the apple harvest).

Pay an extra $3, and you also get admission to the **Rio Grande Zoo** (903 10th St. SW, 505/764-7200, 9 A.M.–5 P.M. daily Sept.–May, 9 A.M.–6 P.M. daily June–Sept., $7); it's not particularly ground-breaking, but kids can run around among trumpeting elephants and screeching peacocks. The window into the gorilla nursery is probably the most fascinating exhibit.

## Albuquerque Museum of Art and History

The museum (2000 Mountain Rd. NW, 505/243-7255, 9 A.M.–5 P.M. Tues.–Sun., $4), which was enhanced by an airy new entrance wing and expanded sculpture garden in late 2004, has a permanent collection ranging from a few choice Taos Society of Artists members (compare Ernest L. Blumenschein's *Star Road and White Sun* with *Acoma Legend,* a painting by his wife, Mary Greene Blumenschein, which use similar colors and allegorical techniques but very different styles) to contemporary work by the likes of Nick Abdalla, whose sensual imagery makes Georgia O'Keeffe's flower paintings look positively literal. The history wing covers four centuries, with heavy emphasis on Spanish military trappings, Mexican cowboys, and Albuquerque's early railroad years. Free guided tours run daily around the sculpture garden, or you can join the informative Old Town walking tour (11 A.M. Tues.–Sun. Mar.–Dec.).

## American International Rattlesnake Museum

You'd never guess this small storefront just off the plaza (202 San Felipe St. NW, 505/242-6569, 10 A.M.–6 P.M. Mon.–Sat., noon–5 P.M. Sun., $3.50) houses the largest collection of live snakes in the world, as you have to wade through an enormous gift shop full of plush snakes, wood snakes, little magnet snakes, and snakes on T-shirts to see the real critters. You'll also see some fuzzy tarantulas and big desert lizards, and the reptile-mad staff are usually showing off some animals outside, to help educate the phobic.

## Capilla de Nuestra Señora de Guadalupe

Tucked away in a side alley off the main street, this tiny adobe chapel (404 San Felipe Rd. NW) is dedicated to the first saint of Mexico; her image dominates the wall facing the entrance. The dimly lit room, furnished only with heavy carved seats against the walls, is still in regular use, and the air is sweet with the smell of votive candles and *milagros* placed at Mary's feet and on the modest altar, along with prayers and testimonies. Despite the building's small scale, it follows the scheme of many traditional New Mexican churches, with a clerestory that allows sunlight to shine down on the altar.

## ¡Explora!

This 50,000-square-foot complex adjacent to the natural history museum (1701 Mountain Rd. NW, 505/224-8300, 10 A.M.–6 P.M. Mon.–Sat., noon–6 P.M. Sun., adults $7, children $3) is dedicated to thrilling—and educating—children; adults may learn something too. Its colorful geodesic dome top sets a circus-like tone, and inside, more than 250 interactive exhibits demonstrate the scientific principles behind everything from high-wire balancing to optical illusions. Kids can even build robots using

Lego systems, and, since this is the desert, a whole section is dedicated to water.

## Indian Pueblo Cultural Center

Just north of I-40 from Old Town, the Indian Pueblo Cultural Center (2401 12th St. NW, 505/843-7270, www.ipcc.org, 9 A.M.–4:30 P.M. daily, $5) is a must-visit before heading to any of the nearby Indian communities. The horseshoe-shaped building (modeled after the Pueblo Bonito ruins in Chaco Canyon in northwestern New Mexico) houses a large museum that traces the history of the first settlers along the Rio Grande, illustrated with some beautiful artifacts. The central plaza hosts dance performances (11 A.M. and 2 P.M. Apr.–Nov., noon Dec.–Mar.), and the extensively stocked gift shop is a very good place to buy pottery and jewelry, as well as Native American music on CD. You can also have a lunch of posole and frybread at the Pueblo Harvest Café. Don't miss the south wing, added in 2004, which contains a gallery for contemporary art. At the information desk, check on ceremony schedules and get directions to the various pueblos.

## Museum of Natural History and Science

This large exhibit space (1801 Mountain Rd. NW, 505/841-2800, 9 A.M.–5 P.M. daily, $6–16) contains three major attractions: a planetarium and observatory; a wide-format theater screening the latest vertigo-inducing nature documentaries; and a presentation of Earth's geological history. The geology section is structured as a walk-through timeline, beginning with the Big Bang (rendered with blacklights and thunderclaps) and meandering through the prehistoric era and age of volcanic activity. Some of the attractions, such as the hokey "evolator" time machine, don't live up to the hype, but there's plenty of space given to the real crowd-pleasers: dinosaurs. New Mexico has been particularly rich soil for paleontologists, and several of the most interesting finds are on display, such as *Coelophysis* and *Pentaceratops*.

## National Atomic Museum

Some Albuquerqueans have bemoaned the 69-foot-tall Redstone missile in front of this museum (1905 Mountain Rd. NW, 505/245-2137, 9 A.M.–5 P.M. daily, $5) as an eyesore, but it's a handy landmark for out-of-towners. Inside, you'll find everything you wanted to know about atomic energy, and probably a lot more, split between nuclear physics' use in daily life and a thorough recounting of the development and use of the atomic bomb, from the first tests at the Trinity Site to its use in Japan to later, less-remembered incidents such as the loss of several warheads over Palomares, Spain, in 1966. The amount of information can feel a bit crushing, but the wonkish displays are interspersed with Cold War–era comic books and other cultural artifacts—just enough colorful detail to entertain the non-science-oriented while others bone up on nuclear history. (Much to the relief of Old Town residents, the museum is slated to move to a new site at Balloon Fiesta Park sometime in 2008.)

## ◖ Rio Grande Nature Center State Park

Familiarize yourself with river ecology at this green haven in the center of town (2901 Candelaria St. NW, 505/344-7240, 8 A.M.–8 P.M. daily, $3 parking). The visitors center (10 A.M.–5 P.M. daily) is a sleek, angular concrete design by local architect Antoine Predock that's surprisingly harmonious with the surrounding greenery; you enter through a drainage culvert to an exhibit on water conservation and river ecology. Beyond, a comfortable glassed-in "living room" lets you watch birds on the pond outside, from the comfort of a lounge chair and with the outdoor sounds piped in over speakers. Outside, you can walk several paved trails across the old irrigation channels and along the river, all shaded by towering cottonwood trees. In the spring and fall, the area draws all manner of migrating birdlife; borrow binoculars from the staff if you want to scout on your own, or join one of the frequent nature walks (including full-moon tours) that take place year-round.

© ZORA O'NEILL

entrance to the Rio Grande Nature Center State Park

## ⟨ San Felipe de Neri Church

Established in 1706 along with the city itself, San Felipe de Neri Church was originally built on what would later become the west side of the plaza but dissolved in a puddle of mud after a strong rainy season in 1792. The replacement structure, on the north side of the plaza, has fared much better, perhaps because its walls, made of adobe-like *terrones* (sun-dried bricks cut out of sod) are more than five feet thick. As they have for two centuries, local parishioners attend Mass here, conducted three times a day, once in Spanish.

Like many religious structures in the area, San Felipe de Neri received a makeover from Euro-centric Bishop Jean-Baptiste Lamy of Santa Fe in the second half of the 19th century. Under his direction, the place got its wooden folk Gothic spires, as well as new Jesuit priests from Naples, who later added such non-Spanish details as the gabled entrance and the widow's walk. The interior, decorated quite grandly for such a small space, has glowing brick floors, a baroque gilt altar, and an elaborate pressed-tin ceiling with Moorish geometric patterns. A tiny museum

(10 A.M.–4 P.M. Mon.–Sat., free) on the east side contains some historical church furnishings.

## Turquoise Museum

This place (2107 Central Ave. NW, 505/247-8650, 9:30 A.M.–4 P.M. Mon.–Fri., 9:30 A.M.–3 P.M. Sat., $4) is more of a consumer's resource than a museum per se. Sure, the less imaginative may see only exhibits on the geology and history of turquoise, along with specimens from all over the world, but most folks can't help but think of all the jewelry they plan to buy on their jaunt around New Mexico. So come here to learn the distinction between "natural" and "real" turquoise and otherwise arm yourself for the shopping ahead.

## DOWNTOWN

Once known as bustling New Town, the downtown area of Albuquerque, stretching along Central Avenue between the train tracks and Marquette Avenue, was the city's commercial center—Central Avenue, first named Railroad Avenue, was crowded with mule-drawn streetcars, bargain-hunters, and fresh-off-the-train wheeler-dealers from the East Coast. Then, in the 1950s and 1960s, shopping plazas in Nob Hill and the Northeast Heights began drawing business away; by the 1970s, downtown was a wasteland of government office buildings that was utterly desolate after 5 P.M. But thanks to an aggressive urban-renewal scheme initiated in 2000, the neighborhood has regained some of its old vigor, and Central is now a thoroughfare best known for its hip bars and lounges. By day, you won't see too many specific attractions, but a walking tour reveals an interesting hodgepodge of architectural styles from Albuquerque's most optimistic era.

### A Walking Tour

To see how far the neighborhood has come, start at the **Civic Plaza,** at Tijeras and 4th Streets. The rather bleak concrete patch was an early attempt to stave off urban decay in the late 1960s; it occasionally hosts international-theme parties on weekends; the rest of the time

ALBUQUERQUE

ALBUQUERQUE

© AVALON TRAVEL PUBLISHING, INC.

# DOWNTOWN ALBUQUERQUE

To University of New Mexico and Nob Hill

25

LOCUST ST

ELM ST

HIGH ST

WALTER AVE

IRON AVE

EDITH BLVD

BROADWAY BLVD

ARNO ST

HIGH ST

HIGH ST

FRUIT ST

ARNO ST

ROMA ST

JOHN ST

COMMERCIAL ST

MARTIN LUTHER KING JR AVE

COPPER AVE

CENTRAL AVE (ROUTE 66)

GOLD AVE

SILVER AVE

ARTICHOKE CAFÉ

1ST ST

1ST ST

2ND ST

3RD ST

4TH ST

5TH ST

STOVER AVE

CONVENTION CENTER

POST OFFICE

Civic Plaza

LA POSADA DE ALBUQUERQUE ★

SUNTRAN DEPOT

AMTRAK DEPOT

GOLD STREET CAFFE

BUS STATION

CONVENTION AND VISITORS BUREAU

KIMO THEATER ★

CATHEDRAL CHURCH OF ST JOHN

PUBLIC LIBRARY

COPPER AVE

PEARL'S DIVE

THE HOTEL BLUE

EL REY THEATRE

GOLD AVE

SILVER AVE

LEAD AVE

COAL AVE

IRON AVE

FLYING STAR

MAUGER ESTATE

Robinson Park

KELEHER ST

7TH ST

8TH ST

9TH ST

10TH ST

11TH ST

12TH ST

13TH ST

14TH ST

LOMAS BLVD

ROMA AVE

MARQUETTE AVE

4TH ST

FRUIT ST

KENT AVE

TIJERAS AVE

CENTRAL AVE (ROUTE 66)

DOG HOUSE

ROUTE 66 HOSTEL

PARK AVE

To Old Town

To National Hispanic Cultural Center

Tingley Park

Rio Grande Zoological Park

0 0.25 mi

0 0.25 km

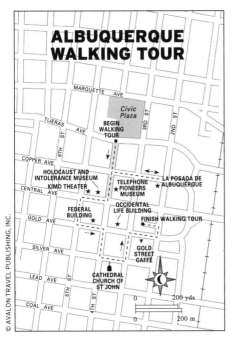

ALBUQUERQUE WALKING TOUR

it during its limited opening hours, but if you do, you get a nice reminder about telecommunications' rapid progress.

Continue on to Central Avenue, where two versions of Route 66 intersect: Between the time the original highway was commissioned in 1926 and when the kinks were worked out of the route in 1937, the road from Chicago to the West Coast ran along 4th Street; after 1937, the route was smoothed so that it ran east–west along Central.

Make a right on Central. In this block, one of the storefronts has been converted into the **New Mexico Holocaust and Intolerance Museum** (415 Central Ave. NW, 505/247-0606, 11 A.M.–3:30 P.M. Tues.–Fri.,. 11 A.M.–4 P.M. Sat., free), a somewhat ad hoc presentation of information about not only the Nazi persecution of the Jews but also the Armenian genocide, the killing of Native Americans during the westward expansion, and the Bataan Death March of World War II, in which a disproportionate number of New Mexican enlistees were killed in the Philippines.

At the corner of Central Avenue and 5th Street is Albuquerque's most distinctive building, the **Kimo Theater.** In 1927, local businessman and Italian immigrant Carlo Bachechi hired Carl Boller, an architect specializing in movie palaces, to design this marvelously ornate building. Boller was inspired by the local adobe and native culture to create a unique style dubbed "pueblo deco"—a flamboyant treatment of Southwestern motifs, in the same vein as Moorish- and Chinese-look cinemas of the same era. The tripartite stucco facade is encrusted with ceramic tiles and Native American iconography (including a traditional Navajo symbol that had not yet been completely appropriated by the Nazi party when the Kimo was built). To get the full effect, you must tour the interior to see the cow-skull sconces and murals of pueblo life; enter through the business office just west of the ticket booth, between 9 A.M. and 4 P.M. on weekdays.

Turn left on 5th Street and continue one block to Gold Avenue, where New Mexico's first **Federal Building,** which included the

it's crossed only by the occasional bureaucrat in search of a lunchtime sandwich. Head south on 4th Street to Copper, where you turn left; two blocks down, at the corner of 2nd Street, is **La Posada de Albuquerque,** a 1939 hotel built by local-boy-made-good Conrad Hilton (who was born in the village of San Antonio, south of Albuquerque, in 1887). Murals in the hallway to the lobby depict the pueblos and other tourist attractions of New Mexico; it's not a stretch to imagine intrepid tourists hopping off the train and getting their first taste of the exotic Southwest in this hotel, all trimmed in territorial brick cornices and finished inside with rustic dark mission-style wood furniture, cattle horns, and war dancers painted over the reception desk.

After checking out the lobby, double back to 4th Street and turn left onto a pedestrian mall, where patio bars face the obscure **Telephone Pioneers Museum of New Mexico** (110 4th St. NW, 505/842-2937, 10 A.M.–2 P.M. Mon., Wed., and Fri., $1); you're lucky if you catch

# NEW LIFE FOR DOWNTOWN

For decades a collection of faded-glory buildings and boarded-up shops on wind-blown streets, Albuquerque's downtown has taken on a new look since 2000. The district has been the recipient of more than $350 million as part of a grand scheme to restore the area to its early-20th-century role as New Town, the hub of Albuquerque's commercial life.

The project is based on the principles of New Urbanism, a planning movement that strives to create mixed-use neighborhoods where residents can live, work, and play without relying on cars – ideally, everything residents need, from bars to grocery stores, should be within a 10-minute walk. New Yorkers or Parisians won't see anything new in New Urbanism – this is the way most dense, older cities already work – but for Albuquerque, a more typical American city where growth has always been out rather than up and people are used to spending hours in their cars every day, the plans are revolutionary and welcome.

Previous, smaller efforts to boost downtown's economy helped establish Central as a nightlife zone, with many small bars and clubs setting up shop in the early 1990s. But the biggest step in the 2000 plan has been to make it not just a destination, but a place people want to live. Rather than just restoring the few apartments that used to sit above the shops, developers have converted whole old office buildings into residential lofts; most famously, the old Albuquerque High School building just east of the railroad tracks on Central Avenue (established in 1914 and the city's only public secondary school until 1946) has had the smell of chalk dust blown out of its lofty halls and now provides chic living space. (As any good gentrified neighborhood requires, this particular section of Central has its own obscure nickname: EDo – that's "east downtown" to you.)

Other major moves include overhauling the bus and train depot to make downtown an easy transit center; welcoming a multiscreen movie theater back to the area that used to hold not just the Kimo but the El Rey and the Sunshine cinemas; establishing a charter high school; and, more controversially, converting the maze of one-way streets downtown back to two-way – a strategy that either encourages New Urbanism or flies in the face of it, depending on whom you talk to.

For all the energy and activity, though, as of 2005 downtown is still not quite there. The holdup? Only food. Pioneering downtowners have a yoga studio, a lingerie boutique, and many sidewalk cafés, but they're still waiting for a big grocery store to invest in the neighborhood; until then, they have to get in their dreaded cars to stock up elsewhere or wait until Saturday morning to shop at the downtown grower's market. But no one's really too unhappy – seeing anyone out in this area on a Saturday morning, much less a vendor of organic carrots, would've been unheard-of just five years ago.

U.S. courthouse, was built in 1930. The two-story rounded-arch doorway has the grandiosity of buildings in Washington, D.C., but the terra-cotta blocks imprinted with thunderbirds and Navajo stepped geometry are distinctly Southwestern; the California mission–style tile roof and cupola add a further not-of-the-east note. Continue on Gold, then turn right on 4th Street; at Silver Avenue, the **Cathedral Church of St. John** was built in 1884, the first grand church in New Town, in a combination of French Gothic and Anglican styles; only the first tier of stone is original, however, as the upper portions of the church were redone in 1951 under the direction of John Gaw Meem, who had by then made a name for himself as principal architect of the University of New Mexico campus. Around the corner on Silver Avenue is the smaller **Cathedral House,** built in 1930 by John Gaw Meem early in his career.

Head east on Silver to 3rd Street and turn left; at the intersection with Gold Avenue, you'll see one of the gems of Albuquerque's downtown: the **Occidental Life**

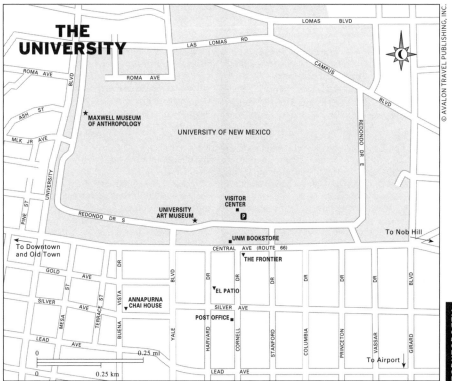

THE
UNIVERSITY

© AVALON TRAVEL PUBLISHING, INC.

LOMAS     BLVD

LAS    LOMAS    RD

CAMPUS    BLVD

ROMA    AVE

ROMA    AVE

REDONDO    DR    E

ASH    ST

MLK JR    AVE

★ MAXWELL MUSEUM
OF ANTHROPOLOGY

UNIVERSITY OF NEW MEXICO

UNIVERSITY ST

PINE    ST

REDONDO    DR    S

UNIVERSITY
ART MUSEUM ★

VISITOR
CENTER
■
P

To Nob Hill

■ UNM BOOKSTORE

To Downtown
and Old Town

CENTRAL    AVE  (ROUTE  66)

▼ THE FRONTIER

GOLD    AVE

ST

DR

VISTA

BLVD

DR

DR

▼ EL PATIO

DR

DR

BLVD

SILVER    AVE

ANNAPURNA
▼ CHAI HOUSE

TERRACE ST

SILVER    AVE

POST OFFICE ■

MESA

BUENA

YALE

HARVARD

CORNELL

STANFORD

COLUMBIA

PRINCETON

VASSAR

GIRARD

LEAD    AVE

0          0.25 mi

0          0.25 km

To Airport ↓

LEAD    AVE

ALBUQUERQUE

**Building.** With its curlicued façade of white ceramic tile gleaming in the sun, the ornate 1917 construction looks like the Doge's Palace in Venice rendered in marshmallow fluff. Following a 1933 fire, the reconstructing architects added even more frills, such as the crenellations along the top. The entire building is surfaced in white terra-cotta; the tiles were made in a factory in Denver, which sprayed the ceramic glaze onto concrete blocks, each individually molded and numbered; the blocks were then assembled in Albuquerque according to an overall plan.

To your right on Gold is a small shopping strip of cool boutiques, and the relaxing Gold Street Caffè. On your way back to your car, head north on 3rd Street half a block, then turn right into the alley next to the parking lot—the backs of the buildings here are finished in some excellent **murals** done by multiethnic arts organization Working Classroom.

## THE UNIVERSITY AND NOB HILL

The state's largest university, another byproduct of the railroad boom, was established in 1889, a tiny outpost on the far side of the tracks. By 1909, under the guidance of president William George Tight, it had acquired the outline of its distinctive pueblo-inspired architecture (though Tight was then fired in part for his non–Ivy League aesthetics). Pueblo revival pioneer John Gaw Meem carried on the vision through the 1940s, and even with crisp-lined contemporary structures now interspersed among the original halls, it's still a remarkably

# THE END OF ROUTE 66?

Route 66, the "mother road," on which so many Dust Bowl refugees made their way west and so many beatniks got into their grooves, is officially no more. The highway, which stretched from Chicago to Los Angeles, was decommissioned in 1985. Sure, you can still drive Route 66 – look for the brown historic-marker signs – but it has lost its zip since it was replaced by larger interstate highways; in Albuquerque, I-40 is the fast conduit for traffic, bypassing Central Avenue, the old Route 66, and the transient-friendly businesses that once thrived there.

Route 66 is one of the biggest repositories of American nostalgia – it symbolizes the country's economic growth in the 20th century, from Depression desperation to postwar optimism to free-wheeling hipness, a little neon-lined ribbon of cool.

But Albuquerque city planners have recently been taking a dry-eyed look at some of the less savory relics of the past, such as the numerous 1950s motels where the dank rooms become hot spots for drug deals and other unsavory business. As part of its aggressive urban renewal program, the city has managed to demolish five such motor courts since 2002. More are on the list, especially those on the east edge of Nob Hill, which already looks like a bit of a graveyard, with dead neon signs standing like tombstones amid the rubble. Residents appreciate the effort, but many people can't help but feel dismay at the end of the "get your kicks" era and all its trappings. So at the same time, others are putting a great deal of effort and money into restoring the route's glow – literally. The signs on the El Rey theater and the Aztec Motel are just two landmarks in Albuquerque that have been taken from dull to dazzling by professional neon artists, creating hope that even if Route 66 no longer exists, some of its more colorful icons will.

harmonious vision, uniting the pastoral sanctuary feel of the great Eastern campuses with a soothing, minimalist interpretation of native New Mexican forms. Surrounding the campus is the typical student-friendly scrum of cheap pizza places, bohemian coffee houses, and dilapidated bungalow rentals. The next neighborhood east along Central is the city's best shopping district, Nob Hill, developed around a shopping plaza in the late 1940s and still showing that decade's distinctive style in streamlined movie marquees and shop facades; it's currently home to eclectic boutiques and relaxed cafés.

## The University of New Mexico

Nearly 25,000 students use this campus, which sprawls for blocks and blocks beyond the old core bounded by Central Avenue and University Boulevard. Visitors can park in a complex just inside the UNM campus across from Cornell Street; the info center, where you can pick up a detailed map, is in the southwest corner of the structure. Just across the way is the **University Art Museum** (Center for the Arts, 9 A.M.–4 P.M. Tues.–Fri., 1–4 P.M. Sun.), which often displays very good work by MFA students and professors, as well as treasures from the permanent fine art collection of more than 30,000 pieces from all over the globe.

Wandering around the grounds, you'll see such classic Meem buildings as **Mesa Vista Hall** (now the Student Services Building) and **Zimmerman Library.** Rest up at the bucolic duck pond, crowded with nappers on land and birds in the water, then head for the **Maxwell Museum of Anthropology** (off University Blvd., north of M. L. K. Jr. Blvd., 505/277-4405, 9 A.M.–4 P.M. Tues.–Fri., 10 A.M.–4 P.M. Sat., free), a John Meem building originally designed as the student union. The museum has a particularly good overview of Southwestern Indian culture and a collection of Native American artifacts from university-sponsored digs all over the state.

## Nob Hill

The **Nob Hill** district is now marked by square frames trimmed in neon on Central Avenue at Girard Street and at Washington Boulevard. The area began to grow after 1937, when Route 66 was rejiggered to run along Central, and the Nob Hill Shopping Plaza, at Central and Carlisle, signaled the neighborhood's success when it opened as the glitziest shopping area in town in 1947. The area went through a slump from the 1960s through the mid-1980s, but it's again lined with brightly painted shop facades and buzzing neon signs, a lively district where the quirk factor is high—whether you want to buy designer underwear or an antique Mexican mask, you'll find it here. The eastern half of the strip hasn't enjoyed quite the same renaissance, but wander down this way to see the **Aztec Motel** (3821 Central Ave. NE), a bizarre art project/flophouse decorated with a weird array of tiles, mannequin parts, plastic Christmas decorations, and rain-worn plush animals. Then head off of Central Avenue on Monte Vista, and keep an eye out for the **Bart Prince house,** the home of the city's most celebrated contemporary architect, whose favorite forms seem to be spaceships and antennas—it's the residential counterpart to the eccentric businesses that flourish in this area.

## ALBUQUERQUE METRO AREA

Beyond the neighborhoods described in the previous pages, Albuquerque is haze of modern tract houses and shopping centers built during the 1960s and later—decades dubbed Albuquerque's "Asphalt Period" by an unkind local journalist. A few sights, particularly along the edges of the city, are well worth seeking out, however.

## National Hispanic Cultural Center

Just south of downtown (but not within walking distance) on 4th Street in the historic, and historically neglected, neighborhood of Barelas, the National Hispanic Cultural Center (1701 4th St. SW, 505/246-2261, www.nhccnm.org, 10 A.M.–5 P.M. Tues.–Sun., $3, $1 on Sun.) is an impressive modern complex that lauds the cultural contributions of Spanish-speakers the world over. It has had a huge positive influence in this down-at-the-heels district: Even the McDonald's across the street mimics its architecture. The central attraction for visitors is the museum, which houses a permanent collection in several large rooms, with work ranging from the traditional santos and *retablos* by New Mexican craftspeople (including Luis Barela, grandson of legendary Taos *santero* Patrocinio Barela) to contemporary painting, photography, and even furniture by artists from Chile, Cuba, Argentina, and more. Three additional rooms house temporary shows—recent exhibits have compared the inspirations of three very different New Mexico artists, for instance. Adjacent to the museum is the largest Hispanic genealogy library in existence, as well as the giant Roy E. Disney Performance Arts Center.

## Sandia Peak Tramway

The longest tramway of its type in the world, the tram (505/856-7325, www.sandiapeak.com, $1 parking, $15 round-trip, $8 one-way)

Zip up to Sandia Peak on the world's longest tramway.

whisks passengers 2.7 miles along a continuous line of Swiss-made cables, from Albuquerque's northeast foothills to the crest in about 15 minutes, a somewhat dizzying trip up the steep and jagged side of the mountain, a 4,000-foot altitude gain. If the wind is blowing, it's especially alarming—or thrilling, depending on your outlook. The service runs frequently all year-round (9 A.M.–9 P.M. in summer; 9 A.M.–8 P.M. in winter), making it a convenient way to get to the ski area; in the summer, you can ride up to the peak, then hike along the crest or even all the way back down the mountain. Even from the base of the tram, the view across the city is very good—you may want to come to the casual Mexican restaurant here, **Sandiago's** (38 Tramway Rd., 505/856-6692, $10), for a sunset margarita (one of which, the Doogie, honors Albuquerque actor Neil Patrick Harris, who attended a nearby high school).

## ◖ Petroglyph National Monument

Albuquerque's west side is bordered by this national reserve area, 7,500 acres of huge black boulders that crawl with carved lizards, birds, and assorted odd beasts. Most of the some 20,000 images, which were created by chipping away the blackish surface "varnish" of the volcanic rock to reach the paler stone beneath, were probably made by ancient Puebloans as part of religious rituals; the bulk are between 400 and 700 years old, while others may date back three millennia. A few more recent examples of rock art include Maltese crosses made by Spanish settlers and initials left by explorers (not to mention a few by idle 20th-century teenagers). The carvings can be found all through the West Mesa, and you can see some of the largest groupings on two major trails: **Boca Negra Canyon,** where a few very short trails lead off a paved loop, and the longer **Rinconada Canyon** trail, a 1.25-mile one-way hike. Boca Negra Canyon is the only fee area ($1 per vehicle on weekdays; $2 on weekends), and there are restrooms and water in the parking area. The Rinconada trailhead is less developed; the trail can be tedious going in some

spots because the ground is sandy, but it's relatively flat—you can see some figures on the rocks along the way (along with some that are a bit more, well, contemporary), but the clearest, most impressive images are in the canyon at the end of the trail. Keep an eye out for millipedes, which thrive in this stark environment; dead, their curled-up empty shells resemble the spirals carved on the rocks—coincidence?

You can also explore in the northernmost section of the reserve, **Piedras Marcadas Canyon,** on a few trails that start in the backyards of the homes bordering the area; maps are available at the **visitors center** on Unser Boulevard at Western Trail (8 A.M.–5 P.M. daily). In any case, stop here first for full park maps, flyers on flora and fauna, and general orientation; on weekends, there's often some interesting free activity, from herb walks to live music.

The back (west) side of the parkland, the **Volcanoes Day Use Area** (9 A.M.–5 P.M. daily), is also a great place to hike and survey the city. Access is via Paseo Volcan (exit 149) off I-40; turn right (east) 4.3 miles north of the highway at an unmarked dirt road to the parking area. Here you'll be at the base of three cinder cones, where you can look down toward the city and see precisely how the lava flow formed the mesa top some 190,000 years ago, flowing in between existing sandstone bluffs that later crumbled away—hence the lava "fingers" that seem to stretch east and the crumbled edges of the escarpment where the petroglyphs are found. If you go in the winter, you'll see that the volcanoes, which were last reported emitting steam in 1881, are still not entirely dead: Patches of green plants flourish around the steam vents that stud the hillocks, particularly visible on the middle of the three volcanoes.

## Los Ranchos and Corrales Scenic Byway

For a pretty drive through these villages that have been all but consumed by greater Albuquerque, head north from Old Town on Rio Grande Boulevard; you first reach Los Ranchos de Albuquerque, then cross the river at Alameda to Corrales Road and continue up the

© ZORA O'NEILL

Corrales and Los Ranchos are horse-friendly districts.

west bank. Despite the subdivisions sprouting all around, Los Ranchos and Corrales remain pockets of pastoral calm where horses gambol and low adobe houses glow in the sun. Both areas are still fed by the traditional acequias Spanish farmers dug in the early 18th century, though now most residents use the water for their organic herb gardens—a practical melding of old agricultural heritage with modern suburban bliss. The only real sights are clustered together in central Corrales, two blocks west of the main road. The folk Gothic **Old San Ysidro Church** (505/897-1513, 1–4 P.M. Sat. and Sun. June–Oct.) stands where the center of the village was in 1868, when its bulging adobe piers were first constructed. Across the road is the village cemetery, a typically New Mexican *camposanto,* where graves are trimmed with plastic flowers and votive candles. Next door, **Casa San Ysidro** (505/898-3915, www.cabq.gov/museum, tours 9:30 A.M. and 1:30 P.M. Wed.–Sat. and 2 P.M. Sun. Feb.–Nov., plus 10:30 A.M. Sat. June–Aug., $4) is a territorial-style *rancho* once owned by obsessive collectors Alan and Shirley Minge, who lived in the place for nearly 40 years, heating with firewood and squirreling away an impressive horde of New Mexican antiques and craftwork. They moved out only in 1997, donating the place and all its furnishing to the Albuquerque Museum, which gives tours several times per week—very much worth planning if you know you'll be coming up this way.

## Coronado State Monument

Though named for Spanish explorer Francisco Vásquez de Coronado, who camped on this lush spot by the river during his 1540 search for gold, the monument (485 Kuaua Rd., Bernalillo, 505/867-5351, 8:30 A.M.–4:30 P.M. Wed.–Mon., $3) is actually a Native American relic, the partially restored pueblo of Kuaua (Tiwa for "evergreen"), which was inhabited between 1300 and the early 1600s. The centerpiece is the large, partially sunken square kiva, its interior walls covered with murals of life-size human figures and animals in ritual poses. What you see are only reproductions—the originals have been removed for preservation, and a few are on display in the visitors center. The setting, too, is worth the visit, especially if you pack a picnic. Seated on a bench facing the river and the mountains, with the city hidden from view behind a dense screen of cottonwoods, you get a sense of the lush, calm life along the Rio Grande in the centuries before the Spanish arrived. To reach the monument, exit I-25 in Bernalillo and head west on Highway 550; Kuaua Road is on your right, before you reach the Santa Ana Star casino.

## Wineries

The Spanish planted the first vineyards in North America in New Mexico in the 17th century, and the industry persisted until a series of floods finally wiped out the vines by the 1920s. So New Mexico's current wine scene, while strong, is still somewhat young. One of the best wineries, **Gruet** (8400 Pan American Fwy., 505/821-0055), began producing its excellent sparkling wines (the Gruet family hails from Champagne) only in 1987; look out especially for its nonvintage sparkling rosé, which is delicious and affordable. Tours run every day but Sunday starting at 11 A.M.; the tasting room (five pours for $5) is open 10 A.M.–5 P.M. weekdays and noon–5 P.M. on Saturday. For contrast, you could also visit **Casa Rondeña** (733 Chavez Rd. NW, 505/344-5911, 10 A.M.–6 P.M. Wed.–Sat., noon–6 P.M. Sun.) in Los Ranchos, which specializes in cabernet franc.

# Entertainment

## BARS AND CLUBS

Albuquerque's downtown renewal program has encouraged nightlife above all—this district is the city's main bar and club scene, all packed in a few square blocks, which makes for handy hopping (or staggering) from place to place. Here and nearer to UNM, a lot of the bars cater to students, with plentiful beer and other happy-hour specials, but a somewhat generic atmosphere. But the more distinctive places are pure Albuquerque: unpretentious, with a remarkably varied clientele. Because there aren't enough members of any one particular subculture to pack a whole bar, even the most chic-appearing places will see an absent-minded professor and a veteran Earth First–er propping up the bar next to well-groomed yuppies.

### Old Town and the Rio Grande

This neighborhood doesn't offer much in the way of nightlife. The few exceptions are the **Q Bar** (800 Rio Grande Blvd. NW, 505/843-6300, 4 P.M.–1 A.M. daily) in the Hotel Albu-querque at Old Town, a decidedly swank little lounge filled with low couches and little nooks for sipping sweet and deadly cocktails. As Albuquerque's most dimly lit non-dive bar, it seems to inspire decadent behavior among those who don't normally indulge.

Just over the west side of the river at Alameda, **Elliott's** (10200 Corrales Rd. NW, 505/898-5555, 11 A.M.–2 A.M. Mon.–Sat., noon–midnight Sun.) is the only bar of any note near Los Ranchos and Corrales. It's tucked in a strip mall, but that's easy to forget on the huge back patio overlooking river-fed greenery; a good chunk of the regulars are staff and patrons of the highly lauded Star Tattoo in the same complex, which means an eclectic jukebox, generous beer specials, and plenty to feast your eyes on (oh yes, there's tasty bar food too). Weekends see occasional oddball dance parties, such as a hip-hop luau.

### Downtown

The best all-purpose bar in the neighborhood is the second-floor **Anodyne** (409

# TRADITIONAL NEW MEXICAN MUSIC

Traditional New Mexican music sounds like a lot of different things: blaring mariachi ensembles, scratchy fiddles accompanying the Matachines dancers, booming tribal drums. The best place to hear the mix is on KANW (89.1 FM) in Albuquerque, a public radio station that devotes most of its day and evening programming to homegrown music, with a heavy emphasis on mariachi, and such stars as Los Reyes de Albuquerque. (There's also a vintage country show on Saturday nights, as a nod to Anglo listeners.) KUNM (89.9 FM) devotes Sunday afternoons to "Singing Wire," where you'll hear traditional Native American music as well as pop anthems like Keith Secola's oft-requested "NDN Kars." And you can catch up on the current sound on KABQ (104.1 FM) – its "Latino and proud" programming fills the speakers of many a lowrider with Spanglish rap and Puerto Rican reggaeton.

If you're out of range of these stations, look for the excellent Smithsonian Folkways CDs *Music of New Mexico: Hispanic Traditions* (which has the Matachines and Comanches dance songs alongside more widespread Mexican songs like "Las Mañanitas") and *New Mexico: Native American Traditions,* which is all traditional drumming.

Central Ave. NW, 505/244-1820), a long, wood-floor room filled with pool tables and a younger crowd sprawled on the thrift-store sofas. Choose from more than a hundred beers, and get some quarters to plug into the good collection of pinball machines. Equally casual, but much cleaner than its name suggests, is **Pearl's Dive** (509 Central Ave. NW, 505/244-9405, 11 a.m.–midnight Mon. and Tues., 11 a.m.–2 a.m. Wed.–Fri., 4 p.m.–2 a.m. Sat.), which has a great patio, serves tasty food, and hosts mellow jazz outfits on weekend nights. Arguably downtown's biggest "scene" is at **Sauce/Liquid Lounge** (405 Central Ave. NW, 505/242-5839 or 505/897-2645, 11 a.m.–2:30 a.m. daily), a combo of chichi pizza parlor and cocktail bar, with moody lighting and a live DJ most nights.

To catch the latest touring indie-rock sensation or the local crew about to hit it big, head to the very professional **Launchpad** (618 Central Ave. SW, 505/764-8887, www.launchpadrocks.com), one of a trio of neighboring live-music outlets. The second is **Puccini's Golden West Saloon** (622 Central Ave. SW), where the sound system is not as good as next door's, but there's constant talk of it returning to its early-'90s punk-rock glory. Then **El Rey Theatre** (620 Central Ave. SW, 505/242-2353), under the same ownership, is Albuquerque's best venue for bigger bands—a former movie theater, the floor is nicely sloped for good sightlines, and there's a balcony as well. Decor is vintage flocked wallpaper and long dark-wood bars, with some bizarre Mediterranean touches, installed by the theater's original Italian owners. For absolutely free live music and a pool table, **Burt's Tiki Lounge** (313 Gold Ave. SW, 505/247-2878, www.burtstikilounge.com, 8 p.m.–2 a.m. Mon.–Sat.) has a funky feel and a very eclectic bill, with everything from British psychedelia to reggae on the roster.

Tired of keeping up with Albuquerque's hipsters? Head to the lobby bar at **La Posada de Albuquerque** (125 2nd St. NW, 505/242-9090), where you can lounge in a low-slung leather mission chair in front of a tinkling Spanish fountain or a roaring fireplace. After a few cocktails from the man behind the dark-wood horseshoe bar, you'll be right back in the hotel's more glamorous era, when Zsa Zsa Gabor was honeymooning here with then-owner Conrad Hilton.

## The University and Nob Hill

**Gulp** (3128 Central Ave. SE, 505/268-4729, 11 a.m.–10 p.m. Sun.–Thurs., 11 a.m.–11 p.m. Fri. and Sat.), the bar end of the restaurant Graze, serves a shortened menu of spicy, wide-ranging snacks along with a few specialty cocktails and a good selection of wines by the glass for just $5. In the Nob Hill shopping plaza, **Gecko's** (3500 Central SE, 505/262-1848, 11:30 A.M.–late Mon.–Fri., noon–late Sat. and Sun.) is a good place for a snack (anything from Thai curry shrimp to chipotle hot wings) and a drink on the patio while you watch the social scene at the adjacent food co-op. **The Martini Grille** (4200 Central Ave. SE, 505/255-4111, 4 P.M.–1:30 A.M. Mon.–Fri., 5 P.M.–1:30 A.M. Sat. and Sun.) offers an unexpected bit of lounge cool in the still-patchy eastern stretch of Nob Hill; cocktail prices are pleasingly low, low, low.

## Albuquerque Metro Area

Albuquerque is ringed with casinos, which provide entertainment not only through gaming but also on their often large stages. The most tastefully done place is **Sandia Casino,** on the north edge of town (I-25 at Tramway, 800/526-9366, www.sandiacasino.com, 8 A.M.–4 A.M. Mon.–Thurs., open 24 hours Fri.–Sun.); the main gaming hall hums and jingles with more than 1,700 slot machines, plus all the table games, including poker. The out-

door amphitheater—a large sunken stage surrounded by more than 4,000 seats—is a very pleasant, and surprisingly intimate, place to hear music on a summer night. Less glitzy is Laguna Pueblo's **Route 66 Casino** (14500 Central Ave. SW, 866/352-7866, www.rt66casino.com, 8 A.M.–4 A.M. Mon.–Thurs., open 24 hours Fri.–Sun.), off I-40 at exit 140, which has a chummier poker room, and its stage is graced by a steady parade of pop stars past, such as the Go-Gos and George Thorogood.

## PERFORMING ARTS

Albuquerque's arts scene graces a number of excellent stages. The most beautiful of them all, the city-owned **Kimo Theater** (423 Central Ave. NW, 505/768-3544, www.cabq.gov/kimo) often hosts locally written plays and dance, as well as the occasional musical performance. Bigger acts visit the **Roy E. Disney Center for Performing Arts** at the National Hispanic Cultural Center (1701 4th St. SW, 505/724-4771, www.nhccnm.org), a modernized Maya pyramid that contains three separate venues, the largest of which is a 691-seat proscenium theater; this is the place to catch a performance by visiting or local fla-

The splendid Kimo Theater is preserved and maintained by the city.

© ZORA O'NEILL

menco artists—with the National Institute of Flamenco headquarters in Albuquerque, there's often someone performing. UNM's **Popejoy Hall** (UNM campus, 505/277-4569, www.popejoyhall.org) hosts the New Mexico Symphony Orchestra (which also plays at the **Rio Grande Zoo** in the summer), while the **Outpost Performance Space** (210 Yale Blvd. SE, 505/268-0044, www.outpostspace.org) books very good world music and dance acts.

You can catch local thespians at **Albuquerque Little Theater** (224 San Pasquale SW, 505/242-4750, www.swcp.com), founded in 1930, and the **Vortex** (2004 Central Ave. SE, 505/247-8600, www.thevortextheater.org), near the university. The latter is Albuquerque's longest-running avant-garde space, putting up everything from Beckett to local playwrights' work in its black box since 1976. Downtown is home to the **Gorilla Tango** theater (519 Central Ave. NW, 505/245-8600, www.gorillatango.com), where improv comedy is the name of the game—a tight-knit crew of versatile comics riffs on audience suggestions Thursday through Sunday.

## Cinemas

The **Century 14 Downtown** (100 Central Ave. SW, 505/243-7469) devotes most of its screens to blockbusters, while the latest indie and art films are shown at **The Guild** (3405 Central Ave. SE, 505/255-1848).

## FESTIVALS AND EVENTS

The city's biggest annual event is the **Albuquerque International Balloon Fiesta** (888/422-7277, www.balloonfiesta.com), 10 days in October dedicated to New Mexico's official state aircraft, with more than 700 hot-air balloons of all colors, shapes, and sizes gathering at a dedicated park on the north edge of town, west of I-25. During the fiesta, the city is packed with fanatical "airheads," who claim this is the best gathering of its kind in the world. If you go, don't miss an early-morning mass ascension, when the balloons glow against the dark sky, then lift silently into the air in a great wave.

You don't have to be in town for the Balloon Fiesta to go up, up, and away: Take a morning **hot-air balloon ride** with **Rainbow Ryders** (505/823-1111, www.rainbowryders.com, 505/823-1111, $180 per person) to get a true bird's-eye view of the city. Typically, you're up in the balloon for an hour or so, depending on wind conditions, and you get a champagne toast when you're back on solid ground.

You'll catch an equally colorful show at the **Gathering of Nations Powwow** (www.gatheringofnations.com), the largest tribal get-together in the United States, with more than 3,000 dancers and singers in full regalia from over 500 tribes crowding the floor of the University Arena. During the powwow, Miss Indian World earns her crown by showing off traditional talents such as spear-fishing or storytelling. The event takes place the last weekend in April.

The state's agricultural roots get their due at the **New Mexico State Fair** (www.exponm.com), a 17-day festival of fried foods and prize-winning livestock that begins immediately after Labor Day. It's your usual mix of midway craziness and exhibition barns, along with really excellent rodeos, which often end with shows by country-music legends like Willie Nelson.

The rest of the year is crowded with specialist get-togethers, such as the **National Fiery Foods Show** in March, where capsaicin fanatics try out hot new products; the **Bernalillo Art Car Parade** in early October; the **Mariachi Spectacular** in early July; and the week-long **International Flamenco Festival** (www.nationalinstituteofflamenco.org) in June, the largest event of its kind in the United States, with performances and workshops sponsored by the National Institute of Flamenco, which has its conservatory here.

Open April–September, the amusement park **Cliff's** (4800 Osuna Rd. NE, 505/881-9373, www.cliffs.net, Apr.–Sept., $21 adults, $18 kids) boasts a respectable assortment of rides, including the venerable New Mexico Rattler, a 3,000-foot-long wooden roller coaster. Hours vary—call ahead for details.

ALBUQUERQUE

# CEREMONIAL DANCES

This is only an approximate schedule for ceremonial dances at Albuquerque-area pueblos – dates can vary from year to year. Annual feast days typically involve carnivals and markets in addition to dances. Confirm details and start times – usually afternoon, but sometimes following an evening or midnight Mass – with the Indian Pueblo Cultural Center (505/843-7270, www.ipcc.org) before setting out.

## JANUARY 1

- Santo Domingo: corn dance

## JANUARY 6

- Sandia and Santo Domingo: various dances

## FEBRUARY 2

- San Felipe: various dances for Candlemas (Día de la Candelaria)

## MARCH 19

- Laguna (Old Laguna): Feast of Saint Joseph

## EASTER

- Most pueblos: various dances; Zia also has dances on Monday

## MAY 1

- San Felipe: Feast of San Felipe

## JUNE 13

- Sandia: Feast of San Antonio
- Santa Clara: Los Comanches

## JUNE 29

- Santa Ana: Feast of San Pedro

## JULY 14

- Cochiti: Feast of San Bonaventura

## JULY 26

- Laguna: harvest dances
- Santa Ana: Feast of Santa Ana

## AUGUST 4

- Santo Domingo: Feast of Santo Domingo

## AUGUST 10

- Acoma (Acomita): Feast of San Lorenzo

## AUGUST 12

- Santa Clara: Feast of Santa Clara

## AUGUST 15

- Laguna (Mesita): various dances
- Zia: Feast of the Assumption of Our Blessed Mother

## AUGUST 28

- Isleta: Feast of Saint Augustine

## LABOR DAY

- Santo Domingo: arts and crafts market

## SEPTEMBER 2

- Acoma (Sky City): Feast of San Estevan

## SEPTEMBER 4

- Isleta: Feast of Saint Augustine

## SEPTEMBER 8

- Isleta (Encinal): Feast of the Nativity of the Blessed Virgin
- San Ildefonso: corn dances

## SEPTEMBER 19

- Laguna (Old Laguna): Feast of Saint Joseph

## SEPTEMBER 25

- Laguna (Paguate): Feast of Saint Elizabeth

**OCTOBER 17**

- Laguna (Paraje): Feast of Saint Margaret Mary

**OCTOBER 24-27**

- Laguna (Old Laguna): harvest dance

**DECEMBER 24**

- San Juan: Los Matachines and torchlight processions

- Acoma (Sky City): luminaria display
- Laguna and Santa Ana: dances after evening Mass

**DECEMBER 25**

- Santo Domingo, San Juan, and Zia: various daytime dances

# Shopping

Albuquerque doesn't have Santa Fe's exotic treasure troves and tony galleries, but it doesn't have the high prices either. Old Town and the environs are where you can pick up traditional American Indian jewelry and pottery for very reasonable prices, while Nob Hill is the commercial center of Albuquerque's counterculture, with body-piercing studios adjacent to comic book shops next to herbal apothecaries.

## OLD TOWN AND THE RIO GRANDE

The slew of galleries and gift shops packed in around the plaza can blur together after just a little bit of browsing, but a few places stand out: **Saints & Martyrs** (404 San Felipe St. NW, 505/224-9323, 10 A.M.–5 P.M. Wed.–Sun. Nov.–Mar., 10 A.M.–5 P.M. Wed.–Mon. Apr.–Oct.) specializes in traditional Spanish colonial religious art and related items. Some one-of-a-kind santos are quite pricey, but other trinkets are more affordable. **Nizhoni Moses** (326 San Felipe St. NW, 505/842-1808, 9 A.M.–9 P.M. daily May–Oct., 10 A.M.–8 P.M. daily Nov.–Apr.) deals entirely in Indian art, with some beautiful big pieces. Prices are a little high, but it's a useful place to see what very good-quality work looks like.

Just outside of Old Town's historic zone, the **Gertrude Zachary** showroom (1501 Lomas Blvd. NW, 505/247-4442, 10 A.M.–6 P.M. Mon.–Sat., 10 A.M.–5 P.M. Sun.) is the place to go for turquoise-and-silver jewelry, whether you want a traditional squash-blossom necklace or a contemporary reimagining of that design studded with other semiprecious stones. Among other things, the shop specializes in rare, antique turquoise—the variety of colors is astounding—but everything's sold at wholesale prices, so you can get some great treasures for cheap. For strictly traditional work, head to the gift shop at the **Indian Pueblo Cultural Center** (2401 12th St. NW, 505/843-7270, www.ipcc.org, 9 A.M.–4:30 P.M. daily); not only are its prices reasonable, but the staff is happy to explain the work that goes into various pieces.

## DOWNTOWN

Sears Roebuck and JCPenney have moved on, but a few interesting shops still occupy the curved show windows along Central. An emporium of American Indian goods, **Skip Maisel** (510 Central Ave. SW, 505/242-6526, 9 A.M.–5:30 P.M. Mon.–Sat.) feels like a relic from downtown's heyday—whether you want a war bonnet, a turquoise-studded watch, or deerskin moccasins, it's all here in a vast, overstocked shop with kindly salespeople. Don't miss the beautiful murals above the display windows in the foyer; they were painted in the 1930s by local Indian artists. Another throwback: **The Man's Hat Shop** (511 Central Ave. NW, 505/239-9871, 9:30 A.M.–5:30 P.M. Tues.–Fri., 9:30 A.M.–5 P.M. Sat.), which stocks just what it promises, with nary a trace of retro kitsch; come here for a homburg, a pith helmet, or one of the countless styles of cowboy hats. Zip back to the present day at **Visiones Gallery** (212 Gold Ave. SW, 505/242-9267, 9 A.M.–5 P.M. Mon.–Fri.), run by a local nonprofit and showing fresh artwork by Latino, African American, and American Indian artists, usually priced quite reasonably.

## THE UNIVERSITY AND NOB HILL

Start your stroll on the west end of the Nob Hill district, near Girard. **Martha's Body Bueno** (3105 Central Ave. NE, 505/255-1122, 10 A.M.–6 P.M. Mon.–Thurs., 10 A.M.–7 P.M. Fri. and Sat., noon–4 P.M. Sun.) deals in lotions, potions, and suggestive underthings; the locally made moisturizers will take the edge off desert-induced dryness and leave you smelling angelic. Across the street, **Masks y Más** (3021 Central Ave. SE, 505/256-4183, 11 A.M.–6 P.M. daily) deals in all things bizarre, most with a south-of-the-border flavor; here's where to get your statues of glamorous skeleton dames or the outfit for your Mexican-wrestler alter ego. Impressively tasteful (and expensive) **Hey Jhonny** (3418-B Central Ave. SE, 505/256-9244, 10 A.M.–6:30 P.M. Mon.–Sat., 11 A.M.–6 P.M. Sun.) stocks gorgeous sushi sets, hip handbags, and travel guides only to the coolest destinations; **Hey Jhonny Home** (118 Tulane Dr. SE), half a block off Central, handles the bigger (and more expensive) items.

On the next corner, **Mariposa Gallery** (3500 Central Ave. SE, 505/268-6828, 11 A.M.–5 P.M. Mon.–Sat., noon–5 P.M. Sun.) is one of the city's longest-established art vendors, dealing since 1974 in jewelry, fiber art, and other crafts, for the most part by

vintage style in the Nob Hill district

© ZORA O'NEILL

local artists. If you're looking for unusual postcards, head south one block to **Papers!** (114 Amherst Dr. SE, 505/254-1434, 10:30 A.M.–6:30 P.M. Mon.–Sat., 11 A.M.–5 P.M. Sun.), which stocks everything from greeting cards to blank books to Japanese origami sheets, so you may be inspired to make your own missives home. **A, the Albuquerque Store** (3500 Central Ave. SE, 505/266-2222, 10 A.M.–6 P.M. Mon.–Sat., noon–5 P.M. Sun.) specializes in home furnishings for the Southwestern hipster—you'll find some pricey items, but also some more affordable bits with excellent design sensibility, such as colorful flower-print Mexican tablecloth fabric and handmade candles; the jewelry here, much of it by local designers, is very good, too.

## ALBUQUERQUE METRO AREA

Every Saturday and Sunday, Albuquerque's **flea market** (505/265-3976, 9 A.M.–4 P.M., $2 parking) takes place at the fairgrounds (enter at Gate 9, on Louisiana just north of Central). Attendance has fallen in recent years, and there aren't so many individuals selling off the contents of their garages, but it's still an interesting outlet where you can pick up anything from new cowboy boots to loose nuggets of turquoise; socks and beef jerky are also well represented. Head to the northwest corner for the better collections of secondhand junk, and stop off at one of the myriad food stands for a snack—refreshing *aguas frescas* (fresh fruit juices, in flavors such as watermelon and tamarind) and Indian frybread are the most popular.

# Sports and Recreation

Albuquerque is a perfect city for outdoor enthusiasts, with several distinct ecosystems and plenty of trails running through them. Late spring and summer are the best times to head to the higher elevations on the Sandia Mountains; once the cool fall weather sets in, the scrub-covered foothills and the bare, rocky West Mesa are more hospitable. The Rio Grande Valley, running through the center of the city, is remarkably pleasant year-round: mild in winter and cool and shady in summer. As everywhere in the desert, always pack extra layers of clothing and plenty of water before you set out, and don't go charging up to Sandia Peak (10,678 feet above sea level) your first day off the plane.

## SKIING

**Sandia Peak Ski Area** (505/242-9052, www.sandiapeak.com) is open from mid-December through mid-March, though there's rarely enough natural snow early in the season—it takes until about February for a good base to build up; the 30 trails, serviced by four lifts, are not dramatic, but they are pleasantly long. The area is open daily in the holiday season, then Wednesday through Sunday for the remainder of the winter.

Sandia Peak also has plenty of opportunities for **cross-country skiing,** if the snow conditions are right. The most popular place is the **Capulin Snow Play Area** ($3 parking), nine miles up Highway 536 to the crest, where there are also big hills for tubing and sledding. About six miles of trails are groomed here, or you can bushwhack—just be wary of sudden drop-offs. Farther up on the mountain, **10K Trail** is usually groomed for skiers, as is a service road heading south to the upper tramway terminal; the latter is wide and relatively level—good for beginners. You can check the status of the trails at the Sandia ranger station (505/281-3304) on Highway 337 in Tijeras.

## HIKING

Between the West Mesa and the east mountains, Albuquerque offers a huge range of day hikes. The easiest option is the *bosque* (the wooded area along the Rio Grande), where level paths lead through groves of cottonwoods, willows, and olive trees; the **Rio Grande Nature Center,** at the end of Candelaria, is the best

ALBUQUERQUE

© ZORA O'NEILL

Elena Gallegos Open Space is the main access point to the Sandia foothills.

ALBUQUERQUE

starting point for any walk around the area. Anyone looking for some elevation gain will want to head to the Sandias; note that camping is forbidden in the borders of the wilderness area, though, so there's really no place for multi-day backpacking trips. On the city side, you can hoof around the foothills, which are ideal in the winter but a little hot and shadeless in the summertime—the best access is at **Elena Gallegos Open Space** (7 A.M.–9 P.M. Apr.–Oct., 7 A.M.–7 P.M. Nov.–Mar., $1 weekdays, $2 weekends), east of Tramway Boulevard and north of Academy, at the end of Sims Park Road.

The foothills are also the starting point for a much more challenging hike: **La Luz Trail,** a 7.5-mile ascent to the Sandia Crest Visitor Center. The trail has a 12 percent grade at certain points, but the views are well worth the effort, as is the experience of hiking through four climate zones (pack lots of layers) as you climb 3,200 vertical feet. The trail is perhaps the best known in the Sandias, so well worn; the only potentially confusing part is after about 2 miles, where the

trail crosses a streambed and makes a sharp turn south. Near the top, you can take a spur that leads north to the Sandia Crest observation point or continue on the main trail south to the ski area and the Sandia Peak Tramway, which you can take back down the mountain. You could conceivably do a full loop, but ideally you'd have someone pick you up at the bottom end of the tram, because the 2.5-mile trail along the foothills from there back to the trailhead is dusty and lacking in shade and generally kills any accomplishment you'd earned earlier. (You might be tempted to take the tram up and hike down, but the steep descent can be deadly to toes and knees.) La Luz trailhead is at **Juan Tabo Open Space** ($3 parking), at the far north end of Tramway Boulevard just before the road turns west.

If you want to enjoy the views without quite so much effort, you can drive up the east face of the mountain (I-40 to Highway 14) via scenic byway Highway 536, a.k.a. the Crest Road, and park at the Sandia Crest Visitor Center at the top ($3 day-use fee). From there, an easy loop of a little more than 2 miles runs south along the **Crest Spur Trail,** which dips below the ridgeline to connect to **La Luz,** which in turn goes on to the tram terminal. Then you can hike back to your car via the **Crest Trail.** This is the single-most-traveled stretch on Sandia Peak; if you want to avoid the crowds, you can continue on the Crest Trail either south of the tram or north of the crest, or drive back down Highway 536 a few miles to where the **10K Trail** crosses. The stretch of trail to the north, through dense aspen groves, is particularly beautiful in the fall. And with some 180 miles of trails crisscrossing the mountains, there's plenty more to explore; visit www.sandiahiking.com for exhaustive trail descriptions and printable maps.

## BIKING

Albuquerque maintains a good network of paved trails for cycling in the city, and the mountains and foothills are lined with challenging dirt tracks. Recreational cyclists need head no farther than the river, where the **Paseo del Bosque,** a 16-mile-long, completely flat biking and jogging path runs through the Rio Grande Valley State Park. The natural starting point is at **Alameda/Rio Grande Open Space** (7 A.M.–7 P.M. daily) on Alameda Boulevard; you can also reach the trail through the **Rio Grande Nature Center** (8 A.M.–8 P.M. daily, $3 parking), at the end of Candelaria and at several other major intersections along the way. For details on this and other bike trails in Albuquerque, download a map from the city's bike info page (www.cabq.gov/bike).

**Mountain bikers** can take the Sandia Peak Tramway to the ski area, then rent a bike to explore the 30 miles of wooded trails. Bikes aren't allowed on the tram, though, so if you have your own wheels, you can drive around the east side of the mountain; advanced riders will appreciate the challenge of rocky **Faulty Trail,** which runs about 11 miles north–south along the lower elevations of Sandia Peak, connecting with other trails that lead down to main roads as well as higher up the mountain. One access point, midway along the route, is from Highway 14: Coming from I-40, turn left after 3.4 miles onto Cañoncito Road, which turns to dirt in about half a mile; bear left, then park outside the locked gate. The next mile of road is private property (which you may cross on foot), then you reach the Cañoncito trailhead. This trail leads up 0.75 mile to the intersection with Faulty, just after Cañoncito Spring—the more challenging sections are to the north, or right (heading left brings you into the Sandia Mountain Wilderness, where mountain biking is prohibited). You can also get access to the trail near its north end, via the Sulphur Canyon Trail that leads out of Doc Long Picnic Ground, off the Crest Road.

Or you can stay in the city and explore the foothills. Locals built the small but fun **Embudo Mountain Bike Terrain Park** at the end of Indian School Road, which is packed with jumps and berms. For a longer cruise, head for the **foothills trails,** a web of dirt tracks all along the edge of the Northeast Heights. **Trail 365,** which runs for about 15 miles north–south from near the tramway down to near I-40, is the best run. You can start at either end (near the tramway is the easiest—park in the lot here, and ask for directions), or go to Elena Gallegos Open Space, off the north end of Tramway Boulevard at the end of Simms Park Road, where there's access to the midpoint of the trail. Elena Gallegos in particular is very popular, so go on a weekday if you can, and always look out for hikers and other bikers. Aside from the occasional sandy or rocky patch, none of the route is technical, nor steep—more complex trails run off to the east; pick up a map at the entrance booth at Elena Gallegos.

For hard-core road bikers, a popular tour is up to **Sandia Peak** via the Crest Road on the east side—you can park and ride from any point, but cyclists typically start somewhere along Highway 14 (the Turquoise Trail) north of I-40, then ride up Highway 536, which winds 13.5 miles along increasingly steep switchbacks to the crest. The New Mexico Touring Society (www.swcp.com) lists

ALBUQUERQUE

descriptions of myriad other ride options and organizes group rides.

## SPECTATOR SPORTS

**Minor-league baseball** thrives in Albuquerque, apparently all because of some clever name: The so-so Dukes petered out a while back, but a fresh franchise, under the name of the **Albuquerque Isotopes,** has been drawing crowds since 2003. It's hard to judge whether the draw is the zippy new Isotopes Park (1601 Avenida Cesar Chavez NE, 505/883-7800, www.albuquerquebaseball.com), the whoopee-cushion theme nights, or just the name, drawn from an episode of *The Simpsons*. Regardless, a summer night under the ballpark lights is undeniably pleasant; it helps that the best seats are just $10.

For an even smaller-scale ball game, you can head up to the ballfield at Santa Ana pueblo (near Bernalillo), home of the Tamaya Tigers, where semi-pro pueblo teams, as well as Navajo teams from Shiprock and Gallup, face off all summer long. (Isotopes Park then hosts the All-Indian All-Star Playoffs when the pueblo tournament season is through in mid-September.)

Albuquerqueans also go crazy for UNM Lobos **basketball,** packing the raucous University Arena, a.k.a. "The Pit" (Avenida Cesar Chavez at University Blvd., 505/925-5626, www

.golobos.com). In the winter, you can catch a **hockey game**, represented by the New Mexico Scorpions (www.scorpionshockey.com), who will inaugurate the new Rio Rancho Events Center arena in fall 2006.

## SPAS AND SPORTS FACILITIES

**Betty's Bath and Day Spa** (1835 Candelaria St. NW, 505/341-3456) is the place to get pampered, whether with a massage and a facial or with an extended dip in one of two outdoor communal hot tubs (private reservations are available most evenings).

Beat the heat at the **Rio Grande Pool** (1410 Iron Ave. SW, 505/848-1397, noon–5 P.M. daily, $2.25), one of Albuquerque's nicest places to take a dip; the outdoor 25-meter pool is shaded by giant cottonwoods and was completely renovated in 2005. Also check out **Tingley Aquatic Park** (505/764-6200, free) just to the north, 18 acres of paths and ponds, including a fishing lake and a model boating lake, dug along the eastern riverbank south of Central Avenue all the way to Iron Avenue; it was also thoroughly rehabbed in 2005, and it's a popular place to stroll and picnic. A narrow-gauge railroad runs through the park, linking the Albuquerque Biological Park with the zoo.

# Accommodations

Because Albuquerque isn't quite a tourist mecca, its hotel offerings have languished a bit. Generic, chain-operated towers are the norm, and some of the bed-and-breakfasts have a haphazard air. But a few places, particularly the inns in the bucolic areas of Los Ranchos and Corrales, on the north edge of the city, are quite nice, and you'll pay substantially less here than you would in Santa Fe for similar amenities. As a bonus, some of the Route 66 motel courts have been kept up with loving care; fans of retro travel style will not be disappointed.

## UNDER $50

Funky and affordable, the ◖ **Route 66 Hostel** (1012 Central Ave. SW, 505/247-1813) is the kind of place you might get settled into and never leave. This century-old house midway between downtown and Old Town has been offering bargain accommodations since 1978, and it's very clean despite years of budget travelers traipsing through. Upstairs, along creaky wood hallways, are private rooms ($20–33) with various configurations, including the tiny "monk cell," perfect for the broke solo traveler; others have bathtubs and room for three to sleep comfortably. Downstairs and in the cool basement area are single-sex dorms ($17), likewise tucked into various nooks and crannies. Guests have run of the kitchen (an optional free dinner is served every night), and there's a laundry and plenty of room to lounge. The most useful city bus lines run right out front.

The only criticism to muster against the **Sandia Peak Inn** (4614 Central Ave. SW, 505/831-5036, www.sandiapeakinn.com, $45 d) is that it's nowhere near the mountain; in fact, it's on the west side of the city, just over the river from Old Town. In all other respects, however, it's more than you could want in a bargain hotel: Newly constructed in 2002, the two-story motor lodge has large, spotless rooms decorated in a homey fashion, all with bathtubs, fridges, microwaves, and huge TVs. (One suite has a whirlpool tub; another has an extra daybed, handy for families.) An indoor pool and hot tub provide year-round relaxation, and breakfast is included in the rate. The near-obsessive owner lives on the premises with his family and is very proud of his creation, which he plans to expand into the neighboring lot in coming years.

**El Vado** (2500 Central Ave. SW, 505/243-4594, $37 d) is a remarkable phenomenon: a motor-court that seems to have persisted at exactly the same level of class since it was built in 1937, neither falling into decrepitude nor getting spruced up with modern comforts—the "steam heat" and "tile baths" advertised in the 1940s are still there, along with viga ceilings and thick, whitewashed stucco walls. The rooms are a bit snug, but that's all part of the authentic Route 66 charm.

Conveniently located in Nob Hill, **Hiway House** (3200 Central Ave. SE, 505/268-3971, $38 d) retains a bit of the Route 66 motel-court flair—particularly in the rooms, which are frozen in 1968, complete with blue shag carpeting and drum-shaped grasscloth lampshades. The place is kept quite clean, however, and you could certainly do worse in this price category; there's a small pool in the parking lot, and you're within easy walking distance

of the university as well as all of the Nob Hill attractions.

If you're on a budget but have your own car, you can also stay in Cedar Crest, on the east side of the Sandias, about a half-hour drive from the city. The **Sandia Mountain Hostel** (12234 Hwy. 14, 505/281-4117) is peaceful and well kept, even if its yard is filled with rusting trucks and live burros; two single-sex dorms ($14) open onto a big shared kitchen with a wood stove, and a separate house has three private rooms ($38) with porches overlooking the back canyon. Just up the road on the west side, the **Turquoise Trail Campground** (22 Calvary Rd., Cedar Crest, 505/281-2005) has tree-shaded spots for tents ($14.50) as well as small cabins ($28), along with hot-water showers and laundry facilities.

## $50-100

**The Hotel Blue** (717 Central Avenue NW, 877/878-4868, www.thehotelblue.com, $89 d) is the best value downtown, with low prices but the concierge services and perks of a much more expensive place: free airport shuttle service, parking, Internet, and bicycles; Tempurpedic beds, refrigerators, and plasma TVs in the rooms; and a staff that's well equipped to give advice and guidance (pick up an exhaustive brochure on New Mexican cuisine). You also get access to a very pleasant pool and spa. Request a room on the northeast side for a mountain view.

Yes, it's a highly standardized and fairly typical chain hotel, but the **Best Western Rio Grande** (1015 Rio Grande Blvd., 505/843-9500, www.riograndeinn.com, $88 d) is a better deal than the Hotel Albuquerque across the street, and one of the cleanest properties in town. A free airport shuttle, a small pool, and laundry facilities are bonuses; request an upper-floor room for a bit of a view.

The heart of **Cinnamon Morning** (2700 Rio Grande Blvd. NW, 505/345-3541, www.cinnamonmorning.com, $95 d), about a mile north of Old Town, is its lavish outdoor kitchen, with a huge round dining table and a fireplace to encourage lounging on

ALBUQUERQUE

nippier nights. Rooms are simply furnished, with minimalist Southwestern detail—choose from three smaller rooms in the main house, each with a private bath, or the guest house across the garden, which has a two-bedroom suite and another separate bedroom with a corner kiva fireplace.

Hidden on a narrow road in Los Ranchos, **Casita Chamisa** (850 Chamisal Rd. NW, 505/897-4644, www.casitachamisa.com, $95 d) is very small—only one bedroom, and one guest house for four people—but it's wonderfully private, and the sort of place that could exist only in New Mexico: The 150-year-old adobe house sits on an old acequia, as well as the remnants of a Pueblo community established seven centuries ago, partially excavated by the owner's late wife, an archaeologist. There's also a heated pool and a glass-covered patio—both lovely in the wintertime.

## $100-150

If you hanker for the romance of the early railroad era, you'll appreciate two conveniently located historical properties (coincidentally, both owned by wool dealers in the early 20th century). Just two short blocks from the plaza in Old Town, **Böttger Mansion** (110 San Felipe St. NW, 505/243-3639, www.bottger.com, $139 d) is the epitome of Victorian, inside and out. In most of the rooms, though, the frills are applied with a relatively light hand. The lavish Stephanie Lynn room features a giant bath lit by a chandelier, while the snug Molly Jane, with two twin beds, has a great view of the mountain and a clawfoot bathtub; it's ideal for friends traveling together.

On the west edge of downtown you'll find the Queen Anne–style **Mauger Estate** (701 Roma Ave., 505/242-8755, www.maugerbb.com, $119 d), which gleams with polished dark wood paneling and floors. Luxe touches like triple-sheeted beds and fresh flowers contribute to an overall feeling of elegance.

Ironically, at Albuquerque's nicest place to stay, you don't feel like you're anywhere near the city. **Los Poblanos Inn** (4803 Rio Grande Blvd., NW, 505/344-9297,

www.lospoblanos.com, $135 d) sits on 25 acres, the largest remaining plot of land in the city, and the rooms are tucked in various corners of a sprawling *rancho* built in the 1930s by John Gaw Meem for city bigwig Albert Simms and his wife, Ruth McCormick, former U.S. legislators who contributed enormously to the city's social and economic life. Luckily, the subsequent owners have been dedicated to maintaining the historic status of the home—even the huge old kitchen ranges are still in place, as are murals by Taos artist Gustave Baumann. Main-house guest rooms, accented with Spanish colonial antiques and arrayed around a central patio, retain their old wood floors and heavy viga ceilings; a big sunny guesthouse is filled with colorful folk art. Guests are welcome in the extensive gardens, as well as the organic lavender farm and the community-supported agriculture plots that take up much of the acreage. Very much worth a splurge (the majority of the rooms are in the $150–250 range).

Another strong choice in the rural-feeling Los Ranchos district: **Sarabande B&B** (5637 Rio Grande Blvd. NW, 505/345-4923, www.sarabandebb.com, $129 d), with six rooms in three configurations—choose from a skylight, brick floors, and a potbelly wood stove; a private garden and a gas fireplace; or a wood-burning kiva fireplace and a soaking tub. Regardless, they're all done in subdued Southwestern style. A small lap pool takes up the backyard, and a flower-filled patio with a fountain is the breakfast venue.

You can save a bit by heading out of the main tourist areas. On the north side of town, **Nativo Lodge** (6000 Pan American Fwy., 877/901-7666, www.nativolodge.com, $109 d) is conveniently located only for the Balloon Fiesta or an early start to Santa Fe, but once you're inside, it's very nice: The place was completely overhauled in 2005, with new pillow-top beds, sepia-tone decor, and a dramatic lobby and atrium, carved and painted with Native American designs. Definitely get a room in the back, so you're not overlooking I-25.

## $150-250

**Hotel Albuquerque at Old Town** (800 Rio Grande Blvd. NW, 505/843-6300, www.hotelabq.com, $209 d) got a facelift in 2005; it's a little pricey, but the location is handy, and the brick-red-and-beige rooms are relatively spacious (though the angular 1970s tower architecture requires creative placement of furnishings in some instances). Opt for the north side (generally, even-numbered rooms) for a view of the mountains.

Historic **La Posada de Albuquerque** (125 2nd St. NW, 505/242-9090, www .laposadadealbuquerque.com, $160 d) is the city's only remaining relic of early 20th-century travel, a glamorous period when New Mexico was still the wild hinterland. The rooms, unfortunately, don't live up to the mood created on the ground floor—they're a bit tattered, and not particularly inspired in their decor, with token Navajo wall-hangings and punched-tin light fixtures but otherwise standard fittings. If you want to be downtown, however, the location can't be beat. (Should you opt for a more sensible lodging option, don't fail to have a drink at the big wooden horseshoe bar in the lobby.)

The smell of piñon smoke and the sound of flute music set the tone at the **C Hyatt Regency Tamaya** (1300 Tuyuna Tr., Santa Ana Pueblo, www.hyatt.com, $235 d), an impeccably designed resort that's a cooperative project between Santa Ana Pueblo and the Hyatt chain; Hyatt supplies training and experience, and the pueblo dictates aesthetic choices. Even the standard rooms are quite large, with either terraces or balconies; a mountain view is worth the small surcharge. Three swimming pools and a full spa offer relaxation; the more active can play golf or tennis, take an archery class, or attend an evening storytelling program with a pueblo member.

# Food

Although Albuquerque has a few dress-up establishments that merit a little bit of credit-card debt, the real spirit of the city's cuisine is in its oddball, low-rent spots where dedicated owners follow their individual visions—whether that means deluxe tea for two or the hottest chile in the state.

## OLD TOWN AND THE RIO GRANDE

Aside from the couple recommended here, the restaurants in the blocks immediately adjacent to the Old Town plaza are expensive and only so-so; better to walk another block or two for real New Mexican flavor, which can be found in a large number of local hangouts around Old Town and up Rio Grande Boulevard in the North Valley.

### Cafés

Stuck on a barren stretch of North 4th, where neighboring businesses are feed stores and car-repair shops, **C Sophia's Place** (6313 4th St. NW, 7 a.m.–3 p.m. Mon.–Fri., 9 a.m.–2 p.m. Sat. and Sun., $8) is a colorful gem that's well worth the drive, the sort of bohemian café that serves fresh farm eggs but doesn't brag about it. Get those eggs on a breakfast sandwich, which you're really ordering for the side of highly addictive red-chile-dusted home fries. If it's lunchtime, you can opt for a big bowl of noodles or a fat sandwich stuffed with your choice of grilled meats. Either way, this is the sort of place you'll want to laze around, reading the newspapers strewn about and musing over the oddball art and vintage calendars on the walls.

Closer to Old Town, **Chef du Jour** (119 San Pasquale Ave. SW, 505/247-8988, 11 a.m.–2 p.m. Mon.–Fri., $8) is a one-room operation, with about a third of the floor space occupied by the open kitchen; decor is limited to vegetable illustrations from *Cook's Illustrated,* perhaps because all the attention has gone into the lunch specials, which change weekly. On the short menu, you might find anything from green-chile meatloaf to (miracle of miracles) a really tasty veggie burger. Bottomless herbal ice tea and service direct from the owner, who calls everyone "dear," are just icing on the cake. (Oh yes—dessert is always good.)

Good for a lunch break, or just a break from chile, **La Crêpe Michel,** tucked in a courtyard on the back side of the art museum (400 San Felipe St. NW, 505/242-1251, 11:30 a.m.–2 p.m. and 6–9 p.m. Tues.–Sat., 11:30 a.m.–2 p.m. Sun., $8), serves French standards—not just crepes, but also quiches and *croque monsieurs*—in a snug front room and a covered back patio.

Even more chile-free: **St. James Tearoom** (901 Rio Grande Blvd. NW, 505/242-3752, $25 per person), a surprisingly nice spot in the back of a shopping plaza that puts out a dazzling spread of tea sandwiches, scones, and more. Every meal is a carefully balanced mix of savory bites and sweet treats, often reflecting a particular region of Britain and changing monthly. You'll have to plan ahead, though: Tea is served only on Friday at 6:30 p.m. and on Saturday at 11 a.m., 1:30 p.m., and 4 p.m.; reservations are recommended.

### New Mexican
Not far from the plaza, **Duran Central Pharmacy** (1815 Central Ave. NW, 505/247-4141, 9 a.m.–6:30 p.m. Mon.–Fri., 9 a.m.–2 p.m. Sat., $6) is an old-fashioned lunch counter hidden behind the magazine rack in this big fluorescent-lit drugstore. Regulars pack this place at lunch for all the New Mexican staples: huevos rancheros, green-chile stew, big enchilada plates.

**Sadie's** (6230 4th St. NW, 505/345-5339, 11 a.m.–10 p.m. Mon.–Sat., 10 a.m.–9 p.m. Sun., $14) is one of those mammoth operations that started as a cozy, out-of-the-way joint (in this case, in the back of a bowling alley) then morphed into a massive phenomenon. Any sense of "secret find" is lost now, but the chile is still plenty hot and served up

in gigantic portions (check out the juicy, chile-slathered pork chop) by an army of staff. The big patio is very pleasant too.

Hybrid New Mexican cuisine, the blend of Indian ingredients like pinto beans into Mexican dishes like enchiladas, is everywhere; **Pueblo Harvest Café** (2401 12th St. NW, 505/843-7270, 9 a.m.–4:30 p.m. daily, $8) is one of the few places you can get "pure" American Indian food, as enjoyed by the state's Pueblo people. Expect earthy flavors, like strong lamb and rich hominy, as well as frybread, the deep-fried delight that transcends all cultures.

### Steaks and Burgers
The first step at the **Monte Carlo Steakhouse** (3916 Central Ave. SW, 505/831-2444, 11 a.m.–10 p.m. Mon.–Thurs, 11 a.m.–11 p.m. Fri. and Sat., $18), a big brown cinderblock building that looks exactly like a package-liquor store, is to get in: Try the southernmost of the two doors in the unmarked east facade. Then you have to navigate through the dim room and slip into a vintage Naugahyde booth. After that, it's easy: Go for the prime rib if you're there for dinner Thursday through Saturday; otherwise, it's another cut of steak or a softball-size green-chile cheeseburger, served with hand-cut fries. Greek ownership means you get a tangy feta dressing on your salad and baklava for dessert. And even though the place adjoins a bar, you're still welcome to buy wine from the package store up front and have it with your dinner, for a nominal markup.

Despite the retro name and the menu of burgers and fountain treats, the **◖ Route 66 Malt Shop** (1720 Central Ave. SW, 505/242-7866, 11 a.m.–8 p.m. Mon.–Sat., $5) is no hokey 1950s-theme diner. It's simply the real deal: an unpretentious short-order-grill place run by really friendly people who work hard to make good food. For lunch, get a big BLT ("lots of bacon!" promises the menu) or a cheeseburger topped with extra-savory green chile. Then wash it down with a "black cow" (a Coke float with chocolate syrup and chocolate ice cream) or any other combo of syrup and ice cream you can dream up. An absolute must: the house-made root beer, an invigorating, not-too-sweet brew that's great on a hot day.

**Dog House** (1216 Central Ave. SW, 505/243-1019, $4) specializes not just in hot dogs, but in chile dogs, and has been doing so since the 1960s. (Don't like wieners? Get a green-chile cheeseburger instead. Or some tater tots.) The place is worth a visit for its neon sign alone: A dachshund wags its tail as it swallows up a link of sausages.

## Fine Dining

By far the best upscale dining experience in Old Town, ⟨ **Ambrozia** (108 Rio Grande Blvd. NW, 505/242-6560, 5:30 P.M.–late Tues.–Sat., 11 A.M.–late Sun., $24) is the product of a decadent and funny chef, who serves up rich inventions like lobster corn dogs and the Duck Duck Goose (duck breast stuffed with duck pâté and goose foie gras). But despite the cute names, the food is seriously good, and it's helped by an excellent wine list with lots of half bottles and rare varietals, which you can also sample in the small side bar along with snacks. On top of it all, there's the stupendous Sunday "brunchies," a four-course prix fixe meal ($20) with treats like bacon-and-apple-stuffed waffles and duck meatloaf with truffled cream corn.

## DOWNTOWN

Lots of downtown's cafés double as bars, so you can easily while away the afternoon sipping beers on the sidewalk or on airy patios, then segue into the lively post-work happy hour.

## Cafés

Equal parts bar and grill, **Pearl's Dive** (509 Central Ave. NW, 505/244-9405, 11 A.M.–midnight Mon. and Tues., 11 A.M.–2 A.M. Wed.–Fri., 4 P.M.–2 A.M. Sat., $7) is a pleasant spot for a varied lunch or light dinner of burgers and big fresh salads—especially out on the sunny back patio.

For either coffee and pastry or a full dinner with a glass of wine, head to **Gold Street Caffè** (218 Gold Ave. SW, 505/765-1633, 7 A.M.–2 P.M. Mon., 7 A.M.–10 P.M. Tues.–Fri.,

8 A.M.–10 P.M. Sat., 8 A.M.–2 P.M. Sun., $10), where you can monopolize a sidewalk table while you sample food that tends toward light and fresh, from tuna niçoise salad to mussels in a red chile broth. It also serves full breakfasts—the de rigueur huevos rancheros alongside innovations like poached eggs on green-chile brioche.

You can pick up a cheap slice at **Al's New York Pizza Department** (215 Central Ave. NW, 505/766-6973, 11 A.M.–11 P.M. Mon.–Thurs., 11 A.M.–midnight Fri., noon–midnight Sat., noon–10 P.M. Sun., $6), which specializes in thin-crust pies named after the five boroughs (Da Bronx: cured pepperoni and mozzarella); hot subs and calzones are also on the menu. Six bucks gets you two slices and a cold drink.

## New Mexican

Cruise down by the railyards to find **El Modelo** (1715 2nd St. SW, 505/242-1843, 7 A.M.–6:45 P.M. daily, $5), a local go-to for a hangover-curing *chicharrón* burrito, chile-smothered spare ribs, or tamales for the whole family. Because it's really a front for a tortilla factory, the flour tortillas are particularly tender, and you can order either a taco or two or a whole platter of food. If the weather's nice, grab a seat at a picnic table outside and watch the freight trains go by.

Just two blocks from the National Hispanic Cultural Center, popular ⟨ **Barelas Coffee House** (1502 4th St. SW, 505/843-7577, 7:30 A.M.–3 P.M. Mon.–Fri., 7:30 A.M.–2 P.M. Sun., $6) is confusing to the first-timer: The attraction is chile, not coffee—especially the red, which infuses hearty, timeless New Mexican standards like posole, *chicharrones,* and *menudo.* The restaurant occupies several storefronts, and even then there's often a line out the door at lunchtime. But it's worth the wait—this is timeless food.

## Mexican

From the outside, **Juanita's** (910 4th St. SW, 505/843-9669, 7:30 A.M.–4:30 P.M. Mon.–Fri., 8 A.M.–4 P.M. Sat., $5.50) looks like an abandoned Dairy Queen. Inside, though, it's all color and activity—flower-print oilcloths on the tables and lots of sizzle from the half-open kitchen, where hairnetted ladies build giant burritos, crispy tacos, and (most recommended) savory Mexican-style tortas on pillowy white rolls. Jarritos sodas and imported, all-cane-sugar Coca-Cola wash it down. If you're getting your order to go, make sure you get some of the sharp red salsa.

### Fine Dining

Since it opened in 1989, the **Artichoke Café** (424 Central Ave. SE, 505/243-0200, 11 A.M.–2:30 P.M. and 5:30–10 P.M. Mon.–Fri., 5:30–10 P.M. Sat., 5:30–9 P.M. Sun., $22) has been top on locals' lists for a dinner treat, largely because the husband-and-wife team have varied the menu with the times without seeming desperately trendy—influences come from all over the globe (five-spice rubbed duck, pumpkin ravioli with ricotta), but dishes remain simple and unfussy. The blue-tinged dining room is simple without being austere, and the crowd is varied. Reservations are recommended.

### Dessert

For a sweet treat, stop in at **Theobroma** (319 Central Ave. NW, 505/247-0848, 10 A.M.–6 P.M. Mon.–Fri., noon–5 P.M. Sat.), a family operation that makes its own hand-dipped bonbons and other chocolaty delights, like the UFO bar, a chocolate disk covered with pecans and covered in white chocolate. The shop also serves up scoops of rich and creamy Taos Cow ice cream.

# UNIVERSITY AND NOB HILL

Due to the high student population, this area has some great and varied spots to grab a cheap bite, but Nob Hill has some upscale options too.

### Cafés

When you walk into **C Flying Star** (3416 Central Ave. SE, 505/255-6633, $8), you'll be mesmerized by the pastry case: Triple-ginger cookies, lemon-blueberry cheesecake, and big fat éclairs are laid out in enticing rows. But try to look up to appreciate the range on the menu boards: Asian noodles, hot and cold sandwiches, mac-and-cheese, and enchiladas. With speedy service and a huge magazine selection, it's a great place to zip in or to lounge around (wireless Internet access is free). This is the original location of what's now a mini-chain—you'll find one in nearly every neighborhood, including the **North Valley** (4026 Rio Grande Blvd. NW, 505/344-6714) and **downtown** (723 Silver Ave. SE, 505/244-8099); the latter is in a hiply restored 1950 John Gaw Meem building.

Just a few blocks from the university, **Annapurna Chai House** (2201 Silver Ave. SE, 505/262-2424, 7 A.M.–8 P.M. Mon.–Wed., 7 A.M.–9 P.M. Thurs.–Sat., 10 A.M.–2 P.M. Sun., $5) is a vegetarian's delight, serving a menu that's completely compatible with Ayurvedic dietary recommendations, with giant *masala dosas* (rice-flour crepes) as well as less strictly Indian dishes such as cardamom pancakes with maple syrup. Or just stop in for a refreshing spicy mango *lassi* or cold *chai*. There's also free wireless access.

On the north side of the university, **Blue Dragon** (1517 Girard Blvd. NE, 505/268-5159, 8 A.M.–11 P.M. daily, $6) is an all-purpose neighborhood hangout dishing up organic coffee, great baked goods (the brownies are super-moist, and the vegan options are tasty, too), veggie-packed sandwiches, creative pizzas, and fresh juices like "rabbit punch" for everyone from counterculture teens—who play video games in a separate room—to aging bohemians. Service can be a little spacey, but it's all part of the mellow coffeehouse vibe.

Pick up goods for a picnic at **La Montañita Co-op** (3500 Central Ave. SE, 505/265-4631, 7 A.M.–10 P.M. Mon.–Sat., 8 A.M.–10 P.M. Sun.), where quinoa salads and stuffed grape leaves are all the rage; look in the cheese section for tiny "sampler" pieces of locally made chèvre and other dairy delights. Most everything's organic, and the co-op arrangement means it's reasonably priced. There's a bigger branch in the **North Valley** (2400 Rio Grande Blvd. NW, 505/242-8800, 8 A.M.–10 P.M. daily).

## Brewpubs

Two places in Nob Hill make their own beer but have more of a restaurant feel. **Kelly's** (3222 Central Ave. SE, 505/262-2739, 8 A.M.–midnight daily, $10), formerly a gas station, is the city's most popular spot for patio dining and schmoozing. The rich Kelly Porter washes down beer-friendly food like bison burgers and curly fries—not entirely inspired, and often served by distracted waitstaff—but you're really here for the scene, the sun, and the suds.

**Il Vicino** (3403 Central Ave. NE, 505/266-7855, 11 A.M.–11 P.M. Sun.–Thurs., 11 A.M.–midnight, Fri. and Sat., $7) has better food but lacks the expansive feel of Kelly's. Order at the front counter from the list of high-grade pizza toppings, and the dough promptly gets slid into the wood-fired oven at the back—or opt for a grilled *panino* sandwich or a big fresh salad. Then squeeze into your seat (space is tight) and enjoy your pint of Wet Mountain IPA while you wait; in keeping with the upscale pizza-joint feel, there's wine, too, and Italian sodas.

## New Mexican

You haven't been to Albuquerque unless you've been to **( The Frontier** (2400 Central Ave. SE, 505/266-0550, open 24 hours, $6), a mammoth diner across from UNM. Everyone in the city passes through its doors at some point in their lives, so all you have to do is pick a seat in one of the five Western-theme rooms—hmm, under the big portrait of John Wayne? or maybe one of the smaller ones?—and watch the characters file in. You'll want some food, of course: a green-chile-smothered breakfast burrito filled with crispy hash browns, or a grilled hamburger, or one of the signature cinnamon rolls, a deadly amalgam of flour, sugar, and some addictive drug that compels you to eat them despite the hydrogenated goo they're swimming in. If you feel a little unhealthy, you can always get some fresh orange juice and restore your balance by vegging out in front of the mesmerizing tortilla machine.

Near the university, **El Patio** (142 Harvard Dr. SE, 505/268-4245, 11 A.M.–9 P.M. Mon.–Thurs., 11 A.M.–9:30 P.M. Fri. and Sat.,

The Frontier is the city's best spot for green-chile stew and people-watching.

noon–9 P.M. Sun., $8) is the kind of old-reliable place that ex-locals get misty-eyed about after they've moved away; the green-chile-and-chicken enchiladas are high on many citywide favorite lists. It doesn't hurt that the setting, in an old bungalow with a shady outdoor space, feels like an extension of someone's home kitchen.

## Fine Dining

The roomy, cheerful 【 **Graze** (3128 Central Ave. SE, 505/268-4729, 11 A.M.–10 P.M. Sun.–Thurs. 11 A.M.–11 P.M. Fri. and Sat., $13) specializes in small plates—great for groups, and fun to mix and match; however, it's adapted to New Mexicans' sensibilities, and portions are not nearly so tiny as at your standard tapas bar, so you can make a good meal of just a few items without inadvertently boosting the check (though this is one of Nob Hill's pricier restaurants). Dishes change seasonally and range from single bites like deviled eggs to items that could almost pass as full entrées, such as lamb loin with a peanut-tamarind sauce. Another adaptation for New Mexican tastes: Almost everything has a bit of heat, whether it's the peppery pomegranate glaze on the roast quail or the pickled-jalapeño garnish on the deviled eggs. Wash it down with carefully paired selections from the affordable wine list; a good selection of half bottles encourages sharing and tasting, just as the food does.

Even if you're not hankering for a big slab of meat, check out the classy **Gruet Steak House** (3201 Central Ave. NE, 505/256-9463, 5–10 P.M. daily, $29), housed in the pueblo-look Monte Vista fire station, built by the WPA in 1937. Though you can pick from six cuts of beef and a very tasty iceberg-and-blue-cheese salad, you might want to stick just to appetizers, like the grilled oysters, and a glass of wine as an excuse to enjoy the great patio that now occupies the spot where the fire trucks used to roll in and out. Local Gruet vintages are the centerpiece of the wine list, but you've got plenty of other options too.

# ALBUQUERQUE METRO AREA

Great places to eat are scattered all over the city, just as often in unlikely looking strip malls as in intimate and luxurious historic properties. These places are worth making a trip for, or will provide a pick-me-up when you're in a strange part of town.

## New Mexican

Don't confuse the old location of 【 **Los Cuates** (5016 Lomas Blvd. NE, 505/268-0974, 11 A.M.–9 P.M. daily, $8) with the newer place across the street. You want the 1979 original, which could be called the ur–New Mexican restaurant. Its red vinyl booths have saggy springs; pebbled plastic water cups scrape on the glass tabletops; and you can hear the clink of ceramic and silverware from the dishwasher. The vinyl-encased menus offer combination plates and smaller choices *para los niños*. Everything's tasty, but do make sure you sample the especially savory chicken, whether in enchiladas or a burrito. And of course you'll need a basket of hot, puffy sopaipillas to mop it all up.

Experts agree: **Mary & Tito's Café** (2711 4th St. NW, 505/344-6266, 9 A.M.–6 P.M. Mon.–Thurs., 9 A.M.–8 P.M. Fri. and Sat., $7) is the place to go for *carne adovada*, the dish of tender pork braised in red chile. The only thing better is the "Mexican turnover," an uncooked flour tortilla filled with *carne adovada*, then deep-fried. But in fact, everything with red chile is delicious at this simple, home-style place north of downtown. You'll see locals cashing in their frequent-diner cards—even if you're in town for a short stay, you might want to get one.

Definitely worth a stop when you're cruising scenic Corrales, **Casa Vieja** (4541 Corrales Rd., 505/898-7489, 5–9 P.M. daily, $12) started out as a much fancier, hip American place, but conceded to customers' demands for real New Mexican food—the restaurant is in a 300-year-old adobe, after all. The place has been packed ever since. Happily for those who might be burned out on chile, you can still get dishes like Baja-style fish tacos, garlicky lamb chops, and even Asian spring rolls.

Finally, **K & I Diner** (2500 Broadway SE, 505/243-1881, 6 A.M.–3 P.M. Mon.–Sat., 8 A.M.–2 P.M. Sun., $6) serves perhaps the most massive meal you will eat anywhere in New Mexico. It's a single dish, the Travis: An enormous burrito, bigger even than the heads of the high-school football players who come here to bulk up, is slathered in chile and topped with French fries. You can order a half-Travis, or even a quarter-Travis, but you'd better have a damn good excuse, like a stapled stomach, if you opt for the eighth-Travis.

## Asian

Vietnamese **Café Da Lat** (5615 Central Ave. NE, 505/266-5559, 10:30 A.M.–9 P.M. Mon.–Sat., 11 A.M.–3 P.M. Sun., $8) has an uninspiring view of an auto-parts store, but inside it's all stylish and serene, with spotlights over the gleaming tabletops. Well-priced, flavor-packed standard dishes like catfish in ginger sauce and lime-dressed beef salad are on the menu, and the spring rolls are bursting with shrimp.

Another hidden gem in a strip mall, **Chow's Chinese Bistro** (1950 Juan Tabo Blvd. NE, 505/298-3000, 11 A.M.–2 P.M. and 5–9:30 P.M. Mon.–Sat., 5–9:30 P.M. Sun., $13) specializes in slightly dressed-up Chinese. Everything's very fresh-tasting, with distinct, strong flavors, and the menu includes both favorites like chicken and cashews and great surprises, such as a lamb stir-fry. Brown rice is an option, the ice tea is great, and the minimalist room, adorned only with large calligraphy scrolls, is very soothing.

Can't decide what kind of food you're craving? Cruise the aisles of **Talin Market World Food Fare** (88 Louisiana Blvd. SE, 505/266-0755, 8:30 A.M.–8 P.M. Mon.–Sat., 9 A.M.–7 P.M. Sun.), a megamarket stocked with items from Bombay to the U.K. Its Asian stock is the largest, though, and you can get a variety of hot Laotian, Korean, and Filipino lunch items from the small cafeteria section in one corner, and sweets like pumpkin custard from the bakery. A bubble-tea joint outside rounds out the meal, and by the time you read this, this corner across from the fairgrounds may be home to other ethnic eateries, as part of the city's plan to develop the zone as a larger internationally flavored district.

## Fine Dining

**Prairie Star** (255 Prairie Star Rd., Santa Ana Pueblo, 5:30–9 P.M. Tues.–Sun., $25) is one of Albuquerque's most respected "date night" places, where the view across the river valley to the Sandias is as valued as the food, which adds Southwestern touches without being overwhelming: Locally raised lamb chops are served with red-pepper-and-chèvre flautas, and the duck breast gets a sweet pecan-cherry tamale on the side. If you're out this way sightseeing, it's worth coming by, if not for an entire splurgey meal, at least for cocktails (drinks service starts at 5 P.M.) and an appetizer. The restaurant is in Bernalillo, just off Highway 44, at the turn for the Hyatt Regency Tamaya.

**ALBUQUERQUE**

# Outside Albuquerque

In every direction from the city, you'll find some natural attraction. Most important is Acoma, an ancient pueblo that seems to have grown out of the tall, windswept mesa on which it's built, and the dramatic, wide-open scenery out this way is the stuff of movie backdrops. To the south, the Rio Grande continues through its fertile valley to the Bosque del Apache, a lush network of marshlands maintained for migrating birdlife; the drive down is a long one, but you can make a day of it with stops at out-of-the-way eateries and a scenic dirt-road route back. To the east is the start of one of three routes to Santa Fe, the Turquoise Trail, which leads through the vestiges of New Mexico's mining past. An equally scenic route north is the more circuitous Jemez Mountain Trail, past red rocks and hot springs. Or you can zip directly up the main highway, where you'll pass another remarkable bit of scenery, the windswept region known as Tent Rocks.

## WEST TO ACOMA PUEBLO

Heading out from Albuquerque, I-40 climbs the West Mesa and heads dead straight across a plateau lined with flat mesas—archetypal Southwest scenery. Although it's somewhat dull freeway driving, the trip out this way is well worth it, as ancient Acoma Pueblo is built on top one of these mesas, an amazing place to visit and meet the people whose ancestors have lived here for nearly a thousand years.

### Laguna Pueblo

About 18 miles west of Albuquerque, I-40 crosses the border onto the 45 square miles of Laguna Pueblo (505/552-6654, www.lagunapueblo.org), on which nearly 8,000 Keresan-speaking Ka-waikah ("lake people") live in six villages. From the highway, the only impression you get of Laguna is its Dancing Eagle Casino, but if you have time, it's worth getting off at exit 114 to visit the **San José Mission Church**

(8 A.M.–4:30 P.M. Mon.–Fri.). Built around 1700, it is immediately distinctive for its stark white stucco coating, but this is a relatively recent addition. Inside is the really remarkable element of the church: Between a packed-earth floor and a finely wrought wood ceiling, the fine late-18th-century altar screen commands the full focus of the room. It's the work of the unknown "Laguna Santero," an innovative painter who placed his icons inside a crowded field of decorative borders and ornately carved and painted columns to create a work of explosively colorful folk art that was copied elsewhere in the state in subsequent decades.

Each individual village of Laguna celebrates its own feast day, then the whole pueblo turns out at the church September 17–19 for the Feast of San José, one of the bigger pueblo events in the Albuquerque area. Along with traditional dances and an arts-and-crafts market, the pueblo hosts the All-Indian Baseball Tournament, in which the very sports-minded pueblo fields five semi-pro teams, pitched against teams from up and down the Rio Grande.

### ( Acoma Pueblo

At exit 108 off I-40, visitors to Acoma turn south on Indian Route 23. The road soon crosses up and over a ridge, and you may feel as though you've crossed through a pass into a Southwestern Shangri-La, for none of this great basin is visible from the highway. The route runs directly toward a flat-topped rock that juts out of the plain like a tooth.

Atop this rock is the original Acoma Pueblo, the village known as Sky City. The community covers about 70 acres and is built entirely of pale, sun-bleached adobe, as it has been since at least 1100; only 50 or so people live on the mesa top year-round, given the hardships of no running water or electricity, but many families maintain homes here, and the place is thronged on September 2, when the pueblo members gather for the feast of San Esteban. The rest of the 2,800 Acomas ("people of the white rock"

# ACOMA VS. OÑATE: GRUDGE MATCH

After more than a decade of slave-labor construction, the Acomas completed the Church of San Esteban del Rey. The Spanish friars, as if to add insult to injury, then presented the church in 1640 to the pueblo people as "restitution" for an earlier brutal incident, which started with a nasty attack on the pueblo in 1599 by conquistador Don Juan de Oñate, the first governor of Spain's newest province. The battle, which Oñate called justice for an earlier ambush on a handful of his men (which in turn was provoked by a previous disagreement), resulted in the deaths of hundreds of Acomas – the hilltop village was more than decimated.

But Oñate was not content. After the battle, he brought his enemies into a makeshift court and tried them for murder. The sentence for the inevitable guilty verdict was that every male in Acoma over the age of 25 would have one foot cut off; everyone between the ages of 12 and 25 was pressed into slavery; and the children were sent to convents in

Mexico. Oñate was at least recalled from his post and chastised for his actions, but it was to this maimed populace that the Franciscans presented the "gift" of a Catholic church 30 years later; as a further gift of salvation, the friars publicly purged and hanged the village's spiritual leaders in the churchyard.

Variations on this treatment happened up and down the Rio Grande (and eventually inspired the Pueblo Revolt of 1680), but Oñate's particular brand of viciousness is probably the most remembered. Shortly after a monument to the conquistador was erected north of Española in 1998, the right foot of the bronze statue turned up missing – someone, or some group of people, had snuck in in the night and sawed it clean off. An anonymous letter to newspapers stated that the act was "on behalf of our brothers and sisters at Acoma Pueblo." Rumor adds that the prankster vandals also left behind at the statue two miniature feet made of clay, attached to a shield inscribed with the words "The Agony of Defeat."

ALBUQUERQUE

in their native Keresan) live on the valley floor, which is used primarily as ranchland.

The very fragile nature of the windswept village accounts in part for the particularly stringent tourism policies. All visitors must stop at the **Sky City Cultural Center** (Indian Rte. 23, 800/747-0181, www.skycity.com, 8 A.M.–7 P.M. daily May–Oct., 8 A.M.–4 P.M. Nov.–Apr.) on the highway; from here, they must join a guided tour ($10), which transports groups by bus to the village—the one concession to modernity has been the carving of this road to the top; previously, all goods had to be carried and hauled up the near-vertical cliff faces. The tour lasts one hour, after which visitors must return by bus, or they may hike down one of the old trails, using hand- and footholds dug into the rock centuries before.

The centerpiece of the village is the **Church of San Esteban del Rey,** one of the most iconic of the Spanish missions in New Mexico. It was

adobe houses in Acoma Pueblo

COURTESY NEW MEXICO DEPARTMENT OF TOURISM

built 1629–1640, and its graceful, simple form has been inspiring New Mexican architects ever since. (Visitors are not allowed inside, however, nor into the adjoining cemetery.) As much as it represents the pinnacle of Hispano-Indian architecture in the 17th century, it's also a symbol of the Spanish brutality exercised in the early colonial period, as it rose in the typical way: through forced labor. The men of Acoma felled and carried the tree trunks for the ceiling beams from the forest on Mount Taylor, more than 25 miles across the valley, and up the cliff face to the village.

Acoma is well known for its **pottery,** easily distinguished by the fine black lines that sweep around the curves of the vessel; on the best works, the lines are so fine and densely painted, they appear almost like a moiré. Additionally, the clay particular to this area can be worked extremely thin, to create a pot that will hum or ring when you tap it. Throughout the village, you have opportunities to buy samples—though this may feel like a scam, given the constraints of the tour, you often have the privilege of buying a piece directly from the artisan who created it.

## SOUTH TO THE BOSQUE DEL APACHE

If you haven't gotten enough of the area's birdlife along the Rio Grande in the city, head to the Bosque del Apache bird sanctuary, which is the site of an awe-inspiring fly-in of giant sandhill cranes during November and hosts hundreds of other migratory species in the fall and winter. On the way there or back, you can strike out into truly remote New Mexico along the Quebradas Scenic Backcountry Byway.

### Lemitar

A great reason (but the only one) to stop in this farming community 45 miles south of Albuquerque is the **Coyote Moon Café** (west frontage road at exit 156 off I-40, 11 A.M.– 8 P.M. Wed.–Sun., $5), in what looks like a former storage barn on the west side of the highway. The New Mexican food served here—all cooked by the owner/waiter/dishwasher—

is of the gringo rancher variety: The meat is kept distinct from the chile and really shines in the green-chile stew and specials such as the lamb burrito; cheese is applied with a light hand. The red chile sauce, made with peppers grown nearby, is velvety and perfectly balanced. You can also get some more obscure (New) Mexican dishes, such as *fideo* (thin noodles with chile-smothered pork) and *quelites,* spicy sautéed greens. If you're driving by early in the week, don't give up—sometimes the place is open for lunch on Monday and Tuesday, between 11 A.M. and 2 P.M.

### Socorro

Once a booming mining town, Socorro now exists largely as an adjunct to New Mexico Institute of Mining & Technology (a.k.a. New Mexico Tech), which has been training engineers since 1893. The town has a small time-warp historic plaza, but the campus is where the real scenery is: Mission-style buildings are set amid rolling green lawns, and the view from the top of the golf course is stunning, taking in the green river valley and red-striped hills along the horizon. There's not much in the way of food in town (**Martha's Black Dog,** at 110 Manzanares Street just west of the main street, is fine), but you can wet your whistle at the **Capitol Bar** on the plaza, which doesn't seem to have changed much in its century of doing business.

### San Antonio

Even though it's just a blip on the map, this town supports two great burger joints: the **Owl Bar & Café** (U.S. 380, 505/835-9946, 8 A.M.–9 P.M. Mon.–Sat., $5), which has always gotten all the press, and the lesser-known **Manny's Buckhorn** (U.S. 380, 505/835-4423, 11 A.M.–8 P.M. Mon.–Sat., $5), just across the street. Both serve beer and green-chile cheeseburgers, both have chummy local staff and plenty of lore, so how to choose? Go to the Owl if you like your burgers thin, to Manny's if you like them a little fatter. Actually, the Owl gets an extra point for historic detail: The bar here is from the world's first Hilton

Hotel—not part of Conrad Hilton's international chain, but the one opened by his father when he moved here in the 1880s; Conrad was born shortly thereafter, grew up to be his father's business partner, and went on to develop hotel properties around the world. The Owl's owners salvaged the bar after the structure surrounding it burned.

If you want to wake up and get straight to the birds, **Casa Blanca B&B** (13 Montoya St., San Antonio, 505/835-3027, www.casablancabedandbreakfast.com, $70 d) can put you up for the night in one of three cozy rooms in an 1880 Victorian farmhouse, or you can camp at the **Bosque Birdwatchers RV Park** (505/835-1366, $15), just 100 yards north of the reserve border on Highway 1.

## Bosque del Apache National Wildlife Refuge

Occupying 57,191 acres on either side of the Rio Grande, this bird sanctuary is in a sense a manufactured habitat: Controlled flooding creates the marshes that draw the birds, which find food on farm plots dedicated to tasty grains. But this is really restoring a process that happened naturally before the Rio Grande was dammed upriver. The birds certainly have no objection: Arctic geese, sandhill cranes, bald eagles, and a whole variety of ducks settle in for the winter, happily ensconced in the rich ponds. The huge flocks of geese take flight simultaneously every morning, in a rush of noise caused by many thousands of wings flapping at once. In the spring, migratory warblers and pelicans stop off on their way back to points north, while great blue herons make their spring nests here. Summer is relatively quiet, as only the year-round species are still here: hummingbirds, swallows, flycatchers, and the like.

Head first to the **visitors center** (7:30 A.M.–4 P.M. Mon.–Fri., 8 A.M.–4:30 P.M. Sat. and Sun.), five miles inside the north border of the reserve, where you can pick up maps and find out what birds have been spotted that day. The main way to see the reserve is via a 12-mile paved car loop that passes through all the marshlands and the grain fields; at certain

Sandhill cranes spend the winter at Bosque del Apache National Wildlife Refuge.

COURTESY NEW MEXICO DEPARTMENT OF TOURISM/JIM ORR

ALBUQUERQUE

points along the drive, you can get out and hike set trails, such as a quarter-mile boardwalk across a lagoon or a trail over to the river proper. Some areas are open to mountain bikers. Although the visitors center is open only during daylight hours, the park accommodates bird-watchers by opening the loop drive when birdlife is at its best, one hour before sunrise; cars need to be out by an hour after dark. With all its marshlands, the *bosque* could just as well be called a mosquito sanctuary—slather on plenty of repellent before you start your drive.

The biggest event of the year is the arrival of the sandhill cranes—they were the inspiration for the refuge, as their population had dwindled to fewer than 20 in 1941, but now more than 15,000 of these graceful birds with six-foot wingspans winter over in the *bosque*. They're celebrated annually at the five-day **Festival of the Cranes** (www.friendsofthebosque.org) in November, when birders gather for lectures and tours, and to witness the awe-inspiring mass morning lift-offs and evening fly-ins.

**THE TURQUOISE TRAIL**

## Quebradas Backcountry Scenic Byway

This 24-mile dirt road cuts across several deep arroyos, or natural drainage channels—these are the *quebradas* ("breaks") in the earth that give the area its name. The rounded hills here are striped with rainbow hues, and the scrub desert teems with hawks, mule deer, and foxes. The route makes a good slow way back to Albuquerque if you've come down early in the morning to see the birds (though you could just as easily drive down this way and hit the *bosque* near sunset). The drive takes between two and three hours, but bear in mind that this is remote wilderness—be sure you have extra food and water, as well as a spare tire. Don't attempt it if it has rained very recently, as the mud can be impossible to pass, and look out for sandy patches at all times.

From the intersection of the *bosque* road (Hwy. 1) in San Antonio, in front of the Owl Café, head east on U.S. 380 for 11 miles; then turn north on County Road A-129, the beginning of the byway. Coming from Albuquerque is a little trickier: Leave I-25 at Escondida (exit 152, south of Lemitar), then go north on the east frontage road; turn east after you pass Escondida Lake, cross the river, and continue for about 2 miles to Pueblito, where you turn right at a T-intersection. After about a mile, you will see a sign for the byway beginning on your left (west).

## THE TURQUOISE TRAIL

This scenic back route to Santa Fe, which runs along the east side of the Sandias and up across high plateaus, revisits New Mexico's mining history as it passes through a series of ghost towns. Take I-40 east from Albuquerque to exit 175. Bear right to go into the village of Tijeras and the **Sandia ranger station** (505/281-3304) if you want to pick up hiking maps to the area, or left to continue directly to the junction with Highway 14, the beginning of the Turquoise Trail.

### The East Mountains

The four-lane road heads north through al-

ALBUQUERQUE

## BIRDING ON THE PEAK

Sandia Peak in the dead of winter does not seem hospitable to life in any form, much less flocks of delicate-looking birds the size of your fist, fluffing around cheerfully in the frigid air. But that's precisely what you'll see if you visit in the iciest months, particularly right after a big snowfall. The feathered critters in question are rosy finches, a contrary, cold-loving variety (sometimes called "refrigerator birds") that migrate from as far north as the Arctic tundra between November and March to the higher elevations of New Mexico, which must seem relatively tropical by comparison.

What's particularly special about Sandia is that it draws all three species of rosy finch, which in turn draws dedicated birders looking to add the finches to their "life lists." *Birder's*

*World* magazine praises Sandia Peak as "the world's most accessible location to see all three species of rosy finches." This is a boon for people who are more accustomed to kayaking through swamps and slogging through tropical forests to spot rare species. So if you see the finches – they're midsize brown or black birds with pink bellies, rumps, and wings – you'll probably also spy some human finch fans. But they might not have time to talk, as it's not unheard-of for the most obsessive birders – those on their "big year," out to spot as many species as possible in precisely 365 days – to fly into Albuquerque, drive to the crest, eyeball the finches, and drive right back down and fly out in search of even more obscure varieties.

ternating communities of old Spanish land grants and modern subdivisions—San Antonito, Cedar Crest, Sandia Park—collectively referred to as the East Mountains. Six miles on, you come to a large triangle intersection—to the left is Highway 536, the Crest Road up to Sandia Peak, a beautiful winding drive through steadily thinning forests until you reach the exposed top of the mountain, more than 10,000 feet above sea level and more than 5,500 feet above the center of Albuquerque. Even if you don't drive to the crest, do head 1.5 miles up the Crest Road to **Tinkertown Museum** (9 A.M.–6 P.M. daily), a temple to efficient use of downtime. Ross Ward, an artist and sign painter who learned his trade doing banners for carnivals, was also a master whittler and creative engineer who built, over 40 years, thousands of elaborate miniature figures and dioramas out of wood, some of which he even animated with tiny pulleys and levers: a man with a cleaver chases chickens in a circle, circus performers soar, the blacksmith's bellows huff and puff. Many of the buildings themselves are Ward's creations as well—undulating walls made of bottles and studded with odd collectibles, for instance; the museum, like an

amoeba, even seems to have taken over a friend and neighbor's 35-foot wooden boat. Ward died in 2002; his family keeps up the museum today, and even though it's no longer growing organically as it used to, it remains a remarkable piece of pure folk art.

### Golden

Back on Highway 14, continue north through rolling hills and ever-broader sky. After 15 miles, you reach the all-but-gone town of Golden—so named because it was the site of the first gold strike west of the Mississippi, in 1825. But all that's left now is a handful of homes, an attractive adobe church, and one store, **Golden General Merchandise** (10 A.M.–3:30 P.M. Tues.–Sat.), open since 1918. Pop in if you happen to be there during its limited opening hours; it's largely given over to Indian jewelry and pottery, but prices are reasonable and quality is generally quite high. Antique trinkets line the upper shelves, remnants of Golden's moment of glory.

### Madrid

Thirteen miles beyond Golden, and about midway along the drive, Madrid (pronounced

MAD-rid by locals) is a ghost town back from the dead. Built by the Albuquerque & Cerrillos Coal Co. starting in 1906, it once housed 4,000 people, but it was deserted by the end of World War II, when natural gas became more widespread. Beginning in the late 1970s, though, a few of the sway-roofed wood houses had been reoccupied by hippies who were willing to live somewhere where indoor plumbing was barely available. Over the decades, Madrid slowly revived; portable toilets are still more common than flush models, but the arts scene has flourished, and a real sense of community pervades the main street, which is dressed in gaudy lights at Christmas and lined with pretty painted bungalows.

You can learn more about Madrid's history at the **Old Coal Mine Museum** (Hwy. 14, 505/438-3780, 9:30 A.M.–5:30 P.M. daily, $4), where you can wander among sinister-looking machine parts and through dusty old workshops, where you'll feel the "ghost" in "ghost town," and even walk partway down an abandoned mineshaft—a great disciplinary tool for kids who've been acting up in the car. And

there's the last remaining intact Richmond Locomotive short-haul freighter, if you care about these sort of things. If the Old West costume photo studio on the lobby doesn't sate your desire for old-timey fun, you can stay for a show at the **Engine House Theatre** (505/438-3780, 3 P.M. and 7 P.M. Sat., 3 P.M. Sun., $10), where local hams play out a classic melodrama inside an atmospherically drafty repair shed (call ahead to reserve).

A more vibrant remnant of Madrid's company-town days is the **Mine Shaft Tavern** (2846 Hwy. 14, 505/473-0743, 11 A.M.–10 P.M. Mon.–Sat.), where you can belly up to a 40-foot-long pine-pole bar, over which hang murals by local artist Ross Ward, who built the Tinkertown Museum in Sandia Park. "It is better to drink than work," reads the Latin inscription interwoven among the mural panels, and certainly everyone in the bar, from long-distance bikers to gallery-hoppers, is living by those encouraging words.

If you'd prefer something nonalcoholic, you can sample history on the small boardwalk at the old **soda fountain,** installed in 1934. The

Belly up to the 40-foot-long pine-pole bar at the Mine Shaft Tavern.

larger space is the **Talking Bridge Gallery,** which carries tie-dyed onesies and one-of-a-kind knitwear, so the man making your egg cream may not be a specialist, but everything turns out sweet and tasty nonetheless.

Scads of other galleries are laid along the main street—a stroll down and back, followed by lunch, is the typical Madrid itinerary. Look out especially for quirky hats at **Woofy Bubbles** (2872 Hwy. 14, 505/471-3837, 11 A.M.–4 P.M. Fri.–Mon.) and the gorgeous rugs at **Seppanen & Daughters** (2879 Hwy. 14, 505/424-7470, 10:30 A.M.–4:30 P.M. daily).

As for food, head straight to **Mama Lisa's Ghost Town Kitchen.** When it's open (seemingly not on a regular basis, but chances are better in the summer), it's a true treat, a cozy place with an all-over-the-map menu: buffalo chalupas, Austrian-style pork chops, rhubarb pie, and hibiscus mint tea, which you can enjoy out on the tree-shaded front patio. When it's closed, all you can do is press your face against the window and dream—or go down the street to **Java Junction** (2855 Hwy. 14, 505/438-2772, from 7:30 A.M. daily) for coffee.

Solace for those cruising through very early: The **Miner's Chuckwagon** in front of the museum sells shockingly cheap and tasty sausage biscuits ($1.50) and coffee in the mornings.

## Cerrillos

By contrast with Madrid, Cerrillos, once the source of turquoise that has been traced to Chaco Canyon, Spain, and Chichén Itzá in Mexico's Yucatán Peninsula, hasn't been gallerified like its neighbor down the road. Well, there is *one* gallery. There's also one church, built in 1922; one cheerful café with organic coffee, **Enchanted on First** (505/474-0112, 7 A.M.–4 P.M. daily); one trading post selling cow skulls, antique bottles, taxidermied jackalopes, and turquoise nuggets; and one petting zoo, with a llama and a sheep. And there's one bar, **Mary's,** whose proprietress is into her 10th decade of life and has been running the place since 1977. The bar doesn't look particularly open from the outside, but do stop in

and have a beer and a chat with Mary Trujillo, who can tell some fine tales of putting unruly drunks in their place (including the cast of *Young Guns,* which was filmed here). You can go **horseback riding** through the canyon (Broken Saddle Riding Co., 505/424-7774, www.brokensaddle.com, $65 for two hours) and in **Cerrillos Hills Historic Park** (www.cerrilloshills.org), more than 1,000 acres of rolling hills and narrow canyons that are particularly good for **mountain biking.**

After ascending from the canyons around Cerrillos onto a high plateau (look out for antelope), you're on the home stretch to Santa Fe—but you'll pass one more dining option, the **San Marcos Café** (3877 Hwy. 14, 505/471-9298, 8 A.M.–2 P.M. Tues.–Sun., $9), which shares space with a working feed store where chickens scratch in the yard. Breakfast in the country-style dining room (a potbelly stove lurks in one corner) is especially delicious, with great cinnamon buns, homemade chicken sausage, and a variety of fresh-tasting egg dishes.

From here, Highway 14 continues on to become Cerrillos Road, the very roundabout and un-scenic way into Santa Fe; the more direct route is via I-25 to Old Santa Fe Trail. Keep an eye out for the highway on-ramp—signs point to Las Vegas.

## JEMEZ MOUNTAIN TRAIL

Beginning just northwest of Albuquerque, the Jemez (HAY-mez) Mountain Trail is an exceptionally beautiful drive, as it passes through Jemez Indian Reservation, the Santa Fe National Forest, and the Valles Caldera National Preserve. It's the most roundabout way of getting to Santa Fe—you actually wind up near Los Alamos and must backtrack a bit south to reach town—but nature lovers will want to set aside a full day for the trip, which is especially beautiful in the fall, when the aspen leaves turn vivid yellow against the rich red stones. Unlike the Turquoise Trail, it's not based on any particular historical route, but rather on the sheer beauty of the scenery. The drive begins on U.S. 550, which goes northwest out of the satellite town of Bernalillo, just west of I-25. At the village of San Ysidro, bear right onto Highway 4, which forms the major part of the route north.

## Jemez Pueblo

This community of some 3,000 tribal members settled in the area in the late 13th century, and Highway 4 runs through the middle of the 89,000 acres it still maintains; before the Spanish arrived, the Hemish people (which the Spanish spelled Jemez) had established more than 10 large villages in the area. One of the few pueblos in the area that has not opened a casino, it's quite conservative and closed to outsiders except for ceremonial dances; because Jemez absorbed members of Pecos Pueblo in 1838, it celebrates two feast days, San Diego's (November 12) and San Persingula's (August 2). It's also the only remaining pueblo where residents speak the Towa language, the rarest of the related New Mexico languages (Tewa and Tiwa are the other two). The pueblo operates the **Walatowa Visitors Center** (505/834-7235, www.jemezpueblo.org, 8 A.M.–5 P.M. daily Apr.–Dec., 10 A.M.–4 P.M. Jan.–Mar.), about five miles north of San Ysidro. The center is easy to miss because you'll be gawking off the east side of the road at the lurid red sandstone cliffs at the mouth of the **San Diego Canyon**; vendors selling traditional Indian frybread are another tasty distraction. The visitors center has exhibits about the local geology and the people of Jemez and doubles as a ranger station, dispensing maps and advice on outdoor recreation farther up the road, such as hiking trails, campgrounds, fishing access points, and the various hot springs that well up out of crevices all through the Jemez Mountains.

## Jemez State Monument

Just before you reach the town of Jemez Springs, you pass this set of ruins (Hwy. 4, 505/829-3530, 8:30 A.M.– 5 P.M. Wed.–Mon., $3), where the ancestors of the present Jemez people settled more than 700 years ago and lived until the Pueblo Revolt of 1680. More striking than the old pueblo, which was named Giusewa, is the crumbling Franciscan mission

that rises up in the middle of it. The convent and church of San José de los Jémez were built around 1620, using forced labor from the pueblo; the result was remarkably lavish, but the friars had abandoned their work by 1640, probably because they'd thoroughly antagonized their would-be parishioners. Today the remnants of the two different cultures have nearly dissolved back into the earth from which they were both built, but the church's unique octagonal bell tower has been reconstructed to good effect. Pay $5 admission, and you can also visit Coronado State Monument, on the north edge of Albuquerque, on the same day.

## Jemez Springs

This charming small resort town—really just a handful of little clapboard buildings tucked in the narrow valley along the road—is the most convenient place to indulge in some of the area's springs, which are a stew of minerals and trace elements like lithium that have inspired tales of miraculous healing over the decades since people began visiting in the 1870s. **Giggling Springs** (Hwy. 4, 505/829-9175, www.gigglingsprings.com, 11 A.M.–sunset Tues.–Sun., $15 per hour or $35 for day use), built in the 1880s, has a luxe-meets-rough feel, with a relatively small spring-fed pool enclosed in an attractively landscaped flagstone area right near the Jemez River. The **Jemez Springs Bath House** (Hwy. 4, 505/829-3303, www.jemezspringsbathhouse.com, 9 A.M.–9 P.M. daily May–Oct., $15 per hour) is operated by the village; here, the springs have been diverted into eight individual private soaking tubs, and massages and other spa treatments are available as well. (Hours are more limited between November and April, especially early in the week; call ahead to reserve a tub in any case.) If you want to stop for a bite to eat, the **Laughing Lizard Inn & Café** (Hwy. 4, 505/829-3108, www.thelaughinglizard.com, 11 A.M.–8 P.M. Tues.–Sat. and 11 A.M.–6 P.M. Sun. June–Nov., $8) serves veggie-friendly fare such as spinach burritos and crisp-crust pizzas on its patio or inside its cozy adobe walls; it also rents four tidy guest cabins ($64). Like the bath house, it scales back in the winter and only opens Thursday–Sunday. If all that seems too healthy and modern, head to **Los Ojos Restaurant & Saloon** (Hwy. 4, 505/829-3547, 11 A.M.–8:30 P.M. Sun.–Thurs., 11 A.M.–9:30 P.M. Sat., $8), where horseshoes double as window grills and the atmosphere hasn't changed in decades; hamburgers are meaty, just the way they should be.

Not quite one mile north of Jemez Springs, you pass the bizarre rocks of **Soda Dam** off the right side of the road. The pale, bulbous mineral accretions that have developed around this spring resemble nothing so much as the top of a root-beer float, with a waterfall crashing through the middle. You can't really dip in the water here, but it's a good photo op.

## Hot Springs

Outside of the town of Jemez Springs, you pass several other opportunities to take a hot bath. Five miles north of town, where the red rocks of the canyon have given way to steely-gray stone and Battleship Rock looms above the road, is the trail to **McCauley Springs;** these re-quire a two-mile hike along East Fork Trail (the parking area for the trailhead is just past Battleship Rock Picnic Area), but are an excellent motivator for a not-too-strenuous climb. Follow the trail until it meets a small stream flowing down from your left (north), then walk up the creek about a quarter mile to the spring, which has been diverted so it flows into a series of pools of ever-cooler temperatures (only 85°F at most points). Because the trail runs along the streambed, though, it's usually impassable in the high-flow winter and spring.

The most accessible pools are **Spence Springs,** about half a mile north of Battleship Rock. A sign marks a parking area on the east side of the road, and the trail to the springs starts immediately south of the dirt pullout. A short hike (0.4 mile) leads down to the river then up the steep hillside to two sets of 100°F pools. The place is well known, and although there are signs insisting on clothing, don't be surprised if you encounter some people bathing nude.

**San Antonio Springs** require the most effort to reach, but again are worth the trek, which is five miles up Forest Road 376 (closed

Soda Dam, the product of mineral deposits from hot springs

to motor vehicles). To reach the road first turn off Highway 4 at La Cueva Lodge, continuing on Highway 126 for about 3.5 miles and parking at the gate blocking the forest road. From there, it's a straight shot until a smaller road near a cabin leads downhill to the right; cross the creek and head straight uphill, about a quarter mile, to the pools, which enjoy great views of the valley.

## Hiking

Several trails run through the Jemez, but the best one for a day hike is the **East Fork Trail** (no. 137), which runs from Battleship Rock Picnic Area to Las Conchas. At 10 miles one-way, the whole route is a bit ambitious for a full day, so it's preferable to start the trail where it crosses Highway 4, about 3 miles after the highway makes its hairpin turn southeast, when you descend a bit and enter a small valley. From this point, the eastern half of the trail, about 4.5 miles one-way, is the most scenic, following a stream up through a pine forest, where wild berries grow in the summer; or you can head west 1 mile to Jemez Falls, where water cascades through a narrow canyon.

## ◖ Valles Caldera National Preserve

Spreading out for 89,000 acres to the north of Highway 4, this protected parkland (www.vallescaldera.gov) is a series of vast green valleys, rimmed by the edges of a volcano that collapsed into a huge bowl millennia ago. At the center is rounded Redondo Peak (11,254 feet). The park was previously a private ranch, which the U.S. government purchased in 2000, then created a unique experimental structure to manage the new preserve: A nine-member board of trustees is charged with designing a plan that will eventually make the area self-sustaining, independent of government funds. To this end, use fees are high (starting at $10 per person), and you must make reservations at least 24 hours ahead of time online, as there are restrictions on how many people may enter the park each day. The reward is a hike through

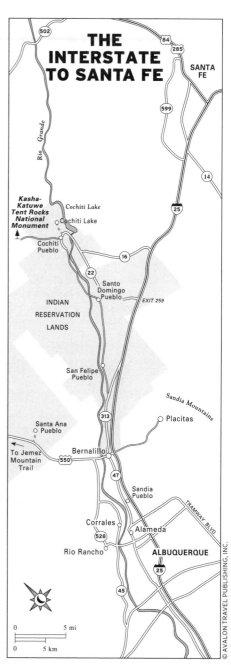

land that feels utterly untouched, where you will see herds of elk grazing and eagles winging across the huge dome of the sky. Hiking is best June–September, but the park is open in winter months for cross-country skiing, and there are limited elk-hunting and fishing seasons. In addition to exploring on your own, a full roster of guided activities is available: group day hikes, full-moon snowshoeing and sleigh rides, overnight winter yurt camping or birding and photography excursions, tracking classes, horseback riding, and more.

If you haven't planned ahead, you can still use the **Coyote Call Trail,** a three-mile loop off the south side of Highway 4, and the **Valle Grande Trail** (two miles round-trip), off the north, without prior reservations.

Past Valles Caldera, Highway 4 goes into Bandelier National Monument (covered in detail under *Outside Santa Fe* in the *Santa Fe* chapter). If you're carrying on to Santa Fe, go through White Rock and join Highway 502, which leads through Pojoaque to U.S. 285, which then goes south to the capital.

## THE INTERSTATE TO SANTA FE

The most direct route north to Santa Fe is along I-25, a drive of about 60 miles. The road, which passes through the broad valley between the Sandia and Jemez mountain ranges, is not as scenic as the more meandering routes, but it does cross wide swathes of undeveloped pueblo lands (Sandia, San Felipe, and Santo Domingo) with impressive vistas. You also have the opportunity to detour to one of the region's most striking natural phenomena, **Kasha-Katuwe Tent Rocks National Monument** (Forest Rd. 266, 8 A.M.–5 P.M. daily Nov.–Mar., 7 A.M.–7 P.M. Apr.–Oct., $5), where the wind-whittled clusters of volcanic pumice and tuff do indeed resemble enormous tepees, some up to 90 feet tall. To reach the parklands, leave I-25 at exit 259 and head west toward Cochiti Pueblo on Highway 22, then turn south in front of Cochiti Dam, which blots out the horizon around mile 15. From the parking area,

Kasha-Katuwe Tent Rocks National Monument

you have the choice of two short trails: an easy, relatively flat loop runs up to the base of the rocks, passing a small cave, while a longer option runs 1.3 miles into a narrow canyon where the rock towers loom up dramatically on either side. The latter trail is level at first, but the last stretch is steep and requires a little clambering.

On your way out from the hike, you can drive through **Cochiti Pueblo,** the northernmost Keresan-speaking pueblo, which claims its ancestors inhabited some of the ruins found at Bandelier National Monument. The traditional core of the community is still two ancient adobe kivas; you can't enter the kivas, but the people who live in the surrounding houses sell craftwork and are happy to tell you more about them. Nearby **Cochiti Lake** (reached by continuing along Highway 22 past the dam) is a popular summer destination for boaters, though it's not particularly scenic. You can, however, drive along the edge of the dam, which affords a slightly unnerving view.

# Information and Services

## TOURIST INFORMATION

The **Albuquerque Convention and Visitors Bureau** (800/284-2282, www.itsatrip.org) offers the most detailed information on the city, maintaining a desk at the airport, an office in the convention center (open only during meetings), and its main office in the Galeria mall (20 First Plaza NW, Suite 601, 9 A.M.–5 P.M. Mon.–Fri.) at the corner of Copper Avenue and 3rd Street downtown. Given the slight inconvenience of the main office, you're better off trawling the website for details and ordering an info packet if you like.

### Books and Maps

Albuquerque's largest independent bookstore is **Page One** (11018 Montgomery Blvd. NE, 505/294-2026, 9 A.M.–10 P.M. Mon.–Sat., 9 A.M.–8 P.M. Sun.), which has given the megachains a run for their money since 1981. More centrally located, the **University of New Mexico bookstore** (2301 Central Ave. NE, 505/277-5451, 8 A.M.–6 P.M. Mon.–Fri., 10 A.M.–5 P.M. Sat.) maintains a good stock of travel titles and maps, along with state history tomes and the like. On the west side, **Bookworks** (4022 Rio Grande Blvd. NW, 505/344-8139, 8 A.M.–9 P.M. Mon.–Sat., 8 A.M.–7:30 P.M. Sun.) is a great resource, with a large stock of New Mexico–related work as well as plenty of other titles, all recommended with the personal care of the staff.

### Local Media

Albuquerque supports two daily newspapers, the morning *Journal* and the afternoon *Tribune;* both publish cultural-events listings in their Friday entertainment supplement. On Wednesdays, pick up the new issue of the free weekly *Alibi* (www.alibi.com), which will give you a hipper, more critical outlook on city goings-on, from art openings to city council debates. *Crosswinds* (www.crosswindsweekly.com) is another free weekly, with a more political bent, and *abqARTS* (www.abqarts.com) is a

monthly dedicated to fine and performing arts, including nightlife—every issue contains a handy map of all the venues.

### Radio

KUNM (89.9 FM) is the university's radio station, delivering eclectic music, news from NPR and PRI, and local-interest call-in shows such as "Native America Calling." KANW (89.1 FM) is a project of Albuquerque Public Schools, with an emphasis on New Mexican music of all stripes, but particularly mariachi and other traditional forms; it also carries a few of the most popular NPR programs.

## SERVICES

### Banks

Banks are plentiful, and grocery stores and pharmacies increasingly have ATMs inside. Downtown, look for **New Mexico Bank & Trust** (320 Gold Ave. SW, 505/830-8100, 9 A.M.–4 P.M. Mon.–Fri.). In Nob Hill, look for **Wells Fargo** on Central at Dartmouth (3022 Central Ave. SE, 505/265-0365, 9 A.M.–4 P.M. Mon.–Thurs., 9 A.M.–6 P.M. Fri., 9 A.M.–1 P.M. Sat.). Both have 24-hour ATMs.

### Post Offices

Most visitors will find the **Old Town Plaza Station** the most convenient (303 Romero St. NW, 505/242-5927, 10 A.M.–6 P.M. Mon.–Fri., 9 A.M.–5 P.M. Sat.). The **Downtown Station** (201 5th St. SW, 505/346-1256, 9 A.M.–5 P.M. Mon.–Fri.) and an office near UNM (115 Cornell Dr. SE, 505/346-0923, 8:30 A.M.–5:30 P.M. Mon.–Fri.) are also handy.

### Internet

The main branch of the **Albuquerque Public Library** (501 Copper Ave. NW, 505/768-5141, 10 A.M.–6 P.M. Mon. and Thurs.–Sat., 10 A.M.–7 P.M. Tues. and Wed.) offers Internet access with the one-time purchase of a $3 card that's good for three months for out-of-towners; wireless access is completely free. **Central Connection** (215 Central Ave. NW, 505/243-1190, 10 a.m.–10 p.m. Mon.–Thurs., 10 a.m.–11 p.m. Fri. and Sat.) has one computer with free Internet access, along with coffee and Italian sandwiches. City-maintained WiFi hotspots are listed at www.cabq.gov/wifi; quite a few businesses around town also provide the service.

## Laundry

**Mountain Road Laundromat** (1134 Mountain Rd. NW, 505/247-0164, 8 A.M.–8:30 P.M. daily) is midway between Old Town and downtown. **Allstar Cleaners** (800 Central Ave. SE, Suite D, 505/242-8888, 7 A.M.–6 P.M. Mon.–Fri., 10 A.M.–1 P.M. Sat.) offers same-day laundry and dry cleaning.

# Getting There and Around

## BY AIRPLANE

**Albuquerque International Sunport** (ABQ) is a pleasant enough single-terminal airport with four runways. It's on the south side of the city, just east of I-25, about four miles from downtown. The Sunport is served by all of the major U.S. airlines; one commuter line offers connecting service to Taos (TSM). As a perk, there's free wireless Internet access throughout the complex and a nice collection of art on the walls; look up while descending to the bag claim to see the original carved wood vigas from the 1965 structure. Also near baggage claim, you'll find a desk maintained by the convention and visitors bureau, if you need to pick up any extra maps.

## BY CAR

All of the major car-rental companies have offices in a single convenient complex adjacent to the airport, and shuttle buses run frequently to it from the main terminal. **Hertz** and **Enterprise** offer service at the Amtrak depot, and Hertz also has several other locations around town—less expensive, because you bypass the airport service fee, but less convenient too.

## BY BUS AND SHUTTLE

**SunTran** (www.cabq.gov/transit; 505/243-7433) public buses serve the greater Albuquerque metro area. It's possible to reach all of the major sights along Central Avenue by bus, but you can't get to the Sandia Peak Tramway or anywhere in the east mountains. Route 50 runs from the airport to the main bus hub, the Alvarado Transportation Center at Central and 2nd Street downtown; buses depart the airport weekdays every half hour 7:30 A.M.–8:30 P.M., but service is much more limited on the weekends: There's none on Sunday, and it's every hour and 10 minutes on Saturday, 9:45 A.M.–7:05 P.M. Tourists also benefit from the **Downtown-Old Town trolley,** an easily identifiable faux-old-fashioned tram that runs every half hour between the plaza opposite San Felipe de Neri Church and the Alvarado Transportation Center, passing the Museum of Natural History on the way. For faster service along Central, hop on one of the double-length **Rapid Ride** buses, which speed between the most popular stops from Unser Boulevard on the west side up to Wyoming in the heights; service runs until 3 A.M. on summer weekends. The fare for all buses, regardless of trip length, is $1; a **three-day pass** is a bargain at $4 from the ABQ RIDE office downtown (100 1st St. SW).

**TNM&O** (806/763-5389, www.tnmo.com) typically runs buses three times daily to Santa Fe and Taos. Schedules can vary, but one departure is typically in the early morning, another around noon, and the last around midnight. Coming from Taos, TNM&O's service leaves once a day in the early evening; the trip takes a little less than three hours.

Cheaper *and* nicer are the bus services that cater to Mexicans traveling across the

ALBUQUERQUE

Southwest and into Mexico, though they offer service only to Santa Fe, not Taos; **El Paso-Los Angeles Limousine Express** (1611 Central Ave. SW; 505/247-8036) is the biggest operator.

## BY TRAIN

**Amtrak** (800/872-7245, www.amtrak.com) runs the Southwest Chief through Albu-querque, arriving daily at 3:55 P.M. from Chicago and at 12:16 P.M. from Los Angeles. The depot, partially integrated into the larger bus travel center, is downtown on 2nd Street, just south of Central Avenue. A few hotels are within walking distance, if you do not have much luggage; otherwise, you can easily hire a taxi or pick up a rental car from a couple of companies.

# BACKGROUND

## The Land

Sharp peaks, windswept cliffs, deep gorges—everything about northern New Mexico's landscape is dramatic and severe. The light glints off surfaces at surprising angles, and the scenery can change at any bend in the road. The altitude ranges from around 6,500 feet in Albuquerque to more than 13,000 (at Wheeler Peak, the state's highest, north of Taos)—so if you're not gasping for breath from the scenery alone, you almost certainly will be from the thin air.

### GEOGRAPHY AND GEOLOGY

Much of northern New Mexico's landscape is the product of volcanic activity, beginning hundreds of millions of years back and ceasing (at least temporarily) only about 3,000 years ago. The region's main mountain ranges are relatively young, pushed up in the Eocene era between 55 million and 34 million years ago, when shock waves from the collision of the North American plate and the Farallon plate caused the continent to heave. Just a few million years later, the **Rio Grande Rift**—one of the biggest rift valleys in the world—formed, as eras' and eras' worth of accumulated rock was pulled apart by shifting faults, leaving the perfect path for the river when it began to flow about 3 million years ago. The water carved deep canyons, perfect slices of geologic time,

where you can see layers of limestone, sandstone, clay, and lava stacked up. The best example is the 800-foot-deep Rio Grande Gorge, cut through the lava plateau that stretches west from Taos. Just 1.2 million years back, a volcano's violent eruption and subsequent collapse created the huge **Valles Caldera,** and the jagged edges of the crater have barely softened in the intervening time. A very tangible benefit of the state's volcanic activity is the numerous hot springs, especially in the very young Jemez Mountains (15 million years old).

Below all this, though, is evidence of a more stable time. For some 4 billion years, the land was completely underwater, then spent hundreds of millions of years supporting a range of prehistoric sea life—hence the marine fossils found at the top of the Sandia Mountains, 10,000 feet above the current sea level. Dinosaurs, too, flourished for a time—in particular, one of the first, *Coelophysis,* a nimble meat-eater, lived during the Triassic area around Abiquiu. In 1947, paleontologists found the largest collection of *Coelophysis* skeletons in the world, about a hundred, all of them seemingly killed at once, perhaps by a flash flood. Another product of the dinosaur age (specifically, the Jurassic) was the lurid red, pink, and orange sandstone. It began as a vast desert, then petrified into the very symbol of the American Southwest, and is visible around Abiquiu and Jemez Pueblo.

## CLIMATE

Much more than simple latitude, the relative altitude determines the climate in northern New Mexico, where river-bottom central Albuquerque can be crisp and cloudless while Sandia Peak, 20 miles away and almost 5,000 feet up, is socked in by a blinding snowstorm. Nowhere, though, is it a particularly gentle or mild climate—expect sudden changes in weather and extremes of heat and cold.

At the lower elevations, winter is cold—days usually between 40°F and 55°F—but rarely cloudy, with a few snowstorms that never add up to quite as much moisture as people hope for. Come spring, which starts in late April or May, the number of wildflowers that dot the hills is a direct reflection of the previous win-

winter on Sandia Peak

© ZORA O'NEILL

ter's precipitation. Little rain falls in May and June, typically the hottest months of the year, with temperatures climbing into the 90s.

But by early July, the "monsoon" season (as locals call it) brings heavy, refreshing downpours and thunderstorms every afternoon for a couple of months. It's remarkable—if a bit dismaying—to see how quickly all the water vanishes after each torrential rain. (If you're out hiking in this season, steer clear of narrow canyons and arroyos during and after rains, as they can fill with powerful, deadly flash floods in a matter of minutes.) September, October, and November are again dry, with the temperature dipping lower each month.

The higher the elevation, the later the spring: At 8,500 feet, snow could still be on the ground in May. Summer nights are rarely warm, and winter chill sets in sooner too, with fresh snow often falling in late October or November, although it usually takes well into December for a good base layer to build up at the ski areas.

## ENVIRONMENTAL ISSUES

New Mexico's unforgiving climate and geography have made it a perpetual challenge for human inhabitants. For thousands of years, New Mexicans have been facing the same dilemma: never enough water. In prehistoric times, farming in the river valley was relatively easy, if subject to erratic flooding, but at higher elevations, mountain streams had to be channeled into irrigation ditches. This system was perfected by the Spanish settlers, who called their ditches acequias, a word they'd learned from the Arabs *(al-saqiya),* who used the system to cultivate the Iberian Peninsula.

But now, as an ever-growing population demands more amenities, the traditional Spanish ways of managing water have given way to more complex legal wranglings. The Pa'ako subdivision east of Albuquerque, for instance, had its boundaries gerrymandered to get at the water supply of another, noncontiguous community farther east—thank goodness its golf course is green again. There's no relief in sight: Some 49 billion gallons of water are pumped out of the middle Rio Grande aquifer every year, and

Modern, paved acequias (pictured) are rare; traditional mud ditches are more common.

only a portion of that is replenished through mountain runoff. Albuquerque is considering using filtered river water, but some areas are already on chronic alert. Santa Fe, for instance, already has the lowest per-capita water use in the country, and doesn't have any more resources to tap. "Smart growth" gets lip service in city council meetings, although construction continues apace on Albuquerque's arid West Mesa. Neo-homesteaders on the fringes are installing cisterns to catch rain and systems to reuse gray water, but these features are still far from standard.

Another result of northern New Mexico's dry climate is that years of relative drought have made tinderboxes of the forests. In 2000, the National Forest Service started a "controlled burn" (a hotly debated strategy for thinning invasive undergrowth in choked woodlands) that got very out of control and nearly destroyed the town of Los Alamos, along with 45,000 acres of trees. It was the largest wildfire ever in New Mexico, and the smoke and flames could be seen in Albuquerque. The mountain behind Los Alamos is now bald and brown, spiked with burnt tree trunks. Pecos Wilderness Area, too, suffered from fire in 2000 and is still recovering. Fortunately, the winter of 2004–2005 was a very wet one, but the issues surrounding forest management will persist.

Visitors to New Mexico can help the picture by complying with local environmental policies—complying with campfire bans in the wilderness, for instance, and keeping showers short. Golfers may want to consider curtailing their play here. New courses are springing up everywhere, especially on American Indian reservations as part of casino resort complexes, and most are intense draws on the water table, with little thought to sustainability (one exception is Santa Fe's municipal course, which was planned with water restrictions in mind).

General environmental protection policies apply as well. Whether you're out for a day hike or a week-long backpacking trek, maintain the ethic of **"leave no trace."** This concept should first guide your trip in the planning stages, when you should equip yourself with good maps and GPS tools or a compass, to avoid relying on rock cairns or blazes, as well as repackage food and other items to minimize the waste you'll have to pack out. Also try to keep your group size under six people, and don't take pets with you.

On the trail, resist the urge to cut across switchbacks, and slog through the center of the trail, even if it's been widened by others trying to avoid mud. Be quiet and courteous, to avoid disturbing wildlife and other hikers. Leave what you find, whether plants, rocks, or potsherds or other relics of the past.

Camp only where others have, in durable areas, at least 200 feet from water sources; dig cat holes 200 feet away, too. Pack out your toilet paper and other personal waste, and scatter dishwater and toothpaste. Safeguard food in "bear bags" hung at least 15 feet off the ground. Campfires are typically banned in New Mexico—please honor this policy, and keep a close eye on camp stoves. Pack out all cigarette butts.

While most leave-no-trace ethics apply to backpackers, day hikers should also maintain a strict policy regarding litter. Tossing an orange peel, apple core, or other biodegradable item along the trail may not cause an environmental disaster, but it reminds other hikers that humans have been there and intrudes on the natural solitude of New Mexico's wilderness.

# Flora and Fauna

Just as humans have managed to eke a life out of northern New Mexico, so have plants and animals—and a rather large variety of them, considering the circumstances. In fact, New Mexico as a whole supports the fourth most diverse array of wildlife in the United States.

## FLORA

Although much of the plant growth in New Mexico is nominally evergreen, the overall aspect of the landscape can skew toward brown, until you get up into the lush alpine elevations.

### Vegetation Zones

New Mexico's **Upper Sonoran** zone, covering the areas between 4,500 and 7,000 feet, is the largest vegetation zone in the state and includes most of Albuquerque and Santa Fe, where the Sandia and Sangre de Cristo foothills are covered with juniper and piñon trees. The **Transition** zone, from 7,000 feet to 8,500 feet, sees a few more stately trees, such as ponderosa pine, and a lot of the state's colorful wildflowers: orange Indian paintbrush, bright red penstemon, purple lupine. Above 8,500 feet, the **Mixed Conifer** zone harbors just that sort of tree—along with clusters of aspens. The **Subalpine** zone, starting at 9,500 feet, is home to Engelmann spruce and bristlecone pine, while 11,500 feet marks the tree line in most places and the beginning of the **Alpine** zone, where almost no greenery survives.

© ZORA O'NEILL

a centuries-old cottonwood tree

## Trees and Grasses

Trees are the clearest marker of elevation. In very low areas—such as on Albuquerque's West Mesa—you'll see very few trees, only some of the more desertlike plants that are more prevalent in the southern part of the state, but not in the northern: assorted cactuses, such as the common **cane cholla;** the spiky **yucca** plant, which produces towering stalks of blooms in May; and the humble **tumbleweed.** Along the river, thirsty **cottonwoods** provide dense shade; many of the biggest trees, with their gnarled, branching trunks, have been growing for centuries. In the spring, their cotton fills the air—hell for the allergic, but source of a beautiful fragrance—and in the fall, their leaves turn pure yellow. Willow and olive are also common.

In the foothills, **piñon** (also spelled pinyon), the official state tree, is everywhere, as a slow-growing, drought-resistant scrub tree tailor-evolved for the New Mexican landscape. Its wood produces the distinctive scent of a New Mexico winter night, and its pinecones yield tasty nuts. Alongside piñon is **shaggy-bark**

**juniper,** identifiable by its loose strips of bark, its soft, fan-like needle clusters, and branches that look twisted by the wind; in season, it's studded with purple-gray berries—another treat for foraging humans and animals alike. On the ground in the foothills, also look for clumps of sagebrush and bear grass, which blooms in huge creamy tufts at the ends of stalks up to six feet tall.

Up in the mountains, the trees are a bit taller—here you'll find the distinctive, towering **ponderosa** pine, the bark of which smells distinctly of vanilla. Look for tall trees with thick, almost crusty chunks of reddish-black bark. At slightly higher elevations, dense stands of **aspen** trees provide a rare spot of fall color in the evergreen forests—the combination of their golden leaves and white bark creates a particularly magical glow, especially in the mountains near Santa Fe. The highest mountain areas are home to a number of dense-needled hardy pines, such as blue-green **Engelmann spruce, corkbark fir, bristlecone pines,** and **subalpine fir,** with its sleek, rounded pinecones. Hike your way up to stands of these, which are all tall but with sparse branches, and you'll know you're close to the peak.

## FAUNA

As with plants, what you see depends on where you are on the mountain slopes. And you'll have to look very carefully, because a lot of the animals that have survived this long in dry, harsh New Mexico are the sort that have blended in with their surroundings—in short, there are a lot of brown animals.

### Mammals

In the open, low-elevation areas on Albuquerque's fringes (and sometimes in the occasional vacant urban lot), look for **prairie dogs,** which live in huge communities of underground warrens. If you're camping, the first little creatures you'll meet are squirrels and chipmunks—at higher elevations, look out for **Aber's squirrel,** with its tufted ears and particularly fluffy tail. Long-haunched **coyotes** roam the lower elevations and are not shy about nosing around backyards; they make a barking yelp at night. On the plains just south of Santa Fe, you may see **pronghorn antelope** springing through the grasses, while hefty **mule deer** flourish in mountain forests, such as the Pecos Wilderness area. Herds of even larger **elk** live in the high valleys—Rocky Mountain elk are common, thanks to an aggressive reintroduction effort in the early 20th century to make up for overhunting. A group of the largest variety, Roosevelt elk, whose fanlike antlers are the stuff of dreams for trophy hunters, roams in Valles Caldera. **Bighorn sheep** live in the mountains around Taos.

**Black bears** crash around the forests, though their name is misleading—at any given time, they can also be brown, cinnamon-red, or even nearly blond. Smokey Bear, the mascot of the National Forest Service, was from New Mexico, a cub rescued from a forest fire in Capitan. Drought has on many occasions driven the omnivorous beasts into suburban trash cans to forage, with tragic results; if you're camping, take thorough measures to keep your food away from your camp and out of reach of animals.

And then there's the elusive **jackalope,** a jackrabbit hare sporting elaborate antlers. Alas, it seems now to appear only on postcards, although you may occasionally see a taxidermied head in a curio shop.

## Birds

New Mexico's state bird is the **roadrunner,** which can grow to be up to two feet long; it lives in the lower desertlike elevations (Coronado State Monument, north of Albuquerque, is home to a few), nesting in the ground and feeding on insects and even rattlesnakes. Blue-and-black **Steller's jays** and raucous all-blue **piñon jays** are some of the most common birds in the foothills and farther up in the mountains, where you can also see bluebirds, black-masked mountain chickadees, and Clark's nutcrackers, which hoard great stashes of piñon nuts for winter. Also look around for varieties of **woodpeckers,** including the

a roadrunner in a rare moment of repose

three-toed variety, which lives at higher elevations. On the very highest peaks are **white-tailed ptarmigans,** which blend in with their snowy environment. But you can't miss the bright-yellow-and-red **Western tanager,** a shot of tropical-looking delight in the Transition zone forests.

In the late summer, keep an eye out for tiny, red-throated **Rufous hummingbirds** on their way to Mexico for the winter. The Sandia Mountains are part of the migratory corridor for **red-tailed hawks,** eagles, and other raptors—they're especially numerous in springtime.

With more than 450 species spotted in New Mexico, this list is only scraping the surface. If you're a dedicated birder, first contact the **Randall Davey Audubon Center** (505/983-4609, nm.audubon.org) in Santa Fe, which leads bird walks, or the **Rio Grande Nature Center** in Albuquerque. **Bosque del Apache National Wildlife Refuge,** south of Albuquerque, is a must-visit, especially in the winter when thousands of sandhill cranes—and even the occasional rare **whooping crane**—rest in the wetlands.

## ATTACK OF THE BARK BEETLES

Piñon is the most prevalent tree in New Mexico's foothills – or it *was*, until the bark-beetle blight of 2002-2003, when the invasive bugs managed to kill an estimated 43 million trees over about 800,000 acres, leaving whole swaths of hillsides an eerie shade of gray. The normally hardy trees were felled not so much by the beetles, which are always present on the trees, as by drought – ordinarily, the piñon's sticky sap protects it by smothering attacking insects, but years of abnormally dry weather meant they were no longer producing as much sap. The beetles were able to bore under the bark and lay eggs; the larvae feasted on the soft inner bark, while the adults spread a blue fungus that also helped kill off the tree.

New Mexicans had to fight the invaders using tactics that seemed straight out of a horror movie: Living trees had to be felled at the first sign of infestation, then chopped into tiny pieces and buried. The other option was to seal the bug-filled wood in heavy plastic and leave it in the sun, to effectively smother and cook the beetles. Fortunately, wet weather in 2004 helped stop the spread of the beetles, so the invasion is abating – but New Mexicans will likely still fear for their trees for years to come.

## Fish

**Trout** are the major endemic fish, found in the cold waters of the Rio Grande as well as the Chama River, the Pecos River, and the Rio Chiquito and Rio Pueblo around Taos. The cutthroat is particularly beloved in New Mexico—the only variety of trout that was originally found on the eastern side of the Continental Divide, whereas the more aggressive rainbow and brown trout are interlopers. The Rio Grande cutthroat, the official state fish, is now quite uncommon. Another local fish in jeopardy is the **Rio Grande silvery minnow,** listed as endangered since 2004. The last of the Rio Grande's five native fish, it's in such a dire state that biologists are scooping them out of the water individually during bad dry spells and taking them to the Albuquerque aquarium for safekeeping. The hope is that they will breed and be able to be returned to their original habitat during wetter conditions.

## Reptiles

One can't step foot in the desert without thinking of **rattlesnakes,** and New Mexico has plenty of them, usually hidden away under rocks and brush, but very occasionally sunning themselves in full view, much to hikers' alarm. The New Mexico ridgenose variety is an endangered species, while the predominant species in the Rio Grande Valley, the **Western diamondback,** can grow to be seven feet long. Although its venom is relatively weak, it has an impressive striking distance of almost three feet. Around Taos and Santa Fe, the main species is the prairie rattlesnake, which is only about four feet long at most.

More benign cold-blooded critters include all manner of **lizards,** including the **short-horned lizard** (a.k.a. horny toad), a miniature dinosaur, in effect, about as big as your palm—you'll see them primarily in the scrubby foothills.

## Insects and Arachnids

Because it's so dry, New Mexico isn't too infested with bugs. The ones that are there, however, can be a bit off-putting to a visitor, particularly if you chance upon the springtime **tarantula migration,** usually in May around Albuquerque—it's not a true seasonal relocation, just all of the male tarantulas coming out of their dens to go on the prowl for mates. The fist-size spiders move in huge waves, hundreds at a time, and occasionally roads are closed to let them pass. Though they're big and hairy, they're not poisonous.

# History

The historical and cultural continuity in New Mexico is remarkable. Although the state has been transformed from ice-age hunting ground to home of the atom bomb, many people claim roots that stretch back hundreds, even thousands, of years.

## ANCIENT AND ARCHAIC CIVILIZATION

New Mexico was one of the first places to harbor humans after the end of the last ice age. Archaeological findings indicate that some 12,000 years ago, people were hunting mastodons and other big game across the state. Mammoth bones, arrowheads, and the remains of campfires have been found in Folsom, in northeastern New Mexico; Clovis in the south; and the Sandia mountains east of Albuquerque. Sometime between 8000 and 5000 B.C., these bands of hunters formed a small temporary settlement just north of Albuquerque, but it was not enough to stave off the decline of that ancient culture, as climatic shifts caused the big game to die off. Nomadic hunter-gatherers, seeking out smaller animals as well as seeds and nuts, did better in the new land, and by 1000 B.C., they had established communities built around clusters of pithouses—sunken, log-covered rooms dug into the earth.

Along with this new form of shelter came an equally important advance in food: Mexican people gave corn kernels (maize) and lessons in agriculture to their neighbors, the **Mogollon,** who occupied southern New Mexico and Arizona; by A.D. 400, the Mogollon had begun growing squash and beans as well, and had established concentrated communities all around the southern Rio Grande basin. This culture, dubbed the Basketmakers by archaeologists, also developed its own pottery, another skill learned from the indigenous people of Mexico. So when the Mogollon made contact with the Anasazi (the people who are the ancestors of today's Puebloans) in the northern part of the state, they had plenty to share.

## THE PUEBLOS FORM

The year 700 marks the beginning of the **Pueblo I** phase—the time when disparate groups began to form larger communities in the upland areas on either side of the northern Rio Grande. Pithouses were still in use, but aboveground buildings of clay and sticks were erected alongside them. Increasingly, the pithouses were sacred spaces, chambers in which religious ceremonies were carried out; these are now known as kivas, and are still an integral part of pueblo life. The **Pueblo II** era dates from 850 and is distinguished by the rise of Pueblo Bonito in Chaco Canyon, northwest of Santa Fe, into a full-scale city and perhaps capital of a small state. It was home to an estimated 1,500 people ruled by a religious elite. But Chaco began to crumble abruptly around 1150 (perhaps due to drought, famine, or warfare), marking the beginning of the **Pueblo III** period, when the people who were to become today's Puebloans began building their easily defended cliff dwellings—most famously in the Four Corners area, at Mesa Verde, but also farther south, on the Pajarito Plateau in what's now called Bandelier National Monument, and in Puyé, on Santa Clara Pueblo land. A drought in the late 13th century cleared out the Four Corners, marking the start of the **Pueblo IV** era and provoking the population to consolidate along the Rio Grande in clusters of sometimes more than a thousand interconnected rooms. These communities dotted the riverbank, drawing their sustenance both from the river water and from the mountains behind them.

## THE SPANISH ARRIVE

These settlements were what the Spanish explorer **Francisco Vásquez de Coronado** and his crew saw when they first ventured into the area in 1540. Their Spanish word for the villages, *pueblos,* stuck, and is still the name for both the places and the people who lived in them. Coronado wasn't all that impressed,

## THE ANASAZI AND THE CANNIBALISM DEBATE

The Anasazi – the culture that established the elaborate condo-like community of Tyuonyi and the cliff dwellings at Bandelier National Monument – have long been a mystery and a topic of debate among archaeologists because their society appears to have collapsed abruptly in the 13th century.

The popular conception of the Anasazi has long been of a peaceful, egalitarian society based on agriculture, an image further enhanced by the Pueblo Indians' push to rename the Anasazi (an old Navajo word meaning "ancient enemies") "Ancestral Puebloans." The Puebloans point out that the Anasazi are not some foreign, archaic people who mysteriously vanished, but the forebears of today's American Indians in the Southwest.

But a theory advanced by physical anthropologist Christy Turner suggests the Pueblo Indians might be better off disavowing their ancestors. In his 1999 book *Man Corn: Cannibalism and Violence in the Prehistoric American Southwest*, Turner proposed that the Anasazi culture was a violent one obsessed with ritual consumption of human flesh. His theory neatly suggests yet another stress that could have contributed to the Anasazi collapse and answers another nagging question: What about all those piles of mangled human bones and fire-blackened skulls found at Chaco Canyon, Mesa Verde, and other Anasazi sites?

Many of Turner's colleagues were highly skeptical, and Pueblo Indians were, and still are, outraged at the accusations about their ancestors – Turner and other archaeologists were banned from their excavations in Mesa Verde. In the years since Turner published *Man Corn*, however, the evidence to support his theory seems to have grown – for instance, he discovered a coprolite (preserved human feces) that tests positive for human proteins. Turner now imagines the cannibalism may have been introduced by a Mexican culture, perhaps the Toltecs, and perhaps used against the Anasazi as a means of terrorizing them into submission. This puts the ancestral Puebloans in a somewhat better light but still paints a bleak and violent picture of life in what today appear to be lush, peaceful valleys and canyons.

however, because the pueblos were made out of mud, not gold as the Spanish had been hoping—so the team turned around and headed back to Mexico City after two years and a couple of skirmishes with the natives. It took another half a century for the Spanish to muster more interest in the area—this time, in 1598, Juan de Oñate led a small group of Spanish families to settle on the banks of the Rio Grande, at a place they called San Gabriel, near San Juan Pueblo. About a decade later, the settlers moved away from their Indian neighbors, to the new villa of Santa Fe. The territory's third governor, Don Pedro de Peralta, made it the official capital of the territory of Nuevo México, which in those days stretched far into what is now Colorado and Arizona.

This time, the colonists, mostly farmers, were motivated not so much by hopes of striking it rich but simply of making a living. More-over, they were inspired by Catholic zeal, and Franciscan missionaries accompanied them to promote the faith among the Puebloans.

It was partly these missionaries and their ruthless oppression of the native religion that drove the Indians to organize the **Pueblo Revolt** of 1680. The Franciscans' "conversion" strategy involved public executions of the pueblos' medicine men, for instance. But the Spanish colonists were no help either. In their desperation to squeeze some wealth out of the hard land, they exploited the only resource they had, the slave labor of the Indians, who were either conscripted for projects or stolen from their families (though the Indians did their share of poaching from Spanish families, creating a sort of cultural exchange program).

The leader of the Pueblo Revolt was a man named **Popé** (also spelled Po'pay), from San Juan Pueblo. Using Taos Pueblo as his base, he traveled among the other communities, secretly meeting with leaders to plan a united insurrection. Historians theorize he may have used Spanish to communicate with other Puebloans who did not speak his native Tewa, and then he distributed among the conspirators lengths of knotted rope with which to count down the days to the insurrection. Although a few of the rope-bearing messengers were captured (Isleta Pueblo may never have gotten the message, which may explain its being the only pueblo not to participate) and word got out, the violence and bloodshed could not be averted. Families and missionaries were killed, crops burned, and churches toppled. Santa Fe was besieged, and its population of more than 1,000 finally evacuated in a pitiful retreat.

The Spanish stayed away for 12 years, but finally a new governor, Diego de Vargas, took it upon himself to reclaim the land the Spanish had settled. He managed to talk many pueblos into peaceful surrender, meeting resistance only in Taos and Santa Fe, where a two-day fight was required to oust the Indians from the Palace of the Governors. The Spanish strategy in the post–Pueblo Revolt era was softer, with more compromise between the Franciscans and their intended flock, and a fair amount of cultural and economic exchange. The threat of raiding Comanche, Apache, and Navajo also forced the Spanish and the Indians to cooperate. Banding together for defense, they were finally able to drive the Comanche away, culminating in a 1778 battle with the Comanche chief Cuerno Verde (Green Horn). The decisive victory is celebrated in the ritual dance called Los Comanches that's still performed in small villages by Spanish and Indian alike.

The other bonding force was trade. The Spanish maintained the **Camino Real de Tierra Adentro** (Royal Road of the Interior) from Mexico City all the way north to Santa Fe—it follows roughly the line carved by I-25 today. Caravans came through only every year or two, but the profit from furs, pottery, textiles, and other local goods was enough to keep both cultures afloat, if utterly dependent on the Spanish government.

© ZORA O'NEILL

The Cross of the Martyrs commemorates the Spaniards killed in the Pueblo Revolt.

## MEXICAN INDEPENDENCE AND THE FIRST ANGLOS

Spain carefully guarded all of its trade routes in the New World, even in a relatively unprofitable territory like New Mexico. Interlopers were not welcome—a few enterprising fur trappers, lone mountain men in search of beaver pelts, slipped in, but spy-explorer **Zebulon Pike** and his crew were captured (perhaps intentionally, so Pike could get more inside information) and detained in Santa Fe for a spell in 1807. But in 1821, Mexico declared its independence from Spain, liberating the territory of Nuevo México along with it—and one of the first acts of the new government was to open the borders to trade. Initially a trickle of curious traders came down the rough track between St. Louis and Santa Fe, but soon a flood of commerce flowed along the increasingly rutted and broad **Santa Fe Trail,** making the territory's capital city a meeting place between Mexicans and Americans swapping furs, gold, rugs, and more.

## THE MEXICAN-AMERICAN WAR AND AFTER

Pike's expedition, conducted just as Lewis and Clark were returning from their march across the Louisiana Purchase, not only gave the U.S. government new information on the locations of Spanish forts and other details, it also helped fuel the country's general expansionist fervor. By the 1840s, **"manifest destiny"** was the phrase on every American's lips, and the U.S. government was eyeing the Southwest. It annexed Texas in 1845, but New Mexico, with its small population and few resources, didn't figure heavily in the short-lived war that resulted—the Mexican governor surrendered peacefully to General Stephen Kearny when he arrived in Santa Fe in 1846. In Taos, though, the transition was not accepted so readily, as a brief but violent uprising instigated by Hispano business leaders with help from Taos Pueblo Indians resulted in the beheading of the first U.S. governor, Charles Bent.

During the **Civil War,** New Mexico was in the way of a Texan Confederate strategy to secure the Southwest, but the rebels were thwarted in 1862 at the Battle of Glorieta Pass. The territory stayed in the hands of the Union until the end of the war, and people were more concerned with the cultural skirmishes caused by the arrival in Santa Fe of Bishop Jean Baptiste Lamy, a tyrannical—or at least very out-of-touch—Frenchman who tried to impose a European vision of the Catholic church on a populace that had been far beyond centralized control for centuries.

More significant to New Mexico's development was the arrival of the **railroad** in 1880, as it was laid through Raton Pass, near Santa Fe, and very close to Albuquerque. Virtually overnight strange goods and even stranger people came pouring into one of the more remote frontier outposts of the United States. Anglo influence was suddenly everywhere, in the form of new architecture (redbrick was an Eastern affectation) and new business. Albuquerque, almost directly on the new railway tracks, boomed, while Santa Fe's fortunes slumped and Taos all but withered away (its peak had been back in the late days of the Camino Real).

But while wheeler-dealers were setting up shop in central New Mexico, some more intrepid souls were poking around in the less-connected areas farther north. These tourists were artists who valued New Mexico not for its commercial potential but for its dramatic landscapes and exotic populace who seemed untouched by American ways. From the early 20th century on, Santa Fe and Taos were cultivated as art colonies, a function they still fulfill today.

## FROM STATEHOOD TO WORLD WAR II

Based on its burgeoning economy, New Mexico became the 47th state in the union in 1912, effectively marking the end of the frontier period, a phase of violence, uncertainty, and isolation that lasted about 300 years, longer here than in any other state. In addition to the painters and writers who were flocking to the new state, another group of migrants

© ZORA O'NEILL

one of Bishop Lamy's anti-adobe churches, in the village of Pecos arrived: tuberculosis patients. Soon the state was known as a health retreat, and countless people did stints in its dry air to treat their ailing lungs. One of these people was J. Robert Oppenheimer, whose mild case of TB got him packed off to a camp near Pecos for a year after high school. He loved northern New Mexico and became familiar with some of its more hidden pockets, so when the U.S. army asked him if he had any idea where it should establish a secret base for the **Manhattan Project,** he knew just the place: a little camp high on a plateau above Santa Fe—its name was Los Alamos. This was the birthplace of the atomic bomb, a weird, close-knit community of the country's greatest scientific minds (and biggest egos), all working in utter secrecy. Only after Fat Man and Littleboy were dropped over Japan was the mysterious camp's mission revealed.

## RECENT HISTORY

With the invention of the A-bomb, New Mexico was truly ushered into the modern era—not just because it produced world-changing technology, but also because the high-paying jobs at Los Alamos and Kirtland Air Force Base in Albuquerque helped pull some of the population out of subsistence farming and into a life of car-driving and electricity-using. Even with these modern trappings, though, the character of the state remained very conservative and closed, so when the 1960s rolled around and New Mexico looked like the promised land to hippies, the culture clash was fierce. Staunch Catholic farmers even took potshots at their naked, hallucinogen-ingesting neighbors who fantasized about getting back to the land but had no clue how to do it. After a decade or so, though, only the hardiest of the commune-dwellers were left, and they'd mellowed a bit, while the locals had come to appreciate at least their enthusiasm. Even if the communes didn't last, hippie culture has proven remarkably persistent—even today, distinctly straight Hispanos can be heard saying things like, "I was tripping out on that band, man," and the state still welcomes Rainbow Gatherings, would-be Buddhists, and alternative healers.

The end of the 20th century has seen unprecedented growth in both Albuquerque and Santa Fe. As usual, Albuquerque got the practical-minded development, such as the Intel plant and the financial headquarters for Gap Inc., while Santa Fe was almost felled by its own artsiness, turned inside-out during a few years of frenzied trendiness when movie stars and other moneyed types bought up pieces of Santa Fe style for themselves. In just a matter of months in the early 1990s, rents went up tenfold and houses were selling for more than $1 million. The city has yet to work out the imbalance between its creative forces, which did save the city from utter decline, and the weird economic ones through which the richest people live in faux-adobe homes on real dirt roads, and the poorest put a fresh coat of mud on their houses every year, but at least the paving runs up to their doors.

Meanwhile, Taos has grown slowly but steadily, as have the pueblos, thanks to the legalization of gambling on their lands, but all of these communities have a touch of old New Mexico about them, where the frontier flavor and solitude can still be felt.

# Government and Economy

New Mexico doesn't look so good on paper, what with high statistics for corruption, nepotism, and poverty. But that has also inspired a good deal of activist sentiment, and politics are lively as the economy slips out of some of its old restrictive patterns.

## GOVERNMENT

New Mexico's political scene is as diverse as its population, a fractious mix of Democrats, Republicans, Greens, Libertarians, anarchists, independents, and irredeemable cranks. The last two presidential contests (2000 and 2004) were both too close to call on election day, requiring recounts to determine the razor-thin margins (Gore in 2000, Bush in 2004). Governor Bill Richardson, a Democrat who previously served as the U.S ambassador to the United Nations and Secretary of the Department of Energy, was elected in 2002 by 17 percentage points (56 percent–39 percent), the widest margin in any race since 1964. Don't be fooled by his Anglo last name: Richardson is Mexican American, born in Pasadena and raised in Mexico City. A fluent Spanish-speaker who has lived in New Mexico since 1978, he's now the only Hispanic governor in the United States, and he has said he intends to run for president in 2008.

The state political scene is an odd mix of entrenched cronyism and wild activism. On the one hand, Senator Pete Domenici (Republican), a former pitcher for the Albuquerque Dukes and a native of the city, has held his seat since 1972; on the other, former governor Gary Johnson now spends his time advocating marijuana legalization, while the Green Party is running a campaign for a living wage, which was gaining momentum in 2005 in notoriously lefty Santa Fe. Environmental activists have also made great gains in preserving some of New Mexico's best natural assets.

COURTESY NEW MEXICO DEPARTMENT OF TOURISM

New Mexico's state capitol building combines Greek revival details with the local-favorite stucco finish.

On a local level, corruption charges are rampant. When any scandal breaks (nepotistic assignment of highway repair contracts, for instance), pundits can't help but comment that the old Spanish *patrón* system, in which small-town bosses dole out benefits to their loyal supporters, seems to still be at work. "New Mexico is a third-world country" is another common quip. And direct democracy isn't even nominally practiced on the state's Indian reservations, which act as sovereign nations. Indians vote in U.S. and state elections, but most domestic issues are decided by each pueblo's tribal governor, war chief, and a few other officials who are elected by a consensus of men in the kiva.

## ECONOMY

New Mexico has always lagged at the bottom of the country's economic ratings: In 2000, 18.4 percent of the population was living below the poverty level, giving the state a bigger proportion of working poor than any other. It's also 46th out of 50 in the number of high school graduates and the number of college graduates per capita.

But at least as of 2005, the state was in an upswing. As the **manufacturing** center for all manner of things, from computer chips to mattresses to specialty running shoes, Albuquerque leads the state's economy. And the city where Microsoft was founded (then Bill Gates and Paul Allen moved back to Seattle to be close to their families) is doing better at fostering **technology** development these days, as home to a range of tech specialists catering to Sandia National Labs and an **aerospace** manufacturing park growing on the west side. On the horizon: a solar farm that would produce electricity for 300,000 homes and, if the New Mexico Space Commission has its way, development of spacecraft by private companies.

Elsewhere the state is not looking so cutting-edge, however; small-scale **farming,** particularly of apples, is still the norm in most of the Rio Grande Valley, and beef jerky is the major product of the **ranching** industry. Small **oil** and **natural gas** reserves, as well as copper ore, send a little boost from the south. And Santa Fe's **arts** sector shouldn't be overlooked—galleries post sales of $200 million every year, though

Beef jerky is a suprisingly large part of New Mexico's economy.

they're criticized for sending much of that money right back out of the state to artists who live and work elsewhere.

Even if the economic situation isn't ideal, it's nothing New Mexicans aren't used to—in fact, a large segment of the population seems content with eking out a living from almost nothing (the average annual income is only $17,261). In this respect, the state hasn't lost its frontier spirit at all.

# The People

## DEMOGRAPHY

New Mexico's 1.8 million people are typically described as a tricultural mix of Indians, Spanish, and Anglos—which really clears nothing up, because the definitions of these labels are unique to the state.

First, **Indians:** New Mexicans generally don't use the term "Native American." So you'll see "American Indian" in formal situations, but even the "American" part is a bit laughable, considering "America" wasn't so named until Christopher Columbus made his voyage west. In any case, "Indian" refers to a number of different peoples who do not share a common culture or language: Navajo on the west side of the state, Zuni, Hopi, Jicarilla Apache, and the Puebloans of the Rio Grande. (The latter term, Pueblo, is another problematic one, as it refers not to a particular tribe, but to a larger group of people who speak four distinct languages but are banded together by a common way of living.) With about 10 percent of the population claiming American Indian ancestry, traditions are still strong—though of course they've changed, as neon-dyed feathers trim kids' ceremonial headdresses, and wealth from casinos funds elaborate museums as well as new housing projects.

**Spanish** really means that: the people, primarily in northern New Mexico, whose ancestors were pure-blood Spaniards, rather than the mestizos of Mexico. For many families, it's a point of pride similar to that of Mayflower descendants. Over the years, particularly during the 20th century, a steady influx of Mexican immigrants has blurred racial distinctions a bit, but also helped preserve the local Spanish culture, in that it has reinforced the use of Spanish as a daily language and spurred pride in the culture's music and other folkways. Increasingly, the word **Hispano** is being used to label New Mexico's distinct culture with centuries-old Spanish roots, though this still doesn't accurately cover the **Basques,** who came here both during the conquest (Juan de Oñate, the first Spanish governor, was Basque) and in the early 20th century as sheepherders. And the recent discovery of families of **crypto-Jews** (Spanish Jews who nominally converted to Catholicism but who fled here to avoid further Inquisitional examination) has added another fascinating layer to the Spanish story.

**Anglo** is the most imprecise term of all, as it means anyone who's not Spanish or Indian. Originally used to talk about the white traders who came to hunt and sell furs and trade on the Santa Fe Trail, it still refers to people who can't trace their roots back to the conquistadors or farther. If you're a Vietnamese immigrant in Albuquerque, you're an Anglo. If you're a Tibetan refugee in Santa Fe, you're an Anglo. And if you're an African American farmer who settled here after the Civil War, you're an Anglo. (According to the 2000 census, about 45 percent of the population is white; Asians are only 1 percent, and African Americans make up 2 percent.) But all Anglo culture is shot through with Spanish and Indian influence, whether among the organic garlic farmers from California who rely on their acequias for water or the New Age seekers who do sweat-lodge rituals.

Even with this liberal application of "Anglo," the tricultural arrangement is a bit limiting, as it doesn't assign a place to contemporary immigrants from Mexico and other Latin American countries, and their numbers are growing steadily. It also doesn't acknowledge the strong Mexican-American **Chicano** culture that's shared across the Southwest, from Los Angeles through Texas. The U.S. census form lumps both newer arrivals and old Spanish under "Hispanic"—a category (distinct from race) that made up about 42 percent of the population in 2000.

## LANGUAGE

**English** is the predominant language, but once you get off the beaten track, you'll hear **Spanish** used more and more—about 29 percent of the population speaks it. Spanish-speakers in northern New Mexico were for centuries only the old Hispano families, speaking a variant of Castilian with a distinct vocabulary that developed in isolation. This "Quixotic" dialect changed little until the 20th century, when immigrants began to arrive from Mexico and elsewhere in Latin America—a development that changed the old-fashioned New Mexican dialect, but also helped encourage the use of Spanish all over the state. For much of the 20th century, though, English was the only permissible class-room language, although many school districts required Spanish as a foreign language. Since the 1990s, education policy has shifted to include bilingual classrooms.

Additionally, you'll occasionally hear the Pueblo Indians speaking their respective languages, of which there are four main ones. **Tiwa, Tewa,** and **Towa** are part of the Tanoan family of languages (Kiowa, spoken by Plains Indians, is the fourth member). They are all somewhat related but mutually unintelligible, roughly equivalent to, say, French, Spanish, and Italian. Tewa is the most widely spoken, used in all of the pueblos just north of Santa Fe: San Juan, San Ildefonso, Santa Clara, Pojoaque, Tesuque, and Nambé. Four pueblos speak Tiwa—Taos and Picurís share one dialect, while Isleta and Sandia, in an odd pocket near Albuquerque, speak a different dialect. Towa is now spoken only at Jemez Pueblo.

**Keresan** (spoken in Laguna, Acoma, Cochiti, Santo Domingo, San Felipe, Santa Ana, and Zia) is what linguists call an "isolate." Like Basque, it is unconnected not only to neighboring languages, but also to any other language. Additionally, each pueblo has developed its own dialect, such that immediately adjacent

## LUMINARIAS OR *FAROLITOS?*

The cultural differences between Santa Fe and Albuquerque don't apply just to the number of art galleries per square block and whether you eat posole or rice on the side with your enchiladas. Every Christmas, an ugly debate rears its head: What do you call a paper bag with a bit of sand in the bottom and a votive candle inside? These traditional holiday decorations, which line the driveways and flat adobe rooftops in both cities in the last weeks of December, are known as luminarias in Albuquerque and most towns to the south, and as *farolitos* in Santa Fe and all the villages to the north.

To complicate matters, another common holiday tradition in Santa Fe and other northern towns is to light small bonfires of piñon logs in front of houses. And Santa Feans call these little stacks of wood … luminarias. *Faro-*

*litos,* they argue, are literally "little lanterns," which certainly describe the glowing paper bags quite well – and under this logic, the use of *farolito* has spread a bit in Albuquerque, at least among people who weren't raised saying luminaria from birth.

But Albuquerqueans have Webster's on their side; the dictionary concurs that luminarias are paper-bag lanterns, and notes the tradition comes from Mexico, where the bags are often colored and pricked with holes. (Perhaps Albuquerque's relative proximity to the border – and its larger proportion of Mexican immigrants – has shaped the language over the years?) In any case, because this author's own loyalties are to Albuquerque, the argument is settled, at least in these pages: Luminaria it is.

COURTESY NEW MEXICO DEPARTMENT OF TOURISM/MARK NOHL

Christmas reenactments in Chimayó of the Holy Family's search for shelter

communities can understand each other, but those farthest apart cannot.

One interesting phenomenon of the Pueblo languages is that their speakers have managed to keep them relatively pure. Despite centuries of Spanish and English influence, Tewa vocabulary is still less than five percent loan words—probably due in part to the way speakers have been forced to compartmentalize it, using it for conversation at home and switching to English or Spanish for business and trade. For centuries, the Franciscan priests, then the U.S. government attempted to stamp out Native American languages—following the Civil War, Puebloan children were moved forcibly to boarding schools, where they were permitted to speak only English, a policy that continued for decades.

Only in 1990, with the passage of the **Native American Languages Act,** were American Indian languages officially permitted in government-funded schools—indeed, they are now recognized as a unique element of this country's culture, and encouraged. This has created an interesting practice in Taos, where the Tiwa language is a ritual secret that outsiders are not permitted to learn. But one Taos school has Tiwa classes for younger students, open only to tribe members and taught only by approved teachers; as an added measure against the language being recorded, the classroom has no chalkboard. Less formal instruction within the pueblos has also helped the Pueblo languages enjoy a renaissance lately.

## RELIGION

Four hundred years after the arrival of the Franciscan missionaries, New Mexico is still a heavily **Catholic** state (KFC offers a Friday-night fish fry during Lent), but the relative isolation of the territory produced some variants that would no doubt disturb the Vatican. In both Indian and Spanish churches, the pageantry of medieval Christianity is preserved. Las Posadas, the reenactment of Mary and Joseph's search for lodging in Bethlehem, is a festive, torchlit tradition every December, and during the annual Holy Week pilgrimage to Chimayó, devoted groups stage the stations of the cross,

# THE SECRET BROTHERHOOD: NEW MEXICO'S PENITENTES

In almost every small Hispanic village in northern New Mexico is a modest one-story building called a *morada* – the meeting place of Los Hermanos Penitentes (The Penitent Brothers), a lay Catholic fraternity with deep roots in medieval Spain and a long and varied history that has often put it at odds with the church itself.

The Penitentes developed in New Mexico in the early colonial era and were at the height of their influence during the so-called Secular Period (1790-1850), when the Franciscans had been pushed out by church leaders in Mexico but no new priests were sent to the territory. The brotherhood, likely modeled after penitential fraternities in the Old World, cared for the ill and conducted funerals as well as settled petty disputes and even elections. They generally maintained the spiritual and political welfare of their villages when there were no priests or central government to do so.

What the Penitentes are best known for, however, is their intense religious ritual, which includes self-flagellation, blood-letting, and mock crucifixion – activities that apparently took place in public processions for centuries but were driven underground following official church condemnation in the late 19th century. The secrecy, along with sensationalist journalism by visitors from the East Coast, fueled gruesome rumor about the brotherhood. Penitentes used real nails in their crucifixion reenactments, people said, and the man drawn by lot to be the *Cristo* had a good chance of dying (no eyewitness recorded the practice on paper, though). One particularly morbid – and well-documented – ritual involves pulling *la carretera del muerte,* an oxcart filled with rocks and a wooden figure of Doña Sebastiana, the Angel of Death. Morbid imagery bred morbid curiosity: Photos in a *Harper's* magazine story from the early 20th century show Anglos looking on agog as Penitentes clad in white pants and black hoods whip themselves.

In 1947, after years of concerted lobbying (but not an official renunciation of its bloody rituals), the Penitentes were again accepted into the fold of the Catholic church; the *hermanos mayores* (head brothers) from all of the *moradas* (meeting houses) convene annually in Santa Fe, and the group, which has an estimated 3,000 members, has the outward appearance of a political and public-service club.

The rituals, though, do continue, most visibly during Holy Week. This is when the group's devotion to the physical suffering of the human Jesus is at its keenest. The Penitentes reenact the stations of the cross and the crucifixion, and although ketchup is more prevalent than real blood now and statues often stand in for the major players, the scenes are solemn and affectingly tragic. On some days during Holy Week, the *morada* is open to non-Penitentes for various rituals – a rare chance for outsiders to see the meeting place of this secretive group.

complete with hundred-pound wood beams and lots of fake blood.

The Pueblo Indians play on church-as-theater too: During Christmas Eve Mass, for instance, it's not uncommon for the service to come to an abrupt end, as the priest is hustled off the pulpit by face-painted clown figures who make way for the parade of ceremonial dancers down the aisle. In both cultures, the Mexican Virgin of Guadalupe is highly revered, and a number of saints are honored as intercessors for all manner of dilemmas, from failing crops to false imprisonment.

Eastern religions have a noticeable presence as well, and even a bit of political clout—a community of American-born converts to **Sikhism** in Española, for example, is a major donor to both major political parties. Santa Fe is home to a substantial number of **Buddhists,** both American converts and native Tibetan refugees who have relocated to this different mountainous land. Stupas can be found up and down the Rio Grande, the largest at Santa Fe's KSK Buddhist Center, which hosts many of the most influential Tibetan teachers.

# Food

New Mexicans love their food so much, they put it on lottery tickets, with scratch cards named Chile Cash, Chips and Salsa, and Sopaipilla Dough (promising "lots of honey and plenty of money"). The state cuisine is a distinctive culinary tradition that shouldn't be confused with Tex-Mex or south-of-the-border Mexican—even though most locals will say they're going out for "Mexican," when they mean they want a bowl of purely *New* Mexican green chile stew.

## ALL CHILE, ALL THE TIME

The cuisine's distinguishing element is the **New Mexico chile pepper,** also called the Hatch chile, for the name of the southern New Mexican town that's the center of the industry. In the north, Chimayó is another big chile-producing town. The chile is picked green, then roasted and frozen, to be used whole to make chiles rellenos (stuffed with cheese and fried in batter) or cut into chunks and blended into sauces or used as the base of a meaty green chile stew. Other batches are left to dry in the sun, where they turn dark red and leathery. The dry red chiles are then ground into powder or strung up whole in long chains called *ristras,* to be used later in sauces or marinades. While some dishes, such as *carne adovada* (pork shoulder braised with red chile), are only ever made with one type, most other items—enchiladas, burritos, and eggs (huevos rancheros), to name a few—can be ordered with either kind of chile, so a standard question in restaurants is "Red or green?"

The chile is coupled with the traditional Native American triad of **corn, squash,** and **beans.** The beans are typically brown, meaty pintos, served whole in a stew or mashed up and "refried" (not actually fried twice—the term is a mistranslation of Spanish *refrito,* which means "really fried"). Corn makes its way into tortillas as well as into hulled kernels of hominy, called posole here and often cooked into a hearty stew with lamb or beef, chile, and

green chile, New Mexicans' staple food

oregano. Ground corn paste (masa) is whipped with lard (or Crisco, if you're "healthy") and wrapped around a meaty filling, then tied in a corn husk and steamed to make a **tamale** (a local corruption of the Spanish *tamal*). Squash comes in a common side dish called ***calabacitas,*** sautéed with onions and a touch of green chile. Spanish settlers brought lamb, which crops up in tacos and stews. Traditional Puebloan cuisine isn't so distinct from what everyone else eats—its one major element is **frybread,** a round of deep-fried dough served with honey or filled with ground meat, cheese, and lettuce to make an "Indian taco"; bread baked in a traditional domed adobe *horno* oven is also popular. Game meat, such as deer, is also a major component of Indian cooking, though you'll rarely see it in restaurants.

Green chile makes its way into standard American fare as well. It's a popular pizza topping (great with pepperoni or ham), and the **green-chile cheeseburger** is a top choice at fast-food restaurants. Try the statewide Blake's Lotaburger mini-chain for excellent fresh

# RED CHILE SAUCE

Use only freshly ground New Mexico red chile for this sauce – not the "chile powder" sold in most grocery stores. The sauce will keep in the refrigerator for a month, and you can use it to top eggs or steaks, or devote the whole batch to a tray of enchiladas. (If you're doing the latter, you'll want to keep the sauce relatively runny, so you can easily coat the tortillas with sauce before filling them.) The flavor is best if it is prepared ahead and left to sit overnight.

1/2 c. New Mexico red chile powder
1 tsp. ground cumin
1 tsp. ground coriander
2 tbsp. all-purpose flour
2 tbsp. vegetable oil (or lard)
2 or 3 cloves garlic, crushed or minced
1 tsp. dried oregano
2 c. water or chicken stock

Measure the chile, cumin, coriander, and flour into a heavy-bottom saucepan and place over medium-high heat. Stirring frequently, toast the spices until they are just fragrant and the flour has darkened slightly. Turn the heat down to medium-low and make a well in the center of the spices, pushing the powder to the sides of the pan so it is not directly over the flame. Pour in the oil, then add the garlic. When the garlic is fragrant, stir the spices into the oil-garlic mixture – you will have a very coarse paste. Stirring constantly, slowly add half of the water or stock. The mixture should thicken and become velvety. Add the remaining water or stock, mix well, turn heat to low, and let sauce simmer for about 20 minutes, until it is somewhat reduced and thickened to your liking. If the mixture becomes too thick, simply add more water.

sage. Some places sell them as on-the-run food, in which case, green chile is added to the mix, and the whole thing is wrapped in foil. At sit-down places, you can opt to get the thing smothered in either red or green chile sauce and topped with cheese.

**Sopaipillas** are another New Mexican invention—they're little square bits of dough that puff up like pillows when deep-fried. They're used to mop up chile and beans during the main meal, then slathered with honey for dessert. (In a disturbing trend, some restaurants are switching to a honey-flavored corn syrup, because it's cheaper and doesn't crystallize—if you encounter this, complain at top volume.) **Bizcochitos,** little anise-laced butter cookies, are the state's official sweet treat. Wash it all down with a **margarita,** which purists insist should involve only lime, tequila, and triple sec and be served on the rocks in a salt-rimmed glass. You can get a slushy frozen margarita, but it's usually the mark of a restaurant that's pandering to tourists.

## HOW TO TAKE THE HEAT

When your server plunks down a heavy white ceramic plate covered in melted cheese and oozing chile sauce, the words "this plate is very hot" cover only half of the story. Every year the harvest varies a bit, and the chile can be mild or so spicy as to blister lips and produce a dizzying (and addictive) endorphin rush. Locals look back on particularly incendiary seasons with that mixture of awe, fear, and longing that junkies reserve for their best scores. In general, green chile tends to be hotter than red, but it's a good idea to ask your server what to expect.

You can protect yourself against chile-induced burns by ordering a side of sour cream with your enchiladas or burrito—although be warned that this is seen as a "Texan" affectation, and may be derided by your fellow diners. Locals usually just reach for a sopaipilla, the starch from which can absorb some of the chile oils. But don't gulp down water, which only spreads the searing oils around your mouth. Beer is a marginal improvement. If all else fails, there's the distracting power of margaritas.

burgers, as well as hand-cut fries and cherry Coke with extra syrup. Also look out for **breakfast burritos,** big flour tortillas filled with scrambled eggs, hash browns, and some kind of meat—bacon, crumbled sausage, or sometimes Mexican chorizo, a spicy pork sau-

## FINE DINING

While there are plenty of time-warp diners and mom-and-pop hole-in-the-wall joints, the dining scene can also be very sophisticated, keeping pace with the national trend toward local and organic produce—a movement that hasn't been such a huge leap in New Mexico, as many small family farms didn't have to "go organic" because they were never industrialized in the first place. At white-tablecloth places, Southwestern fusion is the byword, with chile working its way into foie gras appetizers and even high-concept desserts. The fine dining scene is enhanced by a burgeoning wine industry, the product of Spanish settlers in the 17th century but enjoying a resurgence since the 1980s. Gruet Winery in Albuquerque is the best-known New Mexico producer, known for its excellent sparkling wine. This is a boon to dining out, because you can get inexpensive fizzy wine by the glass almost everywhere. *Local Flavor,* a monthly tabloid magazine, covers the dining and artisanal food scene, which is centered in Santa Fe but has its proponents in Taos and Albuquerque as well.

## VEGETARIAN FOOD

New Mexican food isn't a meat-centric cuisine, but vegetarians will have to be vigilant, as many chile dishes are traditionally made with beef or chicken stock as well as lard for flavoring. Decades of hippie influence, though, have resulted in many menus stating clearly whether the chile is meatless. And quite a lot of restaurants have an unreconstructed 1970s worldview, with alfalfa sprouts and squash casseroles galore.

# Arts and Crafts

Northern New Mexico is a hotbed of creativity, from Santa Fe's edgy contemporary art scene to traditional Spanish folk artists working in remote villages, using the same tools their great-grandfathers did. Here's what to look out for in the more traditional arenas of pottery, weaving, jewelry, and wood carving.

## POTTERY

New Mexico's pottery tradition is perhaps the state's most thriving one, drawing on millennia of craftsmanship. About 2,000 years ago, the **Mogollon** people in the southern part of the state began making simple pots of brown coiled clay. A thousand years later, the craft had developed into the beautiful black-on-white symmetry of the **Mimbres** people. Later, each of the pueblos developed its own style; by the 20th century, some traditions had died out, but almost all felt some kind of renaissance as a result of **María Martinez** in the first half of the 20th century. A San Ildefonso potter, Martinez developed, along with her husband, Julian, a lustrous black pottery painted with geomet-

ric designs to make a subtle matte-shiny finish. The elegant pieces, at once innovative and traditional, inspired Anglo collectors (who saw the couple's work at the 1934 Chicago World's Fair, among other places) as well as local potters. Today, many artists make their livings from pottery, sold both in galleries and out of people's homes in the pueblos.

The various pueblo styles are distinguished by their base clay, "slip" (the clay-and-water finish), and particular shapes. Taos and Picurís, for instance, are surrounded by beds of micaceous clay; the mica helps the pots withstand heat well (they're renowned for cooking beans) and lends the pottery a subtle glitter. Acoma Pueblo specializes in intricate black-and-white painted designs; San Juan's pottery is typically reddish-brown with incised symbols; and Santa Clara Pueblo developed the "wedding jar," a double-neck design with a handle. A whole other field of contemporary design is thriving too, with artists working in glass, for instance, or applying traditional decorative motifs to large-scale sculpture. If you're interested in buying, start by looking around Santa Fe galleries—if there's a particular style that catches your eye, then you can visit the specific pueblo, where you may be able to buy directly from the artisan and perhaps see where the piece was made.

## TEXTILES

After pottery, **weaving** is probably the state's largest craft industry. Historically, Indian and Spanish weaving styles were separate, but they have merged over the centuries to create some patterns and styles unique to the Rio Grande Valley. Prior to the arrival of the Spanish, American Indians had already developed a weaving tradition—the Spanish explorers marveled especially at the Navajo cotton blankets, woven in whole panels on wide looms (Spaniards had been working with narrow looms and stitching two panels together) and featuring patterns of stepped diamonds. Spanish weavers introduced the hardy Churro sheep, with its rough wool that was good for hand-spinning, as well as new dyes, such as indigo (although the blue-tinted rugs are often called **Moki** rugs, using a Navajo word).

In the early 1800s, in an attempt to make a better product for trade, the Spanish government sent Mexican artists north to work with local weavers. Out of this meeting came the distinctive **Saltillo** details (named for the region the Mexican teachers came from), such as the running-leaf pattern, which Rio Grande weavers alternated with solid-color stripes. In the 1880s, New Mexican artisans first saw quilts from the eastern United States, and they adapted the eight-pointed star to their wool rugs; another popular motif from the 19th century is a zigzag pattern that resembles lightning. One item that crops up in antique shops is the **Chimayó blanket,** an invention of the tourist age in the early 20th century, when Anglo traders encouraged local Hispano weavers to make an affordable souvenir to sell to visitors looking for "Indian" blankets. They're handsome, single-width rugs with a strong central motif, perhaps the iconic Southwestern-look rug. Also look for *colcha* work, a Spanish style in which a loose-weave rug is decorated with wool embroidery; it was revived in the 1930s by Mormons, and you will occasionally see beautiful examples from this period in collectors' shops. Contemporary weaving can draw on any and all of these innovations, and can just as easily be practiced by a young Anglo as a Hispano grandmother. A strong small-batch wool industry in New Mexico helps the scene tremendously—expect to see vivid color-block contemporary pieces alongside the most traditional patterns.

## JEWELRY

The Indians of New Mexico have been making jewelry for thousands of years, though the familiar forms seen today date only from the mid-19th century, when the Navajo of western New Mexico pioneered silversmithing and taught it to the Pueblo Indians. The most iconic piece of Southwestern jewelry is the turquoise-and-silver **squash-blossom necklace,** a large crescent pendant decorated with flower-like silver beads. Actually derived from Spanish pomegranate decorations, rather than native plant imagery, it's readily seen in every Santa Fe jewelry store. Look also for shell-shape **concho belts** (also spelled "concha"), silver "shells" linked together or strung on a leather belt, and **heishi,** tiny disks made of shell and threaded to make a rope-like strand. The Zuni carve small animal **fetishes**—bears, birds, and more—which are often strung on necklaces with heishi. In addition to turquoise, opals are a popular decorative stone, along with brick-red coral, lapis lazuli, and black jet and marble. Whatever you buy, the gallery or artisan should supply you with a written receipt of its components—which stones, the grade of silver (sterling, ideally), and so forth.

### Shopping for Turquoise

Although New Mexico's turquoise is now all mined out, the stone is still an essential part of local jewelry-making; most of it is now imported from mines in China. It is available in shades from lime-green to pure sky-blue, and

Don't like any jewelry you see? You can always pick up the raw materials and make your own.

much of it has been subjected to various processes to make it more stable and versatile, which affects the price.

Rare gem-grade turquoise is the top of the line—a piece from now-empty mines like Lander or Lone Mountain can cost $40 per carat. "Gem-grade" applies only to natural stones—those that have not been chemically treated in any way—and is based on the piece's matrix (the spiderweb of dark veins running through it), natural luster, and hardness. Gem-grade turquoise pieces from still-functioning mines in China or Tibet will cost significantly less ($10–20 per carat) but will be of the same quality as some premium American stones. Slightly less splendid natural stones are graded jewelry-quality, high-quality, or investment-quality—but they are not quite hard enough to guarantee they will not change color over decades. They cost $2–5 per carat. If you're buying a natural stone, be sure the seller will provide you with a written certificate of its status.

Turquoise that has been stabilized, or submerged in epoxy resin to prevent color change, makes up the bulk of the market. Because good natural turquoise is increasingly difficult to come by and turquoise is such an unstable stone, stabilization is a perfectly acceptable way of making a great deal of the stuff usable. Because it's less expensive, it allows for a little waste in the carving process, and good-quality stabilized turquoise is often found in expensive jewelry with elaborate inlay. Average-quality stabilized stone, the next grade down, is used by perhaps 70 percent of American Indian artisans—it can stand up to being carved and is very well priced. Though it ranks relatively low in the range of turquoise available, it produces an attractive piece of jewelry—perhaps not with the elaborate spiderwebbing of a rare piece, but with an overall good color and luster.

Below this are low-quality stabilized stones that have been artificially colored (often called "color shot," or, more confusing, "color stabilized"). Synthetic stones are actually real turquoise—small chunks mixed with a binding powder of ground turquoise or pyrite, then pressed into shapes and cut. The result is surprisingly attractive, with natural spiderwebbing, but it should be clearly labeled as synthetic. Treated turquoise has been submerged in water or oil to make it heavier and shinier, a scam with only temporary results—best avoided, but by its nature, it's seldom honestly labeled.

Aside from the treated stuff, don't worry too much about getting "bad" or "cheap" turquoise—because each stone is different, the more important thing is to find a piece that's attractive to you. Shopping in New Mexico provides many opportunities to buy direct from the artisan—under the portal at the Palace of the Governors in Santa Fe, for instance; otherwise, just avoid shopping in too-good-to-be-true stores that are perpetually "going out of business" or "in liquidation."

## WOOD AND TINWORK

When Spanish colonists arrived in New Mexico, they had few resources, little money, and only the most basic tools. The first group of settlers included one carpenter, whose skills helped the group both fill their houses with heavy wood **furniture** (still made today) and worship—for chief among the wood-carvers was (and is) the *santero* or *santera,* who carves images of saints out of wood. These images, called **santos,** can be either flat *(retablos)* or three-dimensional *(bultos)* and are typically painted in lively colors, though some outstanding work has been produced in plain, unpainted wood. Santo styles have shown remarkable continuity over the centuries—the most notable break from tradition was *santero* Patrocinio Barela, whose work, sponsored by the WPA in the 1930s, employed fluid, modernist shapes that utilize the natural curves and grains of the wood. His sons and grandsons practice the art today. For centuries, the piousness of the *santero* was valued at least much as his skill in carving, though many contemporary carvers do their work for a large market of avid collectors. One popular figure is San Isidro, patron saint of farmers, from 12th century Spain.

Look also for **straw marquetry,** another product of hard times in the colonial period, in which tiny fibers of "poor man's gold" replaced precious metals as inlay to make elaborate geometric designs on dark wood. **Tinwork** is another ubiquitous craft, found in inexpensive votive-candle holders as well as elaborately punched and engraved mirror frames and chandeliers.

ARG

# ESSENTIALS

## Getting There

### BY AIRPLANE

**Albuquerque International Sunport** (ABQ) is the main access point to the region. It's served by all major U.S. air carriers; Southwest Airlines runs occasional direct flights from the East and West Coasts, and Continental has one nonstop flight from Newark. Otherwise, you'll have to fly through a hub such as Salt Lake City, Atlanta, Dallas, Denver, or Chicago. Although the airport bills itself as "international," in fact it receives no regular direct flights from other countries. Fares fluctuate on the same schedule as the rest of the country, with higher rates in summer and over holidays; of the major carriers, however, American seems to have oc-casionally lower rates, and the fact that flights are routed through the relatively temperate hub city of Dallas is a boon in the winter.

**Taos** (TSM) and **Santa Fe** (SAF) have tiny municipal airstrips with very limited commuter service—in general, you're better off taking one of the frequent and not terribly expensive shuttle vans from Albuquerque.

### BY BUS AND CAR

**TNM&O** (806/763-5389, www.tnmo.com), the local Greyhound affiliate, connects New Mexico with adjacent states and Mexico—along either I-40 or I-25. If you're coming from elsewhere in the Southwest, you may want to

© ZORA O'NEILL

investigate **El Paso-Los Angeles Limousine Express** (915/532-4061 in El Paso, 626/442-1945 in Los Angeles), the biggest operator of bargain bus service for the Mexican immigrant population—its route runs east–west from El Paso to Los Angeles, but also connects Denver and Albuquerque. It's both less expensive and more comfortable than TNM&O, but it helps to have some basic Spanish when calling.

Arriving by car is very straightforward: I-40 and I-25 cross in the center of Albuquerque; I-25 runs straight north to Santa Fe. Two scenic but well-traveled roads run between Santa Fe and Taos (take the low road, Highway 68, in winter to avoid snow closures, though).

## BY TRAIN

**Amtrak** (800/872-7245, www.amtrak.com) runs the Southwest Chief daily between Chicago and Los Angeles, stopping in **Lamy** (18 miles from Santa Fe) and **Albuquerque.** Traveling by train, if you have the time to do it, is a rewarding experience, as you'll get a great sense of New Mexico's isolation—as well as what a dramatic change the railroad made when it arrived in 1880.

Arriving in Albuquerque, you're in the middle of downtown, but Lamy is no more than a depot and a couple of run-down houses (although as of mid-2005, plans were in the works for a railroad museum and café adjacent to the station). Amtrak provides shuttle service to Santa Fe hotels, or you can connect with a tour run by **Santa Fe Southern Railway** (505/989-8600, www.sfsr.com), though the schedule varies significantly according to the day and the season. If you're coming from Chicago, know that Amtrak pads its schedule heavily between Lamy and Albuquerque—so if the train is running behind, you'll be late arriving in Lamy, but generally will still get to Albuquerque on schedule.

Plans have been laid for commuter train service between Santa Fe and Albuquerque, but that's not likely for some time yet.

# Getting Around

This book covers a relatively small area—about 200 miles from north to south, easily covered by car or bus. Within each city, you can often get around by walking, biking, or public transport. The only regularly scheduled airplane service is between Albuquerque (ABQ) and Taos (TSM), on Westward Airways (877/937-8927, www.westwardairways.com). Two flights run daily, for about $90 one way.

## BY CAR

If you want to explore at all beyond the town centers, you will have to do it by car—but driving New Mexico's scenic byways is definitely one of the pleasures of traveling here. Parking can be somewhat limited in Santa Fe, and you can get around the center of town very easily on foot, so you may want to rent a car only for the days you plan to go out of the city. In Taos, though, only the very dedicated can get around by bus, and in Albuquerque, a car can give you a great deal more flexibility in your day. All of the major car-rental chains are at Albuquerque's airport, in a single convenient center; see the respective city chapters for other rental companies and offices.

All but a few roads described in this book are passable year-round and don't require four-wheel-drive or any other special equipment, though be prepared in winter for ice and snow anywhere other than central Albuquerque. Plan on an hour's drive from Albuquerque to Santa Fe via I-25, and an hour and a half from Santa Fe to Taos via the low road.

## BY BUS

**TNM&O** (806/763-5389, www.tnmo.com) connects Albuquerque, Santa Fe, and Taos, with either two (Taos) or three (Santa Fe) buses daily. The buses run along I-25 between Albuquerque and Santa Fe and up Highway

The Albuquerque trolley runs between Old Town and Downtown.

68 (the low road) to Taos, with stops in Española and Pilar. If you're just going north to Santa Fe, an airport shuttle is preferable. If you're already in downtown Albuquerque, away from the airport, try **El Paso–Los Angeles Limousine Express** (1611 Central Ave. SW, 505/247-8036), which also runs to Santa Fe; unfortunately, it doesn't stop in Taos.

## BY BIKE

With beautiful vistas, often deserted roads, and a strong community of both road cyclists and mountain bikers, northern New Mexico can be a great place to get around on two wheels, as long as it's not your main form of transport. Whether you'll be riding your own bike or renting one in New Mexico, always pack a patch kit—goathead thorns and broken glass are particular scourges of the high-

way shoulder. You may want to install tire liners on your own bike.

Within the towns, central Albuquerque and Santa Fe are both very manageable by bicycle, with separate lanes in many cases; Taos is less accommodating, and traffic on the main street through town can be unpleasantly heavy and fast.

## TOURS

If you have a particular interest, such as art or archaeology, or just a limited amount of time to see the area, you may want to arrange a custom tour. **Destination 505** (505/424-9500, www.destination505.com), a Santa Fe–based company, has a roster of area-savvy experts in archaeology, Pueblo Indian culture, and history to act as guides. Day-long tours or walking tours are recommended in earlier chapters.

# Conduct and Customs

New Mexico is a part of the United States, but it can sometimes feel quite foreign, particularly in the high mountain Spanish villages and in the Indian pueblos. Basic courtesy still rules—starting with limiting your cell-phone use in public, which is not tolerated very well in either the cities or the small towns. Also, women should dress somewhat modestly for visiting the older Catholic churches north of Santa Fe—at least put a layer over a tank top.

New Mexico is not a wealthy state, and the gap between rich and poor can be very wide; in general, people don't appreciate conspicuous displays of wealth, and it's doubly rude to flash cash, fancy gadgets, and jewelry in tiny subsistence-living villages and pueblos. (On the flip side, well-off tourists who dress in tattered jeans and beat-up shoes are also a bit confounding; locals tend to dress as well as they can.) Be thoughtful when taking photos, particularly of people's homes—always ask permission, and consider that some of the more "scenic" ele-

ments of New Mexico are also the products of poverty, which some people may not be proud of your capturing on film.

You can help the local economy by favoring New Mexican–owned businesses, rather than chain operations. Also try to buy directly from artisans wherever possible. In these situations, don't get too bent on bargaining—the item you're purchasing represents not just raw materials and hours of work, but a person's particular talent, skill, and heritage; insisting on an extra-low price belittles not just the item, but the artisan as well.

## PUEBLO ETIQUETTE

Visiting pueblos calls for particular behavior. Remember that you are walking around someone's neighborhood, so peeking in windows and wandering off the suggested route (most pueblo visitors centers will give you a basic map to follow) isn't polite. If you want to take photos, you'll usually need a camera permit, for

drummers at the San Ildefonso Pueblo

COURTESY NEW MEXICO DEPARTMENT OF TOURISM/MARK NOHL

an additional fee; always ask permission before taking photos of people, and ask parents, rather than children, for their consent. Most pueblos ban alcohol as well—if not all the time, then certainly on feast days.

Some pueblos are more welcoming than others—San Ildefonso, for instance, is open year-round, whereas Jemez is completely closed, except for some feast days. It's flawed logic, then, to seek out the less-visited places or go in the off times in order to have a less "touristy" experience, because the more private pueblos will not be at all welcoming to strangers poking around among their homes. The most rewarding time to visit *is* on a big feast day—although you won't be the only tourist there, you have a better chance of being invited into a local's home.

# Tips for Travelers

## STUDY AND VOLUNTEERING

From afternoon cooking classes to a semester-long intensive on adobe building techniques, the opportunities to learn in northern New Mexico are broad. Santa Fe and Albuquerque are both home to renowned alternative healing and massage schools, more than can be listed here; if you're interested, visit www.natural-healers.com for a list.

### General Education

Look first into the extensive art, music, and outdoors programs at **Ghost Ranch** (877/804-4678, www.ghostranch.org), both at the beautiful property in Abiquiu and at the Santa Fe campus; of particular interest is **Zoukfest** (www.zoukfest.com), a world folk-music intensive workshop, in November. Tap into Albuquerque's active alternative health and wellness scene with a class through **Sage Ways** (505/271-7029, www.sageways.org), a course catalog filled with interesting one-off options such as mushroom hunting and creative relaxation—ideal if you're in town for a short time. **Northern New Mexico Community College** (505/581-4115, www.nnmcc.edu), in the village of El Rito, north of Abiquiu, runs the **Heritage Retreat Center,** offering Spanish immersion classes and short-term workshops in traditional crafts.

### Cooking Classes

Of the several culinary schools in northern New Mexico, the **Taos School of Cooking** (123 Manzanares St., 505/751-4419, ext. 206, www.taoscooking.com) is the most diverse, catering both to the local community looking for French technique tips and to visitors with Southwestern fusion classes. A week-long summer program for kids gives parents a couple of hours of alone time every day. **Santa Fe School of Cooking** (116 W. San Francisco St., 505/983-4511, www.santafe-schoolofcooking.com) offers day classes not only in contemporary Southwestern cuisine, but also in traditional Native American cooking (author Lois Ellen Frank instructs) and New Mexican standards; nice farmer's market trips are offered too.

In Albuquerque, learn to fry the perfect sopaipillas at **Jane Butel Cooking School** (125 2nd St. NW, 800/472-8229, www.janebutel.com), downtown in La Posada and presided over by a Tex-Mex maven who has written numerous cookbooks; day, weekend, and week-long classes are available.

### Permaculture and Alternative Construction

**Lama Foundation** (505/586-1269, www.lamafoundation.org) in San Cristobal, north of Taos, hosts a week-long permaculture get-together, with hundreds of people swapping tips on solar design, organic gardening, and water catchment. You can also be a summer steward at the foundation, for two weeks or the full season, and learn organic gardening and land preservation techniques this way, along with plenty of yoga and quiet time. If you're interested specifically in northern New Mexico's solar architecture movement, you can take a three-day **Earthship Seminar** (505/751-0462, www.earthship.org), a crash course in building the off-the-grid rammed-earth houses that are springing up around Taos. The Earthship Biotecture organization also accepts volunteers. If you're very interested in local building styles, look into the intensive semester-long classes in adobe construction at **Northern New Mexico Community College** (505/581-4115, www .nnmcc.edu).

**Seeds of Change** (888/762-7333, www .seedsofchange.com) is an organization dedicated to preserving biodiversity in agricultural products and promoting organic farming practices; the group occasionally calls for volunteers on its six-acre research farm in El Guique, just outside of Santa Fe near San Juan Pueblo.

## FOREIGN TRAVELERS

As for any destination in the United States, check before departure whether you'll need a **visa** to enter; most European and Latin American nationals do not need one, however.

New Mexico uses the **United States dollar,** and currency exchange is available at most banks as well as in better hotels, though the rates will not be as good. For the best rates and most convenience, withdraw cash from your home account through **automatic teller machines** (ATMs), located in bank lobbies and, increasingly, in shops and restaurants; check first, though, what fee your home bank might charge you for the transaction. Otherwise, **travelers' checks** from known brands (American Express, Visa) are widely accepted—it's best if you can buy them in U.S. dollar amounts, though, rather than British pounds, to avoid an additional transaction while traveling.

**Tipping** etiquette is similar to elsewhere in the country: 15–20 percent on restaurant bills (though often restaurants will add 15 percent or more to the bill for large groups); $1 or so per drink when ordered at the bar; 15 percent to cab drivers; $1 or $2 to staff who handle

© ZORA O'NEILL

Don't worry – you can get cash from an ATM almost anywhere.

your luggage in hotels; and $1 or $2 per day to housekeeping in hotels—envelopes are usually left in rooms for this purpose. **Bargaining** is usually accepted only if you're dealing directly with an artisan, and sometimes not even then—it doesn't hurt to ask, but don't press the issue if the seller won't budge. **Electricity** is 120 volts, with a two-prong, flat-head plug, the same as Canada and Mexico.

## TRAVELERS WITH DISABILITIES

Wheelchair access can be a little frustrating in some historic properties and on the narrower sidewalks of Santa Fe and Taos, but in most other respects, travelers with disabilities should find no more problems in northern New Mexico than elsewhere in the United States. Public buses are wheelchair-accessible, for instance, and you can even get out in nature a bit on paved trails such as the Santa Fe Canyon Preserve loop or the Paseo del Bosque in Albuquerque. If you'll be visiting a lot of wilderness areas, you should get the National

Park Service's **Golden Access Pass** (888/467-2757, www.nps.gov), a free lifetime pass that grants admission for the pass-holder and family to all national parks, national forests, and the like, as well as discounts on interpretive services, camping fees, fishing licenses, and more. Apply in person at any federally managed park or wilderness area; you must show medical documentation of blindness or permanent disability.

The **Governor's Committee on Concerns for the Handicapped** (491 Old Santa Fe Tr., 505/827-6465 voice, 505/827-6329 TDD) maintains an online guide, **WebAccess New Mexico** (www.state.nm.us/gcch/accessnm .htm), which assesses major sites, restaurants, and lodging for accessibility, but you may still want to call hotels ahead to make sure they can accommodate you. For general information on traveling with a disability, visit **Disabled Travelers.com** (www.disabledtravelers.com), which provides tips and directories of disability-friendly businesses, information on home-exchange programs and equipment rental, and even hotel-booking services. The site is a member of the **Society for Accessible Travel & Hospitality** (212/447-7284, www.sath.org), another good general resource.

## SENIORS
Senior discounts are available at most museums and other attractions. If you'll be visiting a number of wilderness areas, look into a **Golden Age Passport,** a lifetime pass for people 62 and older that grants free admission for the pass-holder and any additional passengers in the vehicle to national parks, National Forest Service lands, and many other areas, as well as a 50 percent discount on activities such as camping and boat-launching. The pass can be purchased only in person at a federally managed wilderness area for just $10; for more information, contact the **National Parks Service** (888/467-2757, www.nps.gov).

The **Elderhostel** (877/426-8056, www .elderhostel.org) program runs more than 40 group trips in northern New Mexico, from a five-day general introduction to Santa Fe his-

tory to slightly longer tours focusing on the legacy of Georgia O'Keeffe, for instance, or strategies in Native American museum curation and conservation. Prices are very reasonable, and as the emphasis of Elderhostel trips is on education, tour guides are generally excellent.

## TRAVELING WITH CHILDREN
Hispanic and American Indian cultures are typically very child-friendly, so your little ones will be welcome in most environments, including restaurants and hotels. The only exception would be some of the more formal restaurants in Santa Fe and Albuquerque. Kids are sure to be fascinated by ceremonial dances at the pueblos, but be prepared with distracting games and the like, as long waits are the norm. Prep children with information about American Indian culture beforehand, and brief them on the basic etiquette at dances, which applies to them as well. Kids will also enjoy river rafting (relaxing, less risky "floats" along placid sections of the Rio Grande and Rio Chama are best) as well as skiing; Taos Ski Valley in particular has a very strong program of classes for youngsters. Though the specific prices are not listed in this guide, admission prices at major attractions are typically lower for children than for adults.

## GAY AND LESBIAN TRAVELERS
Santa Fe is one of the major gay capitals in the United States, second only to San Francisco in the per-capita rates of same-sex coupledom, and particularly popular with lesbians. There are no designated "gay-borhoods" (unless you count RainbowVision Santa Fe, a retirement community) or even particular bar scenes—instead, gay men and lesbian women are well integrated throughout town, running businesses and serving on the city council. Two weeks in June are dedicated to Pride on the Plaza, a whole array of gay-pride arts events and parades.

Albuquerque also has a decent gay scene, especially if you want to go out clubbing, which is not really an option in quieter Santa Fe. Visit the website **AlbuQueerque** (www.albuqueer-que.com) for news and events—it's also the on-line version of the *New Mexico Voice,* a biweekly newspaper covering the gay and lesbian community statewide. Taos isn't anti-gay in any way—it just doesn't have a big organized community. As for smaller villages and pueblos, they're still significantly more conservative.

Gay culture in the state isn't all about cute shops and cool bars. One big event is the annual **Zia Regional Rodeo,** sponsored by the **New Mexico Gay Rodeo Association** (505/720-3749, www.nmgra.com). It takes place every June in Albuquerque, with all the standard rodeo events, plus goat dressing and a wild drag race.

# Health and Safety

Visitors to New Mexico face several unique health concerns. First and foremost are the simple environmental hazards of **dehydration, sunburn,** and **altitude sickness.** The desert climate, glaring sun, and thin ozone layer conspire to fry your skin to a crisp and drain you of all moisture. (On the plus side, sweat evaporates immediately.) Apply SPF 30 sunscreen daily, even in winter, and try to drink at least a couple of liters of water a day, whether you feel thirsty or not; remember to ask for water in restaurants—it's frequently brought only on demand, to cut down on waste. After you start feeling thirsty, you're already seriously dehydrated, and at risk of further bad effects: headaches, nausea, and dizziness, all of which can become full-blown, life-threatening **heatstroke** if left untreated. It doesn't even take serious exertion—just lack of water and very hot sun—to develop heatstroke, so if you're feeling at all woozy or cranky (another common symptom of a lack of water), head for shade and sip a cold drink. Gatorade or a similar electrolyte-replacement drink is a good option, but avoid caffeine- and sugar-laden soft drinks or iced coffee.

Staying hydrated will also help stave off the effects of the high elevation, which most visitors will not be used to. The mildest reaction to being 7,000 feet or more above sea level is simple lethargy or lightheadedness—you will probably sleep long and soundly on your first night in New Mexico. Some people do have more severe reactions, such as a piercing headache or intense nausea, especially if they engage in strenuous physical activity. Unfortunately, there's no good way to judge how your body will react, so give yourself a few days to acclimate, with a light schedule and plenty of time to sleep.

More obscure hazards include **West Nile virus** (wear a DEET-based insect repellent if you're down along the river in the summer), **Hanta virus,** which is an extremely rare pulmonary ailment transmitted by rodents, and **bubonic plague** (a.k.a. The Black Death), the very same disease that killed millions of Europeans in the Middle Ages. Luckily, only a case or two of the plague crops up every year, and it's easily treated if diagnosed early. **Lyme disease** is so far nonexistent, as deer ticks do not flourish in the mountains.

If you'll be spending a lot of time hiking or camping, take precautions against **giardiasis** and other waterborne ailments by boiling your water or treating it with iodine—even the clearest mountain waterways may have been tainted by cows upstream. **Snake bites** are also a small hazard in the wild, so wear boots that cover your ankles, stay on trails, and keep your feet out of odd holes and cracks between rocks. Only the Western diamondback is aggressive when disturbed; other snakes will bolt, and will certainly not bite if you simply back away quietly.

And the general **outdoor safety rules** apply: Don't hike by yourself, always register with the ranger station when heading out overnight, and let friends know where you're going and when you'll be back. Pack a good topographical map and a compass or GPS device; people manage to get lost even when hiking in the foothills, and if you're at all dehydrated or dizzy from the altitude, any disorientation can be magnified to a disastrous degree. Also pack layers of clothing, and be prepared for cold snaps and snow at higher elevations even in the summer.

## CRIME AND DRUGS

Maybe it's partially the influence of American Indian culture, with its strong tradition of hallucinogen-induced shamanism, but recreational drug use is not uncommon in New Mexico—generally in a relatively benign form, with marijuana fairly widespread (former governor Gary Johnson, though not a user himself, has been a strenuous advocate for its legalization).

But as in much of the United States, crystal methamphetamine is an epidemic, and some villages in northern New Mexico have been decimated by heroin use, with overdose deaths at a rate several hundred times higher than the national average. Drinking and driving is unfortunately still exceedingly common, especially in rural areas; be particularly alert when driving at night. A distressing number of crosses along the roadside (*descansos*) mark the sites of fatal car accidents, many of which had alcohol involved.

# Information and Services

## MAPS AND TOURIST INFORMATION

Before your trip, you may want to contact the **New Mexico Tourism Board** (800/733-6396, ext. 0643, www.newmexico.org) for a free visitors guide; the board's website is packed with background information and listings of special events. It also publishes the monthly *New Mexico* magazine (www.nmmagazine.com), which covers both mainstream attractions and more obscure corners of the state. If you plan to do a lot of hiking, you can order detailed topographical maps from the **National Forest Service** office in New Mexico (505/842-3292) or from the Bureau of Land Management's **Public Lands Information Center** (www.publiclands.org). Santa Fe, Albuquerque, and Taos also have their own tourism agencies—please see the respective chapters for contact details, as well as for local newspapers and radio stations.

## TELEPHONE AND INTERNET

The **area code** for all of New Mexico is 505; however, a call from Albuquerque to Santa Fe, say, is still charged as long-distance, even though it's in the same area code. **Mobile phones** on the GSM network (Cingular, T-Mobile) get very poor or no reception in rural areas, though this is steadily improving. The corridor between Albuquerque and Santa Fe is fine, but if you'll be spending a lot of time outside of these two cities, you might consider a CDMA phone (Verizon is reliable), particularly if you're counting on it for emergency use.

**Internet access** is widespread, though DSL and other high-speed services have not yet become commonplace in Taos and some historic neighborhoods of Santa Fe. There are not many Internet cafés catering to travelers, but you should be able to find one or two places with per-hour rates in each city; when in doubt, head to the public library. **Wireless** hot spots are prevalent, and the city of Albuquerque even maintains a few—most notably in the airport. Thick adobe walls can be a hindrance to consistent reception, however.

## TIME ZONE

New Mexico is in the mountain time zone, one hour ahead of the West Coast of the United States and two hours behind the East Coast. It's –7 GMT during the winter and –6 GMT in summer, when daylight saving time is followed statewide.

# RESOURCES

## Glossary

**abierto** Spanish for "open"

**acequia** an irrigation ditch, specifically one regulated by the traditional Spanish method, maintained by a *mayordomo*, or "ditch boss," who oversees how much water each shareholder receives

**adobe** a building material of sun-dried bricks made of a mix of mud, sand, clay, and straw

**arroyo** a stream or dry gully where mountain runoff occasionally flows

**atrio** the churchyard between the boundary wall and the church entrance, usually used as a cemetery

**bizcochito** anise-laced hard cookie, traditionally made with lard but now more commonly baked with butter

**bosque** Spanish for "forest," referring specifically to the cottonwoods and other wetlands growth along a river

**bulto** a three-dimensional wood carving, typically of a saint

**caldera** a basin or crater formed by a collapsed volcano

**canal** a water drain from a flat roof; pl. *canales*

**cerrado** Spanish for "closed"

**chicharrón** fried pork skin, usually with a layer of meat still attached, incorporated into burritos and bowls of chile

**chile** not to be confused with Texas-style meat-and-beans chili; refers to the fruit of the chile plant itself, eaten green (picked unripe then roasted) or red (ripened and dried)

**colcha** a style of blanket, in which loom-woven wool is embellished with long strands of wool embroidery

**enchilada** a corn tortilla dipped in chile sauce then filled with cheese or meat, then topped with more chile; can be served either rolled or flat (stacked in layers)

**farolito** in Santa Fe and Taos, a luminaria

**genízaro** during Spanish colonial times, a detribalized Indian who lived with Spaniards and followed Catholic tradition, usually due to having been taken as a slave

**heishi** fine disk-shaped beads carved from shells

**horno** a traditional dome-shaped adobe oven

**jerga** a Spanish-style wool blanket or rug, usually loosely woven and barely decorated, meant for daily use

**kachina** an ancestral spirit of the Pueblo people as well as the carved figurine representing the spirit; also spelled katsina

**kiva** the sacred ceremonial space in a pueblo, at least partially underground and entered by a hole in the ceiling. Only men are allowed in the kiva, and outsiders are never permitted to enter.

**latillas** thin saplings cut and laid across vigas to make a solid ceiling

**lowrider** an elaborately painted and customized car with hydraulic lifts

**luminaria** in Albuquerque, a lantern made of a sand-filled paper bag with a votive candle set inside; in Santa Fe and Taos, refers to small bonfires lit during the Christmas season

**menudo** tripe soup, said to be good for curing a hangover

**morada** the meeting space of the Penitente brotherhood

**nicho** a small niche in an adobe wall, usually meant to hold a santo

**Penitente** a member of a strict Catholic brotherhood

**petroglyph** a rock carving

**pictograph** a painting on a rock surface

**portal** the covered sidewalk area in front of a traditional adobe structure; pl. *portales*

**posole** stew of hominy (soaked, hulled corn), pork, and a little chile

**pueblo** literally Spanish for "village," the word for the various communities of American Indians settled along the Rio Grande Valley; also identifies the people themselves, though they are not of the same tribe and speak several different languages

**rajas** rough-hewn slats laid over vigas to form a ceiling

**ramada** a simple structure built of four sapling posts and topped with additional saplings laid flat, to form a shade structure and a place to hang things to dry

**reredos** an altar screen, usually elabor-ately painted or carved with various portraits of Christ and the saints

**retablo** a flat portrait of a saint, painted or carved in low relief, usually on wood

**ristra** a string of dried red chiles

**santo** a portrait of a saint, either flat (a *retablo*) or three-dimensional (a *bulto*)

**sipapu** the hole in the floor of a kiva, signifying the passage to the spirit world

**sopaipilla** square of puffed fried dough, served with honey for dessert, as well as with the main meal, for wiping up sauces

**tamale** a corn husk filled with masa (hominy paste) and a dab of meat, vegetables, or cheese, then steamed; usually made in large quantities for holidays

**terrón** a building material of bricks cut out of sod and dried in the sun – similar to adobe, but much more rare in New Mexico

**Tewa** the language spoken by the majority of Pueblo Indians; others in the Rio Grande Valley speak Tiwa, Towa, and Keresan

**torreón** a round defensive tower built in Spanish colonial times

**vato** a cool Chicano, usually driving a lowrider

**viga** a ceiling beam, usually made of a single tree trunk and cut to extend outside the building walls on either side

**zaguán** a long central hallway

# Suggested Reading

## HISTORY

Hordes, Stanley. *To the Ends of the Earth: the History of New Mexico's Crypto-Jews.* New York: Columbia University Press, 2005. A rather exhaustive but nonetheless intriguing account of the Jewish families who fled the Inquisition and lived in the Southwest as Catholic converts. The communities, some still practicing distinctly Jewish rituals, came to light only a few decades ago.

Horgan, Paul. *Great River.* Middletown, Conn.: Wesleyan University Press, 1991. Two enormous tomes (*Vol. 1: The Indians and Spain* and *Vol. 2: Mexico and the United States*) that won the Pulitzer Prize for history, and deservedly so: They're packed with drama and intrigue, all on a base of meticulous analysis of primary sources. Horgan's *Lamy of Santa Fe* (Wesleyan, 2003) is also highly recommended, as a balanced examination of the contentious archbishop's life in New Mexico.

Martinez, Esther. *My Life in San Juan Pueblo.* Champaign: University of Illinois Press, 2004. Born in 1912, Martinez has a lot of stories to tell. This free-flowing book incorporates her memories with larger pueblo folklore, and a CD with recordings of some of her stories is included.

Poling-Kempes, Leslie. *Valley of Shining Stone: The Story of Abiquiu*. Tucson: University of Arizona Press, 1997. Georgia O'Keeffe fans will like the personal stories of those in her circle in the 1930s, while historians will appreciate the detailed, linear second half of the book, which gives a more objective overview of the transformation of this remote valley into an artists' haven.

Salaz-Marquez, Ruben. *New Mexico: A Brief Multi-History*. Albuquerque: Cosmic House, 1999. A good introduction with an easy-to-follow timeline format; very thorough, though not much analysis.

Simmons, Marc. *New Mexico: An Interpretive History*. Albuquerque: University of New Mexico Press, 1988. The state's historian laureate presents an easy, concise overview of the major historical events. Also look into his more specialized titles, such as *The Last Conquistador: Juan de Oñate and the Settling of the Far Southwest* (Norman: University of Oklahoma Press, 1993).

Usner, Donald J. *Sabino's Map: Life in Chimayó's Old Plaza*. Santa Fe: Museum of New Mexico Press, 1995. A balanced and gracefully written history of the author's hometown, illustrated with fond photos of all the craggy-faced characters involved. Usner's follow-up, *Benigna's Chimayo: Cuentos from the Old Plaza* (Santa Fe: Museum of New Mexico Press, 2001), is equally good, relating his grandmother's story of the village and her trove of folktales.

## LITERATURE AND MEMOIRS

Anaya, Rudolfo. *Bless Me, Ultima*. New York: Warner, 1994. Anaya's story of a young boy coming of age in New Mexico in the 1940s is beautifully told, and an interesting depiction of life in that era. The book, first published in 1973, launched Anaya into his role as Chicano literary hero; his later books, such as *Alburquerque* (1992) are not quite so touching, but they always have a lot of historical and ethnic detail.

Hillerman, Tony. *Skinwalkers*. New York: HarperTorch, 1990. Hillerman's breakout detective novel, set on the Navajo Nation, weaves a fascinating amount of lore into the plot—which all comes in handy when Tribal Affairs police Joe Leaphorn and Jim Chee investigate three homicides. Hillerman spun Leaphorn and Chee into a successful franchise, and all of the books show the same cultural depth.

Nichols, John. *The Milagro Beanfield War*. New York: Henry Holt, 2000. The first title in Nichols's "New Mexico Trilogy" is also the best, a ripping tale of comic intrigue in a small Hispano village, all started by a little dispute over acequia access. It was later made into a film by Robert Redford (1988).

Pillsbury, Dorothy. *Roots in Adobe*. Santa Fe: Lightning Tree Press, 1983. Pillsbury's charming stories (which occupy three other *Adobe*-based titles) capture the strangeness and warmth of Santa Fe culture in the 1940s. The author tells hilarious stories of settling into her little adobe home and all the characters she meets. The books can be hard to find but are worth seeking out for their excellent vignettes.

Silko, Leslie Marmon. *Ceremony*. New York: Penguin, 1988. Silko's classic novel about the impact of the atomic bomb on Native Americans' worldview (and that of all Americans) is brutal, beautiful, and bleak.

Waters, Frank. *The Woman at Otowi Crossing*. Athens, Ohio: Swallow Press, 1987. Longtime Taos resident Waters fictionalizes the story of a woman whose isolated café catered to Los Alamos scientists during the bomb-building years. Waters is particularly fascinated with the often mystical relationship between the land of the Southwest and the people who live on it—his *The Man Who Killed the Deer* (Athens: Ohio University Press, 1970), about a crime in the Taos Pueblo community, does the same.

## ART AND TRADITIONAL CULTURE

Clark, Willard. *Remembering Santa Fe.* Layton, Utah: Gibbs Smith, 2004. A small hardback edition of selections from the Boston artist who stopped off in Santa Fe in 1928 and stayed to learn printmaking and produce a series of charming etchings depicting Santa Fe life.

Gandert, Miguel. *Nuevo México Profundo: Rituals of an Indo-Hispanic Homeland.* Santa Fe: Museum of New Mexico Press, 2000. Like Lamadrid's work (below), but with a slightly broader scope. There's an attempt at scholarly analysis in the text, but it's really about the 130 beautiful photographs.

Lamadrid, Enrique. *Hermanitos Comanchitos: Indo-Hispano Rituals of Captivity and Redemption.* Albuquerque: University of New Mexico Press, 2003. Fascinating documentation, in descriptive prose and rich black-and-white photos, of the traditional Spanish dances of northern New Mexico, such as Los Comanches and Los Matachines.

Padilla, Carmella, and Juan Estevan Arellano. *Low 'n Slow: Lowriding in New Mexico.* Santa Fe: Museum of New Mexico Press, 1999. Lovingly lurid color photographs by Jack Parsons are the centerpiece of this book, which pays tribute to New Mexico's Latino car culture—an art form that has even landed a lowrider from Chimayó in the Smithsonian. In the interviews with the car owners, the painstakingly transcribed *vato* slang is a little distracting at times, but it certainly conveys their enthusiasm.

Robinson, Roxana. *Georgia O'Keeffe: A Life.* Lebanon, N. A.: University Press of New England, 1998. A strong and intimate biography, focusing on the celebrated painter's role as a proto-feminist and her difficult relationships.

## TRAVEL GUIDES

Coltrin, Mike. *Sandia Mountain Hiking Guide.* Albuquerque: University of New Mexico Press, 2005. Basically a print version of Coltrin's meticulously maintained website (www.sandiahiking.com), with thorough trail descriptions, GPS coordinates, and a foldout map of the east and west slopes of the mountain.

Eaton, Robert. *The Lightning Field.* Boulder, Colo.: Johnson Books, 1995. Eaton served as a forest ranger in Chaco Canyon for five years, so his eye is for the empty and the starkly beautiful destinations around the state, including the art installation of the title (in Quemado, in western New Mexico). His essays, each focusing on a different destination, combine history and strong description. Seek this title out if you want to get well off the usual track.

Galloping Galleries. *Audio CD Road Trips.* Santa Fe. These locally produced narratives liven up any car trip; itineraries include the high road to Taos and the Turquoise Trail. Order at www.gallopinggalleries.com.

Price, V.B. *The City at the End of the World.* Albuquerque: University of New Mexico Press, 1992. Journalist and poet Price writes a travel guide to New Mexico's biggest metropolis but disguises it as a discourse on urban theory, recommending his favorite spots in the context of the city's unique position and growth processes—sometimes a little dense as well as overblown, but interesting nonetheless. Black-and-white photographs by Kirk Gittings highlight the stark landscape.

## NATURE AND THE ENVIRONMENT

Julyan, Robert, and Mary Stuever, eds. *Field Guide to the Sandia Mountains.* Albuquerque: University of New Mexico Press, 2005. A thorough guide illustrated with color photographs, detailing birds, animals, plants, even insects of the Sandias—worth picking up even if you'll be in the Santa Fe area, as much of the wildlife the same.

Kricher, John. *A Field Guide to Rocky Mountain and Southwest Forests.* New York: Houghton Mifflin, 2003. A comprehensive book covering both flora and fauna: trees, birds, mammals, you name it. It's illustrated with both color photos and drawings. It's not encyclopedic, but it's a great basic reference. Peterson guides are also available for narrower categories—reptiles and amphibians, for instance, and butterflies.

Reisner, Marc. *Cadillac Desert: The American West and Its Disappearing Water.* New York: Penguin, 1993. Not specifically about New Mexico, but an excellent analysis of the Southwest's water shortage and how the U.S. government's dam-building projects exacerbated it. Apocalyptic, sarcastic, and totally compelling.

Sibley, David Allen. *The Sibley Field Guide to Birds of Western North America.* New York: Knopf, 2003. The New Mexican birder's book of choice, with 810 species listed, some 4,600 color illustrations, and a handy compact format. Generally beats out Peterson's otherwise respectable series.

Tekiela, Stan. *Birds of New Mexico: Field Guide.* Cambridge, Minn.: Adventure Publications, 2003. A great book for beginning birders or curious visitors, with 140 of the state's most common species listed, many illustrated with photographs.

# FOOD

Frank, Lois Ellen. *Foods of the Southwest Indian Nations.* Berkeley, Calif.: Ten Speed Press, 2002. Beautiful photographs are a highlight of this thorough documentation of a little-covered cuisine—they help make an ancient culinary tradition accessible and modern, without subjecting it to a heavy-handed fusion treatment. For good reason it earned a James Beard Award.

Kagel, Katharine. *Café Pasqual's Cookbook: Spirited Recipes from Santa Fe.* San Francisco: Chronicle, 1993. Re-create your best meals from the legendary restaurant that set the standard for Santa Fe fusion cooking. Chef Kagel is a charming contrarian, too, which makes for great reading.

Sharot, Scott. *New Mexico Chow: Restaurants for the Rest of Us.* Branford, Conn.: Intrepid Traveler, 2004. Sharot, a reviewer for Albuquerque's weekly *Alibi,* strikes out all over the state in search of obscure restaurants with proud chefs, whether they're Vietnamese or Mexican.

# Internet Resources

## TRAVEL INFORMATION

Use official sites produced by chambers of commerce and convention bureaus to look up specific businesses, or to find out what special events will be going on during your trip. If you want more opinionated information, look to privately run sites.

### Official Tourism Sites

#### Albuquerque Convention and Visitors Bureau
#### www.itsatrip.org

The basic official intro to the city and surrounding areas, with events listings as well as hotel-booking services. A good starting point for research.

#### New Mexico Board of Tourism
#### www.newmexico.org

The best of the official sites, this one has very thorough maps, suggested itineraries (go to the "Trip Generator"), and background info like weather. You can even do a live online chat with the New Mexico Visitors Center in Santa Fe.

#### Santa Fe Convention and Visitors Bureau
#### www.santafe.org

Near-exhaustive listings of tourist attractions and services on this slickly produced site. Primarily, though, you'll just want to order the CVB's visitors guide.

#### Taos Chamber of Commerce
#### www.taoschamber.com

Nice background information, a thorough business directory, and events listings, but the chamber's visitors center, in Taos itself, is handier.

#### Visit Los Alamos
#### http://visit.losalamos.com

The online version of the chamber of commerce's nice handbook, with business listings and an events calendar.

## Other Sites

#### Digital Abiquiu
#### www.digitalabiquiu.com

A community-maintained website with lots of information about local galleries, as well as good detailed maps and directions around the Chama Valley area.

#### Hiking in the Sandia Mountains
#### www.sandiahiking.com

Mike Coltrin hiked every trail in the Sandias over the course of a year, covering about 250 miles. He detailed each hike, complete with GPS references, here.

#### Public Lands Information Center
#### www.publiclands.org

Buy USGS, Forest Service, and other topographical maps online from the Bureau of Land Management's well-organized website. Good stock of nature guides and other travel books too.

## NEWS AND CULTURE

#### Albuquerque Journal
#### www.abqjournal.com

The state's largest newspaper is available free online only for the day of publication—you must pay an annual subscription fee to read the archives. But skimming the headlines can give you a good idea what the big local issues are.

#### Alibi
#### www.alibi.com

Albuquerque's free weekly has been cracking wise since 1992, taking a critical look at politics as well as restaurants. Sometimes the staff is too hungover to list all the movie times, but otherwise they're right on target. Its annual "Best of Burque" guide is a good listing of local recommendations.

### Free New Mexican
### www.freenewmexican.com

The free online version of the *Santa Fe New Mexican* requires registration, but its archives contain good restaurant reviews, trail descriptions, and weekend outings, as well as all the news about the city.

### New Mexico Passport
### www.newmexicopassport.com

Feeling like you could be a New Mexico native? Apply for your official papers here, to be presented to any baffled American who's not sure what country you've just been to.

### New Mexico Politics with
### Joe Monahan
### www.joemonahan.com

Analyst Monohan's obsessive, snarky blog charts the circus that is state politics, with plenty of examples why New Mexico still can't shake its "third-world country" rep.

### Santa Fe Reporter
### www.sfreporter.com

Santa Fe's weekly, like Albuquerque's, is politically sharp and often funny. Get opinionated reviews and news analysis here.

### Stephen T. Terrell's Web Log
### www.steveterrell.blogspot.com

A music critic for the *Santa Fe New Mexican,* Terrell also watches politics like a hawk, so his blog mixes reviews of new albums with reports on Senate intrigue.

### Taos Horse Fly
### www.taosdaily.com

Rumor-mongering, way-left-of-center political commentary, and listings of activist meetings—check the pulse of Taos here.

# Acknowledgments

While researching *Moon Santa Fe, Taos & Albuquerque,* I relied heavily on my mother's hospitality; thanks to her too for being an enthusiastic and informed travel companion; and extra thanks to her and my father for raising me in such a nifty place. Others who helped immensely include: Jan Mellor at the Taos Chamber of Commerce; Tom Worrell, who gave a fantastically thorough tour, and Sarah Evans, who arranged it; Susan Vernon; Cheryl, Deb, and Connie; Steve Lewis of the Santa Fe Convention and Visitors Bureau; Patty Romero of the New Mexico Department of Tourism; Paul Margetson; Bruce Kuehnle; Matt and Jen Laessig; Walt Wyss; Mindy Mills; Scott Curtis, Sarah Robarts, and Fraser Robertson; Niall Reid and Simone Rathlé; Megan Mayo of the Albuquerque CVB; Jesse Wood; JoAnn Lysne; John, Rain, and Brooks; all the usual dinner crew: Barbara, Tony, Kent, Sandra, Melu; Peter Moskos, chauffeur extraordinaire; and everyone else who divulged their tips and recommendations.

# Index

## CHURCHES

# MUSEUMS

## PUEBLOS

# MAP SYMBOLS

| | | | | | | | |
|---|---|---|---|---|---|---|---|
| ▦ Expressway | ◖ | Highlight | ✗ | Airfield | ⚓ | Golf Course |
| Primary Road | ○ | City/Town | ✈ | Airport | P | Parking Area |
| Secondary Road | ◉ | State Capital | ▲ | Mountain | ⛁ | Archaeological Site |
| Unpaved Road | ⊛ | National Capital | ✛ | Unique Natural Feature | ♠ | Church |
| Trail | ★ | Point of Interest | | | ⛽ | Gas Station |
| Ferry | • | Accommodation | ⚐ | Waterfall | | Glacier |
| Railroad | ▼ | Restaurant/Bar | ▲ | Park | | Mangrove |
| Pedestrian Walkway | ■ | Other Location | ⬗ | Trailhead | | Reef |
| Stairs | ▲ | Campground | ⛷ | Skiing Area | | Swamp |

# CONVERSION TABLES

°C = (°F - 32) / 1.8
°F = (°C x 1.8) + 32
1 inch = 2.54 centimeters (cm)
1 foot = 0.304 meters (m)
1 yard = 0.914 meters
1 mile = 1.6093 kilometers (km)
1 km = 0.6214 miles
1 fathom = 1.8288 m
1 chain = 20.1168 m
1 furlong = 201.168 m
1 acre = 0.4047 hectares
1 sq km = 100 hectares
1 sq mile = 2.59 square km
1 ounce = 28.35 grams
1 pound = 0.4536 kilograms
1 short ton = 0.90718 metric ton
1 short ton = 2,000 pounds
1 long ton = 1.016 metric tons
1 long ton = 2,240 pounds
1 metric ton = 1,000 kilograms
1 quart = 0.94635 liters
1 US gallon = 3.7854 liters
1 Imperial gallon = 4.5459 liters
1 nautical mile = 1.852 km

# www.moon.com

For helpful advice on planning a trip, visit www.moon.com for the **TRAVEL PLANNER** and get access to useful travel strategies and valuable information about great places to visit. When you travel with Moon, expect an experience that is uncommon and truly unique.

*HANDBOOKS • OUTDOORS • METRO • LIVING ABROAD*

# MOON SANTA FE, TAOS & ALBUQUERQUE

AVALON
publishing group incorporated

Avalon Travel Publishing
An Imprint of
Avalon Publishing Group, Inc.

1400 65th Street, Suite 250
Emeryville, CA 94608, USA
www.moon.com

Editor: Erin Raber
Series Manager: Kathryn Ettinger
Acquisitions Manager: Rebecca K. Browning
Copy Editor and Indexer: Deana Shields
Graphics and Production Coordinator:
   Domini Dragoone
Cover and Interior Designer: Gerilyn Attebery
Map Editor: Kat Smith
Cartographers: Kat Bennett, Suzanne Service,
   Christine Markiewicz
Cartography Manager: Mike Morgenfeld

ISBN-10: 1-56691-879-0
ISBN-13: 978-1-56691-879-4
ISSN: 1557-7163

Printing History
1st Edition – April 2006
5 4 3 2 1

Text © 2006 by Zora O'Neill.
Maps © 2006 by Avalon Travel Publishing, Inc.
All rights reserved.

Some photos and illustrations are used by permission
and are the property of the original copyright
owners.

Front cover photo: © Mark Newman/Rainbow
   Albuquerque Balloon Fiesta at night
Title page photo: © Zora O'Neill
   Pecos National Historical Monument

Printed in the United States by Worzalla

# KEEPING CURRENT

If you have a favorite gem you'd like to see included in the next edition, or see anything
that needs updating, clarification, or correction, please drop us a line. Send your
comments via email to feedback@moon.com, or use the address above.